Morning by Morning

Morning by Morning

365 Days of Meditations to Nourish the Soul

Frank R. Shivers

Copyright 2023 by
Frank Shivers Evangelistic Association
All rights reserved
Printed in the United States of America

Unless otherwise noted, Scripture quotations are from
The Holy Bible *King James Version*

Library of Congress Cataloging-in-Publication Data

Shivers, Frank R., 1949-
Morning by Morning / Frank Shivers
ISBN 978-1-878127-52-5

Library of Congress Control Number:
2023907524

Cover design by
Tim King

For Information:
Frank Shivers Evangelistic Association
2005 Congress Road
Hopkins, South Carolina 29061
www.frankshivers.com

Because

I have found Jesus to be everything He promised to be: my Savior, Friend, Guide, Comforter, Helper, Teacher, Shepherd, Sustainer, and much, much more,

I am excited to present this book to

_____

Date

_____

From

_____

with the prayer

that the reading of its pages will enhance your walk with Jesus and be used by Him to minister to the needs and cares of your life.

Scripture quotations taken from the Bible that are unmarked are from the King James Version.

Scriptures taken from the Holy Bible, New International Version®, NIV®. Copyright © 1973, 1978, 1984, 2011 by Biblica, Inc.™ Used by permission of Zondervan. All rights reserved worldwide. www.zondervan.com. The "NIV" and "New International Version" are trademarks registered in the United States Patent and Trademark Office by Biblica, Inc.™

Scripture quotations marked (NLT) are taken from the Holy Bible, New Living Translation, copyright ©1996, 2004, 2015 by Tyndale House Foundation. Used by permission of Tyndale House Publishers, Carol Stream, Illinois 60188. All rights reserved.

Scripture quotations marked (TLB) are taken from The Living Bible copyright © 1971. Used by permission of Tyndale House Publishers, Carol Stream, Illinois 60188. All rights reserved.

Scripture taken from the New Century Version®. Copyright © 2005 by Thomas Nelson. Used by permission. All rights reserved.

Scripture quotations taken from the Amplified® Bible (AMPC), Copyright © 1954, 1958, 1962, 1964, 1965, 1987 by The Lockman Foundation. Used by permission. www.lockman.org.

Scripture quotations taken from the Amplified® Bible (AMP), Copyright © 2015 by The Lockman Foundation. Used by permission. www.lockman.org.

Quotations marked ESV are taken from the ESV, (The Holy Bible, English Standard Version), copyright 2001 by Crossway, a publishing ministry of Good News Publishers. Used by permission.

To

Mike and Karen Shaffer

Enablers to my ministry and encouragers to me

"Fellowhelpers to the truth"
3 John 8

Contents

January	1
February	35
March	65
April	99
May	129
June	163
July	195
August	227
September	261
October	291
November	321
December	351

Morning by Morning is a daily devotional of biblical meditations on various subjects for 365 days to enlighten, edify, and encourage the heart.

January 1

Things That Must Be Forgotten

"I focus on this one thing: Forgetting the past and looking forward to what lies ahead" (Philippians 3:13 NLT).

A secret to a happy new year is forgetting the negatives of the past.

Every man should forget his sins. The past will handcuff the present. Truett said, "If Paul had not learned how to forget those awful sins that mastered him back yonder, if he had not learned how to get past them, then he would have gone with an accusing conscience and broken spirit clear to his grave."[1]

Every man should forget his sorrows. Past sorrows suffocate present mercies.

Every man should forget his shortcomings. Always looking over your shoulder at failures you have experienced weighs the soul down and hinders forward progress. Don't let the past define your future. Chambers states, "Never let the sense of past failure defeat your next step."

Every man should forget his successes. Don't stroke the flesh over past achievements and triumph. Exhibit humility in every success or exaltation, knowing it comes from the hand of God and is not of your own doing.

Every man should forget his suffering. Hurts inflicted by another are grievous and, if not forgotten, infect the heart with poisonous bitterness, resentment, vengefulness, and hatred.

The bottom line: Unpack the hurtful, painful and distressing things of yesterday and leave them at the foot of the Cross.

"The past is over...forget it. The future holds hope...reach for it."
Chuck Swindoll

January 2

The Saint's 'Neglect Nots'

"Be thou faithful unto death" (Revelation 2:10).

The Bible is replete with many 'neglect nots' of spiritual growth for the new year.

Morning by Morning

Neglect not salvation. 'Neglect not so great salvation' (Hebrews 2:3). Apart from Jesus, there is no escape from the penalty of sin.

Neglect not Scripture. Like the Bereans, 'search the Scripture daily' (Acts 17:11). Gather heavenly manna for the soul each day.

Neglect not supplication. "Men ought always to pray, and not to faint" (Luke 18:1). Bunyan exhorts, "Pray often, for prayer is a shield to the soul, a sacrifice to God, and a scourge for Satan."

Neglect not the sanctuary. 'Do not forsake the assembling of yourselves together' (Hebrews 10:25). Without the church, the soul decays and the spiritual walk crumbles.

Neglect not soul winning. "Ye shall be witnesses unto me both in Jerusalem, and in all Judæa, and in Samaria, and unto the uttermost part of the earth" (Acts 1:8). On my way to preach, I noticed a pontoon boat on which was written, "Go" (on the left pontoon) and "Fish" (on the right pontoon). Every Christian is to "Go Fish."

Neglect not stewardship. "Upon the first day of the week let every one of you lay by him in store, as God hath prospered him" (I Corinthians 16:2). He that sows sparingly shall reap sparingly; he that sows bountifully shall reap bountifully (II Corinthians 9:6).

Neglect not self-examination. Like David, the Christian often should pray, "Search me, O God" (Psalm 139:23), regarding his walk with Christ, to detect sin, spiritual laxness, or heresy. Spiritual physicals are imperative in order to assure spiritual health.

Neglect not sacrificing self daily. "I die daily" (I Corinthians 15:31). There must be that daily presentation of the Christian's total self to the Lordship of Christ (Romans 12:1–2). Spurgeon admonishes, "Remember, O Christian, that thou art a son of the King of kings. Therefore, keep thyself unspotted from the world."[2] Ellicott says, "The true position of our natural appetites is that they should be entirely our servants and not our masters; that we should not follow or be led by them, but that they should follow and be led by us."[3]

Neglect not the second coming. "Looking for that blessed hope, and the glorious appearing of the great God and our Savior Jesus Christ, Who gave Himself for us" (Titus 2:13–14). Live in expectation of Christ's glorious return this year. Do soing will impact all you do.

Neglect not service. "For we are his workmanship, created in Christ Jesus unto good works" (Ephesians 2:10). MacArthur asserts, "Good works cannot produce salvation but are subsequent and resultant God-empowered fruits and evidences of it."[4]

Neglect not stirring up that gift God has placed within you (I Timothy 4:14). Keep the flame burning.

"Your priorities must be: God first, God second, and God third, until your life is continually face to face with God."
Oswald Chambers

January 3

Why I Believe the Bible to Be the Word of God (Part One)

"It is in truth, the word of God" (I Thessalonians 2:13).

What is the basis for belief that the Bible is the Word of God? While the Bible validates itself through an array of internal supports of its reliability—consistency, multiple witnesses, verifiable history—it is also validated by many external evidences.

The archaeological reason. The Bible is confirmed to be authentic by over one hundred archaeological discoveries. Scholars formerly denied what the Bible says about the existence of the Hittite nation and the description it gave of them. Then their capital city and public records were discovered at Bogazkoy, Turkey.[5] Skeptics thought Solomon's wealth was greatly exaggerated until recent discoveries revealed that in antiquity wealth was concentrated with the king.[6] Some claimed that there was never an Assyrian king named Sargon (Isaiah 20:1) until his palace was discovered in Khorsabad, Iraq.[7] King Belshazzar (Daniel 5) also was counted as fictitious until tablets were found showing that he was Nabonidus' son who served as coregent in Babylon.[8] Outside of the Bible, no documentation was known to give credence to the existence of Pontius Pilate. But in 1961, archaeologists discovered at Caesarea a stone that bore Pontius Pilate's inscription honoring the Roman emperor Tiberius. Coins have also been discovered dating from Pilate's gubernatorial rule.[9] The discovery of the Dead Sea Scrolls (February 20, 1947), the greatest archaeological discovery in the twentieth century, substantiates the integrity and accuracy of Scripture.

The scientific reason. Francis Bacon said, "A little science estranges a man from God; a lot of science brings him back."[10] The Bible contains scientific facts about the stars, moon, oceans, planets, chemistry of the blood, etc., that were not known to man for hundreds of years. How could that be? The Bible was divinely authored by an all-knowing God. These scientific facts clearly give credence to the authority of the Bible.

"Every graveyard and every cemetery testify that the Bible is true."
　　　　　Billy Graham

January 4

Why I Believe the Bible to Be the Word of God (Part Two)
"It is in truth, the word of God" (I Thessalonians 2:13).

The prophetic reason. "Fulfilled prophecy," states John MacArthur, "is perhaps the greatest proof that the Word of God is true. It carries the weight of proof for the Word of God further than any other single element of Scripture."[11] Micah prophesied the place where Jesus would be born, in Bethlehem Ephratah (Micah 5:2), and He *was* born there—700 years later. Isaiah prophesied Jesus would be born of a virgin (Isaiah 7:14), and He was. Daniel prophesied the exact year that Jesus would die (Daniel 9:24–27), and He died precisely at that time. Isaiah prophesied hundreds of years prior to Jesus' birth that He would be buried with the rich (Isaiah 53:9). This was fulfilled, despite the fact that Jesus was poor. He was buried in the unused tomb of a wealthy man, something unheard of prior to this. The same prophecy declared that Jesus would die with the wicked, something that indeed happened when He was crucified between two thieves. Jeremiah prophesied that the Messiah would be a descendant of King David (Jeremiah 23:5–6). Matthew 1 gives the lineage of Jesus to David. Isaiah foretold the rejection of Christ by His unbelieving people (Isaiah 53). This prophecy was fulfilled (John 1:11). In Christ's first coming to earth He fulfilled dozens of Old Testament prophecies.

The experiential reason. To the objective evidence that Bible is the Word of God found in archaeology, science and prophecy, add the subjective evidence of personal experience. I know the Bible is the divine Word of God due to the Holy Spirit's illumination and confirmation to me that it is, and because it does what it says it will do for me, in me, and through me. Personally, I can point to promises and precepts in the Bible that have been fulfilled in my life regarding salvation, forgiveness, strength, comfort, service, and more, as can millions of other believers.

A little boy had a tummy ache, and his mother asked why? He said, "I've been eating green apples."

The mother inquired, "How do you know it's the green apples that are causing the stomachache?"

"Because," the boy replied, "I have inside information."

How do I know the Bible is the Word of God? I have inside information. Every born-again believer does.

"The Holy Spirit," declares R. A. Torrey, "sets His seal in the soul of every believer to the divine authority of the Bible. Christ says, 'My sheep hear my voice.' God's children know His voice, and I know that the voice which speaks to me from the pages of that Book is the voice of my Father. Everyone can have that testimony. John 7:17 tells you how to get it: 'If any man will do his will, he shall know of the doctrine, whether it be of God.'"

"How unquestionably we must receive its statements of fact, bow before its enunciations of duty, tremble before its warnings, and rest upon its promises!"[12]

B. B. Warfield

January 5

A Prisoner's Dying Word

"I have fought a good fight, I have finished my course, I have kept the faith" (II Timothy 4:7).

Paul sums up his life in three ways. He states:

"I have fought a good fight." It was a good or worthy fight. Knight says, "The struggle is 'good' because he has engaged in it for God and the Gospel."[13] It was a fight well fought. When an athlete can really say he has done his best in a contest, then there is great satisfaction in his heart, whether he wins or loses.[14] Paul, now at the end of his life, looks back without regret, knowing he gave it his best shot. Barrie, upon his mother's death, said, "I can look back and I cannot see the smallest thing undone."[15] Knowledge at the last that we have done our best produces satisfaction like nothing else. Live life to the end knowing that you rolled

up your sleeves and fought every round for God and against Satan to the best of your ability.

"I have finished my course." Paul finished the race well. It is one thing to start a race; another, to finish it. "Endure [persevere] unto the end" (Matthew 24:13). Endurance "is that quality of character which does not allow one to surrender to circumstances or succumb under trial."[16] Wuest says it is "to remain under trials and testings in a way that honors God."[17] It is to not faint in battle, to fight until it's over. Paul epitomizes endurance. He refused to quit. Determinedly he chose to preach the Word "in season and out of season" (II Timothy 4:2) until the end. Many saints that run valiantly at the first of the race, faint toward the end. There is a plentitude of Demas's. There is a rarity of Paul's. A famous man refused to allow a biography of his life to be written while he was yet alive. In defense of the decision he said, "I have seen so many men fall out on the last lap." Be mindful that you don't fall out by the way on the final lap. With Vance Havner, pray, Lord, take me home before dark.

"I have kept the faith." Paul persevered in the whole of biblical truth and its proclamation despite the hardship, hostilely, and hurt suffered. Never betray the Lord or His Word. Simeon surmises. "He had maintained a warfare against the world, the flesh, and the devil: he had run his race with indefatigable zeal and ardor: he had kept the faith with undaunted courage and constancy: he had disregarded life itself when it stood in competition with his duty."[18]

"The only course open to us is to plow right on to the end of the furrow, and never think of leaving the field till the Master shall call us home."[19]
              C. H. Spurgeon

January 6

The Wounded Spirit
"The spirit of a man will sustain his infirmity; but a wounded spirit who can bear?" (Proverbs 18:14).

A wounded spirit (broken, damaged or crushed spirit) is the painful injury to the heart (emotions).

Causes. The wounded spirit results from, among other things, abuse, betrayal, sorrow, desertion, slander, scorn, belittlement, hypercriticism, and insult.

Consequences. Left unchecked, the wounded spirit precipitates plaguing pain and hurt, resentment, retaliation, hostility, feelings of inferiority, and inner turmoil. It is fueled by unrelenting focus on the injury and unforgiveness toward the offender.

Cures. (1) Forgiveness. Stephen Arterburn said, "When we hold fast to resentment, we chain ourselves to a pain we cannot undo. The alternative is to move on, give up our right to resent, and find a way to forgive."[20] MacArthur states, "Forgiveness reflects the character of God. Unforgivingness is therefore ungodly. That means unforgivingness is no less an offense to God than fornication or drunkenness, even though it is sometimes deemed more acceptable."[21] (2) Forgetfulness. When we grant forgiveness, does that entail a promise to forget the offense completely? No, for there is no way to completely erase the bitter past. What it does mean is that we promise not to ever bring the offense up again. Jay Adams characterizes this promise as threefold: "You promise not to remember his sin by bringing it up to him, to others, or to yourself. The sin is buried."[22] (3) Faithfulness. Abide in Christ, and His presence and power will grant healing to the hurt and pain, and deliverance from the affliction.

"Man is a double being: he is composed of body and soul, and each of the portions of man may receive injury and hurt."[23]
–C. H. Spurgeon

January 7

Who Cares for My Soul?
"I looked on my right hand, and beheld, but there was no man that would know me: refuge failed me; no man cared for my soul" (Psalm 142:4).

Who cares if a person is saved from a life of degradation, meaninglessness, despair, and an eternity in Hell?

God cares; that's why He sent His only Son into the world to die upon an old rugged Cross to make possible man's forgiveness for sin and reconciliation to Himself (John 3:16).

Jesus cares; that's why He willingly bore the ridicule, mockery, torture, and crucifixion at Calvary to make atonement for man's sin (Philippians 2:5–8). T. DeWitt Talmage said, "From the first infant step to the last step of manhood on the sharp spike of Calvary, a journey for you—oh, how He cared for your soul!"[24]

The Holy Spirit cares; that's why He convicts man of sin (John 16:8), draws him to Christ (John 6:44), and orchestrates opportunities for the hearing of the Gospel and appeals to be saved.

The Christian cares; that's why he risks rejection and persecution and expends time, treasure, and energy in sharing the Good News with men (Romans 9:1–3). Spurgeon said of John Bunyan that "he often felt while preaching that he could give his own salvation for the salvation of his hearers."[25] And then Spurgeon said, "And I pity the man who has not felt the same."[26]

The Church cares; that's why within her doors, the unadulterated gospel message of Christ crucified, buried, and raised from the dead is preached clearly and soundly, with appeals to be reconciled to God (I Timothy 3:15), and outreach and mission endeavors are implemented to reach the unsaved.

The Sinner in Hell cares; that's why he begs Abraham to send Lazarus or someone else back from the dead to warn family members not to go to that place of eternal torment (Luke 16:27–28).

The Saint in Heaven cares; that's why there is rejoicing about the throne when a lost soul is saved from the jaws of ruination and damnation (Luke 15:10). At the last judgment, no man can say, "No man cared for my soul" (Psalm 142:4).

"God proved His love on the Cross. When Christ hung, and bled, and died, it was God saying to the world, 'I love you.'"[27]
                                    Billy Graham

January 8

Rescue From Divine Judgment

"Like a city that is broken down, and without walls" (Proverbs 25:28).

January

In biblical times walls would be erected about cities to protect against enemy attacks. Sizable broken portions of the wall created a gap through which the enemy could enter, making the city vulnerable. A man was needed to stand in that gap for the city's protection.

God used the analogy of a breach or opening in the wall as a visual aid to indicate man's defenselessness against His judgment upon sin. Men brazenly fortify the gap with religion, humanitarianism, morality, and philosophy.

But the stoutest fence cannot keep back the wrath of God that must be poured out upon sin (Romans 6:23). No man is invincible against the malady of sin and its consequences (Romans 3:23).

Then what is the hope of rescue? Paul answers by saying, "But when the fullness of the time had come, God sent forth His Son, made of a woman, made under the law, to redeem those who were under the law, that we might receive the adoption of sons" (Galatians 4:4–5 KJ21). God's love and pity for man over his wanton estate and damnable plight compelled Him to send His only begotten Son into the world so "that whosoever believeth in Him should not perish, but have everlasting life" (John 3:16).

Jesus stands in the gap against the power and penalty of sin. Receiving Him by faith, coupled with repentance, averts the eternal judgment of God forever (Romans 5:9). Saith John, "But to as many as did receive him, to those who put their trust in his person and power, he gave the right to become children of God" (John 1:12 CJB).

"We are justified, not by giving anything to God—what we do—but by receiving from God what Christ hath done for us."
William Gurnall

January 9

Jesus Holds Your Hand (Part One)

"I the LORD thy God will hold thy right hand" (Isaiah 41:13).

Courson says, "The metaphor of being in someone's hand (or having their hand on someone) was common in the Old Testament and spoke of being in the power of that person or entity."[28] The Sovereign God of all Creation says to His children, 'I will hold thy hand.' The grasp of Jesus' hand conveys His willingness and ableness to help in the time of need.

Knowing that Jesus is clutching your hand tightly brings calm in calamity. A little boy approaching surgery was asked if he could bear up to it. Replied the boy, "Yes, if my father will hold my hand." Saints can bear up to and endure exceedingly more than they imagine, with their Father holding their hand.

Knowing that Jesus holds your hand brings confidence and courage in conflict. The psalmist testified, "My soul clings to You; Your right hand upholds me" (Psalm 63:8 NASB95). "In tough times, we can become so preoccupied with our role in 'clinging to God' that we forget about His promised protection. It's not our fingernails that sustain us—it's His loving, upholding hand."[29] See Psalm 18:35.

Knowing that Jesus holds your hand brings direction in distress. It's not essential that you know the next step if you are clasped in God's hand; He is in control, guiding every footstep (Psalm 37:23*)*. The psalmist said, "If I take the wings of the morning and dwell in the uttermost parts of the sea, even there your hand shall lead me, and your right hand shall hold me" (Psalm 139:9–10 ESV). Wherever the "there" may be (sorrow, sickness, suffering, trouble), His hand shall lead you and uphold you.

Knowing that Jesus holds your hand brings perseverance in pain. The hardship or trial will not prevail against the saint that faces it with Jesus' hand clasped around him. Jesus will turn the pain into great gain (James 1:2–4, 12).

"Storms may be howling and blowing, but Jesus is holding my hand."
Alfred Barrett

January 10

Jesus Holds Your Hand (Part Two)

"So I decided there is nothing better than to enjoy food and drink and to find satisfaction in work. Then I realized that these pleasures are from the hand of God" (Ecclesiastes 2:24 NLT).

Knowing that Jesus holds your hand brings provision in paucity (insufficiency). James reminds us, "Every good gift and every perfect gift is from above, and cometh down from the Father of lights, with whom is no variableness, neither shadow of turning" (James 1:17). All we receive is from the gracious hand of Jesus (even if delivered via friends). His hand is always engaged in supplying our need according to His riches in Glory, whether that need be healing, money, hope, comfort, or peace (Philippians 4:19).

Knowing that Jesus holds your hand brings assurance in apprehension. The hand clutched to ours suffered the nails at Calvary, and its grasp is unbreakable (John 10:29).

Knowing that Jesus holds your hand brings steadiness in shakiness. "I will steady him with my hand; with my powerful arm I will make him strong" (Psalm 89:21 NLT).

Knowing that Jesus holds your hand brings grace in grief. Grief may be beyond measure, rendering you unable to heal yourself, but it is not beyond Christ's grace; He can relieve it, granting peace, comfort, and hope. There is no hell on earth or sorrow of heart that is so deep that His grace cannot go deeper still. Where heartache and despair abound, Christ's grace abounds more (John 1:16).

Knowing that Jesus holds your hand brings delight in death. The same hand that has clasped the saints' hands tightly yet gently in the storms of life will do the same as we cross chilly Jordan into sweet Canaan Land. "I won't have to cross Jordan alone."

"Child of God, see where thou art. Thou art completely in the hand of God. Thou art absolutely and entirely, and in every respect, placed at the will and disposal of Him who is thy God."[30]
C. H. Spurgeon

January 11

Blame the Flame

"So they gave it me: then I cast it into the fire, and there came out this calf" (Exodus 32:24).

A golden calf was being worshipped by the people when Moses descended Mount Sinai. Upon his inquiry, Aaron said, 'They gave me their gold, I put it in the fire, and out came this calf.' In other words, he was saying, "I'm not responsible—blame the flame." He said not a word about the mold that was cast or the tool he personally used to shape the golden calf (Exodus 32:4).

The same excuse for wrongdoing is still used. "'Blame the flame' of my circumstances, my genes, my friends. Don't blame me." Nonetheless, man is solely responsible for his actions and is held accountable by God. 'Whatsoever a man sows, that he will also reap.'

Don't be a foolish Aaron. Stop blaming heredity, culture, family, friends, and circumstances for what you do. Acknowledge sin and personal responsibility for it. And then bring it to Jesus, who awaits your confession and will grant complete forgiveness (I John 1:9).

"The only hope for any of us is in a perfectly honest manliness to claim our sins. "I did it, I did it," let me say of all my wickedness. Let me refuse to listen for one moment to any voice which would make my sins less mine."[31]
Phillip Brooks

January 12

The Power of *Only* One Sin

"When sin completes its work, it brings death" (James 1:15 NLV).

Sin is such a potent pollutant that each time it is engaged in, it colors the person with its vileness and filth. Satan would have man believe that *one* sin won't hurt him. But Satan is a liar, and the truth is not in him. It will hurt man and color his life.

King Saul's one sin bothered him and stripped him of the crown. Though forgiven of the deed, David's sin with Bathsheba colored the rest of his life. Today, hundreds of years later, when David's name is mentioned, the sin is remembered. Only one sin can color a life with a stain that can never be shaken out or forgotten.

How powerful is just *one* sin carelessly committed?

It can alter God's plan. One sin dethroned King Saul. Moses was God's choice to lead the Israelites into Canaan, but one sin thwarted that plan. Throughout history, many have suffered a similar fate following the committing of just one sin.

One sin can spoil the testimony. Just ask David if that's not true.

January

One sin can shorten life. Len Bias, a basketball great, had his life snatched away as the result of taking one dose of cocaine. Fentanyl is snuffing out the lives of tens of thousands, including some first-time users.

One sin can lead to a life of addiction. A beer, a shot of whiskey, a snort of cocaine, the viewing of a pornography video or magazine, or a gamble made on the internet or at the office can all imprison a man for the rest of his life in chains of iron from which he cannot break free (John 8:36).

It takes only *one sin to condemn the soul to Hell* (John 3:18). The sin of unbelief in Jesus Christ, rejecting Him as Lord and Savior, leads to an eternity in eternal torment (Revelation 21:8).

All sin may be forgiven. C. S. Lewis said, "We have a strange illusion that mere time cancels sin. But mere time does nothing to either the fact or the guilt of a sin." It's the confession of the sin that cancels it and cleanses us of it (1 John 1:9).

Don't underestimate the consequences of only one sin. An ocean begins with a drop of water; a stone is first a little pebble, and a rock at first a tiny grain. Just so, a ruined and devastated life begins with just one sin. It's true that any sin but unbelief is forgivable, but its bitter consequences may not be avoided.

"Sin has the Devil for its father, shame for its companion, and death for its wages."
                                  Thomas Watson

January 13

Malfunctioning Watches

"Son of man, I have made thee a watchman unto the house of Israel: therefore hear the word at my mouth, and give them warning from me" (Ezekiel 3:17).

A watchmaker told me that four things caused a watch to malfunction: a cracked crystal, dirt, an imbalanced pendulum, and neglect of winding. A cracked crystal (duplicity of lifestyle), dirt (sin), an imbalanced pendulum (straying from the Bible), and neglect of winding (constant fellowship with Christ in the Word and prayer) likewise cause God's watchman to the world to malfunction.

Inconvenience, tardiness, burnt toast, and perhaps missed opportunities arise when the watch malfunctions. But when God's watchman does, hearts remain broken and hurting and, tragically far worse, die without Christ.

As God's watchmen, all believers must sound the alarm to the lost loudly, clearly, and constantly by staying spiritually in good repair. Stay wound, visible, clean, and accurate. Note: watches have no power to regulate those who read their time or hear their alarm; that's not in their power or design. It is the same with the watchman of God. He is responsible for sounding the alarm and proclaiming the message, not the success or failure of his proclamation (Ezekiel 3:18–21).

"Oh, my brothers and sisters in Christ, if sinners will be damned, at least let them leap to Hell over our bodies; and if they perish, let them perish with our arms about their knees, imploring them to stay and not madly to destroy themselves. If Hell must be filled, at least let it be filled in the teeth of our exertions, and let not one go there unwarned and unprayed for."[32]
C. H. Spurgeon

January 14

What Can the Righteous Do?
"If the foundations be destroyed, what can the righteous do?" (Psalm 11:3).

The "foundations" are the pillars upon which the fundamental principles of law and justice rest in society set in place by Sovereign God at creation and maintained.[33] "The righteous" refers to those who are upright and godly. The question posed is one that has been asked by the righteous time and again in the face of sweeping anti-Christian legislation and cultural reform ("deform"). It is being asked more and more as "political correctness" and "cancel culture" replace biblical and moral values and Christians are being persecuted and ostracized.

What can the righteous do? They must not be dissuaded from insistence on allegiance to Almighty God and His holy decrees in Scripture. They must not succumb to the evil tide, but resist it with every tooth and nail. Like David, they must refuse to 'flee to the mountains,' but be vigilant in the battle for the right, depending upon the power and authority of God for ultimate victory.

January

In the Lord put I my trust. Spurgeon asserts, "David here declares the great source of his unflinching courage. He borrows his light from Heaven—from the great central orb of Deity....'What can the righteous do in an unrighteous government?'" To the question, Spurgeon answers, "What can they not do?" when they trust in God, that reigns supreme in authority and power, praying for His divine intervention and protection (Psalm 11:4–7)."[34]

Matthew Henry remarks, "That which grieved him in this motion was not that to flee now would savor of cowardice, and ill become a soldier, but that it would savor of unbelief and would ill become a saint who had so often said, 'In the Lord put I my trust.'"[35]

J. M. Boice writes, "What can the righteous do? They can go on being righteous. And they can stand against the evil of their society."[36] "When wickedness gets the upper hand in these ways, times are hard indeed for good and faithful men. In such times Elijah, Jeremiah, and others lived and wept, and moaned, and prayed. Many a prophet of the Lord has had to look upon such a state of things, when all day long he stretched out his hands to a disobedient and gainsaying people."[37] The believer can do no less. The righteous must persevere courageously, saying with Edward Mote, "When all around my soul gives way, He then is all my hope and stay."

> His foes a season here may triumph and prevail;
> But ah, the hour is near when all their hopes must fail.
> Henry Francis Lyte

"What can the righteous do?" Methinks the question under any circumstances is not only unbelieving, but atheistical: for if there be a God, and that God be a hearer of prayer, the question would rather be, 'What cannot the righteous do?'"[38]
Charles Simeon

January 15

Lean on Your Staff

"Jacob, when he was a dying, blessed both the sons of Joseph; and worshipped, leaning upon the top of his staff" (Hebrews 11:21).

Morning by Morning

The writer of Hebrews says that as Jacob was dying, he leaned "upon the top of his staff" (Hebrews 11:21). Why? Undoubtedly, it supported his weak and frail body, preventing a fall. But it provided spiritual bracing as well through the memories with which it was associated. Every saint's "staff"—an old picture; a religious book; correspondence from cherished friends that has been stored away; mementos or awards and honors received; a ragged, tattered, and worn-out chair; a diary or journal; a Sunday school lectern or an old country church pulpit; or an altar or rock pile (prayer spot)—when he leans upon it, will do the same. Don't lay your staff aside just yet. Lean on it for the precious remembrances of the mercies, kindness, faithfulness of God, and the loyalty, love, and support of family and friends. And thereby be richly encouraged and deeply consoled.

"God hides inspiration in things of apparently little value and touches the imagination and the faith by books, ministries, churches, altars, which we thought had passed away into desuetude, perhaps oblivion."[39]
Joseph Parker

January 16

How to Come to Jesus
"There came a leper" (Matthew 8:2).

After Jesus had delivered the Sermon on the Mount, "there came a leper and worshipped him, saying, Lord, if thou wilt, thou canst make me clean" (Matthew 8:2). The manner in which the leper came to Jesus serves as a pattern for the sinner's coming to Him for salvation.

He came without pretense. The leper came conscious (fully aware) of his unclean and hopeless sick estate. All that are to be saved must first acknowledge their utter depravity and sinfulness. They must humbly say to Christ, without mask or costume, 'I acknowledge my transgression, and my sin is ever before me. Against thee, and thee alone, have I sinned' (Psalm 51:3–4).

He came without power. The leper was incapable of changing his leprous spots, of healing himself (Jeremiah 13:23). He had no power or control over the disease that ravaged his body. To be cleansed and made whole, the sinner must acknowledge the same about his sinful condition.

January

The leper came without promise. In coming to Jesus, the leper didn't claim a promise of healing, but said, "If thou wilt." What a demonstration of faith! To be saved, cleansed, and forgiven of sin, the sinner must come believing in Jesus' willingness and ability to do this. Unlike the leper, the sinner is promised that "whosoever shall call upon the name of the Lord shall be saved" (Romans 10:13). See John 6:37.

The leper came without people. "There came a leper." The unwillingness of other lepers to come to Christ didn't dissuade or discourage him from going to Him. The refusal of another mustn't hinder a person's reception of the offer of salvation. He must say, "Though none go with me, still I will follow." Methinks that once other lepers witnessed the miracle of healing in their friend, they sought out Christ. Likewise, the miraculous change in one who is saved impacts others to be saved.

The leper came without procrastination. The leper immediately seized the opportunity to be healed. The sinner must do the same with regard to Christ's invitation to be cleansed and forgiven (2 Corinthians 6:2). To delay may mean eternal doom. The leper's coming to Christ resulted in complete healing—nevermore to be a leper, nevermore to be confined to a leper's colony, nevermore having to cry out in the streets, "Leper." As wondrous as that was for him, it pales in comparison to the change Jesus makes in one who cries out, 'Lord, be merciful to me, a sinner.' He goes his way singing, "What a wonderful change in my life has been wrought, since Jesus came into my heart!"

"We come to His blood to be washed, to His righteousness to be cleansed, to His wounds to be healed, to His life for life eternal, and to His death for the death of our sins. We come to Jesus for everything, and the promise is that any man who comes, whoever he may be, shall find that he is not cast out."[40]
C. H. Spurgeon

January 17

The Sin of Not Soul Winning
"Ye shall be witnesses unto me" (Acts 1:8).

In the changing of the guard at Arlington Cemetery, the soldier from the previous hour's watch says only three words to the one taking his place: "Orders remain unchanged." The church was given orders to go and make disciples for Christ two thousand years ago—and "orders remain unchanged." The Christian who fails to win souls is guilty of six terrible sins.

It is a sin against the Savior. To not witness to the unsaved is a direct sin against the main command of Jesus (Acts 1:8), the last command of Jesus (Matthew 28:19–20), and the command dearest to the heart of Jesus (Acts 10:42). There is nothing that we can do to make up for not obeying Christ in this matter. No sacrifice, service, stewardship or study is sufficient.

It is a sin against Scripture. Failure to witness is rebellion against the Bible. Time and again Scripture instructs us to give a witness to the unsaved (Mark 16:15). And Jesus says, "If ye love me, keep my commandments" (John 14:15).

It is a sin against the sinner. To not give the Gospel to unsaved men is to sin against their souls' need for spiritual light—the truth about sin, the means of its forgiveness, and its eternal judgment.

It is a sin against the saved. The believer who neglects to witness hinders the progress of his church, for such disobedience grieves the Holy Spirit, hindering the full manifestation of His power. Further, it promotes complacency about soul winning in the lives of fellow saints.

It is a sin against society. Soul winning is the only cure for a sick and depraved world. Government and religion are unable to make the world better. Christ is the world's only hope.

It is a sin against the soul. Failure to be a soul winner hurts the saint personally. It stagnates his soul, steals his power, stunts his growth, softens his burden, and stains his hands with the blood of those he refused to tell of Jesus.

"There is no greater honor than to be the instrument in God's hands of leading one person out of the kingdom of Satan into the glorious light of Heaven."

D. L. Moody

January 18

Children as Arrows

"As arrows are in the hand of a mighty man; so are children of the youth" (Psalm 127:4).

Shape them. Children, like arrows, must be fashioned with the right components—biblical values, convictions, beliefs, and discipline—to go straight (Proverbs 22:6). Warped arrows lead to wayward lives. Criswell states, "Children must always be looked upon as belonging to the Lord. They are a sacred trust, a holy heritage. The rabbis of old declared that a child has three parents: God, his father, and his mother (Genesis 20:17–18; 30:1–2). Parents, then, are held accountable unto God for their stewardship of parenthood."[41] The shaping, to be of the greatest benefit, is to occur when they are young children.

Secure them. Children, like arrows, are to be kept safely in a quiver (the guardianship and protective custody of strong, godly parents and a Christian home) until the time of their discharge. Arrows mishandled, abused, or reshaped by wrong companions or shot prematurely, bring incalculable harm.

Shoot them. Children, like arrows, are not designed to remain forever in the safety of the quiver but at the proper time placed upon the bowstring and released into the world. Arrows in the quiver, though safe and pretty to behold, are unproductive. Though difficult and perhaps painful, the time arrives when parents must pull back the bowstring and shoot their arrows under divine guidance at the target of God's design and plan, possibly the mission field or other venue of Christian service.

Retrieve them. What is to be done if arrows miss the mark of God's approval? Rescue and restore them by divine enablement. The prodigal went astray but ultimately returned to the straight and narrow way (Luke 15).

"When a son is born into a family, a bow and arrow are hung before the gate."[42]

Chinese Proverb

January 19

Remembering God's Goodness
"Remember the former things of old" (Isaiah 46:9).

An often untapped source of comfort, hope, and peace in trial is remembering the former displays of God goodness. Why remember?

It is a pledge. What God did yesterday on our behalf is an argument for His willingness to do it again. It's the argument (rationale, reasoning) that David used in fighting Goliath. He said to Saul, "The LORD that delivered me out of the paw of the lion, and out of the paw of the bear, he will deliver me out of the hand of this Philistine" (1 Samuel 17:37). Sangster said, "God never gives a blessing just for the hour. Every special blessing is not only for the hour itself, but for the future. It is a pledge; it is as though God were to say, 'I'll do this for you now; then you will always know that you are the object of my love.'"

It is a preventative. Remembered past mercies safeguard us against despair, fear and doubt. Matthew Henry states, "The remembrance of the works of God will be a powerful remedy against distrust of his promise and goodness, for he is God and changes not."[43]

It is a proof. Yesterday's mercies provide evidence for God's dependability and trustworthiness in the present. God is "a very present help in trouble" (Psalm 46:1).

It is a push. The past works of God arouse hope in the dark times that He will intervene and deliver again (Psalm 124:1, 4). God didn't deliver me then to desert me now. In commemoration of success in battle at the hand of God, Samuel erected on behalf of Israel a monument of remembrance and named it Ebenezer, saying, "Hitherto hath the LORD helped us" (1 Samuel 7:12). Its objective was to instill confident trust in God in future conflicts by reminding them of His mightiness and faithfulness that delivered them that day. Our Ebenezer is not a chiseled stone pillar, but a sanctified memory chest. Utilize it.

"One of God's wonders placed before the eyes gives reality also to all the others."[44]

Hengstenberg

January 20

Incomprehensible Peace

"The peace of God that exceeds all understanding will keep your hearts and minds safe in Christ Jesus" (Philippians 4:7 CEB).

The peace of God transcends all understanding in three ways:

1) In the tranquilly it gives when storms shake and rattle life but cannot thrust it into chaos or hopelessness like that which the ungodly experience in such times. Spurgeon asserts, "The Christian is often surprised at his own peacefulness. There is a possibility of having the surface of the mind lashed into storm, while yet, deep down, all is still. There are earthquakes, yet the earth pursues the even tenor of its way. It surpasses understanding, but not experience."[45]

2) In its manifestation regardless of whether or not the believer's prayer is granted.[46] Possessing peace when prayers for healing or deliverance are denied exceeds the mind's ability to understand.

3) In its power to lift the soul that is in deepest despair one moment to a state of almost unbelievable serenity the next, which amazes the saint and gravely confuses the ungodly.

"It [God's peace] transcends human intellect, analysis, and insight."[47]
John MacArthur

January 21

A Handful of Theology

"What is that in thine hand?" (Exodus 4:2).

The hand is helpful as a ready prop to aid in the understanding of fundamental biblical doctrine.

The thumb stands for a theology of God. Since the thumb is the hand's first "finger," it is good to let it stand for God, who ought always to be first in our life. God is omnipotent (all-powerful), omniscient (all-knowing), omnipresent (everywhere), immutable (unchanging), holy, and loving.

The second finger stands for a theology of the Bible. The Bible is the inerrant and infallible Word of God. It has the power to convict a man of sin and bring him to God. No other book in the world can do that. Nothing is said in the Bible that shouldn't have been said, and nothing which God wanted to include is missing.

The tallest finger stands for a theology of Sin and Satan. Sin entered the human race in the Garden of Eden when Adam and Eve disobeyed God (Romans 5:12) and brought the consequence of separation from God presently and eternally (Romans 6:23). This finger also represents the doctrine of Satan. He is for real. The Bible teaches that he possesses intelligence (2 Corinthians 11:3), emotions (Revelation 12:17), and a will (2 Timothy 2:26) and that his avowed purpose is to thwart the plan of God in redemption by every means possible. Disguised as a wily serpent or an attractive angel of light, he is the master deceiver, the wellspring of lies, the evil one, the tempter, a murderer, and the spoiler of good.

The ring finger stands for a theology of Salvation. It is fitting to attach salvation to the ring finger, for this doctrine is all about God's wondrous love for the world. He so loved mankind that He sent His only Son to die on the cross to make possible our forgiveness from sin (John 3:16). When one receives Jesus into his life through faith and repentance, that life is reconciled to God (John 1:12).

The little finger stands for a theology of Last Things. The Bible speaks of three events that will happen in the future. The first is the return of Christ to earth. In John 14:3, Jesus declared that He was going back to Heaven but would return. The second event is that of Judgment. There are two distinct Judgments, one for the unsaved (Revelation 20:11–15) and one for the saved (2 Corinthians 5:10). Every courtroom in America has a judge who sits on a bench and makes people take responsibility for their actions. God will do the same. Next, the Bible speaks of two eternal abodes: Heaven and Hell (Philippians 3:20–21; Luke 16:22–23). Heaven is a glorious place reserved for those in whose lives Jesus is present, while Hell is a place of eternal punishment for those in whose lives He is absent.

"All my theology is reduced to this narrow compass—'Jesus Christ came into the world to save sinners.'"
Archibald Alexander

January 22

Uplifted Eyes

"Behold, as the eyes of servants look unto the hand of their masters, and as the eyes of a maiden unto the hand of her mistress; so our eyes wait upon the LORD our God, until that he have mercy upon us" (Psalm 123:2).

The uplifted eyes to the Master are the testimony of a dependent heart. The servant trusts and relies upon the Master implicitly to supply every need and care.

The uplifted eyes to the Master are the testimony of a submissive heart. The servant awaits instructions from the Master to promptly obey and comply.

The uplifted eyes to the Master are the testimony of a grateful heart. The servant acknowledges with gratitude the Master's abundant goodness. "Every good gift and every perfect gift is from above, and cometh down from the Father of lights" (James 1:17).

The uplifted eyes to the Master are the testimony of a pleasing heart. The servant's goal is to bring delight to the Master in all that is done.

The uplifted eyes to the Master are the testimony of a believing heart. The servant trusts the Master without question, for his best good to be accomplished.

Just so it is with the servant (saint) and his Master (the Lord Jesus Christ). Servants of the Lord should look steadily to His guiding hand for direction, supplying hand for provision, caring hand for comfort and protection, enabling hand for service, and correcting hand when he has done wrong.

Chambers wrote, "This verse is a description of total reliance on God. Just as the eyes of a servant are riveted on his master, our eyes should be directed to and focused on God. This is how knowledge of His countenance is gained and how God reveals Himself to us. Our spiritual strength begins to be drained when we stop lifting our eyes to Him."[48]

Matthew Henry asserts, "Hypocrites have their eye to the world's hand; thence they have their reward (Matthew 6:2); but true Christians have their eye to God as their rewarder."[49]

"Let us keep our eyes fixed on Jesus, on whom our faith depends from beginning to end" (Hebrews 12:2 GNT).

"The lifting up of the eyes implies faith and confident persuasion that God is ready and willing to help us. The very lifting up of the bodily eyes towards Heaven is an expression of this inward trust."[50]
Thomas Manton

January 23

The Positive Side of Death (Part One)

"The day of one's death [for the saved soul] is better than the day of one's birth!" (Ecclesiastes 7:1 CSB).

Amid death's negative aspects (departure from loved ones and friends, cessation of noble and beneficial work for Christ, the horrendous grief to those that remain, etc.), one finds several positive facets.

Death protects from the evil that is ahead. Isaiah states that saints die (at the time they do) to spare them from the evil days ahead (Isaiah 57:1–2). What a thought! Death is God's grace at work protecting saints who die from future heartache of immeasurable proportions. Thus, death is a merciful friend! Our shortsightedness conceals what awaits down the road. Earth's perspective often fails to see Heaven's perspective (Isaiah 55:8–9) regarding death.

Death makes room for others. Parker asserts, "And some great names must be removed to make way for lesser names that have growing sap in them and real capability of beneficent expansion. Some great trees must be cut down to make room for lesser trees that mean to be great ones in their time. We owe much to the cutting-down power of death, the clearing power of the cruel scythe or axe."[51]

Death frees man from sin's vexation and temptation. Saith Spurgeon, "When a man is saved by divine grace, he is not wholly cleansed from the corruption of his heart. When we believe in Jesus Christ, all our sins are pardoned; yet the power of sin, albeit that it is weakened and kept under by the dominion of the new-born nature which God doth infuse into our souls, doth not cease, but still tarrieth in us, and will do so to our dying day." The Christian, in death, ends the battle with the old Adamic nature and is free at last. At death, grace is perfected in man. Death is under the control of God. "My times are in thy hand" (Psalm 31:15). We die when God deems it best for us, perhaps for our family or for others, and for His glory. See Isaiah 46:10.

January

"Never fear dying, beloved. Dying is the last, but the least matter that a Christian has to be anxious about."
C. H. Spurgeon

January 24

The Positive Side of Death (Part Two)

"The day of one's death [for the saved soul] is better than the day of one's birth!" (Ecclesiastes 7:1).

Death ushers the saint to Heaven. Spurgeon said, "The best moment of a Christian's life is his last one, for then he is nearest Heaven." As death shuts one door, it opens another immediately into the presence of Jesus. The outward man is merely a temporary tent, one awesomely and marvelously made, to house the soul (2 Corinthians 5:1). When the tent is no longer habitable, it collapses, and its tenant changes residency to Canaan's fair land. Criswell comments, "While I'm in this house [the flesh], I can't have my new house. God has to tear down this old house first before He can construct my new house, the one made without hands, eternal in the heavens (2 Corinthians 5:1)."[52] A man noticed a house with a sign that read, "This House for Sale." "How is this? Is the former tenant dead?" the man asked.

"Oh, no, sir," said the caretaker; "he has removed to a larger house in a better situation." Similarly, the Christian at death moves into a superior and permanent house, one not built with hands, in Heaven.

Death is the day of cure. That which plagues the body and mind with torment and agony, at death will be healed. There will be no more pain or sorrow. At death, the suffering and sorrowing saint shouts, "Free at last, free at last! Praise God Almighty, I'm free at last."

Death means the end of the battle. At death, the conflict is over, and the conquest is achieved. The sword is forever sheathed, and the saint says, "I have fought a good fight, I have finished my course, I have kept the faith: Henceforth there is laid up for me a crown of righteousness, which the Lord, the righteous judge, shall give me at that day" (2 Timothy 4:7–8).

"Death to the Christian is the funeral of all his sorrows and evils, and the resurrection of all his joys."
James H. Aughey

January 25

Why Pray?

"Men ought always to pray, and not to faint" (Luke 18:1).

Why pray? The preeminent intention of prayer is found in Jesus' prayer in John 12 when He said, "Father, glorify thy name" (John 12:28). Ole Hallesby said, "Prayer is ordained for the purpose of glorifying the name of God."[53]

Why pray? Spurgeon says, "We do not bow the knee merely because it is a duty and a commendable spiritual exercise, but because we believe that into the ear of the eternal God we speak our wants, and that His ear is linked with a heart feeling for us and a hand working on our behalf. To us, true prayer is true power."[54]

Why pray? We pray out of obedience to the Lord (Luke 18:1). We pray, for it's part of worship to Him (Psalm 95:6–7). We pray to have an intimate connection to and communion with God. We pray, for it's God's appointed means of receiving good things at His hand (Luke 11:13). We pray to obtain grace and mercy for every need (Hebrews 4:16).

Why pray? Because prayer is an exchange. "We leave our burdens, worries and sin in the hands of God. We come away with the oil of joy and the garment of praise."[55] We pray, for to it God has attached divine promises (Matthew 7:7) that can only be claimed through engaging in it.

Why pray? Believers pray to acquire the power of the Holy Spirit to live the victorious Christian life. We pray to break down the strongholds of Satan, thwart his devious and malicious work, and drive him back from the ground he has gained in the church, Christian work, and lives.

Why pray? Pray to thrust needed workers into the harvest (Matthew 9:38). A. B. Simpson says, "Prayer is the mighty engine that is to move the missionary work."[56]

Why pray? We pray to solicit the power and grace of God to bind up the brokenhearted, to set the prisoner free, to comfort all that mourn by giving them beauty for ashes and the garment of praise for the spirit of heaviness (Isaiah 61:1–3).

Why pray? We pray to nourish and sustain the soul.

Why pray? We pray, for it is the means of supremest joy and delight. David testified that time spent in communion and fellowship with the Lord filled him with "great" authentic joy.

Why pray? We pray because prayer changes things.

Why pray? Schauffler, says, "When we are on our knees, then light flashes, then the intellect is clarified, then the conscience is aroused, then the spiritual sensibilities are quickened; and we can learn more of our duty and of His will than in hours of argumentation."[57]

"Our prayers lay the track down which God's power can come. Like a mighty locomotive, his power is irresistible, but it cannot reach us without rails."
Watchman Nee

January 26

The Prayer of Nehemiah
"Nevertheless we made our prayer unto our God" (Nehemiah 4:9).

Nehemiah benefited mightily from constant prayer. Prayer revealed the call to him to rebuild the walls about Jerusalem and restore worship in the Temple (Nehemiah 1:4–11). It granted him permission to talk to the king and gain his favor with the project through authorizing it and supplying the material to undertake it. It gave him the strategy and "Holy Spirit engineering" required for the work. (He didn't have a "How to Fix a Wall" handbook. Prayer revealed each step to take in building it.) It fortified him from the harm of railing accusations and assaults of the enemy. It afforded him support in the project from almost all the people in the city. It bolstered his courage not to back down to the enemy's threats and tricks or quit the work out of cowardice. It provided discernment when it would have been ill advised to hide when told of an assassination plot on his life. It gave him a refuge from the slander and lies propagated about him. It kept him focused on the task, unworried by the hostile opposition.

And through it he accomplished the arduous and onerous task assigned in fifty-two days (Nehemiah 6:15). Why was prayer so efficacious and beneficial to him? It was because it, as Redpath says, "was grounded in the Word, founded on the promises, rooted in God's past dealings."[58] Nehemiah was an ordinary man such as you and I. But he was a man who believed in and depended upon prayer to accomplish a heavenly assignment. Let it likewise be employed to benefit us.

"Prayer is the ship which bringeth home the richest freight—the soil which yields the most abundant harvest."[59]

C. H. Spurgeon

January 27

The Night Cometh

"I must work the works of him that sent me, while it is day: the night cometh, when no man can work" (John 9:4).

The mandate. The work of enlightening the lost to the need of salvation through sundry means must be engaged in promptly, without trifling and balking.

The motive. The impetus to do the work is not only its divine directive and divine strength, but its short duration. Our opportunity is fleeting. The day quickly will give way to the night. Time squandered cannot be reclaimed. Souls not warned and won die eternally damned. Note: Christ kept before Him the coming night as He fulfilled His redemptive mission. He used every day, hour, and moment prudently to that end. The urgency of the work necessitates His followers doing the same.

The must. Christ *must* do the work the Father gave Him. Spurgeon says, "With Christ it was not 'I may if I will,' 'I can if I like,' but 'I must.'" The cords of love for the Father and love for sinful man bound Him to the work incessantly. And it likewise *must* bind us. The divine *must* of the work *must* be manifest in us. Work in such a manner that at the coming of night you may exclaim to the Father, as did Christ, "I have finished the work you gave me to do" (John 17:4 GNT).

"'The night cometh.' You cannot put it off, however much you may dread it. It comes for the pastor, missionary, father, mother."

C. H. Spurgeon

January 28

Defense of the Faith

"Earnestly contend for the faith which was once delivered unto the saints" (Jude 3).

Note the traits of the Christian's defensible faith.

It is a common faith, available and sufficient to redeem from sin and its penalty, regardless of face, race, or place (Jude 3a).

It is a complete faith; nothing more needs to be added or can be added (Jude 3b).

It is a certain faith, absolutely authentic, trustworthy, and reliable (Jude 3a). Spurgeon says of Scripture, "These words come from Him who can make no mistake and who can have no wish to deceive His creatures. If I did not believe in the infallibility of the Book, I would rather be without it."[60]

It is a contested faith. Liberalism and heresy threaten its purity, influence, and propagation (Jude 4), while governments seek to silence and/or eradicate it.

It is a combative faith worthy of suffering and dying for (Acts 5:41). Being silent, for whatever reason, against the advancement of antibiblical legislation, antagonism to biblical cultural, and liberal religious ideologies is deplorable. It's imperative that Christians mobilize and fight for the preservation (and restoration) of that which is right morally, ethically, politically, and biblically. With Paul, the Christian should say, "I am set for the defence of the gospel" (Philippians 1:17). Contend for the faith (sound doctrine) earnestly, strenuously, courageously, perseveringly, and fearlessly (not furiously).

It is a conquering faith. Jude says that God "is able to keep you [the defender of the faith] from falling [stumbling, caving in to the pressures of liberalism, damnable heresies, false teachers and the contagion of sin], and to present you faultless [blameless] before the presence of his glory with exceeding joy" (Jude 24). See Ephesians 6:10.

"Many tsunamis are coming against the church today. The pressure to compromise and redefine the Gospel by finding a 'middle way' might well undermine 'the faith which was once delivered unto the saints.'"[61]

Erwin Lutzer

January 29

Nonconformists

"Don't be like the people of this world [conformed], but let God change the way you think [transformed]" (Romans 12:2 CEV).

The "world" is that which is antagonistic to the things of God and His work in the soul of man.

The design of worldly conformity is to have the believer's life governed by carnal principles, pursuits, and pleasures, to the neglect of the spiritual. Graham said, "The pagan world is still trying to put its stamp of conformity on every follower of Jesus Christ. Every possible pressure is being brought to bear upon Christians to make them conform to the standards of the present world...;be a committed follower of Jesus Christ."

The danger of worldly conformity includes worldliness, shipwrecks, and the ravaging of the Christian's walk and life. It ruined Lot's wife, Achan, Haman, Judas, Simon Magus, and Demas. It will devastate and ravage your life as well. It is impossible to serve two masters without loving the one and hating the other (Matthew 6:24).

The directive against worldly conformity. Paul exhorts, "Don't be conformed [molded] to this world" (Romans 12:2 WEB) and "Come out from among them, and be ye separate" (2 Corinthians 6:17). Don't approve of the world. Don't copy the world. Don't compromise with the world. Don't seek the approval of the world. Don't mingle with the world (2 Corinthians 6:14).

The deterrence of worldly conformity. Daily present your body to God as a living sacrifice, crucifying the appetites and allurements of the flesh (Romans 12:1). Live as a separatist (2 Corinthians 6:17–18). Love not the world (1 John 2:15). Pray for the needed grace to resist the pull and pressure of the world to become what it is. Like Paul, exert rigorous discipline to bring your body under strict control lest you become a castaway (1 Corinthians 9:27).

A preacher came to a city to win its people to Christ. At first, they listened to his sermons but then gradually drifted away until no one came to hear him preach. A man passing through the town inquired of the preacher, "Why do you go on preaching?"

He replied, "In the beginning, I hoped to change these people. If I still shout, it is only to prevent them from changing me." We, preachers and laymen alike, have to keep "shouting" the truth to keep the world from changing us.

"We are not to conform. A true Christian, living an obedient life, is a constant rebuke to those who accept the moral standards of this world."
Billy Graham

January 30

The Infilling of the Holy Spirit

"And be not drunk with wine, wherein is excess; but be filled with the Spirit" (Ephesians 5:18).

The infilling of the Holy Spirit (control to a larger measure by the Holy Spirit) is commanded, and therefore attainable. How is the believer infilled with the Holy Spirit?

It takes an understanding. Not to be confused with the baptism or indwelling of the Spirit that occurs once and for all at the moment of salvation, the infilling of the Spirit allows Him to be president, governing the whole of life. "Let me say," writes Oswald Smith, "that it is not a question of us getting more of the Holy Spirit, but rather of the Holy Spirit getting more of us."[62] Watchman Nee asserts, "Just as the right relationship with Christ generates a Christian, so the proper relationship with the Holy Spirit breeds a spiritual man."[63] The Holy Spirit is the power source for victorious Christian living and success in ministry endeavors.

A slow-witted farmer purchased a chainsaw after being told that it was guaranteed to cut down forty trees a day. In a week's time, he returned the chainsaw to the store. The salesman inquired as to the problem, and the farmer replied, "I have been working my head off, and I ain't able ta bring down more than five trees a day." The salesman, with a frown, looked at the chainsaw and then pulled its starter cord. As it roared to life, the farmer jumped back and exclaimed, "What's that noise?"

Sadly, far too many believers, when told about the liberating, illuminating, triumphing, enabling, equipping, and emboldening power of the Holy Spirit available to live the victorious Christian life and accomplish ministry undertakings, exclaim, "What's that?" Such ignorance leads to a life of religious self-effort, which results in defeat, discouragement, and little fruit. Christians who are not walking under the control of the Holy Spirit are like the slow-witted farmer; they are trying to cut down trees with a chainsaw that's not powered on.

It takes a thirsting. The Holy Spirit infills the person who has nothing less than an aching void for more of His fullness and power.

It takes a cleansing. Sin must be confessed and renounced (1 John 1:9). The Holy Spirit will only infill and use a clean vessel.

It takes a surrendering. The total self must be submitted to His fullest control (withholding nothing). In faith, claim the promise of the infilling (empowering, enabling, emboldening, quickening) of the Holy Spirit.

It takes asking. Jesus said, "If ye then, being evil, know how to give good gifts unto your children: how much more shall your heavenly Father give the Holy Spirit to them that ask him?" (Luke 11:13). Pray with Augustine, "O Holy Spirit, descend plentifully into my heart. Enlighten the dark corners of this neglected dwelling and scatter there Thy cheerful beams." Based upon God's command to be infilled, walk in faith, believing the promise that all who meet the condition of the command are infilled (Luke 11:11–13).

"The Spirit-filled life is not a special, deluxe edition of Christianity. It is part and parcel of the total plan of God for His people."
A. W. Tozer

January 31

Dress for Battle

"Put on the whole armor of God, that ye may be able to stand against the wiles of the devil" (Ephesians 6:11).

To battle Satan the saint must dress with spiritual armor (Ephesians 6:10–17). Stormie Omartian wrote, "The Bible would not have told us to take up the whole armor of God in order to withstand evil if evil could have been withstood without doing that." Put the armor on with prayer. Pray, "Heavenly Father, I put on the whole armor provided for my victory over Satan.

January

"*I put on the Belt of Truth.* To the Word of God may I stand faithful and true despite what happens. May Your Word, not my emotions, order my steps this day.

"*I put on the Breastplate of Righteousness.* Help me live a righteous and holy life by heeding Your Word, for it is a mighty shield against Satan's assault.

"*I put on the Gospel Shoes.* In the battle against Satan and in my witness to salvation, help me be surefooted by attachment to Your Word. May I stand ready to plunge into every opportunity to share the Gospel's good news.

"*I put on the Shield of Faith.* I choose to trust YOU with whatever happens because of Your love for me and promises to me. You will repel Satan's fiery darts of doubt and lies that are hurled at me. I will rejoice this day in knowing that nothing can separate me from Your wonderful love and care—nothing!

"*I put on the Helmet of Salvation.* May my mind be kept from carnal and injurious thoughts by staying fixed upon YOU. Keep my mind under Your constant control.

"*I pick up the Sword of the Spirit.* May I use Scripture to drive Satan back, thwart his work, overcome temptation, and win the lost.

"*I resort to Prayer in the Spirit.* May I continuously seek Your counsel and strength about all things as I walk through this day. In Jesus' name I pray, Amen."

"It is only by donning the divine panoply that believers can be properly equipped against the Devil's attacks."[64]
P. T. O'Brien

February 1

A Solemn Assembly

"Blow the trumpet in Zion, sanctify a fast, call a solemn assembly" (Joel 2:15).

In times of extraordinary spiritual decline, a Solemn Assembly is in order for saints to seek God's face through confession of sin, repentance, and fasting.

The compulsion for it. The spiritual declension of God's people—biblical compromise, worldly conformity and lukewarmness—and the world's moral decadence, antagonism toward God, and the Woke agenda necessitate a solemn assembly more than ever.

The convener of it. In the Old Testament, its call usually came from a prophet, priest, or king. In New Testament times, the call comes to the congregation or ministry organization from a spiritual leader.

The cause for it is to be spiritually renewed and restored as God's people by exhibiting humility toward God, seeking God's face and guidance, confessing personal and corporate sin, and aligning with His Word and will (2 Chronicles 7:14). "Who knows? He [God] may turn and have pity and leave behind a blessing" (Joel 2:14. EHV). Joel's call requires a prompt response, "Consecrate a fast, Proclaim a solemn assembly; Gather the elders And all the inhabitants of the land To the house of the LORD your God, And cry out to the LORD" (Joel 1:14 NASB).

"A Solemn Assembly gives God an opportunity to respond to His people at a level He cannot possibly do when they are living in neglect of His Word or in direct violation of His commandments."[65]
John Owens Roberts

February 2

The Devil

"Be sober, be vigilant; because your adversary the devil, as a roaring lion, walketh about, seeking whom he may devour" (1 Peter 5:8).

Reality of the Devil. The primary witness to the reality and existence of Satan is not experience or even the repulsive, shameful, perverted, depraved, and degenerate acts of man, but the testimony of the Holy

Scripture. Both the Old Testament and New Testament unequivocally affirm Satan's reality. Satan is not a mythological character or the comical caricature of one dressed in a red suit with a pitchfork and tail. He is alive and well on planet earth. "The Devil is delighted to be denied!" states Jack R. Taylor. "Face the foe! Find out who he is! Force him to acknowledge the truth! Fight the fight of faith and watch him FLEE!"[66]

A man came to Charles Finney, the well-known evangelist, and said, "I don't believe in the existence of a Devil."

"Don't you?" asked Finney. "Well, you resist him for a while, and you will believe in it."

Roaring of the Devil. Satan roars to demonstrate strength greater than man's, advocate authority over man, and engender fear in man, prompting one to submit to his rule.

He roars through persecution. How Satan roars with the gallows, prisons, guillotines, dens of lions, and burning stakes, seeking to have believers deny the faith!

He roars through evil. With suffering and pain, wrong and indecency the Devil seeks to discourage and undermine the saint's faith.

He roars perhaps the strongest through death. Satan uses death to frighten, disturb peace and cause doubt among believers.

Resolve of the Devil. He aims at nothing short of the believer's complete demise and the destruction of his body and soul (John 10:10) and is relentless to that end. Matthew Henry says, "To this end he is unwearied and restless in his malicious endeavors; for he always, night and day, goes about studying and contriving whom he may ensnare to their eternal ruin."[67]

Resistance to the Devil. Counteract Satan's attack with the truth of God's Word, dependence upon Christ, and the support of other believers (an army stands together against the enemy). Adrian Rogers said, "You might as well be throwing snowballs at the rock of Gibraltar as come against Satan in your own strength."[68]

Removal of the Devil. "And the devil that deceived them was cast into the lake of fire and brimstone, where the beast and the false prophet are, and shall be tormented day and night for ever and ever" (Revelation 20:10). Criswell states, "The Book says that Satan is defeated. We don't have to be afraid. Brethren, it's a temporary thing that he's here. It's a temporary thing that he makes us sick. It's a temporary thing that he tears up our homes. It's a temporary thing that he sows tares and discord among the brethren. It's a temporary thing that he hinders and interdicts. It's for the moment. Our victory is final and forever. Blessed be the name of the Lord who saves us, who sustains us, and who keeps us now and to the end of the way."[69]

"Like a good chess player, Satan is always trying to maneuver you into a position where you can save your castle only by losing your bishop."
C. S. Lewis

February 3

Running from God

"But Jonah rose up to flee unto Tarshish from the presence of the LORD" (Jonah 1:3).

When one is running from God, Satan is always ready to provide transportation. There will always be a "ship" (excuse) docked at port to take you away from where you ought to be, doing what you ought to do. Jonah paid the fare for the ticket to Tarshish and boarded the ship, believing all would be well. But quickly, he discovered otherwise. All who sleepeth, fleeing God, will be shockingly awakened.

The ticket for passage on a ship to Tarshish is expensive, more than anticipated, and often comes in several installments. It will cost erosion of peace of mind, loss of reputation, forfeiture of God's perfect plan, withdrawal of blessing and power, and the chastening rod of God upon oneself, and sometimes his family. Mark it down: fleeing from God's assignment (God has the right to choose the Christian's work) in stubborn disobedience will be prodigiously expensive.

Jonah set sail for Tarshish. But did he get there? Indeed not. By divine order, a violent storm and seasoned seamen above the water and a sea creature beneath the water abruptly changed Jonah's travel destination to Nineveh. With the assistance of a "whale," free transportation was provided for him to Nineveh, where he fulfilled God's assigned task with a short, stirring sermon that bore amazing results.

The fugitive always has a choice. He can allow disruptions and disturbances sent by God to prompt obedience to His call, as Jonah did, or he can ignore them and sail on for Tarshish to live as a castaway and an unprofitable servant. A Christian may choose to run from God, but he cannot choose not to bear the sorrows and sufferings it brings.

The bottom line? No man can escape God. Jonah could not. Adam and Eve could not. King Herod could not. Why not? The psalmist gives the answer: "Is there anyplace I can go to avoid your Spirit? to be out of your sight? If I climb to the sky, you're there! If I go underground, you're there! If I flew on morning's wings to the far western horizon, You'd find me in a minute— you're already there waiting!" (Psalm 139:8 MSG). God is omnipresent. There is no place to hide from Him.

"We should not wish to avoid the doing of the Lord's will, but when we know what our duty is, we ought to follow it out with unswerving determination. We must not wish to leave our post, no, not even to go to Heaven."[70]
C. H. Spurgeon

February 4

The Right Words
"A word spoken in due season, how good is it" (Proverbs 15:23).

Saying the right thing at the right time is as apples of gold in pictures of silver (Proverbs 25:11). Its impact is incalculable. "Due season" is times of adversity and affliction, the season in which the uplifting word ought to be shared. Notice some things about this word.

It is sympathetic. A sympathetic word is compassionate and empathetic. It communicates genuine concern and offers of care.

It is simplistic. Keep the word said light and clear. Another "season" will arrive when deeper theological truths may be shared.

It is scriptural. Frame that which is said in sound biblical theology. "Words which do not give the light of Christ increase the darkness."[71]

It is suited. "Our souls have their seasons, and words that would be suitable in one season to our souls would not be so in another. There are words suited to soul moods."[72] Be mindful of the mood (disposition, frame of mind) of the soul to which you speak.

It is sensitive. Helpful and healing talk involves knowing what not to say and just the right words to say. Ironside comments, "Many a sorrow and heartache has been caused, both to the speaker and others, by repeating what in itself was true enough, but which should never have been passed on to a third party."[73]

It is soothing. Pithy words said in a timely fashion are like the giving of a sunny, radiant smile. They cost little in the giving, "but like morning light it scattered the night and makes the day worth living."[74]

It is Spirit directed. "The Lord GOD hath given me the tongue of the learned, that I should know how to speak *a word in season* to him that is weary" (Isaiah 50:4).

It is seasonable (punctual). Matthew Henry said, "Many a good word comes short of doing the good it might have done, for want of being well-timed. We speak wisely when we speak seasonably. The answer of the mouth will be our credit and joy when it is pertinent and to the purpose and is spoken in due season when it is needed, and will be regarded, and, as we say, hits the joint."[75]

It is suitable. Inappropriate words spoken enhance the pain. Job's sorrow was intensified by the words of his friends (Job 16:2–3).

"We have all felt the brazenness of words without emotion, the hollowness, the unaccountable unpersuasiveness of eloquence behind which lies no love."[76]
Henry Drummond

February 5

Just Use What You've Got

"As each has received a gift, use it" (1 Peter 4:10 ESV).

God uses for His purposes that which man possesses. He used a slingshot to down a giant (1 Samuel 17:50), a jawbone to slay a thousand men (Judges 15:16), twenty loaves of bread to feed one hundred people (2 Kings 4:42–44), a walking stick to swallow the snakes of Pharoah's magicians (Exodus 7:12), a shepherd's rod to bring water from a rock (Exodus 17:6). The most trivial of talents, abilities, and gifts are mighty when submitted to God's use. What's in your hand to use for God's glory and the betterment of the world (Exodus 4:2)?

A boy was courting a beautiful girl on the front porch swing of her home. He looked at her and said, "If I had a thousand lips, I would kiss your rosy cheek; if I had a thousand eyes, I would stare into your beautiful blue eyes; if I had a thousand arms, I would embrace you so tight."

The young girl looked at him and said, "Just use what you've got."

In ministry, don't harp on what you would do if you had the abilities of a Spurgeon or Moody, rather, "Just use what you've got." God takes the ordinary and uses it in the extraordinary. "God hath chosen the weak things of the world to confound the things which are mighty" (1 Corinthians 1:27). "Little is much when God is in it."

"Start where you are. Use what you have. Do what you can."
Theodore Roosevelt

February 6

Salvation Sent

"To you is the word of this salvation sent" (Acts 13:26).

What is it that is sent? It is the message of salvation, the good news that Christ has borne man's sin at Calvary, providing the opportunity for forgiveness of sin and reconciliation with God.

From whom is it sent? Not from man, for the leper cannot cleanse his spots, but from God, who loves and pities man and longs for his salvation. John says, "For God so loved the world, that He gave His only begotten Son, that whosoever believeth in Him should not perish, but have everlasting life" (John 3:16).

To whom is it sent? "To you," whoever you may be, regardless of the measure or blackness of your sin (Romans 10:13).

For what purpose is it sent? To grant pardon and peace to the condemned sinner and set his soul at liberty from the shackles of bondage to sin (Luke 4:18).

How is it sent?

1. It is sent through God's beloved Son, Jesus. If salvation is to be obtained, it must come from Him (2 Timothy 2:10; Acts 4:12).

2. It is sent by the Word of God (2 Timothy 3:15). The Bible is the Word of God's mouth. The reading and proclamation of the Scriptures make plain to man the need and sole means of salvation. "Faith cometh by hearing, and hearing by the Word of God" (Romans 10:17). Lucado

says, "The purpose of the Bible is simply to proclaim God's plan to save His children. It asserts that man is lost and needs to be saved. And it communicates the message that Jesus is God in the flesh sent to save His children." David testified of God's Word, "[It is] more precious than gold, than much pure gold" (Psalm 19:10 NIV).

3. It is sent by the preacher. "How then shall they call on him in whom they have not believed? and how shall they believe in him of whom they have not heard? and how shall they hear without a preacher?" (Romans 10:14). Spurgeon says, "Very especially may you be sent to the preacher, the preacher sent to you, and the special message be sent through the preacher to you."[77] Don't dismiss it as coincidental when the preacher exclaims to you from the pulpit or in private, "What will you do with Jesus, which is called the Christ?" or "Prepare ye to meet the Lord." He is God's messenger boy delivering God's Word of love, instruction, and warning. "To *you* is the word of this salvation sent."

4. It is sent by the believer in the pew. The believers at Thessalonica "sounded out the word of the Lord not only in Macedonia and Achaia, but also in every place..." (1 Thessalonians 1:8). Every believer is tasked with the job of spreading the Good News to the unsaved.

With what power is it sent? "So shall my word be that goeth forth out of my mouth: it shall not return unto me void, but it shall accomplish that which I please, and it shall prosper in the thing whereto I sent it" (Isaiah 55:11). The purpose of God's Word is to bring man to a knowledge and understanding of His divine plan (specifically salvation) and will (not willing that any shall perish but all might have everlasting life) and conformity to it. Saith Spurgeon, "When God sends His grace from Heaven, you may know it by this sign, that it soaks into your soul. It fertilizes it; it makes the soul bring forth and bud. It works in the man whatsoever God pleases, all His Divine purpose."[78] The author of Hebrews testified of the power of God's Word: "For the word of God is quick, and powerful, and sharper than any twoedged sword, piercing even to the dividing asunder of soul and spirit, and of the joints and marrow, and is a discerner of the thoughts and intents of the heart" (Hebrews 4:12).

God has gone to extreme measures to make sure His message of salvation sent to you gets to you. What will you do with it?

"There are only two kinds of people in the end: those who say to God, 'Thy will be done' and those to whom God says, in the end, 'Thy will be done.'"
C. S. Lewis

February 7

Why the Showers Have Been Withholden

"Therefore the showers have been withholden, and there hath been no latter rain" (Jeremiah 3:3).

For God to intervene through depriving one of blessing is not unreasonable. In attempting to correct a child, parents often withhold specific "blessings"—a pleasure, a social event with friends, a toy. As a loving Father, God sometimes works similarly with His disobedient children.

For God to intervene through depriving one of blessing is not unwarranted. The rain was withholden from Judah for their persistent, defiant and dishonoring conduct. They deserved far more severe punishment. The Christian acknowledges that whatever judgment for wrong conduct falls upon him personally, upon the church, or upon the nation corporately, is less than that which is deserved. Recall that the prodigal son anticipated a far greater penalty for departure from the Father than he received.

For God to intervene through depriving one of blessing is not unknowable. It shouts loudly and clearly about God's displeasure over sin and call to immediate repentance. But man, like Israel, often turns a deaf ear to its voice and ignores it, suffering gravely because of it.

For God to intervene through depriving one of blessing is not unalterable. The purpose for the deprivation was to bring Israel to repentance. God said, "Turn thou unto Me. But she returned not" (Jeremiah 3:7). Returning to God in sincerest confession of sin and repentance will be met with forgiveness and the resumption of the "showers [that] have been withholden." Just ask the prodigal son.

"There are reasons for what seems evil which we cannot trace, and perhaps one of the chief causes of the calamities which befall men may be found in their want of regard for the honor and glory of the Divine Name."[79]
Quiver

February 8

Hold Fast

"Don't take the path of the wicked; don't follow those who do evil. Stay away from that path; don't even go near it. Turn around and go another way" (Proverbs 4:14–15 ERV).

An analysis of the condition of the world (and church) reveals just how far we have drifted from apostolic faith and practice. The ancient landmarks have been pushed back or altogether replaced. Bitter is called sweet, and sweet is called bitter. The message of and means to salvation is skewed. Biblical standards are absent or unobserved in the schoolhouse, courthouse, and White House (and shockingly some church houses). Intolerance toward the Christian faith is escalating, and derision toward the Bible is all too common. WOKE culture is working hard to undermine the Judeo-Christian foundation of morality and ethics on which America was built.

Timely is our Lord's mandate: "Hold that fast which thou hast, that no man take thy crown" (Revelation 3:11). This is echoed in Hebrews: "Let us hold fast the profession of our faith without wavering" (Hebrews 10:23). Paul admonished Timothy, "Protect the truth that you were given. Protect it with the help of the Holy Spirit who lives in us" (1 Timothy 2:14 ICB).

By the power of the Holy Spirit, may we remain "untainted by error" and "unstumbling against obstacles, till the Day of Messiah's appearing" (Philippians 1:10 WAY). The truth is to be guarded vehemently and courageously against being adulterated, abused, or abandoned until Christ returns. It's not a time for casual, but robust Christianity. "Hold Fast" to the faith, lest that which remains erode and dissipate.

"Hold fast to the Bible as the sheet-anchor of your liberties; write its precepts in your hearts, and practice them in your lives."
Ulysses S. Grant

February 9

Who Is My Neighbor?
"And who is my neighbor?" (Luke 10:29).

Definition of a neighbor. Who is our neighbor? Jesus gives the answer in the parable of the Good Samaritan (Luke 10:30–37). A neighbor is anyone in *legitimate* need (don't be duped).

Duty to a neighbor. It is encapsulated in the Golden Rule: "As ye would that men should do to you, do ye also to them" (Luke 6:31). In the parable of the Good Samaritan, this rule was not observed by the thieves, priest and Levite, but it was by the Samaritan. The thieves said, "What's thine is mine, and I am going to take it." The priest and Levite said, "What's mine is mine, and I am going to keep it." But the Samaritan (whom we are to imitate) said, "What's mine is thine, and I am going to give it." Martin Luther King, Sr., said, "The first question which the priest and the Levite asked was, 'If I stop to help this man, what will happen to me?' But the Good Samaritan reversed the question: 'If I do not stop to help this man, what will happen to him?'"[80]

Distraction from a neighbor. Hurrying to attend to other matters of life (job, pleasure, school) often prevents us from being involved in the lives of the hurting. Ortberg says, "Love and hurry are fundamentally incompatible. Love always takes time, and time is the one thing hurried people don't have."[81] The Samaritan was just as busy as the priest and Levite. He just chose not to allow his haste to interfere with helping a neighbor in need. Be careful not to be like Martha, who due to hurriedness in the kitchen missed the far better thing (Luke 10:42) in the living room with Jesus. Rushing about is a sin when it impedes our spiritual walk and keeps us from assisting others in need. "He that hasteth with his feet sinneth" (Proverbs 19:2).

"By depicting a Samaritan helping a Jew, Jesus could not have found a more forceful way to say that anyone at all in need—regardless of race, politics, class, and religion—is your neighbor. Not everyone is your brother or sister in faith, but everyone is your neighbor, and you must love your neighbor."
                            Timothy Keller

February 10

Warning About Drifting

"It's crucial [exceedingly necessary] that we keep a firm grip on what we've heard so that we don't drift off" (Hebrews 2:1 MSG).

Drifting is departure from God. There is no standing still; either we are making advancements spiritually or floating downstream. Charles Stanley asserts, "Without an anchor, a 'parked' boat will drift. In a similar way, unless we are anchored in the Word, we can easily slip away from a close relationship with God. The unsecured vessel may float quickly to a new location."[82]

Drifting is effortless. It results when we neglect to abide in and heed spiritual truth (John 15:4). Without godly vigilance, the soul vacillates.

Drifting is clueless. Drifting from our first love and allegiance to Christ is often unnoticed, and we are not unconscious of it until a sin, storm, or sermon alert. "Gray hairs are here and there upon him, yet he knoweth not" (Hosea 7:9). Samson drifted into powerlessness without knowing it (Judges 16:20).

Drifting is gradual. Some abruptly turn their back on God, while most, little by little, day after day, distance themselves from Him (like a slow leak in a tire).

Drifting is dangerous, leading to grave shipwrecks of life and soul and happiness and potential.

*Drifting is avo*idable by embedding the soul's anchor in the rock of the Word of God (Hebrews 6:19). Packer says, "Anchored ships stay steady. Anchored Christians do the same. And the anchor that can and does hold us steady is the hope that is ours in Christ."[83]

"The truth and teaching of the Gospel must not be held lightly. They are of supreme moment; they are matters of life and death and must be cherished and obeyed at all costs. The danger of drifting away from them, and so losing them, cannot be treated too gravely."[84]
F. F. Bruce

February 11

Causes of Drifting

"Therefore, we ought to give the more earnest heed to the things which we have heard, lest at any time we should let them slip" (Hebrews 2:1).

Spiritual undertows threaten to pull the Christian away from the faith once firmly embraced (Jude 3). "Everything that can influence the present temper and future state of the soul is weighty and important."[85]

Religious surfing. This the Bible calls "whoring after other gods" (Judges 2:17)—the search among heretical faiths for something better than the truth embraced.

Past spiritual highs. Spiritual and emotional highs experienced at conversion or summer camp or revival are fleeting. You can't live on them—it can't be done. A daily fresh encounter with God is imperative for spiritual progress (Matthew 17:4).

Distractions. School, sports, work, relationships, entertainment, and clubs or fraternities are potential distractions in living for Jesus. Demas failed to handle distractions successfully and drifted from his first love for Christ (2 Timothy 4:10).

Busyness. The world crowds out time for church, prayer and Bible study, and meditation, which are necessary for spiritual maintenance and progress (Luke 9:56–62).

Disillusionment. This can come by tethering oneself to a church, teacher, preacher, or ministry instead of Christ and His Word (Jeremiah 17:5; Psalm 111:8–9). Man disappoints, but Christ never does.

Carnality. "Lovers of pleasures more than lovers of God" (2 Timothy 3:4)—a Laodicean disposition produces this (Revelation 3:15–16).

Familiarity. Familiarity with the basics of the Christian life tends to breed presumptuous complacency. Havner wrote, "Comfort precedes collapse."

Avarice. Focusing on the acquisition of money instead of the Lord causes a lapse of faith (1 Timothy 6:10). A healthy Christian life stems from holy contemplation and focus on the spiritual, fixing the eyes on Jesus, the Author and Finisher of our faith (Hebrews 12:2).

Discouragement. Some allow unexplained sorrow and suffering to undermine their faith. They are like Peter upon the water who allowed

February

the scary unknown about him to rob him of the security that was with him (Matthew 14:29–31).

Secret sin. Failure to "lay aside...the sin which doth so easily beset us" will eventually slay us (Hebrews 12:1). Sin suffocates the sacred, stagnates the soul, stunts spiritual growth. Because of the Christian's danger of drifting, Jude's instructions are, "Building up yourselves on your most holy faith, praying in the Holy Ghost. Keep yourselves in the love of God" (Jude 20–21).

"The mark of the true child of God is that he does not drift for long."[86]
John Piper

February 12

The Sin of Not Praying for Others

"God forbid that I should sin against the LORD in ceasing to pray for you" (1 Samuel 12:23).

These words of Samuel, who, as Spurgeon says, "is worthy to be placed in the very forefront of intercessors,"[87] suggest five facts about intercessory prayer.

Practice of it. Petition is praying for ourselves; intercession is praying for others. To be an intercessor for others, to bear their sorrows, heartaches, burdens, cares, and needs to the Lord, is the greatest kindness we can do for them. "When we pray for our fellow sinners," says Spurgeon, "we are in sympathy with our divine Savior, who made intercession for the transgressors."[88]

Abraham pleaded for Sodom and Gomorrah, Jeremiah for apostate Israel, Samuel for Saul, David for the Jewish people, Daniel for the Israelites in Babylonian captivity, Paul for the saints at Philippi and elsewhere, Epaphras for the Colossian believers; and Christ prayed for Peter and the disciples. It is commendable to have it said of a believer that "he prayed for his friends" (Job 42:10).

Persistence in it. Habitually and perseveringly prayer is to be made for others, even if they "despitefully use you, and persecute you" (Matthew 5:44).

Power of it. Ole Hallesby said, "Prayer is the conduit through which power from Heaven is brought to earth."[89] Piper asserts, "Prayer causes things to happen that wouldn't happen if you didn't pray."[90] Saith Spurgeon, "It is a very great privilege to be permitted to pray for our fellowmen. Such prayers are often of unspeakable value to those for whom they are offered."[91]

Perimeter of it. Halverson says, "No place is closed to intercessory prayer: no continent, no nation, no city, no organization, no office. No power on earth can keep intercession out."[92] Bach says, "Many of us cannot reach the mission fields on our feet, but we can reach them on our knees."

Perpetuation of it. Paul exhorts, "Pray much for others" (I Timothy 2:1 TLB). Prayer (intercession) for others is to be continuous. Not doing so is more than carelessness; it is a sin ("that I should sin against the LORD in ceasing to pray for you"). As God looks for intercessors among His people, must it again be said as in Isaiah's day, "And he saw that there was no man, and wondered [astonished, appalled] that there was no intercessor" (Isaiah 59:16)?

"So often we pray narrowly, attending only to our own needs. Instead, we should pray broadly for everyone."[93]
D. James Kennedy

February 13

Spiritual Markers

"And he went on his journeys from the south even to Bethel, unto the place where his tent had been at the beginning, between Bethel and Hai" (Genesis 13:3).

After living in Egypt, Abraham returned to the place where he had previously called upon the name of the Lord (Genesis 13:3–4). This was a spiritual marker in his life. Spiritual markers are places and reference points which identify a transition, decision, or direction when God clearly gave guidance.[94] They are life-altering events spiritually.

In looking at these markers (a spiritual turning or transition point, a mountaintop encounter with God, an open or shut door, the introduction to a person that God used to shape your life, the impact of a sermon or book, etc.), one can readily see the direction in which God is moving his life. These markers are important in understanding God's guidance.

February

A good help in knowing that you are walking in the will of God when you encounter another marker (for instance, a call to ministry) is to look at the previous markers. If they all seem to point in the same direction as the new marker, then it is most likely that you are moving in the right direction. It's extremely important to chart spiritual markers to keep track of how they align.

"When God is ready for you to take a new step or direction in His activity, it will always be in sequence with what He has already been doing in your life. He does not go off on tangents or make meaningless detours. He builds your character in an orderly fashion with a divine purpose in mind."[95]
Henry Blackaby

February 14

The Ministry of Hugs

"They were all crying as they hugged him and kissed him good-bye" (Acts 20:37 GNT).

Hugs take the place of a thousand words. Hugs are arms wrapped with love and concern. Hugs are healing medicine when delivered by caring people. Every hug helps dilute the pain. Hugs express emotions too deep to speak. Hugs say, "I'm here and I care." Hugs say, "I wish that I could bear your pain and relieve your sorrow." Hugs bind two lives together. Hugs are huge bandages for hurts and wounds. Hugs transfer hope and strength. Hugs are grease to the wheels of a broken heart. Hugs are spoons and shovels that take a bit of our pain away. Hugs are consolation blankets. Hugs transmit happiness and health. Hugs instill calm and courage. Hugs speak what words cannot.

Paul, when departing Miletus, was hugged by his converts and coworkers (Acts 20:37). It pictured appreciation and gratitude. Jonathan hugged David upon revealing King Saul's intention to kill him (1 Samuel 20:41). It pictured love, support and concern. With arms outstretched upon the Cross, Jesus gave a hug to the whole world (Luke 23:33–34). It pictured loving-kindness, mercy and compassion.

"A hug is always the right size."
Winnie the Pooh

February 15

Stages of Salvation

"For by grace are ye saved through faith" (Ephesians 2:8).

The believer's salvation is in three stages. Justification is a one-time experience, sanctification is a process, and glorification is a future event.

Justification. Salvation occurs instantaneously upon repentance and faith expressed in the Lord Jesus Christ (Luke 7:50) and is an experience that can never be undone (John 10:28).

Sanctification. On the heels of salvation comes sanctification, the process wherein the believer grows or develops in godliness and holiness through the work of the Holy Spirit (2 Thessalonians 2:13). Worldly clothing, connections with the Devil, sinful indulgences, fleshly pursuits, and disdain for that which is holy are continuously discarded. 'All things are in the process of becoming new' (2 Corinthians 5:17).

Solomon compares the believer's progress in sanctification to that of the sun (Proverbs 4:18). He is saved in an instant (sunrise), but godliness is progressive (as the sun rises in the sky) until he is clothed with Christ's perfection in Heaven (sun reaches noonday).

Salvation without change (progressive sanctification) is a contradiction. Every believer, by the enablement of the Holy Spirit, is to 'work out his salvation in trembling and fear,' that is, work out in devoted discipline and allegiance in daily life that which Christ wrought within by amazing grace (Philippians 2:12). Matthew Henry states, "The word ["work out"] signifies working thoroughly at a thing and taking *true pains*."[96]

Glorification. Sanctification ends the moment Heaven begins—"the perfect day" (Proverbs 4:18)—at which time the believer is transformed into the perfect likeness of Christ's righteousness (Philippians 3:21). The glorified body is eternally free from the pollution or power of sin. Hallelujah!

"Wisdom without Christ is damning folly; righteousness without Christ is guilt and condemnation; sanctification without Christ is filth and sin; redemption without Christ is bondage and slavery."[97]
Robert Traill

February 16

Witnessing Tips from Ebed-Melech

"So they pulled Jeremiah up with the ropes and took him up out of the cistern" (Jeremiah 38:13 AMP).

Wound up in the narrative of Ebed-Melech's rescue of Jeremiah are tips on witnessing to and winning the lost (Jeremiah 38:8–13).

Intercession. Ebed-Melech boldly made intercession to the king for Jeremiah's deliverance (Jeremiah 38:8–9). Believers are to intercede on behalf of the lost to God.

Cooperation. Thirty men assisted Ebed-melech in the rescue (Jeremiah 38:10). At times, assistance is required in winning a person to Christ. Believers, like the thirty men, should help in lowering the rope to the lost and/or protecting those who do.

Instruction. Precise direction was given to Jeremiah as to what to do to be rescued (Jeremiah 38:12). The witness's message must be pointed and plain.

Instrumentation. Ebed-Melech made a rope out of "old cast clouts," yanking on each section to make certain of its strength (Jeremiah 38:11). The rope weaved at Calvary is the proven means to save the lost (Acts 4:12).

Compassion. Ebed-Melech acted compassionately in providing soft rags for Jeremiah to put under his armpits to prevent irritation by the rope (Jeremiah 38:12b). Sanders wrote, "Oh, to realize that souls, precious, never dying souls, are perishing all around us, going out into the blackness of darkness and despair, eternally lost; and yet to feel no anguish, shed no tears, know no travail! How little we know of the compassion of Jesus!"[98]

Determination. Ebed-Melech was undeterred by the difficulty of the effort and worked relentlessly until Jeremiah was saved (Jeremiah 38:13). Lost souls depend upon us doing no less on their behalf.

Invitation. Ebed-Melech did not force Jeremiah to be saved; that decision was left to Jeremiah (Jeremiah 38:12a). Christ's witnesses are to extend the invitation to salvation without manipulation.

"There are no easy steps to witnessing! No painless, unembarrassing methods! You must bring men to see that they are filthy sinners under the wrath of God who must flee to Christ for mercy. That is offensive. And there is no way to coat it with honey."
　　　　　　　　　　　Walter J. Chantry

February 17

The Question of Questions

"Examine yourselves whether ye be in the faith. Test your own selves. Know ye not yourselves how Jesus Christ is in you, unless ye be reprobates?" (2 Corinthians 13:5 MSG).

The person addressed. All believers ought to make sure as they approach life's end that they possess genuine salvation, not a counterfeit. This is a divine command, not a suggestion. It is you, not parents, spouse, minister or friends, who must decide the question.

The purpose asked. Were mistaken hope of salvation not possible, we would not have been commanded to make the inquiry. Multiple times in precept and example Holy Scripture confirms the possibility of such a thing. Matthew 7:22–23 indicates the hazardous reality for those in the church. Other biblical texts clearly reveal there are tares among the wheat, professors among possessors, the reformed among the reborn, goats among the sheep, the religious among the redeemed, and the lost among the saved.

One may teach like Nicodemus, be devoted to his religion like Saul of Tarsus, be baptized like Simon Magus, and be a respected and trusted officer among the saints (church) like Judas (disciple band) and still miss Heaven. Unto all who are religious but not reborn, Jesus will say at the judgment, "I never knew you." Make certain that you are not just a believer but a regenerated and converted sinner. Watchman Nee said, "There is nothing more tragic than to come to the end of life and know we have been on the wrong course."[99]

The procedure advised. To obtain assurance of salvation, Paul says to "prove yourselves." It is obtainable, knowable. Question your heart inside and out to determine whether it is genuine or counterfeit based upon the Word of God. Did you repent of sin and exhibit faith in Jesus Christ as Lord and Savior (Acts 20:21)? Does a change in conduct back up that *experience* as genuine (2 Corinthians 5:17)? Implore the Holy Spirit for His help and verdict (Romans 8:16). Be truthful and thorough, for a mistake in examining and proving salvation cannot be rectified upon death.

The profit attained. Seriously examining one's faith is beneficial all the way around. Either it confirms the authenticity and genuineness of faith, enabling the believer to say earnestly, "I know whom I have believed, and am persuaded that he is able to keep that which I have committed unto him" (2 Timothy 1:12), or it reveals a false hope and enables you to embrace genuine salvation through repentance and faith.

"But it's real; it's real. Oh, I know it's real. Praise God, the doubts are settled, For I know, I know it's real."
Homer L. Cox

February 18

Care for the Aging Mother

"Despise not thy mother when she is old" (Proverbs 23:22).

Saith Matthew Henry, "When the mother was grown old, we may suppose the children to be grown up; but let them not think themselves past being taught, even by her, but rather respect her the more for the multitude of her years and the wisdom which they teach."[100]

Make time for her; she needs YOU, not just the stuff you supply. Don't infringe on her personal rights. Treat her as an adult, not as a child. Care for her needs (don't wait for her to tell you). Provide for her security; help her feel safe. Listen to and heed her counsel. Exhibit expressions of love continuously (flowers, meals, gift cards, chores, cards). Try to identify with her world (the sorrow, grief, loneliness and isolation, financial and other struggles) and never let your "world" totally eclipse hers.

Obey her; she's still your mom. Include her on special occasions like Thanksgiving, Christmas, birthdays, and school events for your children. Discover what makes her happy and do it. Hide not behind lame excuses (work, children, spouse, etc.) for neglecting the very lady who went to the brink of death to give you birth; sacrificed that you might have the best possible clothing, education, possessions, medical help; and was always there for you to resort to in times of trouble, heartbreak and need.

"Exuberant youth, self-confident and resourceful, is likely to forget the reverence due to parents when age enfeebles the once bright and active mind."[101]
H. A. Ironside

February 19

A Sure and Safe Refuge

"The name of the LORD is a strong tower [inviolable]: the righteous runneth into it, and is safe [inaccessible to the foe]" (Proverbs 18:10).

The "name of the LORD" (His glorious nature, attributes) is a secure refuge for the troubled and distraught (Psalm 46:1). Saith George Lawson, "In this great name protection is to be found from the distresses of the present life, from the tyranny of sin, from everlasting wrath, from the temptations of the Devil, from the terrors of death, from every evil, and from every fear."[102]

In times of need, run (by prayer) into the Strong Tower of *Jehovah-Jireh*, our provider and supplier.

In times of hurt or sickness, flee into the Strong Tower of *Jehovah-Rapha*, our healer and helper.

In times of temptation or attack by Satan, run into the Strong Tower of *Jehovah-Nissi*, our deliverer and protector.

In times of trouble, grief or fear, run into the Strong Tower of *Jehovah-Shalom*, our peace and hope giver.

In times of needed comfort, run into the Strong Tower of *Jehovah-Raah*, our caring and sustaining Shepherd.

In times of sin, run into the Strong Tower of *Jehovah-Maccad-Deshem*, our sanctifier, and restorer.

In times of despair and bewilderment, run into the Strong Tower of *El-El-Yon*, the sovereign ruler of the universe who controls all that touches our lives (nothing ever catches Him by surprise).

Take no time to prepare for an escape to safety. Quickly to thy knees, if not possible, pray as you run to the strong fortress. Spurgeon asserts, "When a man enters a castle, he is safe because of the impregnability of the castle, not because of the way in which he entered into the castle."[103]

"Our safety is only in the name of the Lord, that God with whom is everlasting strength and sufficiency, and who reveals Himself through His blessed Son, our Savior, as the refuge of fallen men."[104]
George Lawson

February 20

Fellow Helpers to the Truth

"Fellowhelpers of the truth" (3 John 8).

Paul's "fellowhelpers" (Timothy, Titus, Aquila and Priscilla, Barnabas, Epaphroditus, Fortunatus, Achaicus, etc.) undergirded, enabled, and enhanced his ministry. How might we be a "fellowhelper" to a ministry servant?

By praying for them. Paul said to the Corinthian saints, "You also help us by praying for us" (2 Corinthians 1:11 NLV).

By providing for them. Paul says that while he was ministering in Thessalonica, believers sent "contributions repeatedly to take care of my needs" (Philippians 4:16 CEB). In supplying the necessities of the minister, we speed the propagation of the Gospel.

By protecting them. They that lowered Paul in a basket through an opening in the wall in Damascus to save his life were "fellowhelpers of the truth" to whom he preached (Acts 9:25). Delivering the minister from danger (bodily harm and slanderous character assassination) enables him to continue his needed ministry.

"Fellowhelpers of the truth" share in the laborer's work and reward. The fruit borne by a servant is not only credited to his account but also to those of the ones who enabled his work. To the Philippian believers Paul wrote, "Not that I desire your gifts; what I desire is that more be credited to your account" (Philippians 4:17 NIV).

MacArthur comments, "The Philippians were in effect storing up for themselves treasure in Heaven (Matthew 6:20). The gifts they gave to Paul were accruing eternal dividends to their spiritual account (Proverbs 11:25)."[105]

The overarching motivation in being a 'fellowhelper to the truth' is "for His name's sake" (3 John 7)—that is, for the magnification of Christ's person, the proclamation of His message, and the expansion of His kingdom on earth.

"In many ways may the truth be befriended and assisted; those who cannot themselves proclaim it may yet receive, accompany, help, and countenance those who do."[106]

Matthew Henry

February 21

Refusal to Hear God

"See that ye refuse not Him that speaketh. For if they escaped not who refused Him that spoke on earth, much more shall not we escape, if we turn away from Him that speaketh from Heaven" (Hebrews 12:25 WBT).

To refuse the Word of God is to reject it.

Channels of refusing to hear. Man refuses to hear the voice of God through evasion of it ("turn away from Him"), opposition to it, incredulity with it, and procrastination about it.

Causes of refusing to hear. Man gives a deaf ear to God out of ignorance of the truth, indifference to the truth, disagreement with the truth, and disdain for the truth.

Consequences of refusing to hear. "If they escaped not who refused Him that spake on earth, much more shall not we escape if we turn away from Him that speaketh from heaven" (Hebrews 12:25). The Israelites in the wilderness did not escape judgment when they refused to hearken to the voice of God that proclaimed the old covenant statutes. Time and again they failed to keep the commandments and met with severe punishment. Though their judgment was certain and terrible, "much more" so will be the judgment of them that resist and disobey the voice of the Gospel calling them to be reconciled to God through the atoning work of Christ at Calvary. They shall not escape alienation from God presently or separation from God eternally.

The bottom line. Do not toy with or treat lightly the utterances of God. Penalties await them that do. The excellence of the Word spoken by God (Holy Scripture) deserves and demands immediate hearing and heeding. Lawson says, "The matter that He speaks and we hear is the best, the most sweet, the most comfortable, and the most excellent; never better things seen, or heard, or understood by the heart of man. The Gospel is a doctrine of profoundest wisdom, or greatest love and mercy, and of highest concernment, and most conducing to our everlasting good."[107] "He that hath ears to hear, let him hear" (Matthew 11:15).

"We seem to have done with the word as it has passed through our ears; but the word, be it remembered, will never have done with us, till it has judged us at the last day."[108]

Hale

February 22

Small Foxes Spoil the Vines
"The little foxes, that spoil the vines" (Song of Solomon 2:15).

The little fox's representation. They depict the little sins condoned in the believer's life. It might be a little anger. It might be a little vulgarity. It might be a little pornography. It might be a little "white lie." It might be a little booze. It might be a little shadiness in business.

The little fox's ruination. Little sins are just as real and damaging as big ones. They spoil peace, rob power, corrupt doctrine, mar reputation, defile conscience, impede spiritual work, and lead to indulgences that produce greater sins. "Little sins usually are the destroying sins."

The little fox's destruction. The little foxes must be rounded up and slaughtered (Galatians 5:24; Romans 6:11). To save the biggest boat the smallest leak must be plugged. What Samson did physically with three hundred foxes we must do figuratively with ours.

"A great sin cannot destroy a Christian, but a little sin can make him miserable. Jesus will not walk with his people unless they drive out every known sin."[109]

C. H. Spurgeon

February 23

The Sower
"Behold, a sower went forth to sow" (Matthew 13:3).

We are not told whether or not he was an experienced sower, educated or uneducated, a minister or a layperson. Neither are we told the color of his face or his nationality or the method of his sowing. Nothing is said of the man's communication skill, boldness, or timidity. All that is known of him is that he sowed the gospel message.

The sower will encounter four responses (Matthew 13:19–23):

The unknowledgeable hearer. The hearer impulsively receives the Word, but without understanding.

The momentary hearer. The Word is joyfully received, but fails to take root in the soul.

The worldly-minded hearer. The cares and concerns of the world suffocate the Word in the hearer before it takes root.

The sincere hearer. With understanding, the hearer receives it, retains it, professes it, and practices it. The sower and the seed were the same in this case as in the others; the difference was the readiness of the soil.

"The personal evangelist should learn from the parable an ability to sow widely, to avoid discouragement through knowledge, and to proceed confidently with his task, knowing that some will bear fruit."[110]
W. A. Criswell

February 24

Learning to Be Content

"For I have learned, in whatsoever state I am, therewith to be content" (Philippians 4:11).

Paul states that contentment was something he learned ("I have learned"). Based upon the tense of "have," this learning was continual over a period of time, being initiated at his conversion.[111]

1. He learned to be content by the enablement of Christ's power. Continuously abiding in Christ and relying upon His power to meet every adverse circumstance of life victoriously is the secret of true contentment.

2. He learned to be content by exhibiting trust in God's plan. Whatever befalls believers is orchestrated or allowed by sovereign God for their best and His glory. "Contentedness requires that we should believe our condition, whatever it may be, to be determined by God, or at least that He permits it according to His pleasure."[112] To trust God implicitly brings contentment inexplicable.

Joseph Parker said, "'Abraham believed God' (Romans 4:3) and said to his eyes, 'Stand back!' and to the laws of nature, 'Hold your peace!' and to an unbelieving heart, 'Silence, you lying tempter!' He simply 'believed God.'"[113]

3. He learned to be content through hope that was infused into his soul from the Holy Scriptures. Apart from hope, there can be no true contentment.

God's intervention, is doomed for a ruinous life now and destruction in eternity.

Man's provision from God (Savior). "But then the kindness and love of God our Savior was made known" (Titus 3:4 ERV). The remedy to the problem of sin is the shed blood of Jesus at Calvary (Titus 3:4–7). "Jesus paid it all; all to Him I owe. Sin had left a crimson stain; He washed it white as snow." Jeremiah asks a rhetorical question applicable to the sinner. "Can the Ethiopian change his skin, or the leopard his spots?" (Jeremiah 13:23). See Ephesians 2:8–9.

Jonathan Edwards said, "You contribute nothing to your salvation except the sin that made it necessary." The mighty gulf caused by sin between God and man can be bridged only through a personal relationship with Jesus (1 Timothy 2:5). "This salvation includes justification by His grace, adoption into His family by His love, regeneration by the power of the Holy Ghost, the blessed hope of eternal life while here, and the blessed reality of eternal life hereafter."[115]

"You will find all true theology summed up in these two short sentences: Salvation is all of the grace of God. Damnation is all of the will of man."
C. H. Spurgeon

February 26

The Scope of Salvation (Part Two)

"That being justified by his grace, we should be made heirs according to the hope of eternal life" (Titus 3:7).

The scope of salvation includes Man's problem before God (sin), Man's plight without God (separation), Man's provision from God (Savior), and

Man's position in God (sons). Upon justification (forgiveness, mercy, grace), a transformational change takes place. Instantly we become sons of God (John 1:12; Romans 5:1). Let us, therefore, talk and walk like children of the King. A sculptor in southern Georgia was asked about the secret behind his carving of beautiful dogs. He thought a moment and then replied, "I whittle off everything that doesn't look like a dog, and it comes out like this." To live worthy of our position as sons of God, we must whittle off everything in our life that doesn't look like a Christian.

February

Man's part with God (service). Paul says, "They which have believed in God might be careful to maintain good works" (Titus 3:8). Good works don't enter the picture of salvation until after the fact (compare Titus 3:5 to Titus 3:8). Spurgeon said, "Not that our salvation should be the effect of our work, but our work should be the evidence of our salvation."

A factory worker busy at work was asked by a visitor, "How many people work here?" He replied, "About half of them." That ought never to be true with regard to the church and its members. Paul says, "For we are His workmanship, created in Christ Jesus unto good works" (Ephesians 2:10). No greater work can the believer do than to tell another of Christ's free gift of salvation (John 4:29).

"Being a Christian is more than just an instantaneous conversion—it is a daily process whereby you grow to be more and more like Christ."
Billy Graham

February 27

What to Do Until Jesus Comes Back (Part One)

"I will come again, and receive you unto myself; that where I am, there ye may be also" (John 14:3).

There are 318 references in the New Testament that either directly or indirectly point to the return of Christ[116] (more than one out of every thirty verses). All but four of the twenty-seven books in the New Testament make reference to it. Outside the biblical record, the writings of the Early Church Fathers (Clement of Rome, Polycarp, Ignatius of Antioch, Justyn Martyn) testified of their belief in Christ's return. Criswell asserts, "There is no truth more certain in the entire Bible than the personal, literal, and imminent return of the Lord Jesus Christ."[117]

Until He comes back, what ought the Christian to do?

To look expectantly. "Watch therefore, for you know neither the day nor the hour in which the Son of Man is coming" (Matthew 25:13 NKJV). To habitually watch for the Lord's return keeps the believer from foolish indulgences and pursuits, despondency and despair, sin and folly, and slothfulness in duty. McCheyne occasionally would ask people, "Do you believe that Jesus is coming today?" If those whom he asked the question replied in the negative, he would say, "Then you had better be ready, for

He is coming at an hour when you think not!"[118] Look up, brother, "for your redemption draweth nigh" (Luke 21:28).

To testify faithfully. "Occupy till I come" (Luke 19:13). "Occupy" means "to carry on business."[119] Until Jesus comes back, the believer must be vigilant in carrying on His business, which is primarily witnessing, testifying, and soul winning (Luke 19:10). This is the greater work.

To watch guardedly. "Keep alert at all times. And pray that you might be strong enough to escape these coming horrors and stand before the Son of Man" (Luke 21:36 NLT). Matthew Henry exhorts, "Watch against sin; watch to every duty and to the improvement of every opportunity of doing good. Be awake, and keep awake, in expectation of your Lord's coming, that you may be in a right frame to receive Him, and bid Him welcome."[120]

"The main thing about the Lord's return is the Lord. Some are looking merely for something to happen, not for Someone to come. We are not looking for a program of events but for a Person."[121]
Vance Havner

February 28

What to Do Until Jesus Comes Back (Part Two)

"I will come again, and receive you unto myself; that where I am, there ye may be also" (John 14:3).

To stand courageously. Until Jesus comes back, He commands us (Matthew 5:13–16) to be the salt of the earth (preservative against corruption) and lights to the world (to illuminate darkness).[122]

To live virtuously. "Wherefore, beloved, seeing that ye look for such things [the coming of the Lord, v. 12], be diligent that ye may be found of him in peace, without spot, and blameless" (2 Peter 3:14). To live in light of Jesus' coming back keeps the heart pure (clean, undefiled, holy). John says, "This hope makes us keep ourselves holy, just as Christ is holy" (1 John 3:3 CEV).

To submit trustingly. "But of that day and hour knoweth no man, no, not the angels of Heaven, but My Father only" (Matthew 24:36). "It is not for you to know" (Acts 1:7). It is not for the believer to know the

February

time of Christ's return or the reason for every adversity, sorrow, and affliction. They are *hidden* for a divine purpose that will later be revealed. Until Jesus comes back, we must submit the unknowns and unexplainables of life, by faith, to His loving hands confidently, cheerfully, and trustingly (Romans 8:28). Spurgeon says, "I would sooner walk in the dark and hold hard to a promise of God than to trust in the light of the brightest day that ever dawned."[123]

To walk devotedly. Until Jesus comes back, neglect not to pray ceaselessly ("Watch ye therefore, and pray always"—Luke 21:36), read the Word constantly ("If ye continue in my word, then are ye my disciples indeed"—John 8:31), and worship consistently ("so much the more, as ye see the day approaching"—Hebrews 10:25).

To endure triumphantly. "Endure hardness, as a good soldier of Jesus Christ" (2 Timothy 2:3). Pain, suffering, hardship, conflict and fears exhaust strength and threaten our faith. But Christ promises strength to tolerate every intolerable adversity patiently, hopefully and joyfully, to empower victorious warfare against Satan's attacks, and to enable effectual Christian service and ministry. "Therefore, my beloved brethren, be ye steadfast, unmovable, always abounding in the work of the Lord, forasmuch as ye know that your labor is not in vain in the Lord" (1 Corinthians 15:58).

"What will you see when the great event of Christ's return takes place? You will see the eternal Son of God return in the clouds of heaven with power and great glory. He will come to raise the dead saints and to change the living ones, to punish the wicked and to reward the godly."
John Charles Ryle

March 1

To Be Born Again
"Ye must be born again" (John 3:7).

That which Jesus said to the Jewish rabbi, Nicodemus, He says to all—you must be born again.

The new birth is not the outward experience of baptism, reformation or alteration of life, morality, or mere profession of the faith. Graham asserts that the new birth is "the infusing of divine life into the human soul...the implantation or impartation of divine nature into the human soul." It is entering into a right relationship with God through the act of repentance of sin and faith placed in the Lord Jesus Christ. It is a new life complete with a new Ruler, rules, rights, relationships and resolves (2 Corinthians 5:17).

Graham was right to say, "Man can come to Christ by faith and emerge a new man. This sounds incredible—even impossible—and yet it is precisely what the Bible teaches." When Zacchaeus met Jesus in the sycamore tree, he was greedy—and Christ changed him. When John Bunyan came to Christ, he was profane and dishonest—and Christ changed him. When Lee Strobel came to Christ, he was an agnostic—and Christ changed him into an apologist for the Christian faith. When Paul came to Christ on the Damascus Road, he was self-righteous and a persecutor of Christians—and Christ changed him into a preacher of the faith he once denounced. And when Nicodemus met Christ on that Syrian rooftop that night long ago, Christ changed him.

These and all the born-again ones say with Rufus McDaniel, "What a wonderful change in my life has been wrought, since Jesus came into my heart! I have light in my soul for which long I have sought, since Jesus came into my heart!" The new birth—man's sin necessitates it; Calvary provided it; Christ promises it. Christians testify to it; all are invited to experience it.

"As is true of man who is born naturally and receives a human nature from his parents, so man born anew receives a new nature, a new capacity for service and devotion to God."
John F. Walvoord

March 2

Prayer of Jabez

"And Jabez called on the God of Israel, saying, Oh that thou wouldest bless me indeed, and enlarge my coast, and that thine hand might be with me, and that thou wouldest keep me from evil, that it may not grieve me! And God granted him that which he requested" (1 Chronicles 4:10).

The prayer of Jabez reveals four specific things for which to pray.

We should pray for *GRACE*. "Oh that thou wouldest bless me." Jabez prayed for divine enabling. The apostle Paul said, "But by the grace of God I am what I am: and his grace which was bestowed upon me was not in vain; but I labored more abundantly than they all: yet not I, but the grace of God which was with me" (1 Corinthians 15:10). It is God's grace that enables and equips us for effective service, not education, talents, abilities, or charisma.

We should pray for *GROWTH*. Jabez prays, "Enlarge my coast," or my border, my territory of influence and service. Pray for God to enlarge and expand the coast of your influence and ministry opportunity. None have taken possession of all the territory ordained of God for them to acquire. All live in a self-imposed narrow orbit of devotion, discipline and/or duty to some degree.

We should pray for *GUIDANCE*. Jabez prayed, "That thine hand might be with me." The 'hand of God' is an expression that denotes the power of God in action. Pray for God's constant guidance regarding decisions to be made and directions to go (Psalm 139:5).

We should pray for *GODLINESS*. Jabez prayed, "That thou wouldest keep me from evil," that it may not pain me or that it might not spoil my life. Pray that God would keep you from sin and its painful consequences (Matthew 6:13). Pray to be holy and wholesome, free from the stain and stench of sin. Make your prayer that of McCheyne: "O God, make me as holy as a pardoned sinner can be." The kind of praying that Jabez exhibited so impacted his life that he was called an honorable man by God (1 Chronicles 4:9).

The answer to Jabez's prayer: *"And God granted him that which he requested."* Despite the prayer's magnitude, it was immediately completely granted. Success was given to Jabez, he was shielded from evil, blessings supernal were bestowed upon him, and God's hand of strength rested with him.

The God of Jabez is unchanged (Hebrews 13:8). He still hears and answers prayer. Jabez' prayer is no magic formula to blessing, but when personalized and uttered in the right spirit, it will avail mightily with God.

"Simply put, God favors those who ask. He holds back nothing from those who want and earnestly long for what He wants."[124]
Bruce H. Wilkinson

March 3

Never Forsaken

"For he himself has said, I will never leave you or abandon you" (Hebrews 13:5b CSB).

The promise covers all times. It is perpetual. "Never" stretches from infancy to old age until death. Spurgeon says, "Well, if God will never leave me, He will not leave me now. If He will never leave me, no time is excluded from the word 'never.' However dark or however bright, it says 'never.'"[125]

The promise covers all places. Whether at home or abroad, in the hospital ward or hospice care, prison cell, orphanage, battlefield, or ballpark, God's presence is assured.

The promise covers all circumstances. Whatever the trouble, desertion, loss, disappointment, or sorrow, God remains faithful not only to be with you but to sustain you.

The promise instills courage. "So that we may boldly say, The Lord is my helper, and I will not fear what man shall do unto me" (Hebrews 13:6). Our Helper in battle is greater and stronger than the greatest difficulty or foe. Therefore, "be strong and of a good courage; be not afraid, neither be thou dismayed: for the LORD thy God is with thee whithersoever thou goest" (Joshua 1:9).

The promise instills contentment. A little bird alighted on a branch nearly too flimsy to bear him. As the branch swayed to and fro, the bird, unbothered by the weakness of the branch, contently kept singing his song. Why? He knew he had wings! No storm can stifle the Christian's song, for he knoweth the everlasting God, the Maker of heaven and earth abideth with him. He has wings!

The promise instills confidence. The assurance that the promise is inviolable bolsters faith and hope that whatever betide, God will take care of us. "The soul that on Jesus hath leaned for repose, I will not, I will not desert to His foes; that soul, though all Hell should endeavor to shake, I'll never, no, never, no, never forsake."

"It is impossible for that man to despair who remembers that his Helper is omnipotent."
Jeremy Taylor

March 4

Unlikely Friendships

"There is a friend that sticketh closer than a brother" (Proverbs 18:24).

Unlikely friendships are puzzling. They are the "whoever would have thought" relationships. The relationship between Elijah and Elisha was unlikely. Elijah was a popular prophet, and Elisha was an unknown farmer that plowed in the field (1 Kings 19:19). Likewise, the relationship between David and Jonathan was unlikely (1 Samuel 18:1). Jonathan, the "rich kid," next in line for the throne, and David, a poor and lowly shepherd's son. Who would have thought! Despite being cousins, the relationship between Elizabeth and Mary seemed unlikely. They were vastly different in age and life stage (Luke 1:36–40). Similarly, the close-knit relationship between Ruth and Naomi, daughter-in-law with mother-in-law, was rather unusual and unlikely (Ruth 1:16–17).

Unlikely friendships are planned. However, this plan does not come from us. Such friendships are supernaturally birthed. C. S. Lewis wisely observes, "In friendship, we may think we have chosen our peers. In reality, a few years' difference in the date of our birth, a few more miles between certain houses, the choice of one university instead of another, posting to a different regiment, the accident of a topic being raised or not raised at a first meeting—any of these chances might have kept us apart. But, for a Christian, there are, strictly speaking, no chances. A secret Master of Ceremonies has been at work. Christ said to the disciples, 'You have not chosen me, but I have chosen you.' I can, therefore, truly

February

4. He learned to be content through the hardships of life. The invaluable lessons Paul gained from times of pain (a hard schoolhouse) made each successive hardship easier to bear and made him more serene (2 Corinthians 11:24–27). Pink wrote, "Instead of complaining at his lot, a contented man is thankful that his condition and circumstances are no worse than they are. Instead of greedily desiring something more than the supply of his present need, he rejoices that God still cares for him. Such an one is 'content' with such as he has."[114] When faith is exercised and seen to be effective, it produces greater faith for facing future hardships or calamities.

5. Paul also learned how to be content through observing saints who stood immovable in the fires of affliction and trouble, always abounding in the Lord with all eagerness and gladness.

All of Paul's "teachers" taught him that God was dependable to take care of him despite the storm that may assail. Therefore, he could be at rest, peaceful and calm (not anxious or fretting). Paul's contentment may be experienced by all believers, provided they are willing to *learn* from the same able instructors.

"If we have not quiet in our minds, outward comfort will do no more for us than a glass slipper on a gouty foot."
John Bunyan

February 25

The Scope of Salvation (Part One)
"That being justified by his grace, we should be made heirs according to the hope of eternal life" (Titus 3:7).

Paul sets forth the full scope of salvation in Titus 3.

Man's problem before God (sin). Paul says, "All have sinned, and come short of the glory of God" (Romans 3:23). Man's sin is manifest in attitude and action—"foolish, disobedient, led astray, enslaved to various desires and pleasures, spending our lives in wickedness and envy, despicable, hating one another" (Titus 3:3 LEB). The psalmist states, "There is none who does good, not even one" (Psalm 14:3 ESV).

Man's plight without God (separation). Paul says, "The wages [consequences, penalty] of sin is death" (Romans 6:23). Man, apart from

March

say to every group of Christian friends, 'You have not chosen one another, but Christ has chosen you for one another.'"

Unlikely friendships are purposed. "Thou art come to the kingdom for such a time as this" (Esther 4:14). The immediate why of the relationship may be hidden but will in its time be manifest. No close-knit friendship is without divine rhyme or reason, without objective or profit (iron sharpening iron, encouragement, support in affliction and adversity, counsel, accountability, etc.).

Unlikely friendships are permanent. Whereas some friendships come and go, these tend to remain fastened together through thick and thin with eternal glue. They are forged together with unbreakable steel. Jonathan supported and loved his friend David until his death, even as David did for Jonathan. Notice how grievous and painful the severing of such a friendship was at the end. In heart-wrenching grief at the news of his beloved friend's death, David declares, "I cry for you, my brother Jonathan. I enjoyed your friendship so much" (2 Samuel 1:26 NCV). "You were very dear to me" (NIV). An unlikely friendship is rare and is to be highly treasured.

"There is nothing on this earth more to be prized than true friendship."[126]
Thomas Aquinas

March 5

A Family Troubler

"He that troubleth his own house shall inherit the wind" (Proverbs 11:29).

There are numerous ways in which a family member may trouble the household.

A father troubles his family through uncontrolled anger, adultery, greed (withholding from members what is needed), alcohol abuse, gambling (robbing food off the table to play the lottery, etc.), slothfulness, temperament, violence, irritability, bad example and irreligion.

A child troubles the home through an unruly disposition, rebellious attitude, selfishness, idleness (refusal to get a job), party lifestyle, alcohol or drug addiction and temper.

"He shall inherit the wind." There is no profit or gain in creating trouble in the home, only horrendous personal disappointment, sorrow and loss (may be disinherited). The father/husband who mismanages the household certainly will pay the highest toll.

Causing continual vexation to the household is a serious sin that God will judge. Each member's role in the family is to promote unity, love and peace. The psalmist says it's the house that exhibits unity that flourishes mightily under God's hand (Psalm 133:1–2).

"The troubler of his house shall possess vanity, disappointment, and misery."[127]

George Lawson

March 6

For Such a Time As This

"Who knoweth whether thou art come to the kingdom for such a time as this?" (Esther 4:14).

Mordecai was right. God had put Esther in the palace to thwart Haman's holocaust of the Jews. It was the great opportunity of her lifetime, perhaps the reason for her birth (Esther 4:14). Fortunately, she rose to the life-jeopardizing challenge of interceding for the people to the king, and they were saved (Esther 4:15–16).

Throughout life, sometimes suddenly and fleetingly, divine appointments arise to use one's gifts, talents, position, wealth, and/or popularity to intervene on God's behalf against the tidal waves of evil. As Esther's case shows us, redeeming them takes concern, compulsion, and courage—and sometimes, the challenge from a Mordecai (Esther 4:14).

Note six pivotal lessons. The danger looms of doing nothing in the face of evil when divinely positioned to make a difference ("for if thou...holdest thy peace at this time"). It is a serious sin (one of omission) not to stand when we ought to stand. God's judgment will fall on the man that falters in the day of opportunity. God will use another to do what we will not do ("deliverance [will] arise to the Jews from another place"). Fear is overcome by faith. The man that does God's bidding is not without God's presence and power. "Thou needest not fear miscarryng in the enterprise; if God designed thee for it, He will bear thee out and give thee success"[128] Prayer and fasting thwart the plans of the wicked (Mark 9:29).

"We should every one of us consider for what end God has put us in the place where we are and study to answer that end; and, when any particular opportunity of serving God and our generation offers itself, we must take care that we do not let it slip, for we were entrusted with it that we might improve it."[129]

Matthew Henry

March 7

Not Going Your Way
"Preach the word" (2 Timothy 4:2).

Jesus preached evangelistic sermons (Matthew 4:17); Philip preached evangelistic sermons (Acts 8:12); Paul preached evangelistic sermons (1 Corinthians 1:17–18; Galatians 1:16). Despite the ill manner in which some have used evangelistic preaching, it is the time-tested method in reaching the unsaved and is divinely authorized and assigned by Jesus (Luke 24:45–47). Discard it, and the pulpit sounds an "uncertain sound" (1 Corinthians 14:8).

Let the critic of evangelistic preaching sound his protest upon deaf ears. These live in a different spiritual sphere and march to a different drumbeat from us that preach that way. C. T. Studd wrote of the startling contrast in a poem entitled "I'm Not Going Your Way," a frank conversation between a young modernist preacher and an old-time Bible preacher.

> "You're just out of date," said young Pastor Bate
> To one of our faithful old preachers
> Who had carried for years in travail and tears
> The gospel to poor sinful creatures.

> "You still preach on Hades and shock cultured ladies
> With your barbarous doctrine of blood!
> You're so far behind you will never catch up—
> You're a flat tire stuck in the mud!"

For some little while, a bit of a smile
enlightened the old preacher's face;
Being made the butt of ridicule's cut
Did not ruffle his sweetness and grace.

Then he returned to young Bate, so suave and sedate,
"Catch up, did my ears hear you say?
"Why, I couldn't succeed if I doubled my speed;
"My friend, *I'm not going your way!*"[130]

"The ultimate aim of all true preaching is the salvation of men."[131]
J. Henry Jowett

March 8

Hell

"And whosoever was not found written in the book of life was cast into the lake of fire" (Revelation 20:15).

The narrative of the rich man and Lazarus told by Jesus reveals eight insights into the nature of Hell (Luke 16:19–31).

1. There is a place of conscious existence after death. The rich man is representative of the ungodly at death; and Lazarus, the godly. At death, the rich man resides in Hell; Lazarus, in Heaven.

2. There is a place of torment made by God for Satan, the demons, and all who are in league with them. Among other names, Hell is called the bottomless pit, fire and brimstone, the lake of fire, devouring fire, and everlasting fire.

3. The ungodly, at death, go to Hell. The rich man "died and was buried; And in hell, he lift up his eyes" (Luke 16:22–23). This Jesus said, and He "cannot lie" (Titus 1:2).

4. In Hell, blind men are made to see the truth about sin and its consequences. "In Hell, he lift up his eyes." The rich man finally believed and looked up to God, but woefully too late. The inhabitants of Hell pray, but without avail. The rich man's prayer failed to alleviate his suffering or save his brothers. No person in Hell protests God's right to put him there (John 5:40).

5. There is separation from redeemed family members and friends. "There will be weeping and gnashing of teeth, for you will see Abraham, Isaac, Jacob, and all the prophets in the Kingdom of God, but you will be thrown out" (Luke 13:28 NLT). What inexpressible, unspeakable torment it will be to be eternally shut out from those one loved on earth!

6. Indescribable torment is inflicted day and night. They "shall be tormented day and night forever and ever" (Revelation 20:10). Hell is a place of physical and mental torment and punishment in varying degrees and of ravenous, insatiable appetite.

7. It is a place that hath no exit. The door locks upon all that enter its chambers.

8. The present life is connected to the future life. The "one thing…needful" is the care of the soul. Hell with all its agony is avoidable, escapable by the confession of sin and the placing of trust in Jesus Christ as Lord and Savior (Romans 10:9–13). God does not desire any person to go to Hell (2 Peter 3:9).

"Hell is the highest reward that the Devil can offer you for being a servant of his."

Billy Sunday

March 9

Weigh the Cost

"For which one of you, when he wants to build a watchtower [for his guards], does not first sit down and calculate the cost, to see if he has enough to finish it? Otherwise, when he has laid a foundation and is unable to finish [the building], all who see it will begin to ridicule him" (Luke 14:28–29 AMP).

Count Von Moltke, German strategist and general, had as his motto, "First weigh; then venture"; and to this are credited his great victories and successes. The motto is prudent and biblical and worthy of application to every facet of life. But it is most applicable to salvation.

Weigh the cost to be a Christian before making the commitment (receiving Christ as Lord and Savior). Give forethought to the doctrines, difficulties, demands, and challenges of the Christian life. Jesus said, "And whosoever doth not bear his cross, and come after me, cannot be my disciple" (Luke 14:27). Bonhoeffer said, "When Christ calls a man, He bids him come and die."

For lack of "counting the cost," many that spontaneously make the decision to follow Christ flounder or desert the fold (John 6:66). Weigh the cost of followship of Christ before engaging in it. Without serious forethought, a *decision* for Him made today may be abandoned tomorrow. "If any man will come after me, let him deny himself, and take up his cross, and follow Me" (Matthew 16:24).

"Salvation is free, but discipleship will cost you your life."
                                    Dietrich Bonhoeffer

March 10

What Matters Most Near the End

"Even to your old age I will be the same, And even to your graying years I will bear you! I have done it, and I will carry you; And I will bear you and I will deliver you" (Isaiah 46:4 NASB).

Byock's research among the terminally ill revealed the four things that matter most at the end of life. They are saying, "I forgive you"; "Forgive me"; "Thank you"; "I love you."

I forgive you. Don't be a grouchy and critical person due to an unforgiving spirit. Adrian Rogers states, "Guilt imprisons us. Bitterness poisons us. Forgiveness is the answer."[132] Heal the poison of bitterness within by extending forgiveness to the offender. Forgiveness is not extended because the person deserves it, but because God forgave you and instructs you to do the same. "Be kind and compassionate to one another, forgiving each other, just as in Christ God forgave you" (Ephesians 4:32 NIV).

Forgive me. The most difficult words to say in any language are "I am sorry. I was wrong. Please forgive me." The horrendous pain you inflicted upon another by words or actions must be acknowledged to yourself and admitted to them in a spirit of grave humility and godly sorrow. Benjamin Franklin well advises, "Never ruin an apology with an excuse."[133] That is, never attach a "but" to the phrase "I am sorry."

Of whom do you need to ask forgiveness? Seek them out today with heartfelt sincerity to say all nine words: "I am sorry. I was wrong. Please forgive me." Remember, hurts left unattended to by those who inflict them are never fully healed in either the offender or the offended. As long as you stubbornly embrace unwillingness to request forgiveness for a wrong done, an "elephant" will always remain in the room.

Thank you. "Be ye thankful" (Colossians 3:15). Havner eloquently said, "We grow up taking things for granted and saving our flowers for the dead. All along the way, countless hands minister to our good, but rarely do we acknowledge them." Billy Graham said, "Gratitude is one of the greatest Christian virtues; ingratitude, one of the most vicious sins."[134] All have those who have left a huge footprint upon their life, impacting it for the far better. Unexpectedly make other's day by expressing gratitude to them (family members, friends, hospice workers, doctors, nurses and others who provide loving care and comfort to you in times of sickness and distress).

I love you. These words ought not to be shared lightly with all, but sincerely with some. Saying "I love you" tongue-in-cheek demeans, devalues and deflates the term. Its fullest fragrance (blessing) is extracted when used sincerely, reservedly and sparingly. Lucado states, "There is a time for risky love. There is a time for extravagant gestures. There is a time to pour out your affections on one [ones] you love. And when the time comes, seize it, don't miss it."[135]

"Forgive and give as if it were your last opportunity. Love like there's no tomorrow, and if tomorrow comes, love again."[136]
Max Lucado

March 11

"The Lord Is There"

"The LORD is there [or in the Hebrew, *Jehovah-Shammah*]" (Ezekiel 48:35).

What consolation, what encouragement, what hope to know that in every circumstance of life, "The LORD is there." "There" is anywhere that the Christian is. Ponder the wonder and blessing of God's abiding presence with you.

When the physician tells the news of an incurable illness, "The LORD is there." When the choicest friend deserts you and you are left all alone, "The LORD is there." When death steals away the love of life, "The LORD is there." When you are persecuted for righteousness' sake, "The LORD is there." Shadrach, Meshach, and Abednego discovered that even in the fire, "The LORD is there." When the body is writhing with pain, "The LORD is there." When life is left in disarray and all is bleak, "The LORD is there." When God doesn't answer prayer the way you expected, "The LORD is there." When Satan batters with storms that cause our boat to begin to sink, "The LORD is there." When our lot is to dwell in a poor man's dwelling, "The LORD is there."

"Better Paul's inner dungeon at Philippi with his feet fast in the stocks and the presence of the Lord, than the grandest apartments of Caesar's palace and an unknown God."[137] A good marker for the Christian's home is "Jehovah-Shammah, the Lord is here." Even when treading the cold waters of Jordan in death, there is no need to fear (thanks be unto God), for "The LORD is there."

"Oh, it is blessed to think," says Spurgeon, "that if God be there, everything a Christian can want for his final persevering, for his eternal life, is ready at hand."[138] Of all the delights and ecstasies of Heaven, the most sublime is this, "The Lord is there."

What makes Heaven, Heaven is that "the LORD is there." What bliss it will be to "ever be with the Lord." The whole of life and its every step are marked with the words, "Jehovah-Shammah, the LORD is there." Therefore, walk confidently and fearlessly, knowing that "the LORD thy God is with thee whithersoever thou goest" (Joshua 1:9).

> When souls for mercy cry,
> The Lord is there.
> To broken hearts how nigh!
> The Lord is there.
>
> With joy behold Him bring
> Unto such the robe and ring,
> While saints and angels sing,
> The Lord is there"
> —Samuel Peach, 1886

"Beloved, from the first of a Christian's life to the last, the only reason why he does not perish is because "the Lord is there."[139]

C. H. Spurgeon

March 12

The Text That Haunted Charles Spurgeon

"Pray ye therefore the Lord of the harvest, that He will send forth laborers into His harvest" (Matthew 9:38).

Spurgeon said, "This text is laid on my heart. It lies more on my heart than any other in the Bible. It is one that haunts me perpetually and has done for many years."[140] E'er since delving into the text years ago it has also haunted me. Why? Because Jesus says in it that there is a labor shortage impacting the transmission of the Gospel to hungry and thirsty souls around the world.

The dire situation begs the question, whence will the laborers come? To the question, Jesus gives a forthright answer: "Pray ye therefore the Lord of the harvest, that He will send forth laborers into His harvest." Workers will be supplied in answer to requests made to the Father.

Andrew Murray says, "The number of missionaries on the field is entirely dependent on someone praying out laborers."[141] And again, he states, "So wonderful is the surrender of His work into the hands of His Church, so dependent has the Lord made Himself on them as His body through whom alone His work can be done, so real is the power which the Lord gives His people to exercise in Heaven and earth, that the number of the laborers and the measure of the harvest does actually depend upon their prayer."[142]

"The powerful truth is our prayers are being used to send laborers into the harvest."[143]

David Wilkenson

March 13

Questionable Things

"You will hear a voice behind you saying, "This is the way. Follow it, whether it turns to the right or to the left" (Isaiah 30:21 NOG).

Here are some questions that will help decide questionable things.

Does it violate Scripture? "Blessed are the undefiled in the way, who walk in the law [Word] of the LORD" (Psalm 119:1).

Can I do this in Jesus' name? Doing something in His name means to do it under His authority, with His blessing, as His representative.

Will it be a stumbling block to a weaker brother? Love for others overrules personal liberty.

How does it appear to others? The appearance of wrong injuries Christian testimony.

Will it be a temptation? Avoid settings that pose a potential moral or spiritual threat.

Will it wound my conscience? A sanctified mind serves as a helpful "Checkpoint Charlie."

Does it meet with God's approval? "Therefore I urge you, brethren, by the mercies of God, to present your bodies a living and holy sacrifice, acceptable to God, which is your spiritual service of worship" (Romans 12:1 NASB).

Does it jeopardize my spiritual growth? Will this activity be a help or hindrance in my pursuit of holiness, intimacy with God, and building up in the faith?

Will it bring glory to God? Paul instructs, "So whether you eat or drink or whatever you do, do it all for the glory of God" (1 Corinthians 10:31 NIV). "In all actions of moment, although not directly religious, expressly intend the glory of God as the main end."[144]

"When the believer is faced with a decision regarding a questionable matter, he should never proceed unless he has complete peace about it. If there is nothing wrong with it, then God is able to give complete peace."
Curtis Hutson

March 14

Cure for a Heavy Heart

"Heaviness in the heart of man maketh it stoop: but a good word maketh it glad" (Proverbs 12:25).

The cause of a heavy heart. Intolerable burdens cause a heavy heart and rob it of its peace, joy, and drive to press onward. Saith Spurgeon, "The iron bolt...mysteriously fastens the door of hope and holds our spirits in a gloomy prison."

The cure of a heavy heart. "A good word" from the Savior, Scripture, or saint "maketh it glad" (Proverbs 12:25).

The Savior's good word. Jesus beckons the despondent, "Come unto me, all ye that labor and are heavy laden, and I will give you rest" (Matthew 11:28) and says, "I am with thee: be not dismayed; for I am thy God: I will strengthen thee; yea, I will help thee; yea, I will uphold thee with the right hand of my righteousness" (Isaiah 41:10).

The Scripture's good word. "He healeth the broken in heart, and bindeth up their wounds" (Psalm 147:3). Apart from good words such as this, David said, "I should then have perished in mine affliction" (Psalm 119:92). God's Word is designed to lift up the downcast and give hope to him that hath none.

The saint's good word. God instructs His children to speak words of comfort, cheer, and consolation to the distressed (Isaiah 40:1–2). Let the saint along with David say to the heavyhearted, "Come and hear, all ye that fear God, and I will declare what he hath done for my soul" (Psalm 66:16).

"Fits of depression come over the most of us. Usually, cheerful as we may be, we must, at intervals, be cast down. The strong are not always vigorous, the wise not always ready, the brave not always courageous, and the joyous not always happy."

C. H. Spurgeon

March 15

Observance of the Lord's Supper

"This do in remembrance of me" (1 Corinthians 11:24).

The Lord's Supper Pictures Christ. It's all about Christ's sacrificial death, and that is what is to be pondered and reflected upon deeply when it is observed. Its elements symbolize the broken body and shed blood of Christ for the remission of sin.

The Lord's Supper Pictures Calvary. Not only does it reveal the fact of Jesus' death, but it also reveals its manner (the crown of thorns upon His brow, the nails that pierced His hands and feet, the sword that was thrust into His side, the spittle that was hurled upon Him, and all the accusations railed against Him).

The Lord's Supper Pictures Celebration. It's a feast, not a funeral! It's a celebration party about the salvation Christ procured at Calvary.

The Lord's Supper Pictures Communion. At the table the saints sit at *one* table, partake of *one* meal, and drink of *one* cup.

The Lord's Supper Pictures Commission. It's a visible sermon on the message and meaning of the Cross, that which believers are to take to the world.

The Lord's Supper Pictures Consummation. Paul says to observe the Lord's Supper until Jesus returns. When coming to this table, believers are exhorted to "look up...for your redemption draweth nigh" (Luke 21:28).

The Lord's Supper Pictures Confession. The Lord's Supper must be partaken of with a clean heart and proper motive. The believer is to examine himself about both of these and confess that which is found wanting prior to the observance.

Jesus welcomes to the table all His children who meet in accord with these conditions. Note: guard against having the Lord's Supper become a mundane, ritualistic mere formality.

On a dirt road deep in the country, a boy riding his bicycle was struck by a car and was killed. An older brother said, "Later, when my father picked up the mangled, twisted bike, I heard him sob out loud for the first time in my life. He carried it to the barn and placed it in a spot we seldom used. Father's terrible sorrow eased with the passing of time, but for many years whenever he saw that bike, tears began streaming down his face." The older brother continued, "Since then, I have often prayed, 'Lord, keep the memory of Your death as fresh as that to me! Every time I partake of Your memorial supper, let my heart be stirred as though You died only yesterday.'"

"When Jesus wanted to explain to His disciples what His death was all about, He didn't give them a theory; He gave them a meal."
N. T. Wright

March 16

Benefits of Being Mentored (Part One)

"As iron sharpens iron, so one person sharpens another" (Proverbs 27:17 NIV).

March

A mentor is simply someone who empowers others to live up to their potential in Christ. Why is it wise to be mentored?

It Promotes Spiritual Growth. Mentoring will help you be a Spiritual Man by instilling the adaptation and application of spiritual disciplines (Bible study, prayer, quiet time, solitude and fasting, witnessing) which are the Building Blocks of the Faith.

It Provides a Worthy Role Model. Seeing a godly life lived out is of inestimable benefit. Brooks said, "A man who lives right, and is right, has more power in his silence than another has by his words." Benjamin Franklin declared, "Nothing preaches better than the act." Seneca said, "The road to learning by precept is long, but by example short and effective." Timothy learned much by watching Paul. The example of what a godly man looks like and acts like in every "season" of life is invaluable.

It Provides Accountability That Serves as a Spiritual and Moral Safeguard. "Stay alert! Watch out for your great enemy, the devil. He prowls around like a roaring lion, looking for someone to devour" (1 Peter 5:8 NLT). Many and manifold are Satan's hidden landmines designed to destroy our life, ministry, career and family. Having an accountability partner is of invaluable benefit in heading off danger, and avoiding shipwreck.

It Provides the Benefit of Encouragement. Encouragement may be defined as a "Positive Push." There is nothing more powerful than a positive push to someone who is being pushed backward! It was when Timothy was being pushed backward that Paul infused strength to press onward. And to avoid fizzling out, every man needs a positive push from time to time.

It Provides a Confidant/Advisor in Times of Crisis. Mentors provide the comfort of a stable caring relationship on which to lean, as well as counsel and help in navigating to safety through the storms.

"If your actions inspire others to dream more, learn more, do more, and become more, you are a leader."

John Quincy Adams

March 17

Benefits of Being Mentored (Part Two)

"As iron sharpens iron, so one person sharpens another" (Proverbs 27:17 NIV).

You Gain Trusted Counsel in Life Decisions. "Plans are established by seeking advice" (Proverbs 20:18 NIV). Dialog and prayer with a godly saint best enables you in making difficult decisions.

You Get Affirmation. Barnabas affirmed Paul's potential when the church didn't. History reveals they were wrong and Barnabas was right. Walking with someone who sees our potential and affirms it to us and others is of incalculable value.

It Will Shape You into a Better Person. "Iron sharpens iron," making us more useful all the way around at home, work, church, and school.

It Will Help You Tell Others of Jesus. Most people are fearful or timid in talking to others about their relationship with Christ. A mentor will help dispel the hesitations and relieve the fear.

It Compels You to Do What You Know You Should Do to Become the Christian You Ought to Be. Tom Landry, coach of the Dallas Cowboys for three decades, said, "The job of a football coach is to make men do what they don't want to do in order to achieve what they have always wanted to be." A mentor will be like a coach, helping you do what you don't want to do in order to grow in godliness. As a football coach pushes players to engage in certain disciplines that are necessary in order to play their best, so the mentor emphasizes the practice of spiritual disciplines to grow into the best Christian we can be.

The Bottom Line. Having a mentor can provide the kind of help sometimes needed by those scaling a mountain. A climber who is connected to climbers above him will have security and stability. If he should fall, the climbers to whom he is linked will absorb the impact and pull him up to safety. But a lone climber has no one on whom he can depend for help and rescue in the event of a slip and fall.

"I cannot overestimate the impact that a mentor can have in another person's life, and I am reminded of that whenever I look at my own. I am a living legacy to a handful of men who took an interest in me, saw potential where I did not, and encouraged me to become something more."

Chuck Swindoll

March 18

The Pressing Question
"What must I do to be saved?" (Acts 16:30).

This question of the Philippian jailer is every man's pressing question. Why ask the jailer's question?

Because its answer brings escape from what you are. Man cannot fix his despair and misery, emptiness and hopelessness, brokenness and shamefulness, and shackles and chains of addiction by himself. But Jesus Christ can and does that for everyone who turns to Him in faith for help and healing (Romans 10:13). He transforms man from the inside out (2 Corinthians 5:17). What man needs in order to be different is not human resolution but divine regeneration, the new birth (John 3:3).

Because its answer brings entry into what you need. Jesus says, "I am the door: by me if any man enter in, he shall be saved, and shall go in and out, and find pasture" (John 10:9). Outside the door of salvation is a form of Hell on earth, but inside it is a taste of Heaven and all that is needed to fill the empty soul. You can enter into this door by exhibiting belief in who Jesus is and what He did to make possible the forgiveness of sin and acting upon that belief by coming to Him in faith and repentance (turning from sin). In finding Jesus, man finds sufficiency for every need (John 10:10; 2 Corinthians 3:5).

Because its answer brings ease to where you will go. Will your deathbed be peaceful, full of hope and assurance of a future life in Heaven, or wrought with terror, trembling, and anxiety over the prospect of Hell? To live hopefully and happily and die peacefully with the assurance of Heaven, a person must heed the answer stated to the question posed by the jailer. "Believe [turn to Christ in repentance and faith] on the Lord Jesus Christ, and thou shalt be saved" (Acts 16:31). Ask the question and take the answer, and life will never again be the same, for He maketh "all things new" (Revelation 21:5).

"Those who are thoroughly convinced of sin and truly concerned about their salvation will give themselves up to Christ."[145]

Matthew Henry

March 19

Household Salvation

"Thou shalt be saved, and thy house" (Acts 16:31).

Some teach that Paul and Silas promised salvation to all in the jailer's household contingent upon his decision to be saved. But that's wrong. Individual members of the jailer's household were promised salvation contingent upon his or her personal belief (faith) in Jesus Christ as Lord and Savior. J. Vernon McGee suggest this paraphrase of the text: "Believe on the Lord Jesus Christ and thou shalt be saved, and if thy household believes on the Lord Jesus Christ, they shall be saved also."[146]

The jailer's household, in hearing the preaching of the Word (Acts 16:32), believed (Acts 16:34) and were gloriously saved. Of the sermon Paul preached that wrought their salvation Spurgeon asserts, "I have no doubt it was a simple exposition of the doctrine of the cross."[147] Evidence of the sincerity of their belief was manifested through baptism (Acts 16:33), as it is with every new believer. Note: no child in the jailer's household was baptized without having believed.

The jailer and all his household are in Heaven enjoying the raptures of eternity together. Will your family in its entirety be there? Will the family circle be broken by and by? Despite the inability to believe for others for salvation, you can, as the jailer did, get them under the sound of powerful gospel preaching which the Holy Spirit will use mightily to awaken them to the need and urgency of salvation. The Bible says, "So then faith cometh by hearing, and hearing by the word of God" (Romans 10:17).

"They who have embraced the salvation offered by Him in the Gospel will be saved by Him; they who have slighted and neglected it, whatever be their rank or condition in life, will perish."[148]

Charles Simeon

March 20

Ways to Be Sharpened

"As iron sharpens iron, so one person sharpens another" (Proverbs 27:17 NIV).

March

An iron instrument is sharpened (a thin keen edge is put on it) by contact with another piece of iron. A believer is sharpened in primarily six ways.

1. Through the study of Holy Scripture. Paul says, "The whole Bible was given to us by inspiration from God and is useful to teach us what is true and to make us realize what is wrong in our lives; it straightens us out and helps us do what is right" (2 Timothy 3:16 TLB). Hendricks said, "The Bible is the divine means of developing spiritual maturity. There is no other way."[149]

2. Through the example of a godly person (the observation of how a godly man lives). MacArthur states, "Along with the principles for living that the Bible gives us, we need models to follow. An example shows us what principles can't."[150] Whitfield states, "Those who teach by their doctrine must teach by their life, or else they pull down with one hand what they build up with the other."[151] Hendricks states, "You teach what you know, but you reproduce what you are."

3. Through commendation (unexaggerated affirmation of abilities, giftedness, and potential) for a work done or goal achieved. Everyone is enriched and edified by the judicious and generous approval and praise for accomplishments and successes attained. Timothy's heart must have raced when hearing that Paul thanked God for him and believed in his giftedness and call (2 Timothy 1:3).

4. Through the interchange of thought and belief (intellectual and theological discussions). The mind is edified (spiritually benefited, bettered) through its collision with the mind of another. We see what is in our mind more clearly through the manifestation of that which is in another's mind.[152] Matthew Henry says, "Wise and profitable discourse sharpens men's wits."[153] Saith Walvoord, "People can help each other improve by their discussions, criticisms, suggestions, and ideas."[154]

5. Through correction. When godly reproof is heeded, it prevents despair, disdain, and defeat.

6. Through discipleship. Saints are sharpened through the instruction, counsel, and knowledge of a teacher, minister, and mentor. "Two are better than one" (Ecclesiastes 4:9). Upon whose iron will you be sharpened or for whom will you be a sharpener?

"You never graduate from the school of discipleship."
Howard G. Hendricks

March 21

Why I Believe Jesus Is the Son of God (Part One)

"God was manifest in the flesh, justified in the Spirit, seen of angels, preached unto the Gentiles, believed on in the world, received up into glory" (1 Timothy 3:16).

The crux of Christianity is the deity of Christ, which is not without confirmation.

His deity is confirmed by God at His baptism. As He was being baptized in the river Jordan, "a voice from heaven [was heard], saying, This is my beloved Son, in whom I am well pleased" (Matthew 3:17).

His deity is confirmed by equality with the Father. In John, Jesus is shown to be equal with the Father in works, wisdom, judgment, authority, honor and power, even in raising the dead (John 5:17–27). And in Colossians He is shown equal to the Father in creation (compare Genesis 1:1 with Colossians 1:16). T. F. Torrance says, "Christ is not just a sort of *locum tenens*, or a kind of 'double' for God in His absence, but the incarnate presence of Yahweh."[155] R. C. Sproul said, "What we celebrate at Christmas is not so much the birth of a baby, but the incarnation of God Himself."

His deity is confirmed by the virgin birth. Isaiah prophesized 700 years before the birth of Jesus that Messiah would be conceived of a virgin. Christ's immaculate conception and birth in the manger at Bethlehem reveals that He is the promised Messiah, the Son of God who came to earth on a redemptive mission.

His deity is confirmed by sinlessness of life. "He committed no sin, neither was deceit found in his mouth" (1 Peter 2:22 ESV). Pilate could find "no fault in Him," nor can any man. Why? He is the Son of God. Even the unbeliever Strauss said, "Jesus had a conscience unclouded by the memory of sin."

His deity is confirmed by Himself. Christ asserted that He existed before Abraham and that He was the Jehovah of the Old Testament (John 8:56–59). He declared Himself to be the only Way or Door to Heaven (John 14:6; 10:9) and said, "My kingdom is not of this world" (John 18:36). He asserted, "I and my Father are one" (John 10:30). And the clincher to His confirmation of personal deity was the promise that upon His crucifixion and burial, "In three days I will raise [My body] up" (John 2:19), which He did.

March

His deity is confirmed by His miracles. The fact of the miracles of Christ is documented not only in Scripture but in external sources such as the *Acts of Pontius Pilate*, the testimony of the Jewish historian Josephus, and that of the Sanhedrin, Jesus' enemies. R. C. Sproul wrote, "They [genuine miracles] and they alone ultimately prove that Christ is the Son of God and that the Bible is the Word of God. All other 'evidence' is corroborative."[156]

"If Jesus is not God, then there is no Christianity, and we who worship Him are nothing more than idolaters. Conversely, if He is God, those who say He was merely a good man, or even the best of men, are blasphemers. More serious still, if He is not God, then He is a blasphemer in the fullest sense of the word. If He is not God, He is not even good."
Oswald Sanders

March 22

Why I Believe Jesus Is the Son of God (Part Two)

"God was manifest in the flesh, justified in the Spirit, seen of angels, preached unto the Gentiles, believed on in the world, received up into glory" (1 Timothy 3:16).

His deity is confirmed by the disciples. Of Christ, Paul says, "Who is the image of the invisible God, the firstborn of every creature: For by him were all things created, that are in heaven, and that are in earth, visible and invisible, whether they be thrones, or dominions, or principalities, or powers: all things were created by him, and for him: And he is before all things, and by him all things consist" (Colossians 1:15–17). Spurgeon asserts, "How can anyone read this passage, and yet say Jesus is only a man? By what twisting of words can such language as this be applied to the most eminent prophet or apostle who ever lived? Surely, He must be God by whom all things were created, and by whom all things consist." To the question of Jesus to Peter, "Whom say ye that I am?" came the immediate reply, "Thou art the Christ, the Son of the living God" (Matthew 16:15–16). And later, Peter, acting as the spokesman of all the disciples, said, "Lord, to whom shall we go? thou hast the words of eternal life. And we believe and are sure that thou art that Christ, the Son of the living God" (John 6:68–69).

His deity is confirmed by His substitutionary death. Saith Criswell, "The death of Christ makes provision for the propitiation [cancellation of sin's effect] for the sins of the whole world. Men may reject the Lord's substitutionary death, accepting condemnation instead, but Jesus died for all. The word may be translated 'satisfaction' in the sense that Christ's death satisfied the just demands of God's holy judgment of sin."[157]

His deity is confirmed by the resurrection. "And declared to be the Son of God with power, according to the spirit of holiness, by the resurrection from the dead" (Romans 1:4). Proof of Christ's deity is manifest in His being the first to rise from the dead (1 Corinthians 15:20), for which there is a preponderance of evidence.

His deity will be confirmed by His return. The final verification of Christ's deity will be given at His second coming (John 14:1–3). At that moment all men will acknowledge that Jesus is the Son of God and Savior of the world and say with the centurion, "Truly this was the Son of God" (Matthew 27:54).

"The deity of Christ is the key doctrine of the Scriptures. Reject it, and the Bible becomes a jumble of words without any unifying theme. Accept it, and the Bible becomes an intelligible and ordered revelation of God in the person of Jesus Christ."
Oswald Sanders

March 23

The Scissors of Delilah

"She lulled him to sleep with his head in her lap, and they brought in a barber and cut off his hair" (Judges 16:19 TLB).

Five lessons may be gleaned from the weakening of Samson by the scissors of Delilah (Judges 16:16–22).

Even those as strong as Samson must watch out for Delilah's scissors. "Wherefore let him that thinketh he standeth take heed lest he fall" (1 Corinthians 10:12). That which happened to Samson can happen to any man who plays the fool and puts himself in forbidden places with forbidden people engaging in forbidden pleasures.

March

Delilah's scissors are varied. Pornography, drugs, alcohol, gambling, sexual immorality, bad company, and humanism are names of some of the shears with which men are made powerless every day.

Delilah's scissors are deceptive. Whatever the name of the shear or however harmless it appears, be sure that all the Devil's apples have worms.

Delilah's scissors are destructive. They have disgraced, devastated and destroyed many giants (inside and outside the church), leaving them to grind corn in the mill of misery and despair with their locks (consecration) shorn and their eyesight (discernment) gone.

Strength, once shorn, can be regained. Samson confessed his sin, made things right with God, and had the power of God restored. And get this, he was added to the Heroes of Faith listed in Hebrews 11. What encouragement this brings to everyone whose power, peace, potential, and reputation have been clipped by the scissors of Delilah.

A veterinarian was asked if a bird that had its wings clipped and then repaired could ever fly as high as it once did. He responded quite cordially, "It depends on who mends its wings." Our God specializes in mending broken wings. "Despite all your many offenses, He forgives and releases you. More than any doctor, He heals your diseases. He reaches deep into the pit to deliver you from death" (Psalm 103:3–4 VOICE).

"There are a thousand razors with which the Devil can shave off the locks of a consecrated man without his knowing it."[158]
C. H. Spurgeon

March 24

What It Takes to Win Souls

"For the Son of man is come to seek and to save that which was lost" (Luke 19:10).

Jesus' focus while on earth was the salvation of souls. He refused to allow pleasure or schedule or opposition to impede that work. In order to manifest and maintain such heart focus for the unsaved, the believer must do four things.

See as Jesus saw. What did Jesus see? Matthew 9:36 states, "But when he saw the multitudes, he was moved with compassion on them, because they fainted, and were scattered abroad, as sheep having no shepherd." The Christian must look at people through the lenses of Christ, as depraved, hopeless, restless sinners condemned to Hell and in need of eternal salvation.

Feel as Jesus felt. As Jesus looked upon the multitude, He was moved with compassion (Matthew 9:36). John R. Rice said, "He [the soul winner] must go, he must bear precious seed, but the thing so often lacking is the broken heart. It is the broken heart that drives one out, that makes him go."[159]

Pray as Jesus prayed. Pray for the lost to be reconciled to God. "It is doubtful if even a single soul is born again without travail of soul on the part of someone."[160] But specifically in the text Jesus instructs the believer to pray for laborers to be raised up and sent out to the harvest fields of the world (Matthew 9:38). The failure to pray for additional workers will result in a labor shortage.

Go as Jesus went. Jesus is the master soul winner and the saint's example in soul winning. He sought out the lost day and night, seeking to bring them to salvation and light. He first won Andrew, then Phillip. He witnessed to Nicodemus, Zacchaeus, Bartimaeus, and the woman at the well, as well as to the Pharisees, publicans, priests, soldiers, children— even kings. And He tells His followers, "Go...to the lost sheep...And as ye go, preach, saying, the kingdom of heaven is at hand" (Matthew 10:6–7).

"We are concerned here [Matthew 4:19] with the first thought: our Lord Jesus distinctly tells us that if we follow Him, He will make us fishers of men. If then we are not fishers of men, we are not following Jesus."[161]

R. A. Torrey

March 25

The Valley of Decision

"Multitudes, multitudes in the valley of decision: for the day of the LORD is near in the valley of decision" (Joel 3:14).

This place in your life is a valley of decision. What things are you to decide in this valley?

Whether you will prepare to meet God or be found wanting at the judgment. How might a person prepare to meet God? Not by baptism, church membership, a moral life or good deeds. The only way is by receiving Jesus Christ into the heart as Lord and Savior (John 14:6). You alone must decide what you will do with Jesus and His precious invitation of salvation.

Whether you will use your influence for God or the Devil. Failure to lead man to salvation and the right side of life is to abuse and misuse it. Make your cry that of George Whitfield, saying, "O God, forgive me for my wasted influence over other people." And hitherto determine to use it for the good of man and glory of God, not the schemes of Satan. Refuse to influence other people by example or word to gamble, use drugs, drink alcohol, view pornography, be sexually immoral or turn their backs on God and His church.

Whether you will persist in your delay of salvation or settle it now. Delay means doom. "Now is the accepted time; behold, now is the day of salvation" (2 Corinthians 6:2). Deciding the matter tomorrow may be one day too late.

Whether your future life will be with saved loved ones in Heaven or with the wicked in Hell. If you decide against Christ, hug your Christian child and wife/husband closely today, for tomorrow may bring death and an eternity apart from them.

Whether your deathbed will be that of the righteous or the unbeliever. What a vast difference there is between meeting death holding the hand of Jesus in confident assurance that all is well with your soul and facing it empty-handed and in fear.

Here and now bad decisions made in the past in this Valley can be altered for the better. But at death they become final and unchangeable.

"Every choice you make has an end result."
                                        Zig Ziglar

March 26

Devil Stones

"Now unto him that is able to keep you from falling, and to present you faultless before the presence of his glory with exceeding joy" (Jude 24).

A detritus is a loose or crumbling stone that can give way without warning, making it dangerous to mountaineers. It's generally called "the Devil's stone," because stepping upon it may cause a fall to one's death.

There are numerous "Devil stones" in the Christian's path, necessitating carefulness and watchfulness (Proverbs 4:26). The Bible exhorts, "Be careful—watch out for attacks from Satan, your great enemy. He prowls around like a hungry, roaring lion, looking for some victim to tear apart" (I Peter 5:8 TLB).

Matthew Henry says the saint ought to be "suspicious of constant danger from this spiritual enemy, and, under that apprehension, to be watchful and diligent to prevent his designs."[162] When David let his guard down, he was overtaken with the beauty of Bathsheba. When Peter was arrogant, he faltered. When Samson thought he might play with fire (sin) and not be burned, his power was lost. Walk watchfully for Devil stones, lest they be the means of a great fall.

"Strong confidence in God's sovereign care does not mean that the believer may live carelessly. The outside evil forces which come against the Christian demand that the Christian stay alert."[163]

John MacArthur

March 27

Stop Soul Winning—Never

"Let the redeemed of the LORD say so, whom he hath redeemed from the hand of the enemy" (Psalm 107:2).

Some question the merit of soul winning, wondering when it will stop. The answer is, "Never, by the designed will of God." Never—as long as one lost soul remains! Never—as long as souls are perishing! Never—as long as the Lord's edict remains to evangelize the world! Never—as long as the day of grace continues for the unsaved! Never—until the saint stands in the presence of God in Heaven! Never—despite suffering, sacrifice and sorrow for telling! Never—despite new trends that maintain that it's outdated and too intrusive! Never—as long as Satan wages war against God for the soul of man! Never—as long as the tongue can tell of a sinner's danger of eternal Hell! Never—will we quit, shut up, tone down, go away, alter the message, or give up!

March

You ask if the devout believer will ever stop efforts to win souls. I answer, and may all saints answer in one gigantic chorus, "Never!" We are determined to do MORE—more one-to-one soul winning; more evangelistic preaching; more distribution of evangelistic gospel tracts and books; more television, radio and internet gospel presentations; more revival, harvest days, crusades; more recruiting and training of new soul winners. Stop? Never! The church is pressing to do MORE! Why not join us?

"Soul winning is the chief business of the Christian minister; it should be the main pursuit of every true believer."[164]
C. H. Spurgeon

March 28

The Second-Mile Saint

"And whosoever shall compel thee to go a mile, go with him twain" (Matthew 5:41).

The word translated "shall compel" means "to press into service" by request, threat, force, or persuasion. The Persians introduced the courier mail transport system of governmental dispatches. Couriers had the authority of the king to compel any person or take possession of any horse, boat, ship, or carriage needed in transmission of his orders. In Roman-occupied territory the practice referred not to the postal service but to forced transport of a Roman soldier's armor, coat or baggage by a Jew the distance of one mile. A Roman mile was a thousand paces. Note, Simon the Cyrenian was compelled by Roman soldiers to help carry Jesus' cross (a type of "baggage") to Calvary (Matthew 27:32).

Likely, it is the Roman practice to which Jesus makes reference, instructing His followers not only to submit with ungrudging and cheerful compliance, but to generously bear it a second mile. Why? To reflect the love of Jesus to the soldiers and create an opportunity to share the gospel message effectively with them as they walked together the two miles.

We see three significant lessons in this.

1. When unjustly and unfairly treated, respond ungrudgingly and without retaliation, going the second mile in patience and forgiveness

with the offender (Matthew 5:39–41). Francis Bacon asserts, "In taking revenge, a man is but even with his enemy; but in passing it over, he is superior."

2. When compelled by force to do something for someone, the believer can demonstrate the love of Christ by unbegrudgingly doing more than was demanded.

3. The Christian ought to go the second mile not only in relationships (forbearance and forgiveness, love, kindness) but in duty (witnessing, giving, church faithfulness) and discipline (Bible study, prayer, separation from the world).

"There are no traffic jams on the extra mile."
Zig Ziglar

March 29

Keep On Singing (Part One)

"How shall we sing the LORD'S song in a strange land?" (Psalm 137:4).

The "Lord's song" includes the Psalms, hymns and spiritual songs, all of which are the making of melody in the heart to the Lord (Ephesians 5:19). The psalmist asserts that sorrow, suffering and sin ("a strange land") can silence the song and begs the question as to what the saint might do to maintain it under the direst of circumstances.

To keep singing in a strange land takes faith. Saith Spurgeon, "The songs we warble in the night are those that show we have real faith in God. Many men have just enough faith to trust God as far as providence goes as they think right, but true faith can sing when its possessors cannot see; it can take hold of God when they cannot discern him."[165]

In this land God is the same God as He is outside it; not one iota has changed regarding His loving guardianship and tender compassionate care. Every promise of the Bible remains true—possession of forgiveness of sin and eternal life through the Savior's redeeming blood has not been altered, the defiled garments of sin are still washed clean, the saints' citizenship in Heaven is unchanged, God yet remains in sovereign control of all that happens to the saint, the Holy Spirit's ministry of comfort and help to the believer is unabated, and God's mercies are still new every morning.

March

"Suffering may quiet our singing for a time, but God designed singing to sustain our souls."[166]

John Piper

March 30

Keep On Singing (Part Two)

"How shall we sing the LORD'S song in a strange land?" (Psalm 137:4).

To keep singing in a strange land takes focus. Glance at the need; gaze upon God. Fixate on Him. Jesus appeared to the disciples by walking on the water toward their boat (Matthew 14:25). Impetuous Peter asked permission to go to Him. But Peter's calm prayer quickly turned to one of panic when he began to gaze at the waves and water about him instead of looking upon Jesus. "Beginning to sink" he cried out in fear, "Lord, save me" (Matthew 14:30). As long as Peter fixed his gaze on Jesus, only glancing at the water and waves, he successfully walked on the water of the sea of Galilee.

When facing the storms of life, glance at the difficulty, but then in faith steadfastly gaze or focus upon Christ in prayer who hath the power to still the storms with the words, "Peace be still" (Mark 4:39). It's when the principle is reversed that we panic and begin to "sink" and our song is silenced.

To keep singing in a strange land takes fortitude. Like Job of old, the saint that keeps singing in times of trial declares, "Though he slay me, yet will I trust in him" (Job 13:15).

To keep singing in a strange land takes fellowship. Connect with others. First Samuel 23:16 literally reads, "Jonathan helped David strengthen his grip on God." Instilling in the life of another the words of God that will encourage him in times of grave difficulty; enlighten him in times of spiritual darkness; enhance his joy, peace, hope and song, thus strengthening his grip on God, is the invaluable ministry afforded by the saints to each other.

"We may sing beforehand, even in our winter storm, in the expectation of a summer sun at the turn of the year; no created powers can mar our Lord Jesus' music nor spill our song of joy. Let us then be glad and rejoice in the

salvation of our Lord, for faith had never yet cause to have wet cheeks and hanging-down brows, or to droop or die."
Samuel Rutherford

March 31

The Empty Tomb

"He is not here: for he is risen, as he said. Come, see the place where the Lord lay" (Matthew 28:6).

The empty tomb is *a place of Investigation*. 'Come and see; His body is not here.' It was not stolen, but raised from the dead. The chief priests, Pharisees and Pilate sought to keep His body in the tomb by having it guarded by Roman soldiers (trained fighting men of the highest order), covering the mouth of it with a gigantic stone (far too heavy for a few men to roll away, and if they could it would create such a loud noise as to alert the soldiers), and affixing the Roman seal to it (anyone tampering with the seal would be executed). But despite the best effort of these enemies of Christ on Easter morning, the stone was supernaturally rolled away, and up from the grave He arose.

It is a *place of Documentation*. It documents Jesus' fulfillment of the many prophecies concerning the Messiah made hundreds of years earlier. God told us *before* it happened (through prophecies) so we might believe it *after* it happened. The resurrection of Christ is a fact established by the clearest and most verifiable evidence.

It is *a place of Edification*. Come and see and learn what the resurrection of Christ means. It affirms Jesus' deity, that He indeed is the Son of God who has power over death and authority to keep every promise ever made to His followers. It affirms His power to raise our dead bodies from the grave.

It is *a place of Exhortation*. The angel instructs the women, and all who see what they saw through the lens of faith and historical and biblical documentation, to 'go quickly and tell his followers that Jesus has risen from the dead' (Matthew 28:7). And they did, and we must.

It is *a place of Celebration*. The ladies departed from the empty tomb of Jesus "with…great joy" (Matthew 28:8). The Easter message fills the heart with hope, peace, and great joy

March

It is *a place of Invitation*. As the angel invited the women to come and see, so Jesus invites all. Come and see and believe and receive Him by faith as Lord and Savior and live abundantly and live eternally.

"The entire plan for the future has its key in the resurrection."
Billy Graham

April 1

Tetelestai

"It is finished" (John 19:30).

The three words are but one in Greek: *tetelestai*. It was used by merchants. In the market square the people would wrangle with merchants to get a lower price. Once that price was established and paid the merchant would say, *tetelestai*—paid in full. It was used by bankers. In making the final payment on a loan the banker would write over the loan note *tetelestai*—paid in full, the debt is fully settled. It was used by tax collectors. Upon payment of taxes a receipt would be given with the word *tetelestai*—paid in full—written upon it. It was used by servants. In notifying their master of a work done they would say, *tetelestai*—it is completely accomplished.

It was used by Jesus. The last word of Jesus as He hung upon the Cross was *tetelesta*i, signifying that the debt of man's sin was fully paid to Holy God by His shed blood and atoning death (2 Corinthians 5:21). It meant that Jesus' redemptive mission was accomplished, lost man could now be reconciled to Holy God. "Christ himself died for you. And that one death paid for your sins. He was not guilty, but he died for those who are guilty. He did this to bring you all to God. His body was killed, but he was made alive in the spirit" (1 Peter 3:18 ICB). *Tetelestai*—in that one word Jesus was announcing to the world that a way now had been made possible whereby sinners might be saved. And He was that Way. Hallelujah!

"It is finished; that is, the work of man's redemption and salvation is now completed....a full satisfaction is made to the justice of God, a fatal blow given to the power of Satan, a fountain of grace opened that shall ever flow, a foundation of peace and happiness laid that shall never fail."[167]

Matthew Henry

April 2

The Ancient Landmarks

"Remove not the ancient landmark, which thy fathers have set" (Proverbs 22:28).

This directive was given to the Israelites centuries ago regarding property landmarks. Today we apply it spiritually to theological, moral and ethical landmarks God has established for man's protection and greatest benefit.

What the proverb doesn't prohibit. Ancient vocabulary must be replaced by that which is understandable or else preaching, teaching, and witnessing will not connect with the recipients. Ministry methodology must change or be tweaked to be most effective. Landmarks that have shifted must be reverted back to their original placement. We must not condone any aberration from the "faith...once delivered unto the saints" (Jude 3); every departure or change from it must be rectified. Preferences and prejudices must change based upon greater light gained from the moral and ethical principles espoused in the Scripture.

What the proverb does prohibit. Tampering with the ancient biblical landmarks firmly established by God in the Holy Scriptures and embraced by the saints over the centuries (doctrine, principles) is forbidden. God promises judgment upon them that add to or take away from it (Revelation 22:18–19).

Ironside asserts, "Their inheritance [biblical landmarks] is in the precious truth which He has committed to us. To remove the landmarks—the great distinguishing doctrines of Scripture—will be to incur the divine displeasure. Yet, alas, this is the wretched business in which many learned doctors and wiseacres are engaged today. Nothing is too sacred for their irreverent handling. Precious truths like those of atonement and justification by faith—yea, even the mystery of the Holy Trinity and the Person of the Lord Jesus Christ—are, in their eyes, but common things which they may dismiss or ignore as they please. But a day of reckoning is coming when God will judge them in righteousness and when those who have been misled by their removal of ancient and venerable landmarks will curse them for the loss of their souls. Terrible will be the accounting of men who, while posing as instructors of the flock of Christ, have all the while been Satan's instruments for overthrowing the saving truths of Scripture."[168]

"The prevalent evils of today arise from the fact that children of Belial occupy many pulpits and many chairs in theological seminaries and Christian schools. Always they are the advance couriers of disaster to God's cause."

B. H. Carroll

April 3

Give Me This Mountain

"Now therefore give me this mountain" (Joshua 14:12).

In 1546 Michelangelo, at age seventy, consented to the role of chief architect of the Basilica of St. Peter's in Rome, Italy. In a letter to his nephew Buonarotti he wrote, "Many believe—and I believe—that I have been designated for this work by God. In spite of my old age, I do not want to give it up; I work out of love for God and I put all my hope in Him."[169]

Like Michelangelo, identify the mountain (task) of God's plan and then exhibit faith in acquiring it. Don't stagger in unbelief in seeing the Anakim, the gigantic obstacles and hurdles, but like Caleb of old, by faith say, "If so be the LORD will be with me," it will be given to me (Joshua 14:12b). Rejoice in past mountaintop claims and gains. Let them boost your faith and spirit. But don't rest in them. There's a new mountain to scale and champion for Christ—something more to do before your exodus.

Someone said, "God sends His servants to bed when they have done their work." Our journey is not done; it is yet incomplete until God sends us to bed. Take time to take your mountain before it's bedtime. Ardently pray, saying, "Give me this mountain."

"Whatever we undertake, God's favorable presence with us is all in all to our success; this therefore we must earnestly pray for, and carefully make sure of, by keeping ourselves in the love of God; and on this we must depend, and from this take our encouragement against the greatest difficulties."[170]

Matthew Henry

April 4

Death in the Pot

"There is death in the pot" (2 Kings 4:40).

Elisha instructed the students at the Bible College in Gilgal to prepare a pot of stew (2 Kings 4:38–41). One of the students ignorantly sliced into the pot poisonous gourds that looked like squash or cucumbers. While eating, the students tasted foulness in the stew and cried, "O thou man of God, there is death in the pot." Elisha healed the stew by divine power, making it edible. From the story we may draw several lessons that are applicable to bad religious teaching or biblical theology.

1. What looks the same is not necessarily the same. Poisonous gourds (false faiths) look similar to real Christianity but are destructive and deadly.

2. One theological untruth can adulterate the whole.

3. Knowledge is necessary to distinguish the true from the false. The student that gathered the poisonous gourds would have benefited from a study in horticulture, as most believers would from a course in basic theology (Hosea 4:6).

4. Untruth never satisfies the soul once truth is known. In eating the stew, the students discerned it would not satisfy them but would do harm. The blending of truth with poisonous false teaching disturbs the soul rather than delighting it.

5. Heresy in the pot is curable by the intake of the Truth—sap from the true Vine, Jesus Christ (John 15:1–2). Healing is accomplished by the divine means of putting truth ("meal") into the pot to counteract the evil teaching (John 8:32). The Holy Spirit, if hearkened to, will guide the believer into all truth (John 16:13). Jesus said, "He that eateth Me, even he shall live by Me" (John 6:57).

"'There is death in the pot'—everywhere God's truth blended with "wild gourds." In ten thousand different forms it is presented to us—in the Church and in the world, in doctrines, in preaching, in services, in private life and public life, at home and abroad."[171]

F. Whitfield

April 5

Great Mountaintops with God

"Master, it is good for us to be here: and let us make three tabernacles; one for thee, and one for Moses, and one for Elias" (Mark 9:5).

Mountaintop experiences are defining moments in a person's spiritual walk.

April

Mt. Horeb is the place of summons. At the "burning bush" man receives the call of God to Christian service (pastor, evangelist, missionary, singer, professor, etc.).

Mt. Sinai is the place of solitude. It is where we spend protracted time alone with God in prayer and the Word. Moses' face shone with the radiance of God's glory in its aftermath.

Mt. Moriah is the place of surrender and sacrifice. At its altar the believer dies to self and desires of the flesh, surrendering all of life's possessions, relationships, and plans to the will of God.

Mt. Carmel is the place of success. In response to faith and prayer, God sends the "fire" of a miracle, manifesting His great power to deliver, heal or enable us in an undertaking for His glory.

Mt. Tabor is the place of the spectacular. To experience the supernatural hand and presence of God in an unusual, astonishing way in a revival meeting or church service impacts life immeasurably, leading us to say, 'Let's build three booths' and stay here. So few and precious are such encounters that we resist departing from them.

Mt. Calvary is the place of salvation. At the foot of the Old Rugged Cross sin is washed away and the soul is made clean and changed through the blood of the Lamb! "At the cross, at the cross where I first saw the light, and the burden of my heart rolled away. It was there by faith I received my sight, and now I am happy all the day!" Great mountaintops with God—he that experiences them is the richer by far.

"God speaks by the Holy Spirit through the Bible, prayer, circumstances, and the church to reveal Himself, His purposes, and His ways."[172]

Henry Blackaby

April 6

Benefits of Prayer

"Men ought always to pray, and not to faint" (Luke 18:1).

Why pray?

Prayer enables you to reach further. Prayer transcends time and space to accomplish God's purposes. Duwel comments, "Not only can prayer reach Heaven, but the arm of prayer can span the miles to any part of the world; and you in your place of intercession can touch someone who needs you, even thousands of miles away. This is not make-believe. It is spiritual reality."[173] T. J. Bach says, "Many of us cannot reach the mission fields on our feet, but we can reach them on our knees."

Prayer enables you to go deeper. Talking to God forges one's relationship with Him. The Bible says, "Draw nigh to God, and He will draw nigh to you" (James 4:8). Bounds said, "Prayer makes a godly man, and puts within him the mind of Christ, the mind of humility, of self-surrender, of service, of pity, and of prayer. If we really pray, we will become more like God, or else we will quit praying."

Prayer enables you to soar higher. "Prayer lifts the soul into the heavens where it hugs God in an indescribable embrace." David said, "I waited patiently for God to help me; then he listened and heard my cry. He lifted me out of the pit of despair, out from the bog and the mire, and set my feet on a hard, firm path, and steadied me as I walked along" (Psalm 40:1–2 TLB).

Prayer enables you to succeed greater. Bounds says, "The man who truly prays gets from God many things denied the prayerless man."[174] James states, "Ye have not, because ye ask not" (James 4:2). Wesley said, "Every new victory which the soul gains is the effect of a new prayer." Graham said, "A prayerless Christian is a powerless Christian." And Wiersbe says, "Lack of prayer paralyzes us so that we're not able to do anything that will produce lasting fruit to the glory of God."[175]

"There cannot be an answer until there is a prayer."[176]
Woodrow Kroll

April 7

The Memory of Mother
"Who can find a virtuous woman?" (Proverbs 31:10).

Mothers of the Bible reveal traits of successful motherhood.

Eve, the first mother, is remembered for committing the first sin on earth.

The Widow of Zarephath is remembered for trusting God for a miracle in Elijah's turning the little jar of flour into a vast supply.

April

Hannah is best remembered for acknowledging that Samuel was lent to her by God for his spiritual nourishment and physical care.

Eunice is remembered for instructing Timothy in the holy scriptures.

The Proverbs 31 mother is remembered for faithfulness to her husband and excellence in keeping the home, so much so that both husband and children proclaimed her "blessed."

Sarah is remembered for her faith. Mothers like her raise spiritual sons like Isaac.

Jochebed is remembered for risking her life to save that of her son Moses and for training him in the way of God so profoundly that all of Egypt's wealth couldn't remold him.

Eliza Spurgeon is remembered for teaching Charles and the other children the word of God at mealtime, and for her fervent prayers in their behalf. Mother, don't be remembered primarily for being a great cook, having a great garden, or social success, but for being a godly mother who reared her children in the whole counsel of God. "An ounce of mother is worth a pound of clergy." An encouragement for mothers is found in Luther words to them: "What you do in your house is worth as much as if you did it up in Heaven for our Lord God."

"What a mother sings to the cradle goes all the way down to the coffin."
Henry Ward Beecher

April 8

Making the Most of Devotionals

"They received the word with all readiness of mind, and searched the scriptures daily" (Acts 17:11).

Five essential things need be observed to have a meaningful, beneficial devotional time.

The Right Spot. Select a place free from interruption where the heart can focus upon Holy God. Distraction is fatal.

The Ready Soul. Exercise discipline to enter this time alertly, not when you are tired or fatigued. Enter it rightly, with sin confessed and heart clean. Enter it receptively, with mind open to hear and receive from the Lord.

The Regular Span. Set aside sufficient time to read the Word and pray without hurry. The secret to an effective devotional time is not the quantity of time spent but the quality.

The Required Stuff. In addition to a study Bible, a journal and a pen are needed to record truths learned, directives issued, and impressions gained.

The Routine Sequence. Pray for divine illumination and insight. Next, having predetermined the targeted Bible passage, initiate the study, recording truths revealed and lessons gleaned. Adrian Rogers asserts, "It is more important for you to hear from God than even for God to hear from you." Make application of that which was gained. Knowledge says, "Use me or lose me."

"If we don't maintain a quiet time each day, it's not really because we are too busy; it's because we do not feel it is important enough....Late nights kill the quiet time....Quiet time is not just a helpful idea, it is absolutely necessary to spiritual growth."

George Sweeting

April 9

Tongue Sins

"Keep thy tongue from evil, and thy lips from speaking guile" (Psalm 34:13).

In the classic movie *A Christmas Story,* during recess on a cold winter day two boys surrounded by classmates argue whether a person's tongue will stick to the school's flagpole. One of the boys "tripledog dares" the other to stick his tongue to the pole. He does, and it gets stuck. As his classmates returned to class, there he remains with his tongue frozen to the flagpole in great pain. This humorous scene points out how the tongue brings trouble and pain when misused.

Solomon said, "Whoso keepeth his mouth and his tongue keepeth his soul from troubles" (Proverbs 21:23). Saith Spurgeon, "Tongue sins are great sins; like sparks of fire, ill words spread and do great damage."[177]

April

Avoid a *Harsh Tongue*. Harsh words are but an invisible sharp razor that deeply cuts and pains the person on the receiving end (Psalm 52:2).

Avoid a *Belittling Tongue*. "Do not use harmful words, but only helpful words, the kind that build up and provide what is needed, so that what you say will do good to those who hear you" (Ephesians 4:29 GNT). Never speak to others in a way that makes them think they are insignificant nobodies. Words ought to lift others up, not pull them down.

Avoid a *Hasty Tongue*. "Seest thou a man that is hasty in his words? There is more hope of a fool than of him" (Proverbs 29:20). Be slow to speak and learn when to be silent.

How is the tongue muzzled? By placing a diligent guard upon it. David said, "I will guard my ways, that I may not sin with my tongue; I will guard my mouth with a muzzle" (Psalm 39:1 ESV). Matthew Henry says, "He would keep a muzzle upon it, as upon an unruly dog that is fierce and does mischief; by particular steadfast resolution corruption is restrained from breaking out at the lips, and so is muzzled."[178]

"Tongues are more terrible instruments than can be made with hammers and anvils, and the evil which they inflict cuts deeper and spreads wider."
C. H. Spurgeon

April 10

God Uses Broken Things
"Please, God, strengthen me just once more, and let me with one blow get revenge on the Philistines for my two eyes" (Judges 16:28 NIV).

What good news! God uses broken things. He used a morally broken but repentant David to pen the psalms and rule Israel. He used a bitterly weeping, thrice denying, broken but repentant Peter to write two epistles and be the head of the apostles and the first to perform a miracle after Pentecost. He used a discouraged, cowardly suicidal, broken but repentant Elijah to do further great work and to mentor Elisha to take his place. He used the disillusioned, abused, falsely accused, broken but restored Joseph to advise Pharoah and to be second to him in the command of Egypt. He used the rebellious, stubborn-hearted, fleeing, broken but repentant Jonah to bring a mighty revival to Nineveh.

Morning by Morning

"No matter what our situation," says MacArthur, "our suffering, our persecution, our sinful failure, our pain, our lack of faith—in those things, as well as in all other things, our heavenly Father will work to produce our ultimate victory and blessing" (Romans 8:28).[179] God specializes in mending and using flawed people to accomplish His divine purposes. From experience, David exclaimed, "Heart-shattered lives ready for love don't for a moment escape God's notice" (Psalm 51:17 MSG).

"God uses broken things. It takes broken soil to produce a crop, broken clouds to give rain, broken grain to give bread, broken bread to give strength. It is the broken alabaster box that gives forth the perfume."
Vance Havner

April 11

Bethany Is No Longer Bethany

"Jesus wept" (John 11:35).

He wept—not for Lazarus, but for the breakup of the Bethany home; it would never be the same. He wept in compassion for Mary and Martha, Lazarus' sisters.

And this is the element of death that makes it sadder and more grievous. Bethany is no longer Bethany when death enters its gates. And it never will be the old Bethany again. It's not what we want, but the harsh reality is that there is nothing that can be done to alter the fact.

But even with this change, the Lord will give grace to adapt to a new normal step by step. Adjustment to a life without a spouse/child happens in bits and pieces. Baby steps, in time, will turn into big ones. Day by day and moment by moment, spiritual strength is gained to adjust and move forward. Time is not the healer; God is, and He will provide the grace needed to survive and eventually "live" again. "He healeth the broken in heart, and bindeth up their wounds" (Psalm 147:3).

"One way to get comfort is to plead the promise of God in prayer, show Him His handwriting; God is tender of His Word."
Thomas Manton

April

April 12

Misused Time

"Make the most of your opportunities because these are evil days" (Ephesians 5:16 GW).

An end is coming to divinely orchestrated opportunities. Redeem the time! Misspent time is misused time. It forfeits opportunities to advance the cause of Christ. "The night cometh, when no man can work" (John 9:4).

Edison said, "Opportunity is missed by most people because it is dressed in overalls and looks like work." A God-ordained opportunity to a preacher, church, ministry organization, or church member appears suddenly and passes rapidly. John Broadus said, "Opportunity is like a fleet horse that pauses for a moment at one's side. If you fail to mount him in that moment, you can hear the clatter of his hoofs down the corridors of time. That opportunity is gone forever."

Judson, missionary to Burma, wrote that "a life once spent is irrevocable. It will remain to be contemplated through eternity....the same may be said of each day. When it is once past, it is gone forever. All the marks which we put upon it, it will exhibit forever....each day will not only be a witness of our conduct, but will affect our everlasting destiny....How shall we then wish to see each day marked with usefulness! It is too late to mend the days that are past. The future is in our power. Let us, then, each morning, (enabled by God's Spirit) resolve to send the day into eternity in such a garb as we shall wish it to wear forever. And at night let us reflect that one more day is irrevocably gone, indelibly (forever) marked."

"Oh, how precious is time; and how guilty it makes me feel when I think I have trifled away and misemployed it or neglected to fill up each part of it with duty to the utmost of my ability and capacity. Oh, that I might not loiter on my heavenly journey!"

David Brainerd

April 13

All the Promises Art Thine

"Whereby are given unto us exceeding great and precious promises" (2 Peter 1:4).

All of God's promises are in some way applicable and adaptable to *all* of God's children. Spurgeon asserts, "No promise is of private interpretation. Whatever God has said to any one saint, He has said to all. When He opens a well for one, it is that all may drink. When He openeth a granary door to give out food, there may be some one starving man who is the occasion of its being opened, but all hungry saints may come and feed too. Whether He gave the word to Abraham or to Moses matters not, O believer; He has given it to thee as one of the covenanted seed. There is not a high blessing too lofty for thee, nor a wide mercy too extensive for thee."[180] Therefore, claim their promises for thyself and thereby find needed comfort in sorrow, strength in labor, provision in need, and guidance in direction.

Obviously, in some cases a promise is to be adapted to apply to one's personal circumstances (spiritual mountain to climb, river to ford, valley to cross, desert to tread). The promise to Israel of help and strength is but thine (Isaiah 41:10). The promise to David of deliverance from anxiety and fear is but thine (Psalm 34:4). The promise to the disciples of comfort in sorrow is but thine (John 14:18). The promise to Paul of grace to cope with a "thorn in the flesh" (suffering, sickness, etc.) is but thine (2 Corinthians 12:9). The promise to Jeremiah of answer to prayer given is but thine (Jeremiah 33:3). The promise to Joshua not to 'leave nor forsake you' is but thine (Joshua 1:5).

As Spurgeon says, "There is not a brook of living water of which thou mayst not drink."[181] It's not robbery to take that given to another and claimed as thine own.[182] Plenteous are the wells in the Holy Book for the famished saint to partake of and be thereby refreshed and renewed. Note, however, as it was with the people to whom the promise was specifically given, sometimes there are conditions to meet for us to see its fulfillment.

"If, my brother, thou canst in faith lie down upon a promise and take thy rest thereon, it is thine."[183]

C. H. Spurgeon

April 14

When God Tarries
"My God, do not tarry too long!" (Psalm 40:17 ISV).

April

Believers often experience dire affliction or adversity before God intervenes. It was as students at the Bible College at Gilgal were eating poisonous pottage that God's power made it whole (2 Kings 4:40). The wine barrel was empty at the wedding feast in Cana before Jesus made more (John 2:3–9). Abraham's knife was lifted to slay his son at Mt. Moriah before the angel stilled his hand (Genesis 22:11–12). The Israelites walked to the edge of the Red Sea before the waters were drawn back (Exodus 14:21–22). David was delivered from death at the hands of Saul's soldiers by mere hours (1 Samuel 19:11). Hezekiah was on his deathbed before God intervened with healing (2 Kings 20:1–5). The night before Peter was to be put on trial (which probably would lead to being executed, as James had been), an angel delivered him from the shackles and prison cell (Acts 12:6–11).

Tony Evans says, "God's timing is always perfect. Trust His delays. He's got you." He promises grace sufficient unto TODAY. We cannot tap tomorrow's grace for today's use. God is never early, never late, always on time.

"God is never late and rarely early. He is always exactly right on time—His time."[184]

Dillon Burroughs

April 15

The Lost Axe Head

"Where fell it?" (2 Kings 6:6).

Due to lack of room for ministerial students at Elisha's college, an effort was undertaken to build another dormitory, which required the borrowing of at least one axe (2 Kings 6:5–7). And it was lost in the water as a tree was being hewn to the ground.

The axe head symbolizes the power of the Holy Spirit for Christian work in the believer's life, which possibly may be lost. When it is, how might it, the lost axe head of Holy Spirit power, be recovered?

Awareness of its absence. The road to recovery of divine power begins with recognition of its loss. The man that lost the axe head at once detected its absence. Unlike him, believers are often like those of Hosea's day: "Worshiping foreign gods has sapped their strength, but they don't even know it. Their hair is gray, but they don't realize they're old and weak" (Hosea 7:9 NLT).

Acknowledgement of its need. Realizing work was futile apart from the axe head, the man stopped working. It's utterly crazy to attempt to cut down trees (do God's work in preaching, singing, teaching, witnessing, etc.) with only an axe handle. Yet that's what many Christian workers attempt. Eloquence or expertise cannot make up for the loss of spiritual power. Doing the work of God requires the power of God. There was no future work for the man until the axe head was found. And there's no future for us until we discover where we lost our power and recover it.

Admission of its cause. "Where fail it?" Return to the place where the power was lost. Was it in neglect of secret time with God, slackness in church attendance, an impure act, or inflated ego over former successes?

Acquisition of its return. The lost power (axe head) was restored by the man's appropriation of it by faith. Doing what Elisha instructed, "the man reached out and grabbed it" from the water (2 Kings 6:7 NLT). Christ bids all that have lost their axe head (power) to reach out to Him in faith to have it (the fullness of the Holy Spirit) restored (Luke 11:11–13).

"Without the Spirit of God, we can do nothing. We are as ships without wind. We are useless."[185]

C. H. Spurgeon

April 16

Never Stop Learning

"The heart of the prudent getteth knowledge; and the ear of the wise seeketh knowledge" (Proverbs 18:15).

Knowledge is ascertained through diligent discipline ("seeking") and possessing it enables one and enhances success in every facet of life. The knowledge of God, His divine Word and will and assignments is the highest knowledge to gain. The search and acquisition of knowledge is continuous.

Kidner says, "Those who know most know best how little they know."[186] Aristotle wisely said, "Educating the mind without educating the heart is no education at all." Paul declares, "Study to shew thyself

April

approved unto God, a workman that needeth not to be ashamed, rightly dividing the word of truth" (2 Timothy 2:15). Joshua said, "This book of the law shall not depart out of thy mouth; but thou shalt meditate therein day and night, that thou mayest observe to do according to all that is written therein: for then thou shalt make thy way prosperous, and then thou shalt have *good success*" (Joshua 1:8).

Dr. Thomas J. DeLaughter, one of my Old Testament professors in seminary, shared a contrast between the educated and the noneducated that stuck with me. He said the man without an education looks into a well and sees its refreshing water but has no means to reach it. The educated, on the other hand, has a bucket attached to a rope to lower into the well and draw up all the water desired.

Education (religious and secular) gives a person the tools necessary to get to what is needed for highest achievement and success in life. Abigail Adams, mother of John Quincy Adams said, "Learning is not attained by chance; it must be sought for with ardor and attended to with diligence."[187]

"Education will not come of itself. It will never come unless you seek it. It will not come unless you take the first steps which lead to it; but, taking these steps, every man can acquire it."[188]

Henry Ward Beecher

April 17

Old People

"Stand up in the presence of the aged, show respect for the elderly and revere your God" (Leviticus 19:32 NIV).

Old people. Theirs is the buried generation, and among the buried are those by whom they were admired, appreciated, loved and even embraced dearly, and with whom they worshipped, served, and fellowshipped. Their lingering grief and sorrow for a deceased spouse, child, or friend; physical frailty and/or sickness that inhibits; fixation upon one day at a time, loneliness, anxiety over making ends meet, or fear of facing the unknown are all often met with misapprehension, especially among the young.

Old people. Children abandon them, friends desert them, society at large ignores them, the young overlook them, and employers don't want them, while others would euthanize them. How strange it is that relationships often radically change simply by growing older.

Old people. Look out for the needs of old folks. Treat them with the respect and decency they deserve. Splash out sunshine and love upon them. Interact with them. Tap the great store of knowledge and wisdom from their lifetime of experience, observation, and study.

Old People. Stand up before them in honor of their saintly maturity. Rise up before them in honor for the many years spent in service to God. Rise up before them in honor for their nearing the end of life's journey and their entrance to Heaven. Rise up before them in honor for having fought a good fight and having kept the faith, enduring suffering as a good soldier of Jesus Christ. Rise up before them in honor for their godly legacy and sterling example. As they are, you shall soon be.

"Treat the elderly as a nonrenewable resource; they care!"[189]
Woodrow Kroll

April 18

Taste and See

"O taste and see that the LORD is good: blessed is the man that trusteth in him" (Psalm 34:8).

Many see but do not taste of the Lord's goodness and walk away in disbelief or disdain. "To *taste* is to make proof by experience,"[190] says W. S. Plumer. It was when Jonathan tasted the honey that his eyes were enlightened. It is when a person tastes the goodness of the Lord that he discovers Him to be all that He claims.

Taste the comfort He gives in sorrow, the deliverance He gives from a sin's bondage, the friendship He gives in desolation, the hope He gives in despair, the happiness He gives in joylessness, and the calm He gives in the storm, and you will be made to trust in Him. Of this the Psalmist was certain, as I myself am.

Truth about God and the spiritual realm awaits the person that refuses to hear without seeing and refuses to hear and see without tasting.

April

Brady wrote, "Oh, make but trial of His love; experience will decide. How bless'd are they—and only they—who in His truth confide."

"Every taste now influences and engages trust in the Lord."[191]
John Gill

April 19

A Sheltering Tree
"Friends love through all kinds of weather" (Proverbs 17:17 MSG).

Shortly before his death, Samuel Taylor Coleridge wrote the poem "Youth and Age," which compares his old age with that of his youth. In part he writes "Flowers are lovely; love is flower-like; friendship is a sheltering tree." What descriptive language to describe true friends! What an image to describe intimate friendship! The words suggest taking shelter from the raging heat of a July day in an extremely hot place under a gigantic tree whose branches and foliage block the sun, providing a cool shade.

Coleridge is right. True friends provide a refuge from the trials, tribulations, and troubles of life as much as possible by allowing us to sit under their massive sheltering shade to be refreshed in their encouragement, strengthened by their companionship, and helped by their counsel. David's sheltering tree was Jonathan. Thank God for the sheltering tree He placed in the grove of your life.

"Friendship is one of the sweetest joys of life. Many might have failed beneath the bitterness of their trial had they not found a friend."[192]
C. H. Spurgeon

April 20

"Bring the Books"
"Bring…the books" (2 Timothy 4:13).

Paul tells Timothy to "bring…the books" when he comes to visit Paul in prison. Ponder Paul's passion for books. Spurgeon says, "He is inspired, and yet he wants books! He has been preaching at least for thirty years, and yet he wants books! He had seen the Lord, and yet he wants books! He had had a wider experience than most men, and yet he wants books! He had been caught up into the third heaven and had heard things which it was unlawful for a man to utter, yet he wants books! He had written the major part of the New Testament, and yet he wants books!"[193]

If a spiritual giant like Paul wanted books, somehow found time for books, and was profoundly impacted by books, ought we not likewise to make room for choice spiritual books? Paul says, "Bring…the books"—do likewise.

What books ought to be read? Read the Bible, sound biblical devotional material, and sermons. And read Christian biographies (Spurgeon, Brainerd, Gipsy Smith, Praying Hyde, etc.). The story of a spiritual giant reveals how God can take an ordinary man and use him in an extraordinary way for His glory, the secrets that made him what he was for God, and how he battled the agonies and challenges of life and ministry victoriously.

Kimbrough's book, *Words to Die For* gives a brief biography of thirty people whose lives changed the world for God. Note the advice of Thomas à Kempis. "Do not be influenced by the importance of the writer and whether his learning is great or small, but let the love of pure truth draw you to read. Do not inquire, who said this? But pay attention to what is said."

"If all the crowns of Europe were placed at my disposal on condition that I should abandon my books and studies, I should spurn the crowns away and stand by the books."
François Fénelon

April 21

Conquest in Persecution
"Be it known unto thee, O king, that we will not serve thy gods, nor worship the golden image which thou hast set up" (Daniel 3:18).

April

We find the biblical pattern for conquest in persecution displayed by Shadrach, Meshach, and Abed-nego when they refused to bow to the image of gold erected by King Nebuchadnezzar (Daniel 3).

They were confident. "Our God whom we serve is able to deliver us from the burning fiery furnace" (Daniel 3:17). The persecuted saint says with David, "For you have been my hope, Sovereign LORD, my confidence since my youth" (Psalm 71:5 NIV). William Tyndale said, "For if God be on our side, what matter maketh it who be against us, be they bishops, cardinals, popes, or whatsoever names they will?"

They were concrete. "O king, that we will not serve thy gods, nor worship the golden image which thou hast set up" (Daniel 3:18). They were firm in their decision not to compromise belief or dishonor God. Manifest a fixed and steadfast mind not to "bend or bow" to pressure and threats to deny the Lord. Don't waver or wobble.

They were clever. When Nebuchadnezzar asked the Hebrew children to give the reason for their decision not to bow to his image, they wisely replied, "We are not careful to answer thee in this matter" (Daniel 3:16). The word "careful" means "of necessity"; it was unnecessary for them to cite the reasons for refusal to worship the idol or vindicate themselves. Their decision was unalterable and unchangeable. Nothing said by either the king or themselves would change their mind. Deliberating with a persecutor (when one's mind is decided) spawns the chance of caving to compromise.

They were compliant. It was their duty, as it is with with every Christian, to stand for God, regardless of the cost or consequences (Daniel 3:17). And this they did.

They were courageous. Although feeling the heat and seeing the burning furnace into which they were to be cast, Shadrach, Meshach and Abed-nego said boldly, "Be it known unto thee, O king, that we will not serve thy gods, nor worship the golden image which thou hast set up" (Daniel 3:18).

They were congenial. "Be it known unto thee, O king" (Daniel 3:18). In response to the harshness, rage and anger expressed by the king (Daniel 3:13–15), they manifested respect and kindness. Don't dish out what the persecutor gives out. Do the opposite.

They were calm. "Shadrach, Meshach, and Abednego replied, 'O Nebuchadnezzar, we are not worried about what will happen to us'" (Daniel 3:16 TLB). Trust in God banishes fear. The persecuted saint says with Jeremiah, "But the Lord is with me like a mighty warrior; so my persecutors will stumble and not prevail. They will fail and be thoroughly disgraced; their dishonor will never be forgotten" (Jeremiah 20:11 NIV). Saith Spurgeon, "To throw the Christian into the furnace is to put him into Christ's parlor; for lo! Jesus Christ is walking with him."

"That grace which was sufficient for them [the prophets and saints before us], to carry them through their sufferings, shall not be deficient to you."
Matthew Henry

April 22

The Greatest Text in the Bible

"For God so loved the world, that he gave his only begotten Son, that whosoever believeth in him should not perish, but have everlasting life" (John 3:16).

The great subject of salvation. "Not perish." The purpose in God's offer of salvation is to forgive man of sin and release him from its destructive penalty. No subject is of greater importance than that of getting right with God.

The great stimulus of salvation. "For God so loved." God's incomprehensible, immeasurable, and unspeakable love prompted the sacrifice of His Son for man's sin so that we might be saved. Henry Ward Beecher said, "The life and death of Christ was but the working out of the love of God. The affection and the yearning of heart towards His erring creatures was just the same in God before Christ came that Christ showed it to be while He was on earth. It is just the same still. There is no change in God, or in His love."[194]

The great source of salvation. "Only begotten Son." Jesus is God's unique Son who left Heaven to come to earth "to seek and to save that which was lost" (Luke 19:10). He lived sinlessly and died vicariously on Calvary to redeem man from sin. Salvation is only available in and through a personal relationship with Him (Acts 4:12).

The great scope of salvation. "Whosoever." Spurgeon says, "From the moralist to the utterly vile; from the grey-headed sinner to the boy or maiden." All may come who will come. Thankful, I am, that the text reads "whosoever," for had it used the name Frank Shivers, I would not know if it meant me or another with the same name.

The great summons of salvation. "Believeth." Salvation is not automatic. It must be received. The word "believeth" denotes an invitation to gain it by faith. Although salvation is available to all people, it avails only them that take it by faith and repentance.

The great surety of salvation. "Should not perish, but have everlasting life." The good news to him that is perishing in his sins is that God has provided the means to avoid that death. No man needs to die lost, estranged from God in his sin, and enter eternal torment in Hell. In Christ, man is promised abundant life now and eternal life in Heaven (John 10:9–10).

"Here is Gospel indeed, good news, the best that ever came from Heaven to earth. Here is much, here is all in a little, the word of reconciliation in miniature."[195]

Matthew Henry

April 23

A Wonderful Change

"Therefore if any man be in Christ, he is a new creature: old things are passed away; behold, all things are become new" (2 Corinthians 5:17).

At the moment of salvation, a mighty, miraculous change takes place in the sinner's life. A new believer said, "Either the world is altered, or else I am."

It's a change of allegiance. Christ, not Satan, governs and rules life.

It's a change of affection. Worldly appetites are replaced with the heavenly, the sinful with the godly. The new man in Christ loves that which is good and loathes all that is evil. "Old connections with the Devil, the world, and the flesh are broken off; old idols are cast away."[196]

It's a change of actions. Prior to salvation, man's bent is toward evil; in salvation, it's toward the godly. And this is revealed through behavior.

It's a change of association. A new convert asked the famous evangelist D. L. Moody how he might give up old friends who led him astray. Moody replied, "Just live for Jesus and they will give you up." The Bible says, "If we love other Christians, it proves that we have been delivered from hell and given eternal life" (1 John 3:14 TLB).

It's a change of administrators. The manager of an apartment complex harassed a renter continuously. He never allowed the renter a moment of peace, but kept barraging him with things to do—keeping his apartment clean or repairing items he didn't break or demanding rent before it was due. Fortunately for the renter, the complex was sold and the manager was replaced with a new one completely different, making things far superior. The renter one night was surprised to find the former manager at his door demanding early rent and certain repairs.

What was he to do? Was he to do as the old manager asked or tell him to take a hike? No, regardless of the man's threats to raise his rent or kick him out of the apartment, all that was necessary was for him to refer the man to the new manager.

The Christian must respond similarly when his former manager (Satan) comes knocking at the door with a variety of demands, accusations, and temptations. He must boldly, frankly say, "Take the matter up with my new manager (Jesus). That's the end of the matter as far as I am concerned." The believer is no longer under the authority of Satan, his former manager, but completely under that of Jesus Christ.

It's a change of afterlife. The man outside Christ at death will abide in eternal darkness in Hell, but he that is passed from death unto life gains an eternal Home in Heaven with God and all the redeemed.

"After a person is regenerate, old value systems, priorities, beliefs, loves, and plans are gone. Evil and sin are still present, but the believer sees them in a new perspective and they no longer control him."[197]

John MacArthur

April 24

The Greatest "IF"

"And if Christ has not been raised, our preaching is useless and so is your faith" (I Corinthians 15:14 NIV).

Paul argues the absurdity of denying of the resurrection of Christ by stating what that would mean.

April

If Christ was not raised from the dead, it would mean He is still in the tomb (1 Corinthians 15:13). This is absurd in view of the "many infallible proofs" (Acts 1:3) that substantiate that it is empty due to His resurrection. The case for the resurrection of Christ has over 500 eyewitnesses, including both believers and unbelievers (1 Corinthians 15:6).

If Christ was not raised, it would mean the Christian faith is a delusion (1 Corinthians 15:14b). The proof that Jesus is the Son of God and the Savior of the world lies in His resurrection.

If Christ was not raised, it would mean that our preaching is futile (1 Corinthians 15:14a). Literally millions of sermons have been preached about the death, burial and resurrection of Christ by the likes of men such as C. H. Spurgeon, Adrian Rogers, George Whitfield, John Wesley, Billy Graham, and D. L. Moody. If Christ was not raised, all their preaching was meaningless, and so is ours today.

If Christ was not raised, then all who maintain His resurrection are liars (1 Corinthians 15:15). Paul puts his veracity, that of all the apostles and of every other Christian on the line to substantiate the fact of Christ's resurrection.

If Christ was not raised, then it would mean our faith is vain and we are hopelessly lost (1 Corinthians 15:17b). Why? Because apart from the resurrection, there is no remission of sin, and therefore no salvation (Romans 10:9–13). The resurrection of Christ puts the divine seal of God upon what He did on Good Friday to atone for man's sin, showing that it was acceptable and efficacious.

If Christ was not raised, it would mean there will be no reunion with love ones in Heaven (1 Corinthians 15:18). To deny the resurrection is to call God, who promised such a reunion, a liar (1 Thessalonians 4:17).

If Christ was not raised, it would mean that Christians are the most miserable of all men (1 Corinthians 15:19). If the hope of a Christian is untrue, it makes him miserable.

Then Paul emphatically thunders, "But Christ has indeed been raised from the dead" (1 Corinthians 15:20 NIV). And because He has risen, all the absurd propositions Paul suggested are reversed. And that's the game changer!

"The appearances of Jesus are as well authenticated as anything in antiquity....There can be no rational doubt that they occurred."
Michael Green

April 25

The Macedonia Call

"Come over into Macedonia, and help us" (Acts 16:9).

The invitation. Paul's second missionary journey was to be confined to Asia Minor. However, a man appeared to Paul in a vision in the night, begging him to come to Macedonia (the northern and central parts of modern-day Greece). It is speculated that the man was Luke, since afterwards he joins the threesome in the work (Acts 16:10).

The interpretation. Military generals would interpret the vision as a cry for military help; philanthropists, for financial aid; and politicians, for governmental leadership. But immediately, without second thoughts, Paul took it to mean assistance in advancing the cause of Christ. And that's the right knee-jerk reaction for every Christian, preacher or not, called upon to render help to a tribal village in India or the man next door.

The Christian's primary duty is to "preach" the Gospel and accompany it with clothing, food, and shelter, if necessities so demand. The Gospel best rectifies wrong, alleviates despair, heals brokenness of heart, and enables hope, peace, meaningfulness, and joy. Jesus is sufficient to meet man's every need.

Spurgeon says, "The Gospel is a help, not in one way, but in every way. Those who have not the Gospel stand in the greatest need of help; but when the Gospel is carried, you carry everything within it."[198]

The interruption. The Holy Spirit's directive through the vision meant the alteration of Paul's plans. Note, God has the right to interrupt our schedule to put us where we are needed, just at the right time. Interruptions often are divine appointments.

The immediacy of response. Paul and the other three men on the team (Timothy, Silas and Luke) at once obey. "And after he had seen the vision, immediately we endeavored to go into Macedonia, assuredly gathering that the Lord had called us for to preach the gospel unto them" (Acts 16:10). Their certainty of the call prompted immediate compliance. Matthew Henry states, "Ministers may go on with great cheerfulness and courage in their work when they perceive Christ calling them, not only to preach the Gospel, but to preach it at this time, in this place, to this people."[199] The open door today may be a shut door tomorrow.

The outcome. Obedience brings blessings. Paul goes to Macedonia, and Lydia is converted, a demon is cast out of a young girl, a jailer and his family are saved, and the Philippian church is formed. The mighty acts of God accompany the man that obeys the Macedonian call.

"God isn't looking for people of great faith, but for individuals ready to follow Him."

Hudson Taylor

April 26

Divine Visions

"I was not disobedient unto the heavenly vision" (Acts 26:19).

Visions, when used by the Holy Spirit, are purposed for divine communication (commission or call, or confirmation or manner of their fulfillment, etc.). Paul experienced several recorded visions (not dreams): the Macedonia call (Acts 16:9); the heavenly vision of Christ appointing Him to preach the Gospel (Acts 26:19), and the rapturous vision of Heaven about which he was not allowed to speak, not mentioning it for fourteen years (2 Corinthians 12:1–6).

Isaiah's vision of God upon the Throne prompted him to say, "Here am I; send me" (Isaiah 6:8). A blinding vision of the need of India compelled William Carey to take the Gospel to them. David Livingstone's vision of multitudes of Africans without Christ, and Hudson Taylor's of millions of Chinese who needed Christ prompted their going into missionary service to help them. As a teenager, my vision of a vast cotton field ready for harvest and its owner charging me to gather each boll gently and compassionately granted clarity and certainty to my divine call, a call I still endeavor to obey nearly sixty years later.

Don't discount the value and directive of a divine vision. Note, however, that Satan can be a counterfeiter of visions, so test them against the Word of God and the impressions of the Holy Spirit (Lamentations 2:14; Ezekiel 13:9). Make sure the vision is God's vision. Once assured that it is, like Paul, don't be disobedient to it.

"Heavenly visions have a commanding power over earthly counsels, and it is at our peril if we be disobedient to them."[200]

Matthew Henry

April 27

The Grip of God

"For I am the Lord, your God, who grasp your right hand; It is I who say to you, Do not fear, I will help you" (Isaiah 41:13 NAB).

A small boy went for a swim in the old swimming hole behind his home. He didn't know that an alligator was swimming toward him as he swam toward the middle of the lake. But the watchful eye of his father saw what was transpiring, and he quickly ran to the water, shouting to his son about the danger.

The lad made a U-turn to swim to him. Reaching from the dock, the father grabbed his son's arms just as the alligator snatched his legs. An incredible tug-of-war raged. The father would not let go, battling a strength greater than his own.

A farmer passing by in his truck heard the screams, raced to the water, and shot the alligator. Miraculously, following weeks of hospitalization, the young boy recovered. The severe scars on his legs bore witness to the traumatizing and almost fatal encounter with the alligator, while the deep scratches on his arms showed the marks of his father's fingernails that dug into his flesh to hang on to him.

A reporter asked to see the scars. The boy pulled up his pant legs. And then the boy said, "But look at my arms. I have great scars on my arms, too, because my dad wouldn't let go."

Regardless of the *alligators* that afflict and assail you, bringing hurt and pain, the heavenly Father will not let go of you—even when you want to let go, like Elijah (1 Kings 19:4) and Jonah (Jonah 4:3) did. The scars in His hands, feet and side bear indisputable testimony to that. God securely grips your hand in the storms of life, refusing to let go. He says, "I, your God, have a firm grip on you and I'm not letting go" (Isaiah 41:13 MSG).

"Peace comes not from the absence of trouble, but from the presence of God."

Alexander Maclaren

April 28

What to Do with the Bible

"Thy word is a lamp unto my feet, and a light unto my path" (Psalm 119:105).

What to do with the Bible?

Meditate on its pages. To meditate upon the Word is to muse over it (chew it until it is digested) until its truth is absorbed (Joshua 1:8). Mueller states, "I saw that the most important thing I had to do was give myself to the reading of the Word of God—not prayer, but the Word of God; and here again, not the simple reading of the Word of God so that it only passes through my mind just as water runs through a pipe, but considering what I read, pondering over it, and applying it to my heart; to meditate on it, that thus my heart might be comforted, encouraged, warned, reproved, instructed; and that thus, by means of the Word of God, whilst meditating on it, my heart be brought into experimental communion with the Lord." Mediation is essential for spiritual growth.

Memorize its parts. David declared, "Thy Word have I hid in mine heart, that I might not sin against thee" (Psalms 119:11). Scripture verses will keep believers from spiritual reverses. The Word stored in the heart provides a ready answer for those who ask for a reason for the faith, a shield of protection against temptation, and a balm of Gilead in times of sorrow and trial. Fanny Crosby, though blind, memorized five chapters of the Bible each week. By the time she was 15, she had memorized Matthew, Mark, Luke, John, Genesis, Exodus, Leviticus, Numbers, Deuteronomy, Proverbs, Song of Solomon, and many of the Psalms. This she did by hearing them read.

Model its precepts. Meditating upon its pages and memorizing its parts is not enough; its precepts must be modeled. The Word must become incarnate in its reader. James admonishes the believer not to be a hearer of the Word only, but also a doer of what it teaches (James 1:22).

Read the Word, receive the Word, and then by faith appropriate the Word. Spurgeon said, "Those who are hearers only are wasters of the Word. What poor creatures hearers are, for they have long ears and no hands!"[201]

"Nobody ever outgrows Scripture; the book widens and deepens with our years."
Charles Spurgeon

April 29

Dipper or Abider

"Abide in me, and I in you" (John 15:4).

"To 'remain' in Jesus has a deeper significance than simply to continue to believe in Him, although it includes that; it connotes continuing to live in association or in union with Him."[202] It means "to stay put" in fellowship with Him and His Word. It's imperative that we abide, *stay put,* in Jesus, or else we will fizzle out spiritually.

There are two ways that one can make instant tea. The first is by dipping the tea bag in and out of the hot water. The second is allowing the tea bag to remain (abide) in the hot water until it becomes totally saturated.

Don't be a dipper spiritually, dipping in and out of fellowship with Christ; rather, be an abider, remaining steadfast, "unmovable, always abounding in the work of the Lord" (1 Corinthians 15:58). Hindson and Kroll say, "When the Christian fails to abide in Christ, he withers, dries up, and his fruit or works will be judged by fire (1 Corinthians 3:12–15)."[203]

"Abide in Christ, and let His words abide in you. Closer, closer, closer—this is the way to spiritual wealth."[204]

C. H. Spurgeon

April 30

The Landmine of Pride

"Pride goeth before destruction, and an haughty spirit before a fall" (Proverbs 16:18).

Pride is an ugly sin that goes neither unnoticed nor unpunished by God. It is counted an abomination unto the Lord (Proverbs 16:5). "The nose is in the heavens; the seat is in the mire" (Arabic proverb).[205]

Its nature. Pride has lofty and flattering thoughts of oneself, often based upon education, intellect, talent, ability, appearance and/or possession. It is repulsive and detestable to man.

April

Its consequence. Pride separates man from God, causes disdain for and harm to others, and leads to ruin. Colton says, "Pride, like the magnet, constantly points to one object, self; but, unlike the magnet, it has no attractive pole, but at all points repels."[206]

Its detection. Pride is hidden from him who displays it but is known widely to others. Signs of pride are boastfulness, the exaltation of self, and disdain for others.

A kite flying high in the sky moved as stately as a person of royalty. In looking down with contempt on that which was below, it said, "What a superior being I am now! Who has ever ascended so high as I have? What a poor groveling set of beings are all those beneath me! I despise them." And then the kite shook its head in sneers and wagged its tail, moving onward and upward, thinking everything must make way for it. Then, suddenly, the string broke, bringing the kite down with greater speed than that with which it had ascended, and it was badly hurt in the fall.[207]

With pride, what goes up, always comes down, and what is inflated will always be deflated.

"Often Satan injects pride into the believer's spirit, evoking in him an attitude of self-importance and of self-conceit. He causes him to esteem himself a very outstanding person, one who is indispensable in God's work. Such a spirit constitutes one of the major reasons for the fall of believers."

Watchman Nee

May 1

The Appraisal of the Scriptures

"All scripture is given by inspiration of God" (2 Timothy 3:16).

We appraise its credibility and say, "It is in truth, the word of God" (1 Thessalonians 2:13). Its hundreds of fulfilled prophecies and kept promises attest to its authenticity. "There hath not failed one word of all His good promise" (1 Kings 8:56).

We appraise its preservability and say, "Thy word is true from the beginning" (Psalm 119:160). H. L. Hastings wrote, "Infidels of eighteen hundred years have been refuting and overthrowing this book, and yet it stands today as solid as a rock. Its circulation increases, and it is more loved and cherished and read today than ever before. Infidels, with all their assaults, make about as much impression on this book as a man with a tack hammer would on the Pyramids of Egypt."

We appraise its reliability and say, "We also have the completely reliable prophetic word. You do well to pay attention to it, as to a lamp shining in a dark place" (1 Peter 1:19 EHV). The reliability of the ancient manuscript (from which we get the English Bible) is attested by the large number of them—over 5,000 of the New Testament and over 10,000 manuscripts or parts of manuscripts of the Old Testament.[208]

We appraise its availability and say, "The Word of God is not bound" (2 Timothy 2:9). The courier of the word may be fettered, but it cannot be.

We appraise its capability and say, "Many of them which heard the word believed; and the number of the men was about five thousand" (Acts 4:4). It rescues, comforts, guides, edifies, revives, convicts, corrects, changes, emboldens, and much more.

We appraise its infallibility and say, "The Scripture cannot be broken" (John 10:35). Criswell says, "Jesus believed and taught the infallibility of Scripture. He regarded it as the divine authority and as the final court of appeal concerning all questions. He sets His seal to its historicity and its revelation from God."[209]

"The Bible is not only divinely inspired, but it is divinely protected in its present shape."

T. DeWitt Talmage

May 2

What Was Finished at Calvary?

"It is finished" (John 19:30).

The meaning of the Greek word translated here is "to pay in full" or "the price is all paid." Much speculation has been made about what the "it" in this statement meant.

Did it refer to the completion of the sufferings and torment of Christ? Possibly so. Did it mean that all the prophecies about Messiah's death were fulfilled? Possibly so. Did it mean that the atonement for man's sin by animal sacrifice was finished? Likely so. Might it have meant that the battle with Satan and the power of sin were over and Christ was the Victor (Colossians 2:15)? Probably so. Did it mean Christ's physical life was about to end? Maybe so. Or might it have meant that the redemptive mission of Christ to save the world from the power and penalty of sin was fully accomplished "once for all" (Hebrews 10:10)? Surely so.

Prior to the Cross, Christ exhaustingly labored sharing the Gospel *to man*. He endured the bodily torture and death of the Cross *for man* to make his reconciliation with God possible (Romans 5:10). Whatever else is meant in the words, "It is finished," it means that Christ accomplished all God assigned Him to do and all that was necessary to save man from his sinful estate and damnable plight.

And Calvary's results or accomplishments by Christ are continuous. "He hath finished the transgression, and made reconciliation for iniquity, and brought in everlasting righteousness, and sealed up the vision and prophecy, and anointed a holy of holies" (see Daniel 9:24). With this view, MacArthur agrees, stating, "The verb here carries the idea of fulfilling one's task and, in religious contexts, has the idea of fulfilling one's religious obligations. The entire work of redemption had been brought to completion."[210]

"The resurrection is God's 'Amen' to Jesus' loud cry "It is finished," and therefore the guarantee that by Jesus' death the believer has indeed been reconciled to God and made righteous."[211]

J. A. Schep

May

May 3

A Balm in Gilead

"Is there no balm in Gilead; is there no physician there? why then is not the health of the daughter of my people recovered?" (Jeremiah 8:22).

There is balm in the blood of Christ Jesus. Although there is *no physician* here that possesses healing balm for a sin-sick soul, there is such a physician in Heaven. It is the Great Physician, Jesus. Simeon states, "Has not God sent us a Physician from Heaven, even His only dear Son, who perfectly knows the extent of our disorders and is able to prescribe a remedy for them? Other physicians find their remedies in the productions of nature and of art, but this blessed Physician 'heals His people with His own stripes.' He shed His own precious blood for us upon the cross that it might be applied, as a sovereign balm, to our souls to restore us to perfect health."[212] The Bible says, "The blood of Jesus Christ His Son cleanseth us from all sin" (1 John 1:7).

There is balm in the Holy Scriptures. Spurgeon wrote, "Within the Scriptures there is a balm for every wound and a salve for every sore!"[213] Whatever might be the hurt or hardship, grief or difficulty, anxiety or trauma, Christ provides and dispenses the needed medicine through Holy Scriptures to comfort, console, calm, combat, and cheer, and to help cope victoriously.

There is balm in Christ's personal touch. "He [Christ] is the only universal doctor," Spurgeon writes, "and the medicine He gives is the only true catholicon [a cure-all], healing in every instance. Whatever our spiritual malady may be, we should apply at once to this Divine Physician. There is no brokenness of heart which Jesus cannot bind up. We have but to think of the myriads who have been delivered from all sorts of diseases through the power and virtue of His touch, and we shall joyfully put ourselves in His hands. We trust Him, and sin dies; we love Him, and grace lives; we wait for Him, and grace is strengthened; we see Him as He is, and grace is perfected forever."[214]

The balm of Gilead must be appropriated. The "healing balm" must be sought and applied in order to be beneficial. Jeremiah's complaint and grief were that the people of Judah neglected it when they sorely needed it, even though they knew where to find it. Avoid being like them. Seek it, seize it, and be sustained by it in time of deepest need. The psalmist declared, "He healeth the broken in heart, and bindeth up their wounds" (Psalm 147:3)—and "what He's done for others, He'll do for you."

"Christ is the Good Physician. There is no disease He cannot heal, no sin He cannot remove, no trouble He cannot help. He is the Balm of Gilead, the Great Physician who has never yet failed to heal all the spiritual maladies of every soul that has come unto Him in faith and prayer."
James H. Aughey

May 4

The Abiding Life

"Abide in me, and I in you" (John 15:4).

Abiding in Christ is linked intrinsically to the infusion of supernatural power that is imperative if we are to bear fruit, engage in effectual prayer, and live the victorious Christian life.

The metaphor of the Vine and its branches well illustrates the abiding life. The branch depends upon the sap of the Vine for nourishment and strengthening to prosper and bear fruit. It must abide in the Vine, and draw sap from it, moment by moment, day by day, to be healthy and productive. To rely upon sap received today for tomorrow's need leaves the branch weak and fruitless.

The application to the Christian is apparent. Jesus says, "I am the vine, ye are the branches: he that abideth in me, and I in him, the same bringeth forth much fruit: for without me ye can do nothing" (John 15:5). To be infused with supernatural sap or power to live victoriously, healthily, and productively, the branch must abide in the Vine (Christ). It must continuously draw from the life-empowering sap of the Vine.

What does it mean for the branch to *abide* in the Vine? It means consistent compliance with Christ's teaching and commandments. "He that keepeth his commandments dwelleth in him, and he in him" (1 John 3:24). It is to walk in unison with Him, without vacillating, experiencing the manifestation of His holy presence in the sweetest of communion (John 14:21).

The posture of the abiding life may be summed up in four words: "Keep looking to Jesus." McConkey says, "Keep looking to Jesus, moment by moment, until such abiding in faith becomes the constant attitude of the soul."[215] The branch that fails to abide in the Vine withers, dries up, is fruitless and good for nothing (John 15:6).

"It is the great concern of all Christ's disciples constantly to keep up a dependence upon Christ and communion with Him, habitually to adhere to Him, and actually to derive supplies from Him."[216]

Matthew Henry

May 5

The Dead Yet Speaketh

"He being dead yet speaketh" (Hebrews 11:4).

The reference is to ministers of the faith, though it is applicable to all. In what ways "speaketh" the departed preacher to the living?

Through the souls that he won. The converts of the preacher's ministry transmit his message to others. They keep it alive. Mordecai Ham's message echoed decades after his death through Billy Graham, who was saved under his preaching.

Through the example that he left. Henry Wadsworth Longfellow remarked, "Lives of great men all remind us we can make our lives sublime, and departing, leave behind us footprints on the sands of time." It's not that which is generously given but that which is genuinely instilled by walk and talk which bears lasting impact. Spurgeon said, "A good character is the best tombstone. Those who loved you and were helped by you will remember you. So carve your name on hearts and not on marble."

Through the books that he wrote. The writings of Spurgeon, who died in 1892, have allowed him to influence millions for the cause of Christ. E. P. Whipple states, "Books are lighthouses erected in the great sea of time."[217] Books continue to flood out spiritual light long after the minister's departure, providing guidance, edification and encouragement.

Through the sermons that he preached. That which beloved men of God have said which makes Christ dearer to us is always remembered and recalled.

Through the ministries that he founded. Bible colleges, orphanages, churches, rescue missions, missionary societies, etc., keep their founder continually speaking for the cause of Christ.

Through the disciples that he taught. Biblical instruction and training to others multiplies the preacher's influence and witness and enables them to continue after his death (2 Timothy 2:2). The minister faithful to the call is effectual in life and even in death in its fulfillment. Spurgeon is dead, but his thunderous voice is heard worldwide. John Bunyan is dead, but his ministry lives on through *Pilgrim's Progress*. Richard Baxter is dead, but saints find comfort and solace in the *Saint's Rest*. D. L. Moody is dead, yet his work continues through the Moody Bible College that he founded. Hudson Taylor is dead, but the missionary movement he initiated continues to impact the world.

"The influence of a man never ceases through all of the eternities that are to come; personality never dies, and influence never perishes."[218]
W. A. Criswell

May 6

The Meaning of Death

"For I am now ready to be offered, and the time of my departure is at hand" (2 Timothy 4:6).

The word "departure" is used by some to refer to the loosing of a ship from its moorings or the lifting of its anchor to be freed to sail. This is what death is for Christians. It's being loosed from earth's moorings. It's pulling up one's anchor from this world. It's setting sail for the new country of Heaven, having been made free from the cares and trials of this life (Philippians 1:23).

Spurgeon asserts, "When we loose our cable and bid farewell to earth, it shall not be with bitterness in the retrospect. There is sin in it, and we are called to leave it; there has been trial in it, and we are called to be delivered from it; there has been sorrow in it, and we are glad that we shall go where we shall sorrow no more. There has been weakness and pain and suffering in it, and we are glad that we shall be raised in power; there has been death in it, and we are glad to bid farewell to shrouds and to knells. But for all that there has been, *there is* such mercy in it, such lovingkindness of God in it, that the wilderness and the solitary place have been made glad, and the desert has rejoiced and blossomed as a rose. We will not bid farewell to the world, execrating it, or leaving behind us a cold shudder and a sad remembrance, but we will depart, bidding adieu to the scenes that remain and to the people of God that tarry therein yet a little longer, blessing Him whose goodness and mercy have followed us all the days of our life, and who is now bringing us to dwell in the house of the Lord forever."[219]

"I am the resurrection, and the life: he that believeth in me, though he were dead, yet shall he live" (John 11:25). The military guard at funerals play "Taps," the universal signal that the day is over. At the death of a Christian, it would be appropriate for "Reveille," the signal to awake and get going, to be sounded immediately afterward.

To the Christian, death is not a period, but a comma. In English grammar, a period at the conclusion of a sentence means "the end; nothing more is coming; the thought has been completed." In contrast, a comma loudly states, "Take a breath; relax a moment. Get prepared, for there is more to come."

What a wonderful description of death! Death is not a period to one's life (not "Taps"), only a comma indicating "the best is yet to be." When everything seems to cry out that death is the end for your loved one, remember when Jesus rose from the dead, He forever made it a "comma." It's "Reveille." Dietrich Bonhoeffer said, "After death something new begins over which all powers of the world of death have no more might."

"How awful to die out of Christ! How blessed to die in Christ!"
William Tipaft

May 7

Second Chances

"The Lord can always be trusted to show mercy each morning" (Lamentations 3:23 CEV).

As a child, I played with a magic slate that enabled a drawing to be totally erased with the lifting of a thin plastic screen. The lifting of the screen gave me a second chance to do a better job with my drawing.

Similarly, grace grants us a clean slate and fresh start when we confess and repent of our sin. God relishes opportunities to offer second chances (Joel 2:13). His grace affords the one who falters the opportunity for a second chance (or multiple chances) for recovery and restoration to Christian walk and service. This is made crystal clear in Scripture.

God says in Jeremiah 15:19, "If you return to me, I will restore you so you can continue to serve me" (NLT). Max Lucado says, "Second chances are the specialty of our Savior!"[220]

Peter's three denials of Christ on the eve of His crucifixion wasn't final. Grace was extended (John 21:15–19), a second chance was received, and in several days, he was back preaching (Acts 2). Jonah was given a second chance. The Bible says that following Jonah's disobedience, "The word of the Lord came to Jonah a second time" (Jonah 3:1 NIV), and this time, he obeyed. The prodigal son got a second chance, of which he took advantage (Luke 15:21–22). Moses, who murdered an Egyptian soldier, got a second chance (Exodus 2:11–15) and became the leader of the Israelites, bringing them out of Egyptian bondage. David, who committed murder and adultery (2 Samuel 11:14–17), got a second chance and penned the Psalter that has comforted and consoled millions throughout history. After lying about Sarah being his wife (Genesis 12:10–20), Abraham got a second chance and became the Father of many nations.

And what God did for these, He's desirous to do for all that stumble.

"A returning penitent, though formerly bad as the worst of men, may by grace become as good as the best."[221]

John Bunyan

May 8

"Ready to Be Offered"

"I am now ready to be offered" (2 Timothy 4:6).

Paul, realizing that death was imminent, tells Timothy, "I am now ready to be offered."

What makes it somewhat easy to say what Paul said?

1. The relief from sorrow and suffering it grants. Matthew Henry says, "All the effects of former trouble shall be done away. They have been often before in tears, by reason of sin, of affliction, of the calamities of the church; but now all tears shall be wiped away; no signs, no remembrance of former sorrows shall remain, any further than to make their present felicity the greater."[222]

May

2. The reunion with Christian friends it affords. "There will be a happy meeting in Heaven, I know, when we see the many loved ones, we've known here below. Gathered on that blessed hilltop with hearts all aglow, that will be a glad reunion day."

3. The royal residence that it provides. "We may speak about a place," says Lucado, "where there are no tears, no death, no fear, no night; but those are just the benefits of heaven. The beauty of heaven is seeing God."

4. The rapturous delight that it entails. Heaven is a city free of sin, pain, fear, sickness, sorrow, and death, and one with eternal joy and praise.

5. The completion of life's work that it means. "I have finished the race" (NIV).

6. The reward that it promises. Five possible crowns await the believer in Heaven.

What makes it difficult to say what Paul said?

1. Attachment to friends and family. Corrie ten Boom says, "Don't hold onto anything so tightly that Jesus can't take it from you"—or you from it or them.

2. Being unprepared to meet God. Man shuns death, dreads death, and the very thought of death because of his soul's alienation from God.

3. Fearfulness of what the grave holds.

4. Pleasures and possessions of the world.

5. The anticipated pain and discomfort that accompanies it.

6. The destiny to which they will go. Death is unwelcome to him that is to meet it unprepared (not born again), for after it is eternal torment in Hell (Revelation 21:8).

"Death to a good man is his release from the imprisonment of this world and his departure to the enjoyments of another world; he does not cease to be, but is only removed from one world to another."[223]

Matthew Henry

May 9

The Greatness of Salvation

"How shall we escape if we neglect so great a salvation" (Hebrews 2:3 NKJV).

The salvation spurned is great.

It is great because of its benefits.

1. Its recipient gains justification from sin (1 Corinthians 6:11).

2. It's recipient gains reconciliation to God (Romans 5:10).

3. Its recipient gains liberation from sin (Romans 6:6, 14).

4. Its recipient gains reservation for Heaven (Psalm 16:11). Believers are saved from Hell and its torments and given access to the City of God at death.

It is great because of its means. "The law of Moses was unable to save us because of the weakness of our sinful nature. So God did what the law could not do. He sent his own Son in a body like the bodies we sinners have. And in that body God declared an end to sin's control over us by giving his Son as a sacrifice for our sins" (Romans 8:3 NLT). Jesus made a bridge to God for man out of the timber of the Cross. Salvation is a great salvation because of the great cost of providing it—the torturous death of the Son of God on a cruel cross (John 3:16; 2 Timothy 1:10).

It is great because of its availability. Salvation is every man's privilege and possibility. All who will be saved may be saved, "even me with all my sin." It's not a white man's salvation. It's not a black man's salvation. It's the world's salvation. None are excluded, regardless of face, race or place. It is a great salvation for great sinners.

"Jesus is not one of many ways to approach God, nor is He the best of several ways; He is the only way."

A. W. Tozer

May 10

Neglecters of Salvation

"How shall we escape if we neglect so great a salvation" (Hebrews 2:3 NKJV).

To spurn this great salvation bears inescapable consequences. It brings restlessness to the soul. "But the wicked are like the troubled sea, when it cannot rest, whose waters cast up mire and dirt. There is no peace, saith my God, to the wicked" (Isaiah 57:20–21). It brings the wrath of God upon man. "For the wrath of God is revealed from heaven against all ungodliness and unrighteousness of men, who by their unrighteousness suppress the truth" (Romans 1:18 ESV). They that neglect salvation are already under the condemnation of God (John 3:18). It brings damnation in the lake of fire. "And whosoever was not found written in the book of life was cast into the lake of fire" (Revelation 20:15).

The spurners of this great salvation are not deniers or rejecters but ignorers of salvation. They are the sinners that hear the Gospel proclaimed and recognize its truth and necessity, but without making a decision to embrace it. They know what to do but fail to do it. Christ is man's only refuge from that which awaits him at the end of a Christless life (Hebrews 6:18).

Neglect not this so great salvation any longer. Heed that which is heard. Matthew Henry says, "There is no escaping out of this condemned state, but by accepting the great salvation discovered in the Gospel; as far those who neglect it, the wrath of God is upon them, and it abides upon them; they cannot disengage themselves; they cannot emerge; they cannot get from under the curse."[224]

"I urge you without delay to accept the truth about Christ, and to humble confession and repentance and faith. It would be tragic for you to persist in your unbelief and eventually go to eternity without hope and without God."[225]

Billy Graham

May 11

A Sudden Step

"There is but a step between me and death" (1 Samuel 20:3).

A step is taken in mere seconds, and death in its nature is said to be as a step.

A separating step. At death, the wheat is separated from the tare (Matthew 13:30), the sheep from the goat (Matthew 25:31–33), and the twain shall never meet again. The rich man in Hell was separated from Lazarus and the redeemed in Heaven by a great, uncrossable divide.

A sealing step. At death, the door to salvation (reconciliation to God, eternal life, Heaven) is permanently shut. Jesus said, "Make every effort to enter through the narrow door, because many, I tell you, will try to enter and will not be able to. Once the owner of the house gets up and closes the door, you will stand outside knocking and pleading, 'Sir, open the door for us.' But he will answer, 'I don't know'" (Luke 13:24–25 NIV). There are no second chances to be saved beyond the grave. Saith Spurgeon, "What I am when death is held before me, that I must be forever. When my spirit departs, if God finds me hymning His praise, I shall hymn it in Heaven; if He finds me breathing out oaths, I shall follow up those oaths in Hell."[226]

A stinging or singing step. To meet death without Christ is insufferable and horrifying. But with Christ clasping the hand, the journey is peaceful, serene, and fearless. If you are unprepared for the "step," make ready now. To quote Spurgeon again, "If there is but a step between you and death, yet there is only a step between you and Jesus. There is only a step between you and salvation. God help you take that step."[227]

"All mankind is sitting on death row. How we die or when is not the main issue, but where we go after death."[228]

Billy Graham

May 12

The Proverbs 31 Woman

"A truly good wife is the most precious treasure a man can find!" (Proverbs 31:10 CEV).

Proverbs 31 is a divinely inspired description of a godly wife and mother, to which every woman should aspire. No other is her equal in all of Scripture.

She is a valiant woman. "Virtuous" (KJV) means "strong, brave, and competent." The Proverbs 31 woman rises to the task of being a courageous and capable wife and mother.

She is a devout Christian. The model wife and mother have been born again and avidly heed Christ's teaching and instruction.

She is a faithful bride. The godly woman manifests inviolable faithfulness to her husband. There is no fear of impropriety or indiscreet conduct by her. She is his best ally and helper behind the scenes, enabling him to succeed and maintain an honorable reputation.

May

She is a loving mother. A godly mother speaks love and shows it to her household.

She is an instructor. A godly mother rears her children in the counsel and admonition of the Lord. She nurtures them with the milk and meat of God's Holy Word. Upon her knees, her children first learn about God, prompting them to sing, "Jesus loves me this I know, for my mother tells me so." Beecher said, "What a mother sings to the cradle goes all the way down to the coffin."

She is a protector. The Proverbs 31 woman protects and safeguards her children hawkishly from the evil that abounds in the world. Her guardianship spares them from untold harm and hurt.

She is kind and gentle in her speech. Godly wisdom and restraint control her tongue, enabling it to provide consolation, encouragement, tranquility, and guidance to all in the family, and extinguish rather than exacerbate disruption in the home. Her tongue is not rash, harsh, or injurious, but kind and gentle.

She is a hard worker. Idleness is unknown to her. All that is necessary for the welfare of the home (including work outside the home) she does tirelessly and without murmuring.

She is a radiant beauty. A God-fearing woman is beautiful from the inside out.

She is thrifty and frugal. The dollar is stretched to its furthest extent by her hand. She manages the finances of the household prudently.

She is a sympathizer. She serves others with love, tenderness, thoughtfulness, and kindness.

She is unselfish. The Proverbs 31 woman is a charitable and generous mother who gladly does without so that her children may have all that is needed and even wanted, if it is deemed appropriate.

She is a strong soldier. The Proverbs 31 woman has the tenacity to withstand the severest trouble and disappointment, for her trust in God is unshakable.

She is a happy home builder. The godly woman's sphere of work primarily is in the home, and it is her delight and duty to make it an environment of pleasure, peace, provision, and protection.

She is persistent in her role. The godly woman does her husband and children good "all the days of her life." This type of wife and mother is lauded by her children and praised by her husband (Proverbs 31:28).

She is a rarity and should be valued, embraced, and treasured more than precious diamonds and pearls.

"There is more power in a mother's hand than in a king's scepter."
  Billy Sunday

May 13

Lessons from the Elder Brother

"The older brother was so angry that he would not go into the house; so his father came out and begged him to come in" (Luke 15:28 GNT).

Why did Jesus include the elder brother's reaction to the prodigal son's return in the parable? Perhaps for six reasons.

1. To warn the saint against allowing prejudice, jealousy, self-importance, and the monster of selfishness to despise the salvation or restoration of a soul.

2. To show that He counts salvation a big deal and to encourage us to celebrate it. Christ's chiefest joy is in the salvation of the lost and the restoration of the saint. "It was meet that we should make merry, and be glad: for this thy brother was dead, and is alive again; and was lost, and is found" (Luke 15:32).

3. To warn against peevishly staying outside the house (church) in protest when someone who is disliked or detested gets saved or restored (Luke 15:28).

4. To warn against hypocrisy. MacDonald says, "The older son is an eloquent picture of the scribes and Pharisees. They resented God's showing mercy to outrageous sinners."[229] No genuine Christian will look unfeelingly or indifferently upon him who staggers from the Far Country to the Father's house in confession and repentance. He will join the celebration over the transformation.

5. To warn against the sin of condemning the speck in another's eye when there's a beam in one's own (Matthew 7:5). The elder brother was arrogant, self-righteous and pompous, saying he deserved more of the Father's love, treasure, and celebration than did his disobedient brother (Luke 15:29–30), while he himself harbored hostility, bitterness and anger toward his brother. He pictures the Pharisee in the Temple whom

May

Jesus condemned for self-righteousness (Luke 18:14). MacArthur asserts, "This son's self-righteous behavior was more socially acceptable than the younger brother's debauchery, but it was equally dishonoring to the father—and called for repentance."[230]

6. Sin remains sin and is loathsome to God despite its form of dress (attitude or action) or place (the Far Country or the Father's house—the church) or the person's face (saint or sinner).

"Where God's happiness is, there self-righteousness cannot come. If God is good to the sinner, what avails my righteousness?"
J. N. Darby

May 14

Encouragement in Failure

"Master, we worked hard all night and caught nothing" (Luke 5:5 NET).

Failure happens to the best of workers. Peter's words are echoed by the godliest of pastors, evangelists, teachers, soul winners, and missionaries the world over who have labored tirelessly for weeks, months, or years with little or no success.

Failure begets weariness and discouragement. Jeremiah frequently felt despondent and at times wanted to quit over not seeing any visible fruit of his labor for decades. But he didn't abandon the work. Yates said, "The highest form of obedience is to continue to remain at our post of duty when we cannot see why we are kept there."[231] Christ says to the distraught workman that has pulled his boat to shore and has all but quit the work, "Toil on. Faint not. Launch out into the deep and let down your nets for a great catch." He is the saint's best encourager and enabler in the work. Failure (fruitlessness) doesn't mean God is done with you.

Failure often precedes success. The lack of success in the night becomes triumph in the morning. And what success it was, so great that the multitude of fish they caught in their net broke it (Luke 5:6)! Jeremiah, after toiling fifty-one years without a soul, wins someone. How often it is that the Christian worker, after treading in the desert of famine, marches on the mountaintop, basking in the blessings of fruitfulness. Note, failure in one task is not indicative of the same happening in other undertakings.

Failure in the night can come from God as much as the success of the morning does. "The steps of a good man are ordered by the LORD" (Psalm 37:23). See Romans 8:28. God at times ordains failure in order to bring success. One door is closed so that another can be opened.

Failure can bring humility, greater faith, and earnest prayer for victorious achievement. The bottom line is that in failure we should listen for and hearken to the Word of the Lord for a directive. It was Peter's acting upon Jesus' word that brought success: "At thy word" (Luke 5:5–6). Despite the difficulties and failures of the past when you were doing the same task, say with Peter, "Nevertheless at thy word I will let down the net" (Luke 5:5).

Saith Matthew Henry, "We must do our duty, and then leave the event to God."[232] General Wellington gave a command to another general who thought it would be impossible to execute. Wellington told him, "You go ahead and do it, because I don't give impossible commands."[233] Our Lord never gives a command that cannot be done.

"It is not work that tries men and women half as much as it is the disappointment which unsuccess brings."[234]
                                       E. E. Johnson

May 15

Launch Out into the Deep

"Launch out into the deep, and let down your nets for a draught" (Luke 5:4).

Launch out into the deep with regard to the Word of God. Minnows feed in the shadow water, but the big fish in the deep. Row into deeper waters and feed upon the meat of the Word and thereby grow in knowledge and power.

Launch out into the deep with regard to ministry. A "shallow water" ministry (where work is easier, hardships and risks smaller) is a noble undertaking for some, but others God calls to the deeper waters where greater opportunities and challenges abound for His cause. Launch your

May

ship into the deep waters of missionary, pastoral, evangelistic or apologetic work.

Launch out into the deep with regard to giving. Increase what you give to kingdom work. Be more generous and sacrificial. Go deeper into your pocket or bank account, that the Gospel may go further. Spurgeon said, "It is beyond the realm of possibilities that one has the ability to outgive God. Even if I give the whole of my worth to Him, He will find a way to give back to me much more than I gave."

Launch out into the deep with regard to witnessing. Speak up for Christ loudly and clearly at work, school, social gatherings, and play. Stop tiptoeing through the tulips with the Gospel. Brazenly share the faith!

To sail into the deeper waters, the anchor (the hindrance) that holds the boat in the shallow water must be raised. Don't forestall launching out a little further into the deep, for when you do, like Peter, you will be "astonished...at the draught of the fishes" taken (Luke 5:9).

"If you wonder why you aren't in the deeper waters of ministry, maybe it's because you haven't been obedient in launching out in the little things, the simple callings, the unnoticed tasks."235

Jon Courson

May 16

To Make the Wrong Decision

"And he...went away grieved" (Mark 10:22).

Note the rich young ruler's quest for salvation.

He came to the right person: Jesus (Mark 10:17a). He sought Jesus out, not only because He is the door to salvation, but also because He loves the down and out, the broken and weary, the sinful and guilty. "Jesus beholding him loved him" (Mark 10:21). No one loves man or desires his best good and end like Jesus does (John 3:16).

He came with the right attitude: kneeling (Mark 10:17b). Saith Matthew Henry, "He kneeled to Him in token of the great value and veneration he had for Him as a Teacher come from God, and his earnest desire to be taught by Him. He bowed the knee to the Lord Jesus as one that would not only *do obeisance* to him now but would *yield obedience* to him always; he bowed the knee as one that meant *to bow the soul to him.*"236

He came with the right question: "What shall I do that I may inherit eternal life?" (Mark 10:17c). Man's most important question is how to be made right with Holy God and gain Heaven at death.

He got the right answer: "Come, take up the cross, and follow me" (Mark 10:21). To follow Christ requires repentance and faith and an unrivaled love for Him.

But sadly, *he made the wrong decision: "He...went away grieved"* (Mark 10:22). He chose to cling to the world and its possessions. Steeped in legalism, the youth thought keeping the commandments and good deeds would gain him eternal life. When told that such was not the case, that it required the placeing of one's entire life upon the altar in surrender to Christ as Lord and Savior, he was sorrowful, "for he had great possessions" (Mark 10:22b)." The desire to gain eternal life was overtaken by the want of the stuff of the world.

*"Sinners cannot hang on to their sins and at the same time reach out to Jesus. There must be sincere repentance before sinners can turn to God and be saved by His grace."*237

Warren Wiersbe

May 17

A Song to Sing in a Strange Land

"By the rivers of Babylon, there we sat down, yea, we wept, when we remembered Zion. We hanged our harps upon the willows in the midst thereof. For there they that carried us away captive required of us a song; and they that wasted us required of us mirth, saying, Sing us one of the songs of Zion. How shall we sing the Lord's song in a strange land?" (Psalm 137:1–4).

The "Lord's song" includes the Psalms, hymns and spiritual songs, all of which are the making of melody in the heart to the Lord (Ephesians 5:19). The "Lord's song" may be "sung" verbally or mentally. It was this song that was silenced among the saints in Babylonian captivity due to heaviness of heart (grief and sorrow over their estate and that of Jerusalem). Without a "song" to sing (in a "strange land," a solemn place

May

where the believer's song is silenced by tribulation and trials), he hangs his "harp" upon the willows at the river's bank (for he has no heart to use it) and tearfully inquires "How shall we sing the Lord's song in a strange land?"

What a good question! While languishing upon a sickbed ("a strange land"), approaching death, or gripped with great sorrow over the death of a loved one, how is the saint to "sing" the song of Zion? How is it that martyrs of old, while dying for the faith, still had a "song" as they were nailed to a cross, thrust into a den of lions, beheaded by the guillotine, or burned at the stake? How is it that saints like Fanny Crosby, blinded in infancy by a medical mistake; Joni Eareckson Tada, who through a swimming accident became a quadriplegic; Horatio Spafford, whose children were drowned at sea when crossing the Atlantic all maintained their "song" despite the pain, suffering, sickness, and sorrow? Along with multitudes of others, in their "strange land," these testify with Job, "Though he slay me, yet will I trust in him" (Job 13:15). Sword, guillotine, lion, disease, sorrow, and even death were unable to silence their song.

Suffering saints like these answer the question, "How shall we sing the Lord's song in a strange land?" with the question, "Why shouldn't we sing the Lord's song in a strange land?" They continue, "In this land God is the same God as He is outside it; not one iota has changed with regard to His loving guardianship and tender compassionate care. Every promise of the Bible remains true—possession of forgiveness of sin and eternal life through the Savior's redeeming blood has not been altered; the defiled garments of sin are still washed clean; the saints' citizenship in Heaven is unchanged; God yet remains in sovereign control of all that happens to the saint; the Holy Spirit's ministry of comfort and help to the believer is unabated; and God's mercies are still new every morning."

These stupendous facts ought to cause the heart to erupt in praise songs to the King, even while sojourning in a "strange land," and to say with David, "I will bless the LORD at all times: his praise shall continually be in my mouth" (Psalm 34:1).

"Any man can sing when the prison doors are open and he is set free. The Christian soul sings in prison. I think that Paul would probably have sung a solo had I been Silas; but I nevertheless see the glory and grandeur of the Spirit that rises superior to all the things of difficulty and limitation."[238]

G. Campbell Morgan

May 18

Five Invitations of the Church

"And the Spirit and the bride say, Come. And let him that heareth say, Come. And let him that is athirst come. And whosoever will, let him take the water of life freely" (Revelation 22:17).

There are five specific invitations the church extends on behalf of the risen Lord.

That to be saved. This is the primary and foundational invitation of the church to him that is unsaved, and it is issued consistently each time the Gospel is preached.

That to be a church member. The church beckons the born-again ones to unite with a local body of believers to facilitate their spiritual growth through worship, fellowship, service, and giving. A person is invited to join the church by profession of faith and baptism; statement of faith (declaration of salvation and New Testament baptism in a fellowship of like-mindedness), or transfer of letter (membership) from a former church to a new church home.

That to baptism. Not all who are saved have been baptized or baptized biblically. Baptism is to follow conversion when its purpose has been understood. Baptism follows salvation; it does not precede it. Baptism demonstrates the believer's identification with and love for Christ, and his intention to serve Him.

That to vocational Christian work. The Holy Spirit uses the church to extend the call to Christian ministry (pastor, evangelist, missionary, musician, chaplain, etc.). The Antioch church called out Paul and Barnabas to serve as missionaries (Acts 13:2–3). Making this appeal is often neglected by the pastor, but it's always on the table for man's prayerful consideration and response.

That to rededication. This invitation of the church is directed to the believer who has pushed Christ into a secondary place in his life, drifted from his first love and allegiance to Christ, is entangled in a sinful indulgence, or is neglecting prayer, Bible study, witnessing, giving, or being faithful to church. What might be the invitation to which you ought to submit?

"In the New Testament it is obvious that evangelistic preaching and compelling invitations were virtually inseparable."[239]

Roy Fish

May

May 19

The Gospel Is Good News

"Christ died for our sins according to the scriptures" (1 Corinthians 15:3).

The Gospel is divine good news. It is the good news of God's intervention in man's deplorable, depraved and damned estate, providing him a means of deliverance (salvation) from the mastery and penalty of sin through His son, Jesus Christ. Salvation is all God's work from start to finish. God ordained it. He orchestrated it. He offered it. He oversees it.

The Gospel is delightful good news. What makes it such elating good news? It provides forgiveness from sins and reconciliation to God. It provides access to God. It provides escape from Hell and an eternal Home in Heaven. It delivers from the captivity of sin. It grants hope beyond the vale of death. It provides a peace that passes all understanding in trial and calamity. It delivers from the misery of a sin-bruised and crushed life.

The Gospel is dangerous good news. All who embrace it are told to "endure hardness, as a good soldier of Jesus Christ" (2 Timothy 2:3). Of the early saints, the author of Hebrews says, "They were stoned to death, they were cut in two, and they died by being murdered with swords. They went around wearing the skins of sheep and goats, needy, oppressed, and mistreated" (Hebrews 11:37 CEB). Jesus forewarned, "The servant is not greater than his lord. If they have persecuted me, they will also persecute you" (Matthew 15:20).

The Gospel is dispersible good news. "Ye shall be witnesses unto me" (Acts 1:8). The Gospel is to not to be hoarded but shared with the whole world.

The Gospel is dependable good news. It will do exactly what it advocates, promises, and proclaims.

The Gospel is durable good news.

1. Neither Satan, nor anything else, can undo that which Christ wrought in a man's heart. The person who is born again is never unborn (John 10:28).

2. The Gospel is so powerful that nothing can interfere with its transformation of sinners until the age of grace comes to an end at the coming of the Lord (Acts 17:31). Pondering these six facts about the Gospel, it's no wonder that it is called the "Good News"!

"The good news is bigger, better, fuller than you ever imagined."[240]
N. T. Wright

May 20

False Conversions

"Not every one that saith unto me, Lord, Lord, shall enter into the kingdom of heaven" (Matthew 7:21).

False conversions have deceived multitudes.

Intellectual conversion is based solely upon that which is believed mentally about Christ. Many will miss Heaven by eighteen inches, the distance from the head to the heart.

Establishment conversion is based upon uniting with the church or synagogue or mosque. It's not one's name on the church roll down here that gets people into Heaven; it's their name in the Book of Life in Heaven.

Religious conversion is based on baptism or keeping a set of rules and regulations, moral conduct or good deeds. Paul said, "Not by works of righteousness which we have done, but according to his mercy he saved us, by the washing of regeneration, and renewing of the Holy Ghost" (Titus 3:5). Man is not saved by his good works, but by Christ' work on the Cross.

Biblical conversion, the true conversion, is based upon a turning from sin (repentance) and placement of faith in Jesus Christ as Lord and Savior. It is a work that is rooted in regeneration by the Holy Spirit in the soul. "Examine yourselves to see if your faith is genuine. Test yourselves. Surely you know that Jesus Christ is among you; if not, you have failed the test of genuine faith" (2 Corinthians 13:5 NLT).

"Is Christ in you? It's not a matter of religion, but of relationship. It's not a question of theology, but of intimacy. It's not knowing about Jesus intellectually, but knowing Him personally."[241]
Jon Courson

May

May 21

Growth Takes Work

"Work out your own salvation with fear and trembling" (Philippians 2:12).

Christian growth is *work*. Note that Paul says "work out," not "work for" salvation. The work for salvation was done by Christ at Calvary and is wrought within man by the Holy Spirit at conversion. MacArthur asserts, "It cannot refer to salvation by works (Romans 3:21–24; Ephesians 2:8, 9), but it does refer to the believer's responsibility for active pursuit of obedience in the process of sanctification."[242]

The words *work out* are used by the first-century author Strabo to refer to digging silver out of silver mines, a task that required diligent and exhausting labor. The Christian is to *dig out* of his salvation its fullest blessings, beliefs and benefits. "Let your roots grow down into him, and let your lives be built on him. Then your faith will grow strong in the truth you were taught, and you will overflow with thankfulness" (Colossians 2:7 NLT).

You were saved in the twinkling of an eye the moment you confessed Christ as Lord and Savior, but it will take months of *heart work* to mature in the faith. Failure to work out salvation deprives the believer of its richest treasures and benefits, and stagnates the soul while stunting growth (like the proverbial old-timer that lived impoverished all his life without realizing there was a gold mine on his property).

"Many Christians remain stunted and dwarfed in spiritual things, so as to present the same appearance year after year. No upspringing of advanced and refined feeling is manifest in them. They exist but do not 'grow up into him in all things.'"[243]

C. H. Spurgeon

May 22

Treasures in Heaven

"But lay up for yourselves treasures in heaven, where neither moth nor rust doth corrupt, and where thieves do not break through nor steal:

For where your treasure is, there will your heart be also." (Matthew 6:20–21).

Place much on deposit in Heaven's bank. Its structure is impenetrable by thieves and incorruptible by moth or rust. Its banker is the wisest, assuring the deposits' best dividend. It's the only bank that guarantees accelerating interest rates daily on investments. It's the only bank that pays dividends to its depositors personally at death.

Note several ways the Christian might lay up treasures in Heaven.

By the souls that are won. Every person the believer wins to Christ is an actual increase to the treasure awaiting them in Heaven. They are the believers' trophies of grace. "And they that be wise shall shine as the brightness of the firmament; and they that turn many to righteousness as the stars for ever and ever" (Daniel 12:3).

By the deeds that are done. The deposit made in Heaven's bank will be determined by how we use our time, talent, influence, knowledge, giftedness and monetary assets for the cause of Christ. Five heavenly crowns will be awarded by our Lord to believers in Heaven based upon their life on earth. Everything done for "Christ's sake" and the expansion of His kingdom on earth is a deposit in the bank of Heaven that will appear again to the investor's credit and joy.

By the wrong that is shunned. A life of nonconformity (separation from the world and its lusts) has both cost and consequence, and these make great deposits in the bank of Heaven.

By the race that is run. The Christian course, run by faith in and obedience to God, is one of trial, hardship, distraction, and persecution. Persevering to the finish line takes a fixed focus on Jesus and spiritual stamina and discipline (Hebrews 12:1). He that can say with Paul when the race is done, "I have fought the good fight, I have finished the race, I have kept the faith," can also say with him, "Now there is in store for me the crown of righteousness, which the Lord, the righteous Judge, will award to me on that day" (2 Timothy 4:7–8 NIV). Faithfulness to Christ and His cause to the end will deposit great treasures in Heaven's bank (Revelation 2:10b).

"Have a deposit on earth, if you must or can; but let your chief banking be in Heaven."[244]

Henry Ward Beecher

May 23

The Broken-Down Wall

"I went by the field of the slothful, and by the vineyard of the man void of understanding; And, lo, it was all grown over with thorns, and nettles had covered the face thereof, and the stone wall thereof was broken down" (Proverbs 24:30–31).

Slothfulness leads to broken down walls for failure of discipline to keep them maintained. Laziness tears down the wall of good habits—Bible study, prayer, Scripture memorization, journaling, witnessing. It tears down the wall of biblical principles—godly companions, industry, stewardship. It tears down the wall of faithfulness to church. It tears down the wall of strength of character—integrity, dependability, trust. It tears down the wall of ministry—teaching, preaching, missions, singing, writing. It tears down the wall of restraint—when the wall is broken down bad things enter in that bring destruction and misery. It tears down the wall of productivity—the life that once bore bountiful fruit for the Lord now is overtaken with the rankest thistles and weeds. The law of degeneration states that all that is necessary for something to decay is to leave it alone.

Lessons gleaned:

1. Spiritual decay and demise happen unnoticed. The wall of the owner, which Solomon referenced, decayed gradually, perhaps impercertibly, until it crashed to the ground.

2. The slothful one (idler) is a waster of time, influence, giftedness, money, and opportunity.

3. Excuses for idleness and neglect of duty are futile. No excuse prevented the wall from tottering and eventually falling to the ground.

4. Slothfulness leads to unexpected ruin. It seizes man "as an armed man" (Proverbs 24:34).

5. Walls crumble and fall due to two things: "Ignorance that will not learn and slothfulness that will not work."[245] (Proverbs 24:30). The "sage" or wise observer says in beholding the broken-down wall that he "considered it well" and "received instruction" (Proverbs 24:32). May we do likewise.

"Many, I fear, would like glory, who have no wish for grace. They would [want to] have the wages, but not the work; the harvest, but not the labor; the reaping, but not the sowing; the reward, but not the battle. But it may not be."
J. C. Ryle

May 24

Narrow Escapes

"But as for me, my feet were almost gone; my steps had well nigh slipped" (Psalm 73:2).

Narrow escapes are instances in life when a person barely avoids defeat, failure, death, or injury physically, or shipwreck of ministry and testimony spiritually. Narrow escapes ought to engender gratitude to God for the gracious deliverance. "You have grazed rocks on which others were broken; slipped on precipices on which others have fallen; singed your wings in flames by which others have perished. Oh, how you ought to contemplate your 'narrow escapes' and shudder in fear for what may have occurred and thank God that it did not!"

They ought to engender sympathy for them that didn't escape the same fall we evaded. With compassion we should join Bradford in saying about them, "There but for the grace of God go I."

They ought to engender caution with regard to slippery slopes (improper companions; undisciplined eyes; foolish counsel; tantalizing sin; strong temptation). Remember the mercies of God that enabled the "narrow escape" but simultaneously let the escape serve as a caution to avoid such "slippery places" in the future. Heed their admonition and prosper, or ignore it and suffer. A narrow escape today doesn't promise the same tomorrow. Presumptuous arrogance about invincibility to sin puts the foot on a slippery place. "Let him that thinketh he standeth, take heed lest he fall" (1 Corinthians 10:12). "Neither give place [a foothold or beachhead] to the devil" (Ephesians 4:27).

They ought to engender dedication. Narrow escapes reveal the saint's need for greater devotedness to and dependence upon God and the embracing of disciplines (prayer, Bible study, worship, godly restraint, accountability, etc.).

May

"Great is our debt of gratitude to Him who renders our venial errors innocuous; who sustains us as we unwittingly step on slippery place or giddy brink; who delivers us from our inexperience, shortsightedness, and frailty, not permitting our infirmity to work its natural issue of woe."[246]

W. L. Watkinson

May 25

Ordered Steps

"The steps of a good man are ordered by the LORD" (Psalm 37:23).

There are divinely ordered steps in life.

The condition. Not all may claim the promise, only he that qualifies as a "good man." The psalmist clearly identifies the "good man" as a man that trusts in the Lord and does good (Psalm 37:3), delights in the Lord (Psalm 37:4), commits (consents) his way unto the Lord (Psalm 37:5), and shuns evil (Psalm 37:8).

The cause. The path in which the Lord guides the saint is not arbitrary but consists of purpose and design for his best good and God's utmost glory.

The comprehensiveness. The divine governance of the godly man's steps is all-inclusive, from the time of his going out and coming in to his lying down and rising up. Spurgeon said, "All his course of life is graciously ordained, and in lovingkindness, all is fixed. No fickle chance rules us; every step is the subject of divine decree."[247] Neither a joy nor a sorrow is known without first passing through the sovereign hand of God.

The consolation. God orchestrates all things (the good and bad) in the "good man" to work for good (Romans 8:28). That knowledge (promise) produces comfort, peace, and hope in the worst of trials and heartbreaks.

The constraint. To get off the track that God has laid for life (which man is free to do) is to miss or forfeit that beneficial and blessed plan which He intended. Matthew Henry says, "He has all hearts in his hand, but theirs [those that are righteous] by their own consent. By His providence, He overrules the events that concern them so as to make their way plain before them, both what they should do and what they may expect."[248] Note, the psalmist states that on this path, even the good man will suffer falls as a result of battle with sin, but the falls are not permanent (Psalm 37:24).

The channel. God orders man's steps in general, but specifically by the whispers (sometimes shouts) of the Holy Spirit to the soul, Holy Scripture, a sanctified or holy conscience, open and closed doors, interruptions to schedule and plans, the counsel of others, adversity and affliction, and even failure (Psalm 37:24).

"'And the stops too.' It is a sad mistake for someone to break through God's hedges. It is a vital principle of the Lord's guidance for a Christian never to move from the spot where he is sure God has placed him until the 'pillar of a cloud' (Exodus 13:21) moves."[249]

George Müller

May 26

A Joash Chest

"All the leaders and all the people were glad to bring in their contributions and put them in the box, until it was full" (2 Chronicles 24:10 CJB).

A locked box or chest with a hole cut in its lid was prepared for the people's offerings to underwrite the repair of the house of God. The chest was placed at the entrance gate to the Temple (2 Chronicles 24:8). When the chest became full, the Levites would send a scribe with King Joash's secretary to count (weigh) it and store it in bags (2 Chronicles 24:11). Note, accountability for every cent given ruled out any chance of misuse of that which was given and contributed to the Temple fund-raising plan's success.[250]

Not only did the people give as requested, but they gave bountifully and joyously (2 Chronicles 24:10). The king and Jehoiada (the priest) expended the money for the very purpose for which it was designated (2 Chronicles 24:12), and when the task was finished, they used the remaining funds to provide holy vessels for the Temple (2 Chronicles 24:14).

Fund-raising tips from Joash's Chest.

1. Help Christian causes and specific projects of the church through a Joash Chest placed in the church.

May

2. State specifically the purpose for the Chest and the offerings placed within it.

3. Be accountable to the people that contribute.

4. Take the steps necessary to prevent the misuse of funds.

5. The novelty of something new in fundraising sometimes works better than traditional methods. Joash's Chest or offering box had never been used until this time in the Temple, and it met with great success.

"I do not believe one can settle how much we ought to give. I am afraid the only safe rule is to give more than we can spare."
C. S. Lewis

May 27

Losing Your Faith in College

"[Joash] did what was right in the eyes of the LORD all the days of Jehoiada the priest" (2 Chronicles 24:2 ESV).

But within ten years after Jehoiada's death, Joash is a different man. Instead of listening to godly advisors, he hearkens to the princes of Judah, who influenced him to deny God and erect altars to idols in the groves (2 Chronicles 24:17–18). He even slew the son of Jehoiada when he questioned Joash's transgression against God (2 Chronicles 24:20–21).

Judgment fell on Joash. God did forsake him, just as Zechariah had proclaimed. The Syrians devastated Joash's kingdom, and his own men murdered him (2 Chronicles 24:23–25). He died in such dishonor and disgrace that he was not buried with the kings in Jerusalem, as Jehoiada had been (2 Chronicles 24:16, 25).

Joash pictures the young who depart to a secular college from a Christian home, evangelical church, and flourishing faith, only upon graduation to return a different person spiritually than they were when they left. Barna Research reveals that over seventy percent of high school students who enter college as professing Christians will leave with no faith or very little faith. When Jehoiada is replaced with the princes of Judah, their faith collapses.

At a secular college, the Christian faith is mocked, derided, made light of, vilified, and attacked by professors and classmates alike. At college, the Devil whispers, "Eat, drink, and be merry." Decadent ones encourage the consumption of drugs and strong drinks. Deviant ones subtly lure the Christian into the snare of immorality. The slothful or idlers disrupt study time with the invitation to parties or some other pleasure. Pornography introduces obscene and vile material to them, filling their minds with its trash and their souls with great shame. Humanistic professors contemptuously ask, "What think ye of Christ?"

These and other such things pressure the Christian student to discard faith, morals, and biblical values. To remain true to the faith in college or the armed services requires roots deep in the faith. Know what is believed and why. Be prepared to give an answer to all who ask the reason for your faith (1 Peter 3:15). Align with an evangelical church off campus and with a Christian group on campus. Maintain a disciplined devotional life. Choose Jehoiadas as the closest companions, not "the princes of Judah." And never forget that what happened to Joash and multitudes since can easily happen to you as well.

"See your soft clay, how hard and coarse and rough it has become! I have seen this change come over young men."[251]

C. H. Spurgeon

May 28

"There"

"The word which came to Jeremiah from the LORD, saying, Arise, and go down to the potter's house, and there I will cause thee to hear my words" (Jeremiah 18:1–2).

It was "there," not just anywhere, that God would speak to Jeremiah. Oh, the importance of being "there" at the place divinely assigned to hear from God. The "there" may be the prayer closet, the house of God, a religious book, a spiritual retreat to the ocean or mountain, or a post of duty. Are you "there" at the place to which God said to go in obedience and submission?

Only *there*, "I will cause thee to hear my words." Listen to the voice of the Lord as to the location of the "there" and get "there." It was when Moses went "there" to Mount Horeb that he saw the bush burn and he heard God's commission to deliver the Israelites from Egyptian captivity.

May

It was in going "there" to the potter's house that Jeremiah learned that Judah was in the hands of God, just as clay was in the hands of the potter. It was in going "there" to the brook Cherith that Elijah was told to minister to the widow at Zarephath.

"If you have trouble hearing God speak, you are in trouble at the very heart of your Christian experience."
                                    Henry Blackaby

May 29

A Bible Christian
"I will delight myself in Thy commandments" (Psalm 119:47).

A Bible Christian is Saved (Psalm 1:3a). Like a tree that is transplanted into new soil, the Bible Christian has been transplanted from being a child of darkness to being a child of the Light. MacArthur says, "Trees do not plant themselves; neither do sinful people transport themselves into God's kingdom. Salvation is His marvelous work of grace."[252]

A Bible Christian is Satisfied (Psalm 1:1a). "How completely happy is the man."[253] The Bible Christian is "blessed" (happy, content). None are as happy as he who has tasted of the joys of the Lord. Trapp said quaintly, "The Psalmist hath said here more to the point respecting happiness than all the philosophers; for while they beat the bush, he hath put the bird into our hand."[254]

A Bible Christian is Separated (Psalm 1:1b). He is separate from the counsel and conduct of the ungodly.

A Bible Christian is Sound (Psalm 1:2a). The Bible Christian holds fast to sound teaching of the Word of God and avoids the venue where suspicion is sown regarding its credibility (2 Timothy 1:13).

A Bible Christian is Studious (Psalm 1:2b). As a student of the Word, he "soaks in, digests, absorbs" (meditates) in it "day and night," making application of its truths.

A Bible Christian is Steadfast (1:3a). His consistency is "day and night"—consistent in his walk before God and with God; consistent today, but also tomorrow. He is not wishy-washy.

A Bible Christian is Successful (Psalm 1:3). "Godliness…is great gain" (1 Timothy 6:6). He bears fruit "in his season," in God's timing (John 15:5). Fruit in the life is proof of grace in the soul.

"Regenerating grace creates a new world in the soul; all things are new. The renewed man acts from new principles, by new rules, with new ends, and in new company."[255]

Matthew Henry

May 30

Tell Your Story

"Come and hear, all ye that fear God, and I will declare what he hath done for my soul" (Psalm 66:16).

Refine your story. Confine the testimony to the when, where, how, why, and now of your salvation, and to a timeframe of three to four minutes. The Apostle Paul's testimony unto Agrippa serves as a worthy pattern (Acts 26:3–29).

1) My life before meeting Christ (Acts 26:3–11).

2) How I came to realize my need of Christ (Acts 26:12–14).

3) What I did to become a Christian (Acts 26:15–18).

4) My life since I became a Christian (Acts 26:19–23).

5) Appeal—would you be willing to do as I and receive Christ into your life as Lord and Savior? (Acts 26:27–29).

Rehearse your story. Review it for accuracy and rehearse it for conciseness, clarity and conveyance.

Recite your story. Barnes says, "It is right and proper for a converted sinner to call on others to hear what God has done for him."[256] Tell it privately to people on the streets and publicly in the church and public arena when the opportunity avails.

Retell your story. Roland Q. Leavell states, "It is experience, not logic, which grips the heart of a seeking sinner. To tell one's spiritual experience is more convincing than a thousand theories."[257] Blackwood said, "Many times the believer may feel that his testimony is feeble, foolish, and ineffective. Still, he is to continue bearing witness, knowing that he is not the one to decide whether or not his words will win a soul for Christ."²⁵⁸

"I love to tell the story; 'tis pleasant to repeat, what seems each time I tell it, more wonderfully sweet. I love to tell the story, for some have never heard the message of salvation from God's own holy Word."

"If lips and life do not agree, the testimony will not amount to much."
H. A. Ironside

May 31

Biblical Worldview

"Set your mind and keep focused habitually on the things above [the heavenly things], not on things that are on the earth [which have only temporal value]" (Colossians 3:2 AMP).

A biblical worldview is the integration of sound biblical teaching in a person's attitude, standards, ambitions, values, opinions, beliefs, and lifestyle, and allowing that knowledge to define his being and view of life.

In coffee preparation, it's important to strain out what isn't good by using a great filter to obtain a superior taste. To live rightly and godly, a person must have a superior filter to strain untruth from entering the mind, preventing it from corrupting morals and sound doctrine. This filter is the Bible.

Francis Schaeffer wrote, "People function on the basis of their worldview more consistently than even they themselves may realize. The problem is not outward things. The problem is having, and then acting upon, the right worldview—the worldview which gives men and women the truth of what is."²⁵⁹ That worldview is Christianity.

"God's people need to unashamedly and uncompromisingly stand on the Bible. We need to unashamedly proclaim a Christian worldview and the Gospel, all the while giving answers for the hope we have."
Ken Ham

June 1

Identifiers of False Teachers

"Some people may contradict our teaching, but these are the wholesome teachings of the Lord Jesus Christ. These teachings promote a godly life. Anyone who teaches something different is arrogant and lacks understanding" (1 Timothy 6:3–4 NLT).

Note five identifiers of a false belief (cult).

1. It refutes Christ's deity—the virgin birth, sinless life, bodily resurrection, and that He is fully God.

2. Its means of salvation or going to Heaven are based on works, morality, or merit (something other than Christ's atoning death alone).

3. Its source of authority is outside the Bible. Its founder(s) claim their personal revelations from God as more authoritative than the Bible, or on the same plain as it (Revelation 22:18–19).

4. It sprinkles just enough Christianity into its heretical mix to allure and deceive (Galatians 1:8; 1 John 4:2; 1 Timothy 1:6–7). MacArthur said, "Mixing sacred truth with myths corrupts the Word of God. And the cults have done it for years."[260] The jargon of a cult in some regards may be the same as that of Christianity, but upon close examination of its belief, it is revealed to be worlds apart.

5. Its doctrines—salvation, eternity, Heaven, Hell, Judgment, the second coming, the Trinity, Calvary, and Christ's atonement—differ in part or totally.

"Just as bank tellers need a thorough knowledge of legitimate currency in order to spot counterfeit bills, so Christians need a thorough knowledge of the Bible in order to spot bogus religious teachings."[261]
Charles Swindoll

June 2

The Glory of Old Age

"It shall come to pass, that at evening time it shall be light" (Zechariah 14:7).

Tholuck said, "The glory of the old age of the godly consists in this, that while the faculties for sensuous, no less than mental enjoyment, gradually decline, and the hearth of life gets thus deprived of its fuel, the blessings of godliness not only continue to refresh the soul in old age but are not until then most thoroughly enjoyed. The sun of piety rises the warmer in proportion as the sun of life declines (2 Corinthians 4:16)."[262]

In the sermon "At Evening Time It Shall Be Light," Spurgeon says, "Dread not thy days of weariness; dread not thine hours of decay, O soldier of the cross. New lights shall burn when the old lights are quenched; new candles shall be lit when the lamps of life are dim. Fear not! The night of thy decay may be coming on, but 'at evening time it shall be light.' At evening time *the Christian has many lights* that he never had before, lit by the Holy Spirit and shining by His light."[263]

There is the light of godly remembrance of work done and fruit borne, the light of matured hope based upon knowledge of that which awaits at death, the light of increased wisdom into the dark mysteries of life, the light of utmost confidence in the Word of God and its promises. W. A. Newman says, "Remember that some of the brightest drops in the chalice of life may still remain for us in old age. The last draught which a kind Providence gives us to drink, though near the bottom of the cup, may, as is said of the draught of the Roman of old, have at the very bottom, instead of dregs, most costly pearls."[264]

"Autumn is really the best of the seasons; and I'm not sure that old age isn't the best part of life."[265]
C. S. Lewis

June 3

The Price of Fear

"Fear hath torment" (1 John 4:18b).

There was a farmer once who was sitting in front of his shack smoking his pipe. A stranger came by and said, "How is your cotton coming along?"

The farmer said, "I don't have any cotton. I did not plant any because I was afraid of the boll weevil."

The man said, "Well, how is your corn doing?"

June

He said, "I didn't plant any corn; I was afraid of the drought."

The stranger said, "Well, how about your potatoes?"

The farmer said, "I don't have any potatoes; I was too scared of the potato bugs."

The stranger said, "Well, just what did you plant?"

The farmer said, "Nothing, I just played it safe."

Fear constrains a person to play it safe, withholding them from new relationships, joys, and achievements. The ghost of fear imprisons and impairs man from attaining God's happy and wondrous intent. It pains the heart, petrifies the mind, and paralyzes life.

John says that the answer to fear is love, that "perfect love" thrusts fear outside the door, for the two cannot coexist in the same house (1 John 4:18a). The influence of God's love (bold confidence in His immeasurable, indescribable, and immutable love) delivers the mind from fear and all its distressing apprehensions.

It is this awesome love, the psalmist says, that is the reason the saint will "not be afraid for the terror by night; nor for the arrow that flieth by day" (Psalm 91:5). We can trust the love of God to safekeep us despite the danger that stalks us. Graham says, "Focus on Christ instead of your fears, and your fears will begin to fade."

"How very little can be done under the spirit of fear."
Florence Nightingale

June 4

The Love of Christ

"This is my beloved, and this is my friend" (Song of Solomon 5:16).

These words of the Shulamite woman echo the words the Christian has for Christ. Presented in the Song of Solomon are five statements about love that may be applied to Christ.

The power of love. Solomon says love is "strong as death" (Song of Solomon 8:6). Real love is as strong as death in that it cannot be removed from or diminished toward him to whom it is directed, even in the direst of difficulty or adversity. It is invincible.

This type of love is manifested supremely by Christ, who loves His own with everlasting love (Jeremiah 31:3). There is no fear that Christ's love will be diminished or extinguished, for it is not fueled by man's works and goodness, but by the eternal torch of Christ's nature. The love of Christ for His own will not fail; so says the text: "Many waters cannot quench love, neither can the floods drown it" (Song of Solomon 8:6).

"The oil which is poured upon the fire by the hand that is unseen is mightier than the water which is dashed upon it by the carnal, cold, and unbelieving world."[266] The believer has been "set as a seal (unbreakable) upon *Christ's* heart" (Song of Solomon 1:6). Christ, as the believer's High Priest, has engraved on the breastplate near His heart the names of His own (Exodus 28:12), and also upon the palms of His hands (Isaiah 49:16). Spurgeon states, "Death is but weakness itself when compared with the love of Christ."[267]

Oh, the deep, deep love of Jesus! vast, unmeasured, boundless, free,
Rolling as a mighty ocean in its fullness over me.
                S. Trevor Francis, 1931

The push of love. "Eat, O friends; drink, yea, drink abundantly, O beloved" (Song of Solomon 5:1). Love compels a person, despite the risk or cost, to do or attempt to do (if feasible) what another needs or wants, especially when others won't or cannot. "For the love of Christ puts us into action" (2 Corinthians 5:14 NLV). Christ's love compelled Him through a life of ridicule, suffering, rejection, and the torturous death at Calvary to reconcile man to God. And that same love constrains Christ to intervene with aid in man's pain, suffering, sorrow, guilt, and hardship. Let him that is hungry and thirsty come and dine at His table.

The perfection of love. "He is altogether lovely" (Song of Solomon 5:16). Man's love is flawed due to a sinful nature. The best of friends will disappoint us—but not Christ's love, for it is untainted with hypocrisy and inferior, unjust, or selfish motives. Pilate found no fault in Christ. No man can.

The purchase of love. "If a man would give all the substance of his house for love, it would utterly be contemned [scorned; rejected]" (Song of Solomon 8:7). Love is priceless. It is unpurchaseable. The effort to buy His love or that of another is futile. The Beatles are right: "Money can't buy me love." "Any attempt to 'buy' love depersonalizes it."[268] It would be worth the whole world to gain the love of Christ, but it is given and acquired freely (Isaiah 55:1; Ephesians 2:8–9). Note, Christ didn't purchase our love with gifts; we don't love Him for what He has given us. We love Him for who He is (1 John 4:19).

The pursuit of love. "By night on my bed, I sought him whom my soul loveth: I sought him, but I found him not" (Song of Solomon 3:1). Regrettably, the love that some seek in others is not found or proves to be disingenuous. But it is not so with Christ. His love is true and readily available and accessible to one who seriously seeks it. He says, "You will seek me and find me when you seek me with all your heart" (Jeremiah 29:13 NIV).

"Lord Jesus, let me feel that love; let me see Thine arm nerved with it, and Thine heart affected by this strong love which all my enemies cannot defeat, which all my sins cannot overturn, which all my weakness cannot gainsay."[269]

C. H. Spurgeon.

June 5

The Bible (Part One)

"All scripture is given by inspiration of God" (2 Timothy 3:16).

It's a different book. The Bible is unique. There's no other book like it. It was written by 40 men over a period of 1,500 years and consists of 66 books, 39 in the Old Testament and 27 in the New Testament. It is God's only written revelation to man. Hebrews states, "The Word of God is quick, and powerful, and sharper than any twoedged sword, piercing even to the dividing asunder of soul and spirit, and of the joints and marrow, and is a discerner of the thoughts and intents of the heart" (Hebrews 4:12). The Bible is fully alive. It is life-giving communication from God to man. It has the power to convict a man of sin and bring him to God. No other book in the world can do that.

It's a dependable book. It is totally true in fact and doctrine (Psalm 12:6). It has no contradictions. It is trustworthy. Criswell says, "Through the Holy Spirit's agency, God is involved in both the production and interpretation of Scripture. Men of God in antiquity spoke as they were moved by the Holy Spirit. 'Moved' means literally 'to bear along.' Scripture is infallible precisely because the Holy Spirit 'bore along' the prophets who spoke and wrote" (2 Peter 1:20–21).[270] The biblical text is better preserved than the writings of Plato and Aristotle. "There is not one single proved inaccuracy," says Francis Dixon, "in the whole Bible. The Bible is accurate historically, geographically, genealogically, scientifically, psychologically, typologically, and verbally."[271]

It is a durable book. Of the Word of God, the Lord says, "Heaven and earth shall pass away, but my words shall not pass away" (Matthew 24:35). Moody remarked, "When Christ said, 'The Scriptures cannot be broken,' He meant every word He said. Devil and man and Hell have been in league for centuries to try to break the Word of God, but they cannot do it. If you get it for your footing, you have a good footing for time and eternity. My friends, that Word is going to live, and there is no power in perdition or in the earth to blot it out."[272]

"The Bible is one of the greatest blessings bestowed by God on the children of men. It has God for its author, salvation for its end, and truth without any mixture for its matter. It is all pure."
John Locke

June 6

The Bible (Part Two)

"All scripture is given by inspiration of God" (2 Timothy 3:16).

It's a directional book. "Thy word is a lamp unto my feet, and a light unto my path" (Psalm 119:105). It is not within man to know how to traverse the dangerous landscape of life; therefore, a lamp is provided to show the way (Jeremiah 10:23; Proverbs 14:12).

It's a delightful book. The Psalmist testifies that God's Word is "sweeter than honey to my mouth" (Psalm 119:103). Saith Spurgeon, "They were unutterably sweet: 'How sweet!' but he does not tell us how sweet they were. There is no describing the flavors of a royal banquet; there is no picturing to a man who has not the sense of smell the fragrance of a delicious perfume; and you must personally know the sweetness of the Word of God, for to us it is positively unutterable."[273] Jeremiah said, "Your words were found, and I ate them, And Your word was to me the joy and rejoicing of my heart" (Jeremiah 15:16 NKJV).

It's a devotional book. The Bible is the primary means of receiving nourishment for the soul. Jesus said, "It is written, 'Man shall not live by bread alone, but by every word that proceeds from the mouth of God'"

(Matthew 4:4 NKJV). A person need not go outside the Bible for heavenly manna, theological dogma, or guidance about holy living.

It's a deliverance book. W. S. Plumer wrote about the Bible, "It alone can solve a thousand doubts. It alone gives effectual comfort in the day of distress. It alone preserves our feet from forbidden paths."[274]

It is a dynamite book. The Bible is a hammer that breaks (Jeremiah 23:29), a sword that cuts (Hebrews 4:12), a fire that burns (Jeremiah 20:9), and a light that illuminates (Psalm 119:105). Given the chance, the Word will break up the hardest soil, cut the most stubborn heart asunder, burn and consume the dross of the most hideous sin, sift from one's life every pollutant, and illuminate the darkest mind of its need of Jesus. "The B-I-B-L-E, yes that's the BOOK for me. I stand alone on the Word of God—the B-I-B-L-E."

"Nobody ever outgrows Scripture; the Book widens and deepens with our years."
Charles Spurgeon

June 7

The Hands of Jesus

"Behold my hands" (John 20:27).

An examination of the hands of Jesus reveals much about His character, attributes, and nature.

Jesus has the hands of a redeemer. The nail-scarred hands of Jesus testify of His love that took Him to Calvary to atone for man's sin.

Jesus has the hands of a keeper. Enveloped within the hand of Jesus, the believer is forever safe and secure (John 10:28 NIV).

Jesus has the hands of a healer. There is miraculous healing power in the hands of Jesus. Jesus healed Bartimaeus (Mark 10:46–52) and Jairus' daughter (Luke 8:41–56).

Jesus has the hands of a comforter. Jesus soothes doubts, calms fear and dries tears. He beckons, "Come unto me, all ye that labor and are heavy laden, and I will give you rest" (Matthew 11:28).

Jesus has the hands of a provider. Says Paul, "But my God shall supply all your need according to his riches in glory by Christ Jesus" (Philippians 4:19).

Jesus has the hands of a high priest. Robert M. McCheyne said, "If I can hear Christ praying for me in the next room, I would not fear a million enemies. Yet the distance makes no difference; He is praying for me."

Jesus has the hands of a deliverer. Jesus' mighty grasp upon Peter saved him from the raging sea. In the hands of Jesus is delivering power from the gravest sickness, most tumultuous trial and strongest addiction.

Jesus has the hands of a Judge. What He will do with us at the Judgment is contingent upon what we do with Him now.

Jesus has the hands of a wooer. The nail-scarred hand of Christ knocks compassionately at every man's heart's door seeking an entrance to forgive sin and reconcile to God (salvation).

The instruction to Thomas from Jesus is for all: "Behold my hands" and be challenged, convinced, and changed, as he was. "Place your hand in the nail-scarred hand."

"Surrender the thing you fear into the hands of God. Turn it right over to God and ask Him to solve it with you. Fear is keeping things in your own hands; faith is turning them over into the hands of God."
E. Stanley Jones

June 8

Keep Your Fork

"And God shall wipe away all tears from their eyes; and there shall be no more death, neither sorrow, nor crying, neither shall there be any more pain: for the former things are passed away" (Revelation 21:4).

A lady told her pastor, "When you lay me in my casket, please put a fork in my right hand."

The pastor inquired, "Why?"

Replied the lady, "At our fellowships, you tell us to keep our forks because the best is yet to come."

And she was right. At the return of Christ for the believer (Second Coming) or the believer's return to Him (death), he will experience unspeakable joy in Beulah Land—spectacular mansions; eradication of evil and persecution; rest; reunion with saints; continuous praise and worship; enjoyable work; absence of tears, sorrow, pain and death. But most especially, the believer will see and be with Jesus forevermore.

So, keep your fork. The best is yet to come. Saith Spurgeon, "Brethren and sisters, regard the object of our expectations! See the happiness which is promised us! Behold the Heaven which awaits us! Forget for a while your present cares; let all your difficulties and your sorrows vanish for a season and live for a while in the future which is so certified by faithful promises that you may rejoice in it even now!"[275]

Soon and very soon, we are going to see the King through the conveyance of death or His return. Hallelujah! All then will be everlasting bliss and joy! So, keep your fork.

"Heaven is all that the loving heart of God would desire. Heaven is all that the incredible mind of God can conceive. And Heaven is all the Almighty Hand of God can create."[276]
Adrian Rogers

June 9

Promise of Divine Guidance
"And the LORD shall guide thee continually" (Isaiah 58:11).

God's guidance is sure. "The LORD *shall* guide thee." To all, the path ahead is unknown. None have passed its way heretofore (Joshua 3:4). But don't worry or become fearful. God will lead or guide through it. And "he goes not amiss who goes in the company of God."[277]

God's guidance is personal. "The LORD shall guide thee." Calm, comfort and peace in that which lies ahead (snares, adversities, dangers, sorrows, sicknesses, suffering, death) rests in knowing it is God (not an angel) that "shall guide" us. Whatever the dilemma, He will give consolation and courage to bear it and counsel and direction to get through it.

God's guidance has conditions. "*Then*...thy darkness [shall] be as the noonday" (Isaiah 58:10). Note that the word "then" in verse 10 precedes the word "shall" in verse 11. To have life sovereignly directed, the believer must abide (continually dwell) in the Vine (John 15:4).

God's guidance is perpetual. "The Lord shall guide thee *continually*." Spurgeon remarked, "We are not merely to be guided sometimes, but we are to have a perpetual monitor; not occasionally to be left to our own understanding and so to wander, but we are continually to hear the guiding voice of the Great Shepherd; and if we follow close at His heels, we shall not err."[278] Matthew Henry wrote, "While we are here, in the wilderness of this world, we have need of continual direction from Heaven; for, if at any time we be left to ourselves, we shall certainly miss our way."[279]

Anxiety, frustration and fear are all swallowed up in the confidence that God is present in the highs and lows of life. With Him in the equation, even when the clouds are filled with gloom and despair, there is radiant sunshine in the soul. The bottom line is that God's sovereign guidance is the antidote to wearisomeness and worry about what awaits on the horizon.

"For it is better, with closed eyes, to follow God as our guide, than, by relying on our own prudence, to wander through those circuitous paths which it devises for us."[280]
John Calvin

June 10

The Vacant Chair (Part One)

"Thou shalt be missed, because thy seat will be empty" (1 Samuel 20:18).

Jonathan's words to David are ours to family, friends and religious leaders whose death is nigh or who have died: "Thou shalt be missed because thy seat will be empty." How we miss husband, wife, child, parent, sibling, friend, or religious leader because their seat is now empty at the table. But thankfully their vacant chair is not silent. It still speaks and ministers.

Vacant Chairs preach. They warn of coming death, divine judgment and eternity, urging immediate preparation. An epitaph (vacant chair) states, "As I am, so must you be; so be prepared to follow me." The vacant chair says, "It is appointed unto men once to die, but after this the judgment" (Hebrews 9:27). Vacant chairs proclaim, "You don't even know if you will be alive tomorrow! For all you are is a mist that appears for a little while and then disappears" (James 4:14 CJB). The vacant chair says, "In a moment shall they die" (Job 34:20), and, "Prepare to meet your God" (Amos 4:12 NIV). Vacant chairs shout, "Set thine house in order: for thou shalt die" (Isaiah 38:1). Vacant chairs ought to prompt us to pray, "Teach us to number our days and recognize how few they are; help us to spend them as we should" (Psalm 90:12 TLB).

Vacant Chairs plead. They beg for the soul's return to God. The plea of a religious leader, a godly politician or a conservative radio host to the unrighteous to return to God and Judeo-Christian values still resounds from their vacant chair. A departed friend's urging to abstain from alcohol, drugs, or pornography remains relentless from his vacant chair. The admonition to redeem the time, to use it wisely and profitably for the glory of God, echoes from the vacant chair of the pastor and evangelist. "He being dead yet speaketh" (Hebrews 11:4).

Give heed to that which the vacant chair of the righteous speaketh.

"Those who have left us are still with us by their posthumous influence."[281]
E. B. Cole

June 11

The Vacant Chair (Part Two)

"Thou shalt be missed, because thy seat will be empty" (1 Samuel 20:18).

Vacant Chairs pray. We are benefited by the vacant chair of him that prayed for us when he was alive. Widows are being strengthened and sustained by the empty seat of their husband's former prayers. Children are being protected and/or converted through the former prayers of a loving mother and father uttered from their once-occupied chair. Friends are prospering in health and happiness in answer to the former prayers of departed friends that are still flowing heavenward. Ministries yet flourish upon the former prayers of saints that long since entered into their rest in Heaven. Though their chair be empty now, prayers uttered while they sat in it yet ascend to God. In this sense it may be said that though the chair of a loved one, friend, minister, or politician is vacant, it yet prays.

Vacant Chairs pacify. They console, and comfort through recalled memories. J. M. Barrie said, "God gave us memories that we might have roses in December."[282] Memories are medicinal. The empty chair of a loved one and friend is loaded with treasured memories that soothe and assuage our broken hearts. Lewis Carroll (the author of *Alice's Adventures in Wonderland*) wrote, "In the garden of memory, in the palace of dreams…that is where you and I shall meet."[283]

Vacant Chairs promise. They assure us of a coming reunion. Their empty chair testifies with Isaiah Martin, "I will meet you; I will meet you just inside the Eastern Gate over there."

Vacant Chairs prescribe. They counsel and advise. Instruction instilled in children will echo from their empty chairs when they depart to Heaven (Ephesians 6:4). Let ministers instruct the Word of the Lord faithfully in the pulpit, and it will "replay" unceasingly through their vacant chair to the pew.

Billy Graham yet speaketh. Adrian Rogers yet speaketh. C. H. Spurgeon yet speaketh. The encouragement, counsel, and admonition of departed family and friends continue through their vacant chairs (memories, books, sermons, conversations, instructions).

What will your vacant chair speak at death? You are presently writing its script. Write it well.

"Every Christian is useful in his life, but the goodly cedars are the most useful afterwards."[284]
Biblical Illustrator

June 12

Why Christians Love the Church

"LORD, I have loved the habitation of thy house, and the place where thine honor dwelleth" (Psalm 26:8).

Why do Christians love the church?

We love its place. We love the church, "the most amiable object on earth, because it is the nearest resemblance of Heaven, where is the true 'habitation of God's house.'"[285]

We love its preaching. Truth that nourishes the soul and enriches life is proclaimed within its doors.

We love its people. "In the congregation we enter into the communion of saints and are mentally incited to keep our vows. We join a brotherhood possessing the same frailties and having the same needs. The inequalities of life, so apparent in the world, vanish here, where all are drawn with the same bonds of love and inclined to encourage and assist each other on the way of life."[286]

We love its purpose. Its main business is to magnify Christ. Its secondary purpose (linked to the first) is to introduce men to Him, induct them into its body through baptism, and instruct (disciple) them in the teachings of Christ, and send them out into the world as His witnesses (Matthew 28:18–20).

We love its provision. It is loved for the pardon, joy, guidance, accountability, restraint, and sweet fellowship it affords. It is loved for the comfort, hope and peace it instills in times of trouble and sorrow and when we feel abandoned by God in a season of grave despair (Psalm 42:3). It is treasured for the protection it affords the young from the wrong path and ungodly habits.

We love its plea. Christians love the church because it is there where the unsaved are compelled to come to the Cross, backsliders are challenged to return to their first love (Revelation 2:4–5), and the godly are exhorted to walk in holiness and godliness.

We love its praise. We delight in its adulation to Christ through singing, praising and rejoicing in holy worship (Psalm 95:3).

We love its petition. We love the church because its members believe in the power of prayer and intercede on behalf of one another, the unsaved and global concerns (Acts 2:42).

We love its peace. The church is an oasis of tranquility, love, rest, serenity, and calm in an ocean of conflict, confusion, criticism, corruption, cruelty and condemnation.

We love its permanence. The "gates of Hell" are not strong enough to prevent the church's existence or the fulfillment of its mission (Matthew 16:18). It has and will forever survive the vicious assaults of the wicked.

"Churches, organized assemblies or communities of professing Christians, are being shaken on every hand; but the Church, which is the Body of Christ, cannot and will not be shaken."[287]

Francis Dixon

June 13

Reasons to Go to Church

"And let us not neglect our meeting together, as some people do, but encourage one another, especially now that the day of his return is drawing near" (Hebrews 10:25 NLT).

There are six good reasons to attend church.

Go to Grow. Church participation wards off spiritual stagnation and straying and enhances the believer's spiritual state, godly knowledge and walk with God (2 Timothy 2:15).

Go to Show. Faithfulness to a local church is a witness to the world of a believer's allegiance, obedience, and devotion to Christ (Hebrews 10:25).

Go to Know. In the church, believers are aligned with people who love Jesus and spur each other onward in the Christian journey both in word and example (Acts 2:42). The house of God also provides the opportunity of building a network of and relationship with people who are dependable and willing to come to your assistance in the time of need (Galatians 6:2), and to become a mentor if desired (Titus 2:2–6). Your faithfulness to church enables its spiritual leaders to "watch out for your soul," providing accountability and protection from heresy and straying (Hebrews 13:17 NKJV).

Go to Bestow. A primary purpose in attending church is to engage in corporate worship rendering to God the adoration, praise and thanksgiving He deserves (Psalm 100:4–5). The Christian ought to say, "But as for me, I will come into thy house in the multitude of thy mercy: and in thy fear will I worship toward thy holy temple" (Psalm 5:7).

Go to Sow. The church affords the opportunity to discover one's spiritual gift(s) and then exercise it (them) through its varied discipleship, evangelistic and missionary ministries, locally, and even globally (Romans 12:4–8). The church is also a place to sow financially into God's kingdom work liberally and consistently (2 Corinthians 9:6).

Go to Glow. The ministry of the church enables the Christian to be "examples to all that believe" (1 Thessalonians 1:7 WBT) and penetrating lights to those in spiritual darkness (Luke 11:36). "This little light of mine" will shine brighter and further through consistent gathering with fellow believers who make up the body of Christ, the New Testament church.

June

"The church is a hospital for sinners, and not a museum for saints."
Vance Havner

June 14

Fear of Death

"My heart is sore pained within me: and the terrors of death are fallen upon me" (Psalm 55:4).

Most live in slavish bondage to the fear of death (Hebrews 2:15). Death is often a terrifying experience for any of five reasons.

1. Death is feared because of the uncertainty of what's beyond the grave, the unknown.

2. It is feared because it means separation from spouse, children and friends.

3. It is feared because of the future judgment that awaits.

4. It is feared because of the dying process.

5. It is feared because ultimately it is something man faces alone.

By His death at Calvary Christ nullified the true reason to fear death: the curse and condemnation of the law of God (1 Corinthians 15:56).[288] Richard Sibbes states, "Why should we then fear death, which is but a passage to Christ? It is but a grim sergeant that lets us into a glorious palace, that strikes off our bolts, that takes off our rags that we may be clothed with better robes, that ends all our misery and is the beginning of all our happiness. Why should we therefore be afraid of death? It is but a departure to a better condition. It is but as Jordan to the children of Israel, by which they passed to Canaan. It is but as the Red Sea by which they were going that way. Therefore, we have no reason to fear death."[289]

Relating the safe passage of the priests bearing the ark of the covenant across the Jordan River (Joshua 3:17) to the Christian at death, T. DeWitt Talmage remarks, "Obstacles that may appear tremendous in the distance depart when we advance upon and touch them with courage. Many now are afraid of the *Jordan of death*. But when you come up to it, when your time has come to cross it, it will disappear. Christ your Priest, with bruised feet will go ahead of you. His feet touching the waters will cause them to roll away (as did the touch of the priests' feet with the ark), and you will go through on dry ground."[290]

A father's business required him to take a long walk through the Alps early in the morning and back home after dark. As his son grew up, he begged to be taken on these trips, but the father thought his little legs too weak to make the journey.

Finally, after years of refusal, the father gave in and agreed to take him on the next trip. In the early morning walk they crossed a high rope bridge with a few missing slats, suspended over the valley. With daylight and dad leading the way it posed no problem for the young boy to cross.

Once completing their business in the city, they set out for home. The boy began to worry about crossing the rope bridge in the dark and shared that fear with his father. The missing slats, the deep gorge, and the thick darkness were all of grave concern.

The father was unable to give the boy assurance that everything would be just fine. But when they arrived at the bridge, the father lovingly placed his son on his back with his strong arms and started across with him.

The next thing the boy remembered was awaking to early rays of sunlight and seeing a silhouette of his father standing in the doorway. "Dad, what happened?" the boy inquired. "What about the bridge?" he worried out loud.

"Well, Son, you fell asleep with your arms around my neck. I carried you across the bridge and laid you safely in your own bed. You've just awakened on the other side."[291]

What a beautiful picture of the death of a child of God!

"To overcome the fear of death, we must look to Jesus Christ on the cross atoning for us, in the resurrection rising for us, in the Glory taking possession of our home for us, and at the right hand of God preparing our place for us, possessing all power and using it so that He may bring us unto His eternal Kingdom."[292]

C. H. Spurgeon

June 15

Our God Is a Can-Do God

"They said, *Can God* furnish a table in the wilderness?" (Psalm 78:19).

June

Amidst hardships, the Israelites in the wilderness murmured, asking a foolish question: "Can God?" Foolish, I say, because God had already proven that He could during the Exodus. He had delivered them from the plagues, Pharaoh and his army, the mighty waters of the Red Sea, thirst (water from the rock and pure water at Marah), hunger (manna and quail), and led them by the cloud by day and pillar of fire by night (Psalm 78:12–16).

Yet despite these miraculous deeds, unbelief in God's ability to provide "a table in the wilderness" (Psalm 78:19) was expressed. They "unbelievingly and defiantly demanded, instead of trustfully waiting and praying" (Delitzsch).

The saint that trusts God need not question the ability and readiness of God to intervene in times of trouble or sorrow. Spurgeon states, "To question the ability of one who is manifestly Almighty is to speak against him."[293] Says Matthew Henry, "Those that set bounds to God's power speak against him."[294] To the question, "Can God?" the saint readily responds, "Yes, God can!"

The curious servants of Hezekiah perhaps asked about the possibility of his recovery, "Can God?" Before Isaiah was hardly out the door, it was thundered, "God can" (2 Kings 20:1–5).

When the three Hebrew children were cast into the fiery furnace, Nebuchadnezzar and soldiers alike asked, "Can God?" When they witnessed the fourth man in the fire and all walking around unharmed, they answered, "God can" (Daniel 3:25).

When Daniel was put into a den of lions, Darius asked, "Can God?" Early the next morning he learned, "God can."

When the widow of Zarephath and her son were famished with hunger, she asked, "Can God?" Long afterwards the miraculous jar of oil and flour still provided the need. She found out, "God can" (1 Kings 17:7–16).

Our God is a God that can!

"Though I know that God can remove the hardship, sorrow and pain. It is based upon His awesome plan, upon which my hope and trust remain."[295]
Frank Shivers

June 16

The Fifth Commandment

"Honor thy father and thy mother: that thy days may be long upon the land which the LORD thy God giveth thee" (Exodus 20:12).

To "give honor" to one's parents is to obey them, respect them, esteem them, love them, and, when they are old and frail, sustain and support them. It is to place them in "a position of preeminence, dignity, importance."[296]

Father and mother are to be honored equally. Children ought to honor their parents in obedience to the Lord (Exodus 20:12); for their counsel and instruction; for imparting life to them; for the faithfulness of their love, care, and support; for sacrifice made to provide needs and wants; for guardianship (preservation from evil). Parents that shield their children from the poison of pornography, alcohol, drugs, gambling, profanity, sexual sins, and cancel culture are deserving of double honor.

Additionally, children are to honor their parents because they are God's representatives to raise them "in the nurture and admonition of the Lord" (Ephesians 6:4). Note that the fifth commandment is reflexive. It says to the child "to honor" father and mother, but it immediately springs back to the parent, saying, live honorably so that your child will count you worthy of honor.[297] Kroll said, "Honor your parents and the Lord will honor you."

"A child who is allowed to be disrespectful to his parents will not have true respect for anyone."
Billy Graham

June 17

Tomorrow Has Two Handles

"A tranquil heart is the life of the flesh" (Proverbs 14:30 ASV).

"Serenity will preserve the disciple's life, but irritation will kill him."[298] Serenity evolves from a heart that is fixed on Jesus and free from noxious passions and cares (Isaiah 26:3). "A person's emotions", states Buzzell, "affect his physical condition. A heart at peace (or "a mind of health," i.e., a healthy disposition) helps produce a healthy body."[299] In contrast, stress and worry jeopardize health and well-being.

Beecher said, "Every tomorrow has two handles. We can take hold of it with the handle of anxiety or the handle of faith."[300] Swindoll remarked, "Let's get six words clearly fixed in our minds. These six words form the foundation of God's therapeutic process for all worrywarts. *Worry about nothing; pray about everything.* Turn your worry list into your prayer list. Give each worry—one by one—to God."[301] Peter advises the same when he says, "Casting all your care upon him; for he careth for you" (1 Peter 5:7).

He that empties burdens into the lap of God, trusting Him to handle them (Psalm 37:5), exhibits a healthy and peaceful heart (mind) that benefits physically; the man who doesn't do so bears a broken and crushed spirit that injures his physical well-being (Proverbs 12:25).

Beecher is right. Tomorrow has two handles: fear and faith. Take it by the handle of faith to experience a peace that passeth all understanding regardless of calamity, crisis or circumstance it may bring. Max Lucado said, "Faith is not the belief that God will do what you want. It is the belief that God will do what is right."[302] And upon that undeniable and unchanging truth you may confidently rely.

"Oh, how great peace and quietness would he possess who should cut off all vain anxiety and place all his confidence in God."[303]
Thomas à Kempis

June 18

Overcoming Loneliness

"For He hath said, I will never leave thee, nor forsake thee" (Hebrews 13:5).

Loneliness, states Adrian Rogers, is "a painful sense of being unwanted, unneeded, uncared for, maybe even unnecessary."[304] It is a feeling of being unloved and invisible to others. James Dobson says, "Most loneliness results from insulation rather than isolation. In other words, we are lonely because we insulate ourselves, not because others isolate us."[305] The psalmist likens the lonely one to the "pelican of the wilderness" and "the owl of the desert" (places like the wastelands or abandoned ruins where no one lives). See Psalm 102:6.

Oh, the agony of dwelling in a place where there is no one with whom to socialize, no one to care for you or help bear your burdens. There are no letters, no phone calls, no emails, and no visits. Lord Byron, from experience, said, "What is the worst of woes that wait on age? What stamps the wrinkle deeper on the brow? To view each loved one blotted from life's page and be alone on earth, as I am now."[306]

Here are four tactics to defeat loneliness.

Cling to Christ. Embrace Christ personally as Lord and Savior and as the all-sufficient One in your life. James says, "Draw near to God, and he will draw near to you" (James 4:8 ESV). Say to Him, "I am lonely and afflicted. relieve the troubles of my heart and free me from my anguish" (Psalm 25:16–17 NIV). Until the loneliness is completely lifted, He will give the grace to tolerate it.

Claim the promises. Appropriate the promises of God to your life (Hebrews 13:5; Isaiah 41:13).

Connect with Christian friends. Paul says, "So it is with Christ's body. We are many parts of one body, and we all belong to each other" (Romans 12:5 NLT). Trust God to connect you with those that matter most. Expand your Christian social network by cultivating new relationships.

Consult with a Christian advisor. In the case of acute or chronic loneliness, seek guidance from a pastor or licensed Christian therapist.

"There are no words to express the abyss between isolation and having one ally."
                        G. K. Chesterton

June 19

Never Quit

"God, with his mercy, gave us this work to do, so we don't give up" (2 Corinthians 4:1 NCV).

Never quit on God. Paul shares specific reasons for not quitting in Second Corinthians 4:2–6.

Because of the Name we bear (v. 1). The believer bears the name "Christian," a name that directly links him with and identifies him with

Jesus Christ. To fall by the way, to desert our post and go AWOL, would bring dishonor to that name and Him whom it represents.

Because of the testimony we have (v. 1). Paul didn't quit, because he never forgot what happened on the Damascus Road, how God saved him and the change it brought about in his life. It so impacted him that he never stopped testifying and telling His Story. The work of grace that saved us prompts eternal loyalty and allegiance to Christ and a continuous testimony to it.

Because of the truth we share (v. 2). What we possess in our hand (Bible) and heart (biblical values, teaching) is what a lost world (evangelization) and fellow believers (edification and encouragement) need. Don't extinguish your torch; keep shining out the infallible and inerrant truth, imploding the darkness.

Because of what the lost face (v. 3). Paul says, "If the Good News that we preach is hidden, it is hidden only to those who are lost." If we quit, souls that could have been won at our hand may be forever lost to eternal damnation. The fields are white unto harvest, and they cannot reap themselves. Every believer must remain diligent with sickle in hand to harvest it.

Because of the triumph that is ours (vv. 14, 18). Paul says, "So we do not give up. Our physical body is becoming older and weaker, but our spirit inside us is made new every day. We have small troubles for a while now, but they are helping us gain an eternal glory that is much greater than the troubles. We set our eyes not on what we see but on what we cannot see. What we see will last only a short time, but what we cannot see will last forever" (vv. 16–18).

"Wars are not won by evacuations. Battles are won in the trenches, in the grit and grime of courageous determination."
Winston Churchill

June 20

"We Have Found Him"

"Philip findeth Nathanael, and saith unto him, We have found him" (John 1:45).

Phillip's witness to Nathaniel illustrates the type of witness the believer should share (John 1:45–49).

It was a Spoken Testimony. He said, "We have found him." It's important to live a Christlike life, but that does not exempt one from the responsibility of "speaking" the Gospel.

It was a Simple Testimony. A child could have understood. Be careful not to make complicated what God made simple. Simply tell what He has done for you.

It was a Sure Testimony. Phillip was certain of the message from personal experience; he was saved and knew that what Christ had done for him He could do for Nathanael. Not until you are sure of salvation can you convincingly share your faith with others.

It was a Sufficient Testimony. Some witnesses may require more detail, but not this one. Phillip shared all that was needed. While witnessing, stay sensitive and discerning as to what ought to be included and what ought not to be.

In the afterglow of a revival service at which I spoke, a youth under conviction of sin made inquiry about salvation. The pastor took the *How to Have a Full and Meaningful Life* booklet and began sharing the plan of salvation with him. Soon the youth interrupted, asking, "Do I have to listen to all that before I get saved?" Immediately the pastor stopped the presentation and led the student to Christ. The boy had heard enough.

"Testimonies are wonderful. But so often our lives don't fit our testimonies."
Leonard Ravenhill

June 21

Biblical Grit

"So, my dear brothers and sisters, be strong and immovable. Always work enthusiastically for the Lord" (1 Corinthians 15:58 NLT).

Resolve to show biblical grit. Grit is the tenacity to stay at your post when all that is in you wants to desert (1 Kings 19:3). It is spiritual spunk to move forward despite the brokenness, pain, and despair. It is the fortitude to trust God when a loved one is snatched away through death and your world crumbles. It is a resolution to be steadfast in hope amidst the storm of despair or defeat. It is immovable decidedness not to allow the difficulty, confusion, despondency, or disappointment of the hour to impede allegiance to Christ (Luke 21:19). It is unshaken firmness to maintain integrity and purity in opposing the strongest of carnal desires or lustful appetites. It is enduring perseverance in suffering. It is an unbending belief in God's Word when confronted with heresy (2 Peter 3:17). It is Job-like determination that says, "Though He slay me, yet will I trust in Him" (Job 13:15). Biblical grit (steadiness) under fire is essential.

Therefore, be immovable, unchangeable, and steadfast, and "endure hardness [hardship], as a good soldier of Jesus Christ" (2 Timothy 2:3). Remain immovable when you are assailed with doubt; influenced by a bad example; assaulted by skeptics; disillusioned at the conduct of another Christian; persecuted for the sake of Christ; burdened with heaviness, sorrow and hurt; pressed hard with temptation to return to a former sinful habit or addiction; and when the present Christian station or position is barren. Chown said, "Be 'steadfast' when all goes well and 'unmovable' when it goes otherwise."[307]

"Over time, grit is what separates fruitful lives from aimlessness."
John Ortberg

June 22

The Church's Strength (Part One)
"Put on thy strength, O Zion" (Isaiah 52:1).

The admonition is timely. By and large, the church has weakened and needs a reviving of her strength and former glory. There is a misconception about church strength. It is not indicated necessarily by a church's attendance numbers or the size of its facility. "Small" churches may be far stronger spiritually than megachurches. Nor is it to be equated to a large budget. Some churches in poverty accomplish far more than those with greater bank accounts. Church strength is not synonymous with pastoral strength or preaching skill, and neither is it to be equated to an array of ministry functions, activities, and programs. Strong churches may manifest these traits, but the traits in and of themselves do not make the church strong.

Jesus said a church may have a reputation in an area that it is fully alive and flourishing when it is actually "dead" (Revelation 3:1). Wherein does real church strength lie?

Affection for the Savior. Devotion to Christ is manifested in a heart that seeks to please Him above all others (Mark 12:30; Luke 16:13). The branch that abides in the Vine "bears much fruit" (John 15:5). This is essential to the infusion of supernatural strength to individual Christians as well as to the body of Christ.

*Allegiance to the Scripture (*Acts 2:42); that is, loyalty to the Truth regardless of cost and consequence. It is one thing to embrace the Truth, but quite another to adhere to it (practice it). A church faithful to the Word (not in part, but the whole) will be blessed with divine strength. They that are not will have *Ichabod* (the glory has departed) inscribed upon their doors.

"The Church has power in her testimony to truth, in her intercession before God, and in her character as the leaven of society and the salt of the nations."[308]

S. Martin

June 23

The Church's Strength (Part Two)
"Put on thy strength, O Zion" (Isaiah 52:1).

Accord with the Saints (Psalm 133:1). Holy union (agreement) with the brethren with regard to God's plan and purpose for the church infuses strength. A house divided against itself cannot stand (at least not for long). Dissension, discord, and faction suffocate strength. God refuses to bless with His power and presence people who disparage His name.

Attendance to Supplication (Colossians 4:2). The church that prays well, succeeds well.

Anointing with the Spirit. Apart from the unction, anointing, and empowerment of the Holy Spirit upon the minister and people, the church will flounder (regardless of even the good things attempted). It's "'not by might nor by power, but by my Spirit,' says the LORD Almighty" (Zechariah 4:6 NIV). Therefore we are admonished, "Quench not the Spirit" (1 Thessalonians 5:19).

June

Attitude for Service. Sovereign strength possessed increases in practice. The working church that seeks to win the lost will be blessed with added strength.

Assembly in the Sanctuary (Hebrews 10:25). "Enter into His gates with thanksgiving, and into His courts with praise: be thankful unto Him, and bless His name" (Psalm 100:4). Where true and sincere worship goes up, divine power comes down. Formalism stifles strength; hearty worship instills it.

Acknowledgment of Sin. "Carry forth the filthiness out of the holy place....by the words of the LORD...cleanse the house of the LORD" (2 Chronicles 29:5,16). Whatever there is in the church that is found to be "unclean" must be confessed and cleansed if strength is to be regained (2 Chronicles 7:14). From pulpit to pew, clergy to the layman, small to enormous sized church, let's lay aside the fleshly strength housed in our frail personality, skills, abilities, and even giftedness and put on Sovereign strength that is equal to the task to be done. Pray for revival in the church, that her former strength and glory may be returned.

"Saints are weak in themselves, but they have strength in Christ, and on Him should they wait, to Him should they look, and on Him should they exercise faith for it; they should put on the whole armor of God, clothe themselves with it, resume courage, pluck up a good heart and spirit, and not fear any difficulties, dangers, and enemies."[309]
John Gill

June 24

Church Hurt

"Not forsaking the assembling of ourselves together, as the manner of some is" (Hebrews 10:25).

Barna Research states, "Most unchurched people—more than four out of five—were formerly regular participants in church life, many of whom departed after an ugly incident that hurt them deeply."[310] The church's mission field includes these wounded soldiers, and effort must be undertaken to restore them to fellowship with Christ and His people.

The causes of church hurt are varied, including grave disappointment with a pastor/church leader's conduct; exclusion from the inner circle of fellowship (not being accepted); unjust treatment (criticism, slander, or excessive church discipline); detrimental church policy change and/or a negative biblical doctrinal shift (straying from sound theological teaching); removal from a church office held or denial of a position sought; judgmentalism toward status, class, or race; and ministry neglect in the hour of grief, grave illness or suffering.

What's the cure for church hurt? Healing of the bitter wounds of church hurt begin with a redirection of focus—stop focusing on the hurter and focus on the Healer. "He healeth the broken in heart, and bindeth up their wounds" (Psalm 147:3). Bring every verbal barb, emotional shard, and contemptuous smirk to Him. Grant forgiveness to the offender, even if it is undeserved (Ephesians 4:32).

And return to church. Sometimes that means attending a new church. The fact that other churches look the same doesn't mean they are the same. Don't judge all churches by a painful experience in one, or all Christians by the bad behavior of a few.

"Relatively minor church hurts can leave us with a burned-out feeling during service, while the more serious wounds can leave us soul-scarred and physically sick at the thought of walking in the church doors. Far from being innocuous, the pain can open us up to various temptations."[311]
John Piper

June 25

Blow the Bugle

"Ask, and it shall be given you; seek, and ye shall find; knock, and it shall be opened unto you" (Matthew 7:7).

In medieval legend, Roland was a knight that served King Charlemagne. When Roland was dispatched to battle an invading army outside the castle's fortress, he was given a bugle to sound if he "ran into trouble." The blast of the horn would alert the king to send immediate help. As the story goes ("Song of Roland"), Roland's army was ambushed and overwhelmed by enemy forces. Sadly, Roland failed to blow the bugle for help, resulting in the needless massacre of his army.[312]

Every Christian has been given a bugle to blow by their Commander in Chief, the Lord Jesus Christ. It is to be blown when they or others about them are threatened by the forces of evil, sickness, sorrow, and

June

suffering. It is the bugle of prayer (the cry to God for divine help and reinforcements).

Spurgeon said, "Prayer is the lisping of the believing infant, the shout of the fighting believer, the requiem of the dying saint falling asleep in Jesus. It is the breath, the watchword, the comfort, the strength, the honor of a Christian."[313] David said, "The righteous cry out [blow the bugle], and the Lord hears them; he delivers [rescues] them from all their troubles" (Psalm 34:17 NIV). Keep your bugle polished and well-tuned. Play it often. Play it loudly. Play it privately and publicly (James 4:3).

"Prayer lays hold of God's plan and becomes the link between His will and its accomplishment on earth. Amazing things happen, and we are given the privilege of being the channels of the Holy Spirit's prayer."
Elisabeth Elliot

June 26

Superiority of Grace

"For from his fullness we have all received, grace upon grace" (John 1:16 ESV).

Grace is superior to works. Matthew Henry says, "Man in his depraved state under the power of such corruption could never by any works of his own gain acceptance with God, but it must be resolved purely into the free grace of God given through Jesus Christ to all true believers that receive it as a free gift."[314]

Grace is superior to the law. The purpose of the law is to reveal sin, but it has no power to forgive it or reconcile the sinner to God (Romans 8:3–4). Grace alone enables man's trespass against God to be forgiven and him to be reconciled (made right) to Him (Romans 5:20).

Grace is superior to legalism. Legalism entangles man in bondage and fear with its insistence on conformity to rules, regulations, and religious rituals in order to be acceptable to God, while grace brings freedom and liberty. Don't live by a list of *dos* and *don'ts*. All that man needs for reconciliation to God is provided at Calvary, not Sinai (Colossians 2:11–17). Ferguson states, "Grace highlights legalism's bankruptcy and shows that it's not only useless; it's pointless; its life breath is smothered out of it."[315]

Grace is superior to "religions," philosophies, and the help of man. "Don't let anyone capture you with empty philosophies and high-sounding nonsense that come from human thinking and from the spiritual powers of this world, rather than from Christ" (Colossians 2:8 NLT)

"Change won't happen through 'trying harder' but only through encountering the radical grace of God."
                                    Timothy Keller

June 27

Salvation of a Family

"And they said, Believe on the Lord Jesus Christ, and thou shalt be saved, and thy house" (Acts 16:31).

The narrative of the salvation of the jailer's household indicates five tracks (independently or unitedly) by which households may be won to Christ.

1. The first track to household salvation is through its head (Acts 16:31). Fathers and husbands must be proactive as the head of the home in bringing it to Christ (Joshua 24:14–15). This is the fastest track.

2. A second track to household salvation is through the conversion of one of its members (Acts 16:31). God uses solitary believers (spiritual lights) in the nonreligious home to expose its darkness and express the need of Jesus Christ (Matthew 5:16). How great and grave is the darkness in households without any witness. But how penetrating and effectual even the smallest of lights can be to the deepest darkness!

3. A third track to household salvation is to bring its members under the ministry of the Word (Acts 16:32). Get the household under the sound of good old-fashioned preaching and watch the power of God's Word empowered by the Holy Spirit do its work in the conviction of sin and conversion (Romans 1:16). "Faith cometh by hearing, and hearing by the Word of God" (Romans 10:17). Spurgeon said, "Though it may seem a very trite thing to say, it is nevertheless exceedingly important, if we are to have household conversion, that there should be a household hearing of the Word. This is the chosen instrumentality, and we must bring all under the instrumentality if we wish them to obtain the blessing."[316]

June

4. A fourth track to household salvation is calamity and crisis (Acts 16:26). People are more receptive to the Gospel in crisis than in calm. It is when life is disrupted that people become open to new ways of seeing, thinking, and acting.

5. A fifth track to household salvation is intercession (Acts 16:25). Make entreaty to the Lord for each family member's conversion to Christ.

"Every father of a family should consider himself as charged with the souls of those with whom he hopes to leave behind him, and as contributing to the future propagation of the truth, by every act of devotion performed in his house."
James Alexander

June 28

Battlements for the Home

"When thou buildest a new house, then thou shalt make a battlement for thy roof" (Deuteronomy 22:8).

Oriental homes had flat roofs which posed danger of accidental falls off their four sides, causing serious injury. It was for this reason that a "safety wall" was to be built around its edges. Likewise, parents ought to construct spiritual and moral battlements about the home for the welfare and safety of their children.

Erect the battlement (safety wall) of a matchless foundation. A home built upon the shifting sands of irreligion and anti-God values will in time collapse (great will be the fall of it), whereas one built upon the Solid Rock (Jesus Christ and biblical values) will stand firm regardless of the storms encountered (Matthew 7:24–27).

Erect the battlement of moral sanction. Prohibit the profane, irreligious, and corrupt from entering into the home.

Erect the battlement of ministerial instruction. Biblical values and principles must be taught soundly and consistently (Proverbs 22:6).

Erect the battlement of modeled example. Father and mother must serve as worthy patterns of godliness for their children to imitate.

Erect the battlement of measured discipline. Children learn through discipline that there are consequences to disobedience and wrongdoing (Proverbs 22:15 NLT).

Children may climb over these battlements, being drawn away by the beckoning call of sin and wrong companions. But if you wall them up well now, they will have a ladder forever attached to their back to use one day to climb back into the arms of God.

"Battlement your houses, then; do not be afraid of being too strict and too Puritanic. There is no fear of that in these days; there is a great deal more danger of bringing solemn judgments on our families through neglecting the worship of God in our households."
C. H. Spurgeon

June 29

A Theological Schoolhouse in the Home

"And thou shalt teach them diligently unto thy children, and shalt talk of them when thou sittest in thine house" (Deuteronomy 6:7).

The Bible states that if there are children in the home, then there must be a school for their spiritual instruction and training.

Timothy's house had a schoolhouse. Paul said of him, "And that from a child thou hast known the holy scriptures, which are able to make thee wise unto salvation through faith which is in Christ Jesus" (2 Timothy 3:15). Timothy's mother, Eunice, and grandmother, Lois, taught him to know and love the Lord.

Samuel's house was a schoolhouse. Hannah's faith and godliness were instilled in young Samuel.

John and Charles Wesley's house was a schoolhouse. Their mother, Susannah, devoted several hours a week with them (each alone) regarding spiritual things. Someone has said, "The Methodist Church began at Susannah Wesley's knee, when she rocked Charles in a cradle and held John on her lap while she patiently taught him to read, 'In the beginning God created the heaven and the earth.'" Homes like Timothy's, Samuel's and John and Charles Wesley's produce godly men and women who enhance the kingdom of God.

June

What curriculum ought the home schoolhouse embrace? Expound the Word (teach doctrines, attributes of God, commandments). Teach sound biblical principles to govern all of life. Teach them right from wrong. Clarify Christian beliefs and values. Instruct them on the importance of faithfulness to the church. Instill good, noble, and honorable habits. Teach them the importance of prayer, daily devotions, and Scripture memory. Warn them about the dangers of wrong companions, dishonesty, disobedience to God, and immorality. Encourage them to witness to friends and serve the Lord regardless of cost or consequence.

"Let no Christian parents fall into the delusion that Sunday School is intended to ease them of their personal duties. The first and most natural condition of things is for Christian parents to train up their own children in the nurture and admonition of the Lord."
C. H. Spurgeon

June 30

Clutch to Hope

"Why art thou cast down, O my soul? And why art thou disquieted within me? Hope thou in God" (Psalm 42:11).

Steadfastness in hope during trials is possible by embracing four truths.

1. The believer retains hope in distress by remembering that God can be trusted to keep His promises. The author of Hebrews says, "Let us hold tightly without wavering [unbending] to the hope we affirm [expectation; basis of hope in the Christian faith], for God can be trusted [dependable, reliable] to keep his promise [that which He personally promised to the believer recorded in the Holy Scriptures]" (Hebrews 10:23 NLT). MacArthur states, "God's promises are reliable. With that confidence, the believer can persevere."[317]

2. The believer retains hope in distress by the enablement of the Holy Spirit. Paul says, "Guard well the splendid, God-given ability you received as a gift from the Holy Spirit who lives within you" (2 Timothy 1:14 TLB). Depend upon the influences of the Holy Spirit to expose irrational and erroneous thoughts sowed by the enemy and confirm the

hope possessed in Christ Jesus. Jesus says, "He, the Spirit of Truth...will guide you into all truth" (John 16:13).

3. The believer retains hope in distress by grace. Whatever the trial, God says, "my grace is sufficient for you." Therefore, "Let us therefore come boldly unto the throne of grace, that we may obtain mercy, and find grace to help in time of need" (Hebrews 4:16).

4. The believer retains hope in distress by discernment. John warns, "Beloved, believe not every spirit, but try the spirits whether they are of God: because many false prophets are gone out into the world" (1 John 4:1). The believer's safeguard against "seducing spirits, and doctrines of devils" is spiritual discernment (1 Timothy 4:1). When the waters of trouble overtake you and the mind is attacked with the darts of doubt hurled by the enemy, put all the force of your soul into clinging to that which is known to be true. Never doubt in the dark what is believed in the light. Hold fast to God's unchanging hand, trustworthy promises, helping grace, power of the Holy Spirit and spiritual discernment.

"Hope is called the anchor of the soul because it gives stability to the Christian life. But hope is not simply a 'wish'; rather, it is that which latches on to the certainty of the promises of the future that God has made."
R. C. Sproul

July 1

A Dark and Painful Place

"Though he slay me, yet will I trust in him" (Job 13:15).

Spurgeon says of Job, "When others despair, he trusts in God. When he has nowhere else to look, he turns to his heavenly Father; and when for a time, even in looking to God, he meets with no conscious comfort, he waits in the patience of hope, calmly expecting aid, and resolving that even if it does not come, he will cling to God with all the energy of his soul."[318]

The narrative of Job's trial suggests how we ought to trust God.

Trust God without Consideration. Don't allow calamity or crisis to alter trusting faith. Watchman Nee states, "Faith looks not at what happens to him, but at Him Whom he believes."[319]

Trust God without Reservation. Man's extremity is the time to express unquestionable trust in God's sovereignty, despite the measure of the adversity or affliction.

Trust God without Explanation. Across some of our days, God marks, "Will explain later."[320] Until then, we trust His heart and live by His promise that "all things work together for good to them that love God" (Romans 8:28).

Trust God without Manipulation. Against people with disparaging, pessimistic, gloomy, and ungodly counsel, be as surefooted in faith as Job was. Let not their flowery rhetoric coated with disbelief and despair impact faith negatively (Isaiah 28:23).

Trust God without Limitation. Chambers says, "Faith never knows where it is being led, but it loves and knows the One who is leading."[321]

Trust God with Anticipation. Anticipating the resurrection and Heaven helps make the present hardship and pain endurable (Luke 21:28). When it's your lot to be in a dark and painful place, adopt Job's approach to faith and like him, be consoled, comforted, and helped. Resolve to stand firm, saying with Job, "Though He slay me, yet will I trust [place my hope for deliverance] in Him."

Fair-weather faith proves worthless in bad weather. Develop a faith that may withstand the worst of storms (Romans 10:17; 1 Peter 2:2).

"Believers talk about trusting in the Lord with their whole heart and refusing to lean on their own understanding, but no one really knows what that means until circumstances cast them headfirst into a dark and painful place."[322]
David Jeremiah

July 2

The Backslider

"The backslider in heart shall be filled with his own ways" (Proverbs 14:14).

Backsliding is departure from God to satisfy the worldly, lustful desires of the heart. It's not to be equated with a spiritual stumble that is only momentary.

Reason for Backsliding. To cause a believer to backslide, Satan uses improper associations and unequally yoked companions in friendship, dating, marriage, and business partnerships (2 Corinthians 6:14), opposition and persecution from friends and family for living the Christian life (John 16:33), unconfessed sin (Psalm 38:3–6), disappointment in a Christian admired (1 Peter 2:21), neglect of abiding fellowship with Christ and the church (John 15:4), severe hardship and sorrow that causes despair and discouragement (Deuteronomy 1:27–36), change in priorities from the spiritual to the material (Matthew 6:33), busyness (Luke 9:57–62), worldly pursuits (Philippians 2:21), habitual indulgence in a known sin (Song of Solomon 2:15), "weights" that easily entangle us (Hebrews 12:1), unconcern for the lost (Acts 1:8), egotism (Proverbs 16:18), infrequent and unpassionate prayer (Luke 18:1), and acts of moral impurity (Isaiah 52:11).

The bottom line? Spiritual casualness, fleshly carelessness, devotional coldness, immature contentedness, arrogant conceitedness, evangelistic callousness, and fearful cowardliness lead to worldly compromise and corruption which result in spiritual relapse. Spurgeon said, "If you want to know how to backslide, leave off going forward. Cease going upward and you will go downward of necessity. You can never stand still."

Result of Backsliding. Turning from God damages testimony. It disrupts marriage and family life. It brings divine judgment (chastisement). It delivers sorrow and havoc ("buyer's remorse"). Packer wrote, "Unregenerate apostates are often cheerful souls, but backsliding

July

Christians are always miserable."³²³ It destroys ministry. It devastates friends and family. It disappoints God. It disturbs peace, hope and joy. It decays the soul. It disdains and defiles the holy and sacred. It drives unbelievers away from the church. It disillusions would-be followers of Christ.

*"A believer may sometimes lapse into sin and stray from intimacy with the Lord and with His people. But unless the Lord disciplines him and takes him to Heaven, he will come back. He will be too much under conviction to stay away permanently. In the meanwhile, he will be robbed of joy and peace and of many other blessings."*³²⁴
John MacArthur

July 3

Remedy for Backsliding

"Return, ye backsliding children, and I will heal your backslidings. Behold, we come unto thee; for thou art the Lord our God" (Jeremiah 3:22).

It was when the prodigal son "came to himself" (awoke from spiritual lunacy) that his resolve was made to return home to the father without delay (Luke 15:17–18). Recovery from the "far country" is initiated when the backslider says, "I have gone astray like a lost sheep; seek thy servant; for I do not forget thy commandments" (Psalm 119:176), and, "Oh, that I were as in months past, as in the days when God watched over me" (Job 29:2 NKJV). It is consummated when he says, "Have mercy upon me, O God, according to thy lovingkindness: according unto the multitude of thy tender mercies blot out my transgressions. Wash me thoroughly from mine iniquity, and cleanse me from my sin. For I acknowledge my transgressions: and my sin is ever before me. Against thee, thee only, have I sinned, and done this evil in thy sight....Create in me a clean heart, O God; and renew a right spirit within me....Restore unto me the joy of thy salvation" (Psalm 51, selected verses).

John Owen states, "There is only one way to be revived and healed from our backslidings so that we may become fruitful even in old age. We must take a steady look at the glory of Christ in His special character, in His grace and work, as shown to us in the Scripture."

"Remember that if you are a child of God, you will never be happy in sin. You are spoiled for the world, the flesh, and the Devil. When you were regenerated, there was put into you a vital principle which can never be content to dwell in the dead world. You will have to come back, if indeed you belong to the family."[325]

C. H. Spurgeon

July 4

Get Back Up

"The godly may trip seven times, but they will get up again" (Proverbs 24:16 NLT).

In the 1929 Rose Bowl, Roy, a player for Southern California (playing against Georgia Tech), ran the football back the wrong way. A teammate tackled him just before he scored a touchdown for the wrong team. At halftime, Roy sat alone in the locker room amid speculation of teammates as to what the coach would say to him. Finally, just prior to the end of halftime, the coach announced that all who started the game would start the second half. Roy remained seated and sobbing, prompting the coach to say, "Come on, Roy."

Roy replied, "I can't coach. I embarrassed the team and myself. I can never face the crowd again."

The coach responded, "The game is only half over."

What a coach! But greater still what a Savior who says when we have failed that the game of life is not over, that there are opportunities in the second half to do better. He is the God of the second chance. A paralyzing past or a magnificent future are your choices. Failure doesn't have to be fatal or final—not with God in the equation.

Enter into the restoration He provides through Christ Jesus, and get back to intimate communion and fellowship with Him, a full and meaningful life, joyfulness and peace, vibrant worship and profitable spiritual service. Upon restoration you will testify with David, "He brought me up also out of an horrible pit, out of the miry clay, and set my feet upon a rock, and established my goings. And he hath put a new song in my mouth, even praise unto our God: many shall see it, and fear, and shall trust in the Lord" (Psalm 40:2–3).

July

"The voice of sin is loud, but the voice of forgiveness is louder."[326]
D. L. Moody

July 5

Hardships

"Every day is hard for those who suffer" (Proverbs 15:15 NCV).

An artist on a lofty scaffold painting the dome of a cathedral stepped back to behold his work when he unconsciously neared the edge and was about to fall. He would have fallen to his death had not a friend quickly dashed paint on his work, prompting him to dart forward to safety.

To save us from backward and precarious steps God sometimes seems to deal with us severely, allowing things to happen that are painful and grievous. Hardships are in reality blessings designed to foster God's sovereign plan in and through us (Jeremiah 29:11).

The hardship sometimes is a protracted one. It was for Job. "Month after month I have nothing to live for; night after night brings me grief" (Job 7:3 GNT).

The hardship sometimes is a profound one. It was for the Shunammite mother. "The child sat on her lap till noon, and then he died" (2 Kings 4:20 ESV).

The hardship sometimes is a passing one. It was for Joseph. His unjust time in Potiphar's jail ended when he interpreted the king's dream.

The hardship sometimes is a permanent one. It was for Paul. "There was given to me a thorn in the flesh....For this thing I besought the Lord thrice, that it might depart from me" (2 Corinthians 12:7–8).

The hardship sometimes is a preparatory one. It was for Jeremiah. "Then Pashur smote Jeremiah the prophet, and put him in the stocks" (Jeremiah 20:2). That trial only prepared Jeremiah (mentally and spiritually) for a second trial that threatened his life (Jeremiah 38:6).

The hardship sometimes is a parting one. It was for Mary and Martha. "Lazarus is dead" (John 11:14). To be severed from family and friends by death is a heart-wrenching trial.

The hardship sometimes is a profitable one. It was for David. He testified, "It is good for me that I have been afflicted; that I might learn thy statutes" (Psalm 119:71).

Whatever the type of hardship trust God to make a way through it.

"Faith endures as seeing Him who is invisible, endures the disappointments, the hardships, and the heartaches of life by recognizing that all comes from the hand of Him who is too wise to err and too loving to be unkind."
A. W. Pink

July 6

Anxious Fear

"Heaviness in the heart of man maketh it stoop" (Proverbs 12:25).

"Heaviness" (anxiety and fear, i.e., anxious fear[327]) in the heart of man "maketh" (causes) it "stoop" (bows it down, or weighs it down with despair, dejection, depression [effects documented by psychologists]). Anxious fear is symptomatic of mistrust in God's care and provision. It is the thief of man's peace, serenity, joy and comfort.

Spurgeon says, "Anxiety does not empty tomorrow of its sorrows, but only empties today of its strength." Müller said, "The beginning of anxiety is the end of faith, and the beginning of true faith is the end of anxiety."[328] "A Christian's freedom from anxiety," writes Stott, "is not due to some guaranteed freedom from trouble, but to the folly of worry and especially to the confidence that God is our Father, that even permitted suffering is within the orbit of His care."[329] "Peace is the fruit of believing prayer."[330]

Peace stems from the promises. "The cure of it [anxious fear or worry]," says Matthew Henry, is "a good word from God, applied by faith. It makes it [the heart] glad; such a word is, 'Cast thy burden upon the LORD, and he shall sustain thee.' The good word of God, particularly the Gospel, is designed to make the hearts glad that are weary and heavy-laden."[331]

Peace thwarts anxiety through spiritual breathing. Use Scripture to refute and dismiss negative and anxious thoughts (exhaling), and its truth to bolster rest, serenity, and peace (inhaling). Peace permeates the heart when it is fixated on Jesus.

July

"I am no longer anxious about anything, as I realize the Lord is able to carry out His will, and His will is mine. It makes no matter where He places me, or how. That is rather for Him to consider than for me; for in the easiest positions, He must give me His grace, and in the most difficult, His grace is sufficient."[332]

Hudson Taylor

July 7

Footprints of Jesus

"Thou [God] wilt keep him in perfect peace, whose mind is stayed [focused, fixated] on thee: because he trusteth in thee" (Isaiah 26:3).

The News reported that an aged lady's car was stopped on a bridge, halting traffic. Police were summoned. The lady informed the police officers that she was terrified to drive over bridges and couldn't drive any further. The policemen graciously told her that they would ensure her safety in crossing the bridge—that one of them would drive slowly in front of her and the other behind her. Calmly, she then drove over the bridge.

Whatever may be facing you presently that terrifies and perhaps paralyzes you, remember that Christ goes before and behind you to ensure your safety. Therefore, let the anxiety give way to calmness. Stanley said, "As you walk through the valley of the unknown, you will find the footprints of Jesus both in front of you and beside you."[333] With Spurgeon I say, "Away, then, with dark suspicions and anxieties! Is it care about past sin? 'The blood of Jesus Christ, God's dear Son, cleanses us from all sin.' Is it present temptation? 'There has no temptation happened to you but such as is common to men: but God who is faithful, who will not suffer you to be tempted above what you are able; but will with the temptation also make a way to escape, that you may be able to bear it.' Is it future peril? Oh, leave that with Him, for neither 'things present, nor things to come, nor height, nor depth, nor any other creature, shall be able to separate us from the Love of God, which is in Christ Jesus our Lord.'"[334]

Therefore, "Be strong and courageous. Do not be afraid or terrified because of them, for the Lord your God goes with you; he will never leave you nor forsake you" (Deuteronomy 31:6 NIV).

"Where does your security lie? Is God your refuge, your hiding place, your stronghold, your shepherd, your counselor, your friend, your redeemer, your savior, your guide? If He is, you don't need to search any further for security."[335]

Elizabeth Elliot

July 8

Is There No Comforter?

"And they had no comforter; and on the side of their oppressors there was power; but they had no comforter" (Ecclesiastes 4:1).

Is there no comforter? No comforter! Imagine—no believer to be a refuge, shelter, or fortress to which to run for consolation and encouragement in the time of adversity, suffering, and sorrow; no God to which to turn for strength, hope and peace; no friend to listen, confide and advise and to support in the storm; no promises upon which to rest for assurances of God's presence—His peace that passeth all understanding, the ultimate triumph in Heaven over all that pains and grieves, and resurrection upon death; no Holy Spirit on which to plead for holy comfort and power to make it through the struggle; no minister to uplift the soul in bereavement or make the sick-bed lighter or the final step easier; no Bible upon which wearied and worn souls can rest their head for light in the darkest and bleakest of nights; no Calvary upon which the soul might cling for forgiveness of sin, rightness with God, and eternal life. Is such the case?

Is there no comforter in the land to minister to the people in their deepest sorrow and despair? The answer is both "Yes" and "No." Though a comforter is present in the land, that presence is unknown or hidden to the billions that sit in spiritual darkness. The Bible explains, "For the god of this world [Satan] has blinded the unbelievers' minds [that they should not discern the truth], preventing them from seeing the illuminating light of the Gospel of the glory of Christ [the Messiah], Who is the Image and Likeness of God" (2 Corinthians 4:4 AMPC).

"There is no balm in Gilead, but there is balm in God. There is no physician among the creatures, but the Creator is Jehovah-rophi."

C. H. Spurgeon

July

July 9

Behold the Tears

"And behold, the tears of those who were oppressed" (Ecclesiastes 4:1 KJ21).

Behold the tears of the disparaged and damned, and compassionately weep for them.

Jesus beheld those tears. Upon seeing a host of nonbelievers, He "was moved with compassion on them, because they fainted, and were scattered abroad, as sheep having no shepherd [comforter, protector, caretaker]" (Matthew 9:36).

Paul beheld those tears. He wrote, "Many people live like enemies of the cross of Christ. I have often told you about them, and it makes me cry to tell you about them now. In the end, they will be destroyed. They do whatever their bodies want, they are proud of their shameful acts, and they think only about earthly things" (Philippians 3:18–19 NCV). In the farewell address to the Ephesus believers, he said, "Therefore watch, and remember, that by the space of three years I ceased not to warn every one night and day with tears" (Acts 20:31).

Jeremiah beheld those tears. And he said, "Oh, that my head were a spring of water and my eyes a fountain of tears! I would weep day and night for the slain of my people" (Jeremiah 9:1 NIV).

David beheld those tears. He said, "Rivers of waters run down mine eyes" (Psalm 119:136).

L. R. Scarborough beheld those tears. He cried, "Lost—it means separation from God. It means the opposite of Heaven. It means Hell. It means no peace. It means no happiness, no joy. It means all there is in the punishment of sin, in the wrath of God, in the indignation of a wrathful sovereign. Lost! Lost! Lost!"[336]

Spurgeon beheld those tears. He said, "I believe that much of the secret of soul winning lies in having bowels of compassion, in having spirits that can be touched with the feeling of human infirmities."

Hyman Appelman beheld those tears. "Cry unto God, beloved. Cry unto God for the gift of passion, the gift of tears. Compassion for souls must be developed, or our work will become matter-of-fact and mechanical."[337]

John Welch beheld those tears and soaked his pillow with tears over them as he prayed.

"Put your ear down to the Bible and hear Him bid you go and pull sinners out of the fire of sin. Put your ear down to the burdened, agonized heart of humanity and listen to its pitiful wail for help."
William Booth

July 10

The Ministry of Tears

"And behold, the tears of those who were oppressed" (Ecclesiastes 4:1 KJ21).

Why the ministry of tears?

1. Because of the sinner's deception. They are blinded by Satan from seeing the truth of their need of God (2 Corinthians 4:4). Men are like the lost silver in the parable of the lost coin. Does the silver know that it is lost? Neither do most souls (Luke 15:8–10).

2. Because of the sinner's despair. Fulfillment for man's emptiness (absence of meaningfulness, satisfaction, peace, hope and happiness) is only supplied by God.

3. Because of the sinner's desolation. They live in isolation from Him that alone provides comfort in adversity, a crown of beauty instead of ashes, festive oil instead of mourning, and splendid clothes instead of despair (Isaiah 61:3 CSB).

4. Because of the sinner's disposition. They are "enemies of the Cross" (Philippians 3:18).

5. Because of the sinner's disappointment. Ignorant of the truth or disdain it, they anticipate a meaningful and peaceful life and death, only to realize too late that they were on the wrong road.

6. Because of the sinner's destiny. With William Burns, the believer ought to say, "The thud of Christless feet on the way to Hell is breaking my heart." Visualize the hopelessness and despair of the eternally damned. Agonize in prayer for them. Prioritize taking healing medicine to them. Tell the good news to them, that there is a comforter in the land that heals the brokenhearted, mends broken and shattered lives, and instills meaning and peace to life. Packer said, "Christians are sent to convert, and they should not allow themselves, as Christ's representatives in the world, to aim at anything less."[338]

July

"The shortest verse in the Bible tells the story: 'Jesus wept.' Oh, that great Weeper is just the one to silence all earthly trouble and wipe out all stains of earthly grief."[339]

DeWitt Talmage

July 11

Satan's Sabotage

"By mercy and truth iniquity is purged" (Proverbs 16:6).

Satan seeks to sabotage God's promise to forgive sin when we confess and repent.

Tactic of the sabotage. The Devil questions God's promise to thoroughly cleanse from the soul the sin that is sorrowfully acknowledged and renounced, inciting doubt and distrust in what God said (Genesis 3:1), thereby causing fear, anxiety and despair.

Triumph in the sabotage. The stronghold of false, unhealthy guilt is torn down by counteracting what Satan says with that which God says, the "renewing of your mind" (Romans 12:2). Tozer stated, "Are you still afraid of your past sins? God knows that sin is a terrible thing—and the Devil knows it, too. So he follows us around and as long as we will permit it, he will taunt us about our past sins. As for myself, I have learned to talk back to him on this score. I say, 'Yes, Devil, sin is terrible—but I remind you I got it from you! And I remind you, Devil, that everything good—forgiveness and cleansing and blessing—everything that is good I have freely received from Jesus Christ.'" Tozer continues, "Why do we claim on one hand our sins are gone and on the other act just as though they are not gone? Brethren, we have been declared, 'Not Guilty!' by the highest court in the universe....Now, on the basis of grace as taught in the Word of God, when God forgives a man, He trusts him as though he had never sinned."[340]

Satan is right to say that forgiveness is undeserved and unmerited, that man ought to pay for the sin engaged in. BUT God overrules that reasoning, saying, "I, even I, am he that blotteth out thy transgressions for mine own sake, and will not remember thy sins" (Isaiah 43:25).

"Guilt of sin is taken away from us by the mercy and truth of God—mercy in promising, truth in performing—the mercy and truth which kiss each other in Jesus Christ the Mediator."[341]

Matthew Henry

July 12

Miserable Comforters (Part One)

"I have heard many such things: miserable comforters are ye all. Shall vain words have an end?" (Job 16:2–3).

In Job's distress friends did much wrong in their effort to console him. "They were none at all, and worse than none," says Gill, in their effort to comfort him. Job testifies the friends were 'deceitful brooks' (Job 6:15) and "worthless physicians" (Job 13:4, NIV), but also, he calls them "miserable comforters" (Job 16:2).

What was said was Well-meaning. Job's friends tried to console him. When they heard of the tragedy, they immediately got together to pray for him and to talk of how they might grant him consolation. Their grief was so heavy for Job they could not speak for seven days. Despite saying unfounded and distressing things, credit them for their compassionate heart for Job.

What was said was Wrong. To suggest that the affliction was the consequence of a crime or secret sin or hypocrisy necessitating immediate repentance for recovery was not only insensitive but grossly fallacious. There had been no such sin or wicked deed done. "The patient's case is sad indeed when his medicines are poisons and his physicians his worst disease."

What was said was Wordy. "What have I said that makes you speak so endlessly?" (Job 16:3 TLB). "The ear groans at the quantity of windy talk, irrelevant observation, impertinent argument, and pointless discussion to which it is obliged to listen." It is always safer, and probably more effective, to say less than more.

What was said was Witless. Its abruptness, insensitivity, rashness, and pompousness were out of line. The words of the friends were "vain words" (Job 16:3), "literally, words of wind; words which pass by a man 'as the idle wind which he regards not.'" Unlike them, couch what is said based upon the promises of God, enveloped with sympathy and caring concern.

"Job desires his friends in imagination, for a little while, to change conditions with him, to put their souls in his soul's stead, to suppose themselves in misery like him and him at ease like them. Whatever our brethren's sorrows are, we ought by sympathy to make them our own, because we know not how soon they may be so."

Matthew Henry

July 13

Miserable Comforters (Part Two)

"I have heard many such things: miserable comforters are ye all. Shall vain words have an end?" (Job 16:2–3).

What was said was Wearisome. All that Job's friends said brought irritation and agitation, compounding the sorrow borne. Instead of their words being healing salve to his wounded heart, they were as salt upon a grievous injury, prompting Job to say, "What miserable comforters all of you are. Won't you ever stop your flow of foolish words? (Job 16:2–3 TLB).

What was said was Wanting. "Eliphaz, Bildad, and Zophar had only proved 'comforters of trouble,' broken reeds that pierce the hand of those who lean upon them." That which Job's broken heart needed (like all who are afflicted), sympathy, sincerity, sagacity, and support, were sadly lacking. That which is said to the sorrowing, though it may be sincere and true, may not be the most profitable at the moment or that which they want to hear.

What was said was Wasted. Job's friends squandered and misused their opportunity to instill comfort and hope. Spurgeon says, "Cold comfort some ministers render to afflicted consciences; their advice will be equally valuable with that of the Highlander who is reported to have seen an Englishman sinking in a bog on Ben Nevis. 'I am sinking,' cried the traveler. 'Can you tell me how to get out?'

"The Highlander calmly replied, 'I think it is likely you never will,' and walked away."

Safeguard against being a miserable comforter by adaptation of seven primary counseling traits.

1. Be clear in the message.
2. Be sound in theology.
3. Be sympathetic in heart.
4. Be concise in talk.
5. Be focused on hope.
6. Be governed and empowered by the Holy Spirit.
7. Bathe the comforting encounter in prayer from start to end.

"Sometimes we have to experience misunderstanding from unsympathetic friends in order to learn how to minister to others."
Warren Wiersbe

July 14

Ministry Outside the Box

"Peter answered, 'I can't do that, Lord! I've never eaten anything that is impure or unclean'"(Acts 10:14 GW).

It was on a Saturday evening that a team of students was sent from the CSU campus to minister at the Salvation Army chapel in Charleston, South Carolina. No one showed up except the team. I suggested to the rest of the team that we walk down into the neighborhood and conduct an open-air meeting. The singer attracted a crowd. Billy Cashion shared a personal testimony, and I preached. At the conclusion of the invitation, thirty professions of faith had been made. Everyone on the team well realized that changing the venue of ministry was a "God thing" that resulted in this glorious harvest.

Don't stubbornly be set on doing ministry in the traditional way. Dare to think outside the box. Think unconventionally under the constraint of the Holy Spirit. This Jesus did. For example, He preached in a boat upon a lake instead of in the pulpit in a synagogue (Mark 4:1–2).

Had the team that Saturday seen the chapel door locked and simply returned to campus, we would have missed God's divine assignment and souls would have missed their opportunity to be saved.

The seven last words of the church are, "We've never done it that way before." Sometimes, as it was with Peter, God has to force us out of the box (Acts 10:9–16).

"Think outside the box about methodology, not the message."
Frank Shivers

July 15

Perseverance in Persecution

"Thou therefore endure hardness, as a good soldier of Jesus Christ" (2 Timothy 2:3).

When persecuted, the Christian is to persevere as a good soldier of the Lord Jesus Christ, undaunted by the adversary. Perseverance is the capacity to bear up in the face of antagonism, persecution and the temptation to compromise biblical tenets. It involves fortitude, steadfastness, patience and endurance amidst trials and trouble.[342]

The Must to Persevere. "You have obeyed my command to persevere" (Revelation 3:10 NLT). Ironside says, "The denial of His Name is the increasing apostasy around us on every hand."[343] Resolve under every circumstance without consideration of cost or consequence to keep His Word and confess His Name (Revelation 3:8).

The Motive to Persevere.

1. It is to magnify Christ (Matthew 5:10).
2. It is to merit reward (Revelation 3:11).
3. It is to message truth (Acts 3:1–8; Acts 4:4).
4. It is to marshal right (Ephesians 5:11).

The Mind to Persevere. "Hold that fast which thou hast" (Revelation 3:11). Tenacity to hold fast to the Bible, Christian duty and discipline and allegiance to Christ under fire must be exhibited bravely, patiently, prayerfully, and, hopefully, until the end. Criswell says, "Nothing but vigorous counter-contention *is* sufficient."[344]

The Might to Persevere. "For thou hast a little strength" (Revelation 3:8). Isn't it wonderful that into weak believers (like the Philadelphia saints that are somewhat weak-kneed in standing up for biblical values and convictions) Christ infuses His might to make it possible to persevere! Christ says, "I also shall keep thee" (Revelation 3:10; Jude 1:24).

"In one way or another, the Christian church is always being persecuted. The persecution can be political, personal, or religious. The greatest persecutor of evangelical Christianity is probably liberal Christianity."[345]
John MacArthur

July 16

Refusal to Be Comforted
"In the day of my trouble I sought the Lord: my sore ran in the night, and ceased not: my soul refused to be comforted" (Psalm 77:2).

Have you ever sought to console another in the time of sorrow or suffering, only to be chided or ignored? It is a futile effort and brings sore grief. Spurgeon says, "One man can lead a horse to the water, but a thousand cannot make him drink if he will not; and when a man in trouble refuses to be comforted, then lover and friend are put far from him, and his acquaintance into darkness."[346]

The psalmist, despite seeking comfort from God, refused it when it was supplied (Psalm 77:2). How foolish! Why are people unwilling to be comforted?

Is it due to anger with God over the death of a loved one? Is it due to their seemingly endless suffering or sickness? Protracted illness or suffering or distress has stifled any hope of improvement. Is it due to hardheartedness toward God for not granting quicker relief, remedy, or rescue? Is it that sin is enjoyed to the degree that the absence of peace seems better than denial of the sin?

Whyte says, "You do not really care for God's mercy or His comfort either, so long as you live in any sin. And it is well that you do not; for you can have neither. Your peace will be like a river when you put away your sin; but not one word of true peace, not one drop of true comfort, can you have till then."[347] Whatever may be the reason for refusing God's consolation, "refuse not to be comforted, I pray you; you are only driving the dagger deeper and deeper into your wounds. You are making the bitter waters more bitter."[348]

"One way to get comfort is to plead the promise of God in prayer, show Him His handwriting; God is tender of His Word."
                              Thomas Manton

July 17

Peace (Part One)

"Peace I leave with you, my peace I give unto you: not as the world giveth, give I unto you" (John 14:27).

Source. When He departed to Heaven, Jesus left the saint a prized gift. It's a gift that protected Him in a thousand battles, calmed Him in persecution, prevented His anxiety in trouble, consoled Him in grief, enabled His tranquil composure in pain and suffering, granted Him contentment in adversity, and granted Him solace in dying. The gift is that of His peace ("My peace I give unto you").

MacArthur says, "No individual without Jesus Christ can ever have peace, and no world without God can ever know peace."[349] Wiersbe says, "Psychologists talk about 'peace of mind,' but Christ, through His death, resurrection, and ascension, gives 'peace with God' (Romans 5:1)."[350] C. S. Lewis remarked, "God cannot give us a happiness and peace apart from Himself, because it is not there. There is no such thing."[351] "Know God; know peace—no God, no peace."

Supply. "He has opened for the believer sources of tranquility and joy amidst all the calamities and afflictions of life."[352]

Scope. Possessors of this peace know quietude in trouble, serenity in sorrow, placidness in suffering and sickness, and solace in death. Joseph Irons said, "No wonder that a Christian man has peace when he carries the title deeds of Heaven in his bosom!"

"If God be our God, He will give us peace in trouble. When there is a storm without, He will make peace within. The world can create trouble in peace, but God can create peace in trouble."[353]
Thomas Watson

July 18

Peace (Part Two)

"Peace I leave with you, my peace I give unto you: not as the world giveth, give I unto you" (John 14:27).

Surety. Spurgeon says the saint's peace "is not built upon a pleasing fiction of his imagination, a delusive dream of his ignorance; but it is built on facts, on positive truths, on essential verities; it is founded upon a rock, and though the rains descend, and the winds blow, and the floods beat upon that house, it shall not fall, because its foundation is secure. When a man hath faith in the blood of Christ, there is but little wonder that he hath peace, for indeed he is fully warranted in enjoying the most profound calm which mortal heart can know."[354]

Superiority. "Not as the world giveth, give I unto you." The world's peace is hollow, frail, and empty, devoid of power to calm and comfort. God's peace is the only true and effectual peace. The peace of God is invaluable. Matthew Henry said, "Peace is such a precious jewel that I would give anything for it but truth."[355] It's worth all you have to buy it, but it's not something one can purchase. It's available freely to all that request it through the riches of God in Christ Jesus (John 1:12).

Solicitation. Paul says, "Don't worry about anything; instead, pray about everything; tell God your needs, and don't forget to thank him for his answers. If you do this, you will experience God's peace, which is far more wonderful than the human mind can understand. His peace will keep your thoughts and your hearts quiet and at rest as you trust in Christ Jesus" (Philippians 4:6–7 TLB). Although its Christ's peace, it is dispensed by the Holy Spirit to the troubled soul. It's His work to take the things of Christ and give them to us (John 16:14).[356]

Therefore, in times of adversity or infirmity, cry out to the Holy Spirit for Christ's calm, comfort, and consolation. MacArthur comments, "If we lay hold of the promise of the very peace of Christ, we will have calm, untroubled hearts, regardless of external circumstances."[357]

"No confidence that a man can have in his own powers, no reliance which he can repose on his own plans or on the promises or fidelity of his fellow men, and no calculations which he can make on the course of events can impart such peace to the soul as simple confidence in God."
Albert Barnes

July 19

The Pillars of Faith

"Yes, the word of the Lord is right, and everything he does is trustworthy" (Psalm 33:4 EHV).

Faith (trust, confidence) in God to help in time of need is built upon five unshakeable pillars.

1. God's lovingkindness (Jeremiah 31:3). God's love encompasses the believer, constantly bearing assurances of His steadfast concern and control.

2. God's faithfulness (Psalm 119:90). Regardless of what happens (good or bad), God is dependable and trustworthy to sustain and keep us safe.

July

3. God's promises (Joshua 21:45). All that He promised will come to pass according to His timetable.

4. God's manifestation (1 Corinthians 12:7). Christ manifests Himself to believers in a way in which He is not manifested to the world. How? Through times in which an awesome and unusual awareness of His presence is felt, divine illumination is received, and Scripture verses blossom and unravel as never before.

5. God's sovereignty (Isaiah 46:10). The Christian's life is divinely orchestrated and ordered by God. That which He orders will come to pass (Lamentations 3:37). "The steps of a good man are ordered by the LORD" (Psalm 37:23).

The five foundational doctrines of the church are known as the five *sola*s: *Sola Gratia*—"grace alone"; *Sola Fide*—"faith alone"; *Solus Christus*—"Christ alone"; *Sola Scriptura*—"Scripture alone"; *Soli Deo Gloria*—"to the glory of God alone." Christians are saved by grace alone, through faith alone, by Christ alone, as declared in Scripture alone, to the glory of God alone.

"We have been given the peace of Jesus Christ. Even though I might not understand what's going on, I have a peace that bypasses my brain and permeates my heart. I might not know why things aren't working out or why things are coming down. But in the midst of it all, Jesus offers me His peace."[358]

Jon Courson

July 20

Are the Consolations of God Too Small?

"Are the consolations of God small with thee?" (Job 15:11).

This is the question of every man who knows hardship and heartache. Is the comfort that God supplies in the midst of bodily suffering, incurable illness, grievous sorrow, and excruciating trouble enough? If it is too small, why is it?

It is not because of the lack of a bountiful supply. Innumerable consolations are proffered and promised in the Holy Scriptures to all who will believe and receive. Therefore, if the consolations of God be found too small and inefficient to calm and console the bleeding and hurting heart, its man's fault, not God's.

What reasons prompt a man to count God's consolations too small to help?

1. *The consolations of God are Undervalued.* Failure to recognize and acknowledge the greatness of the divine consolations prompts indifference to them.

2. *The Consolations of God are Untried.* Man finds the consolations of God inadequate to calm and comfort because of an unwillingness to put them to the test. "Taste and see that the Lord is good. Oh, the joys of those who take refuge in him!" (Psalm 34:8 NLT).

3. *The consolations of God are Unpreferred.* The comfort of God's consolations are limited when we prefer the consolations of man (human resources) above His.

4. *The consolations of God are Unknown.* Ignorance of the vastness and riches of the consolations of God prompts dismissing them as insufficient.

5. *The consolations of God are Unsought.* James rightly says, "Ye have not, because ye ask not" (James 4:2).

6. *The consolations of God are Unsuccessful.* Impatience with affliction or infirmity and disappointment over a slow resolution prompt a person to count the consolations of God as insufficient.

All reasons for counting God's consolations as inadequate (too small) are slanderous and inexcusable, as is failure to depend upon them in the dark night of trial. To discount or belittle the consolations of God is to speak contrary to God's nature, God's Word, and human experience. Rely upon them, rest in them, and be refreshed by them.

"The consolations of God not being small in themselves, it is very lamentable if they are small with us. It is a great affront to God, and evidence of a degenerate depraved mind to disesteem and undervalue spiritual delights."[359]
Matthew Henry

July 21

Haunting Fears
"Say to them that are of a fearful heart, Be strong, fear not" (Isaiah 35:4).

The Face of Fear. Some fears are healthy and helpful, such as avoiding the edge of a cliff or playing with snakes. Equally, there are hurtful and hindering fears that paralyze, pain, perplex, and pulverize. Are they mastering you presently? If so, what are they specifically? What fears make you shake in your boots and cower? Is it the fear of a negative medical diagnosis? The fear of loneliness? The fear of death? The fear of eternal separation from God and loved ones? The fear of launching out afresh following the death of a loved one or after bitter failure and defeat?

The Father of Fear. A. B. Simpson said, "Fear is born of Satan, and if we would only take time to think a moment, we would see that everything Satan says is founded upon a falsehood."

The Folly of Fear. The most frequent command in the Bible is "Do not be afraid. Do not fear." To fear is to sin; it violates hundreds of God's commands. Fear in its nature is the manifestation of mistrust in God to care for you.

The Fester of Fear. Fears left unattended to fester into dominating fears which are difficult to escape. Elijah's fear of Jezebel led to his flight into the wilderness. Unsettled, it then led to depression and desire to die (1 Kings 19:4).

The Fruit of Fear. It paralyzes progress, jeopardizes health, terrorizes the mind, and demoralizes the soul.

The Freedom from Fear. The antidote to fear is trust in God and His many promises.

The Fate of Fear. Though fear couches at every saint's door, the time is coming when it will be eradicated (Revelation 21:4).

"Faith, which is trust, and fear are opposite poles. If a man has the one, he can scarcely have the other in vigorous operation. He that has his trust set upon God does not need to dread anything except the weakening or the paralyzing of that trust."
        Alexander Maclaren

July 22

The Days Should Speak (Part One)
"Days should speak" (Job 32:7a).

The days of our lives should speak of grace in the past. Grace is the book ends of the Christian's life. "Grace is my story from salvation to glory."

Life is full of sin, failure, and wasted opportunities, all covered by the blood of Jesus Christ. Paul underscores this point by saying, "Do not be deceived: neither the sexually immoral, nor idolaters, nor adulterers, nor men who practice homosexuality, nor thieves, nor the greedy, nor drunkards, nor revilers, nor swindlers will inherit the kingdom of God. And *such were some of you*. But you were washed, you were sanctified, you were justified in the name of the Lord Jesus Christ and by the Spirit of our God" (1 Corinthians 6:9–11 ESV).

Every devoted follower of Christ joins Newton in declaring, "I am not what I ought to be, I am not what I want to be, I am not what I hope to be in another world; but still I am not what I once used to be, and by the grace of God I am what I am."[360] We humbly, and with the greatest of gratitude for the grace received, say with Bradford, "There but for the grace of God go I" as we look out upon the lifestyle of the wicked and ungodly. Lucado says, "The meaning of life, the wasted years of life, the poor choices of life—God answers the mess of life with one word: 'grace.'"

"When we sin and mess up our lives, we find that God doesn't go off and leave us—he enters into our trouble and saves us."
Eugene Patterson

July 23

The Days Should Speak (Part Two)
"Days should speak" (Job 32:7a).

The days of our lives should speak of grace today. Grace not only wrought freedom from sin's chains and shackles yesterday, but it also works today to accomplish deliverance in the believer's life from sin's power to bring defeat, despair, and defilement. "Through many dangers, toils, and snares, I have already come; 'tis grace hath brought me safe thus far, and grace will lead me home."

The days of our lives should speak of grace in the future when the body of decay and sin will be replaced with an incorruptible body and we will be transitioned to our Home in Heaven. And the way that the days of our lives can speak of this is by singing of Heaven, preaching about Heaven, talking about Heaven, and, yes, writing about Heaven. "Sing the wondrous love of Jesus; sing His mercy and His grace. In the mansions bright and blessed, He'll prepare for us a place."

Jonathan Edwards asserts, "Grace is but glory begun, and glory is but grace perfected." Martyn Lloyd-Jones comments, "It is grace at the beginning and grace at the end. So that when you and I come to lie upon our deathbeds, the one thing that should comfort and help and strengthen us there is the thing that helped us in the beginning. Not what we have been, not what we have done, but the Grace of God in Jesus Christ our Lord. The Christian life starts with grace, it must continue with grace, and it ends with grace. Grace, wondrous grace—by the grace of God, I am what I am, yet not I, but the Grace of God which was with me."

"Grace is free sovereign favor to the ill-deserving."
Benjamin B. Warfield

July 24

Profitability of Scripture

"All scripture is given by inspiration of God, and is profitable for doctrine, for reproof, for correction, for instruction in righteousness: that the man of God may be perfect, thoroughly furnished unto all good works" (2 Timothy 3:16–17).

All of the Scripture (its every component in both the Old and New Testaments) is profitable in a four-fold way to enable the Christian to execute his four-fold duty: "preach the word…reprove, rebuke, exhort" (2 Timothy 4:2), and the believer to live righteously.

Scripture is profitable in teaching what is right (truth about salvation, Heaven, Hell, Judgment, Second Coming, Trinity, eternity, morality). Scripture is profitable in refuting what is not right (theological error, wrong thoughts, and beliefs). Scripture is profitable in setting things that are wrong right (convinces of and destroys heretical views, and does the same with sinful conduct). Scripture is profitable in training to *do* what is right (righteousness, honor, holiness).

"No Scripture is exhausted by a single explanation. The flowers of God's Garden bloom not only double, but sevenfold; they are continually pouring forth fresh fragrance."
       C. H. Spurgeon

July 25

A Coming Rest (Part One)
"There remaineth therefore a rest to the people of God" (Hebrews 4:9).

A parallel is made between the Israelites' exodus from Egypt, wilderness wandering, and entrance into Canaan, and the life of the redeemed believer (Hebrews 3:1–4:10). Moses was the Israelites' deliverer from the cruel Egyptian bondage; Jesus Christ is the believers' Deliverer from the bondage of sin through His atoning work at Calvary (Ephesians 1:7). The Israelites wandered in the wilderness for forty years, awaiting the time for the promised rest in Canaan (Hebrews 4:7); the believer sojourns in the wilderness of widespread antagonism to their faith, facing hardship and weariness, while awaiting their eternal rest in Heaven (1 Peter 1:17; 1 Peter 2:11). The Israelites that believed God (exhibited faith) crossed over Jordan into the promised land of rest and plenty (Hebrews 3:16–20); genuine believers in Christ Jesus will either by death or His return enter into their heavenly rest (Hebrews 4:1–3). Paul describes this coming utopia of eternal rest in Romans 8:19–23.

The excellence of the rest is indescribable.

It is a patterned rest. The rest of God's people is modeled after the traditional sabbath.[361] God rested on the Sabbath (Genesis 2:2; Hebrews 4:10) and commanded His people to do likewise (Exodus 20:8). It was for His children a time of cessation of labor (Exodus 16:30) and engagement in worship (Leviticus 23:3). It symbolizes, but not fully, the eternal rest for the child of God in Heaven.

It is a purchased rest. Paul says that this eternal rest is the purchased possession of God, the believer's everlasting inheritance (Ephesians 1:14). Calvary makes it possible, and Calvary alone. Therefore, it belongs only to him who belongs to Christ Jesus through the new birth (John 3:3).

It is a prepared rest. "There remaineth therefore a rest." It exists now but is a future rest. It will be manifest later upon entrance into Heaven. Delitzch says, "The final Sabbath will not, therefore, be realized

July

till time is swallowed up of eternity and mortality of life. It will be the eternal conclusion of the week of time, as seven is the numeric symbol of perfection and rest."[362]

"Jesus Himself, and Captain of our salvation, notwithstanding all that fulness of grace and strength that dwells in Him, will not, cannot give to final unbelievers either spiritual or eternal rest. It remains only for the people of God; others by their sin abandon themselves to eternal restlessness."[363]
Matthew Henry

July 26

A Coming Rest (Part Two)
"There remaineth therefore a rest to the people of God" (Hebrews 4:9).

It is a promised rest. The rest is a certainty, for He that promised it cannot lie (Numbers 23:19; Titus 1:2). Multitudes of saints are presently experiencing that rest, and soon we shall join them.

It is a peaceful rest. It is a rest from hardship, pain, anxiety, sickness, disappointment, persecution, temptation, sin, evil, care, and sorrow. John, in describing the rest, writes, "And God shall wipe away all tears from their eyes; and there shall be no more death, neither sorrow, nor crying, neither shall there be any more pain: for the former things are passed away" (Revelation 21:4).

Due to frailty, affliction, sorrow, or infirmity, you may presently agree with Talleyrand, who wrote in his journal on his eighty-third birthday, "Life is a long fatigue."[364] If so, I bear great uplifting news. Beyond the veil of this life of trouble and heartache awaits a land flowing with milk, honey, and blissful rest. "Weary eyes droop, weary shoulders bend, weary hands tremble, weary feet drag heavily along, weary brows burn, weary hearts faint everywhere."[365] But these very eyes that droop, shoulders that bend, hands that tremble, feet that stagger, and hearts that faint will be gloriously transfigured and renewed upon entering Heaven's domain of eternal rest.

It is a perfect rest. All those in Heaven are thoroughly at rest, not partially. Spurgeon states, "There, all are at rest; they have attained the summit of the mountain; they have ascended to the bosom of their God. Higher they cannot go. Ah, toil-worn laborer, only think when thou shalt rest forever! Canst thou conceive it? It is a rest eternal, a rest that 'remaineth.' Here, my best joys bear 'mortal' on their brow, my fair flowers fade, my dainty cups are drained to dregs, my sweetest birds fall before Death's arrows, my most pleasant days are shadowed into nights, and the floodtides of my bliss subside into ebbs of sorrow; but there, everything is immortal. The harp abides unrusted, the crown unwithered, the eye undimmed, the voice unfaltering, the heart unwavering; and the immortal being is wholly absorbed in infinite delight. Happy day! happy! when mortality shall be swallowed up of life, and the Eternal Sabbath shall begin."[366]

"There is a land where everlasting suns shed everlasting brightness, where the soul drinks from the living streams of love that roll by God's high throne! Myriads of glorious ones bring their accepted offerings there. Oh! how blest to look from this dark prison to that shrine, to inhale one breath of Paradise divine, and enter into that eternal rest which unites the sons of God." [367]

Sir John Bowring

July 27

A Coming Rest (Part Three)

"There remaineth therefore a rest to the people of God" (Hebrews 4:9).

It is a plenteous rest. God's provision of eternal rest is totally complete and tranquil. The rest provided is that which He manifests (Hebrews 4:10); it is Divine in nature and absolute in possession. In Heaven, we rest in the rest of God (Hebrews 4:3). Therefore, there is no way it can be unpleasing or insufficient.

It is a perpetual rest. Jesus said, "And I give unto them eternal life; and they shall never perish" (John 10:28). Unlike the Sabbath presently that lasts only a day, the rest for the believer in Heaven is perpetual, never-ending. Hallelujah!

It is a praising rest. In Heaven, the believer will rest in utter gratefulness to Jesus that made it possible through His vicarious suffering and death at Calvary. John says, "Because of this, they are before the throne of God. They worship him day and night in his temple. And the One who sits on the throne will be present with them" (Revelation 7:15 NCV).

It is a peculiar rest. W. W. Westcott comments, "We make a great mistake if we connect with our conception of Heaven the thought of rest from work. Rest from toil, from weariness, from exhaustion—yes; rest from work, from productiveness, from service—no. 'They serve God day and night.'"³⁶⁸ Rest is not depleted in the least by Heaven's toil.

It is a possessed rest. The Israelites would have to cross over Jordan to possess the promised rest in Canaan; saints must likewise cross the chilly Jordan of death to gain this rest in Heaven. The instant the saint breathes the last breath here, his eternal delight in God's rest begins in Heaven's fair land. Presently, Jesus bids all that need rest from the cares of this life to come to Him. With open arms, He says, "Come unto me, all ye that labor and are heavy laden, and I will give you rest. Take my yoke upon you, and learn of me; for I am meek and lowly in heart: and ye shall find *rest unto your souls*" (Matthew 11:28–29). It is a calming rest, a taste of the rest that awaits in Glory.

"Has this world been so kind to you that you should leave with regret? There are better things ahead than any we leave behind."
C. S. Lewis

July 28

Soul Winning

"In the morning sow thy seed, and in the evening withhold not thine hand: for thou knowest not whether shall prosper, either this or that, or whether they both shall be alike good" (Ecclesiastes 11:6).

Soul winning is a habitual work. It is to be done "in season, out of season." It is always in season. Saith Spurgeon, "We have enough of Christian garnishing, but solid, every day, actual work for God is what we need."³⁶⁹ Soul winning is not to be done in "fits and starts," but with consistency.

Soul winning is a hard work. The labor for men's souls meets with stern resistance, opposition, and discouragement. All of Hell rises to thwart the soul winner's effort. It takes blood, sweat and tears to battle and conquer.

Soul winning is a hasty work. Solomon states, "He that gathereth in summer is a wise son: but he that sleepeth in harvest is a son that causeth shame" (Proverbs 10:5). Why is it a shame to sleep in harvest time? Because the harvest will not wait. It will rot on the stalks unless hastily harvested into the barn. Delay in soul winning and harvesting means the eternal doom of multitudes. Oh, "Awake thou that sleepest" to the cry of the harvest, to the cries of the eternally dammed (Ephesians 5:14).

Soul winning is an honorable work. "He that winneth souls is wise" (Proverbs 11:30). The Bible never says that he that preaches, sings, or teaches is wise, but the man that winneth souls is thus described.

Soul winning is a heart work. Spurgeon says, "I believe that much of the secret of soul winning lies in having bowels of compassion, in having spirits that can be touched with the feeling of human infirmities."[370]

Soul winning is a happy work. To witness a life shackled to the chains of sin set free by the power of God is the greatest joy on earth. It is incomparable. The psalmist states, "They that sow in tears, shall reap in joy" (Psalm 126:5).

Soul winning is a harvest work. Witnessing is the sowing of the precious seed of the Gospel. But soul winning is the harvesting of that seed into the barn (salvation).

Soul winning is a holy work. John "Praying" Hyde said, "Holiness precedes soul winning." God uses only clean instruments in the harvest field (Psalm 139:23–24).

"Look on soul winning as a business, not an incidental matter; as work, not play; as time well spent, not wasted; as a privilege, not a boresome duty."
R. G. Lee

July 29

Confession of Christ

"Whosoever therefore shall confess Me before men, him will I confess also before My Father which is in Heaven" (Matthew 10:32).

Peter confessed Jesus to be the Christ, the Son of the Living God (Matthew 16:16). Nathanael confessed, "You are the Son of God! You are the King of Israel!" (John 1:49 ESV). Martha confessed, "I believe that You are the Christ, the Son of God" (John 11:27 ESV). Thomas confessed saying, "My Lord and my God" (John 20:28). Christian confession is necessary for four reasons.

To receive Christ. Without the confession that Jesus is Lord (Savior, ruler, Master), there is no resulting salvation (Romans 10:9).

To reveal Christ. In confession, the saint declares the deity of Christ that certifies and authenticates His mission to save man from their sins. Hear Paul's confession of Christ: "Christ was revealed in a human body and vindicated by the Spirit. He was seen by angels and announced to the nations. He was believed in throughout the world and taken to heaven in glory" (1 Timothy 3:16 NLT). And, second, the saint reveals acceptance of Christ as Lord and Savior. Sincere confession affirms salvation to the world (1 John 4:2; Matthew 10:32).

To revere Christ. Failing to confess Christ openly and boldly, such as Peter did thrice, is to dethrone Him and disown Him. The Christian is to exalt, honor and reverence Christ by the confession of life and lip that He is Lord. Matthew Henry states, "It is our duty, not only to believe in Christ, but to profess that faith. We must never be ashamed of our relation to Christ, our attendance on Him, and our expectations from Him. Hereby the sincerity of our faith is evidenced, His name glorified, and others edified."[371]

To resemble Christ. Paul states that "Christ Jesus...before Pontius Pilate witnessed a good confession" (1 Timothy 6:13). When Pilate asked, "Are you the King of the Jews," Jesus answered, "It is as you say" (Luke 23:3 NKJV). Even under the threat of torturous death, Jesus didn't walk back His confession. Let us walk in His steps.

"It is probably true that far more people deny Jesus Christ by cowardly silence than by deliberate words."[372]
William Barclay

July 30

Three Kinds of People

"And I, brethren, could not speak unto you as unto spiritual, but as unto carnal, even as unto babes in Christ" (1 Corinthians 3:1).

There are three kinds of people (1 Corinthians 2:14–3:1).

The natural man is he who is dead in trespasses and sin and blind to either the reality or need of Christ.

The carnal man, though saved, lives a life centered on the appetites of the flesh, to the neglect of that which is spiritual. Disobedient, thus dwarfed, this believer fails to grow, mature, or develop spiritually. He is a defeated Christian, not knowing the victory that walking under the control of the Holy Spirit enables. He is dependent upon another to do what he cannot or will not do spiritually for himself—like a baby's dependency upon a parent. Further, the carnal Christian is a disappointing Christian, failing to live up to God's design. Sadly, many believers fit into this category.

The spiritual man is the believer who lives under the control and dominion of the Holy Spirit. This believer continuously crucifies the lusts of the flesh, the lust of the eyes, and the pride of life, denying self to the obedience and pleasure of the Lord.

With which type do you identify?

"If you have not chosen the Kingdom of God first, it will, in the end, make no difference what you have chosen instead."
William Law

July 31

Raising Globally Mission-Minded Kids

"Bring up a child by teaching him the way he should go" (Proverbs 22:6 NLV).

Parents must instill in their children a global mission-mindedness that will impassion them to serve as a vocational or volunteer foreign missionary when they are of age. How can this be done?

Explanation of the Great Commission. Teach your child that the "go" in the Great Commission is a command that applies to all believers, including them. Bill Bright said, "There is no higher calling or greater privilege known to man than being involved in helping fulfill the Great Commission."

Parental Example. Interest in and concern for the unsaved in foreign lands is created and fueled by being displayed by parents. Though the missionary heart ought to be taught, it is more often caught. Sadly, only one percent of Americans have engaged in missionary trips as a family.[373]

Missionary Biographies. Place in the hands of your child stories of missionaries like Adoniram Judson (Burma), William Carey (India), David Brainerd (the American Indians), and Hudson Taylor (China) to infuse passion for the lost and incite openness to missionary service.

July

Missionary Pen Pals. Connect your child with the son or daughter of a missionary sent out from your church with whom they can communicate as a pen pal.

Family Prayer for Missionaries. At mealtime, pray specifically for a missionary by name as well as the people group they serve. On a globe, show the location of the country. SBC Virginia provides "52 Sundays" that may be adapted for this purpose.[374]

Entertain Missionaries. Invite missionaries into the home or to a restaurant for the purpose of interaction with your children.

Local Age-Appropriate Missions. Involve your child in mission work at the downtown rescue mission, food bank, or homeless shelter. Enlist them to assist the church in raising funds to supply the needs of missionaries (Bibles, food, clothing, radios, etc.).

Support Them. Fan the flame of interest and concern for missions; encourage their involvement.

Intercessory Prayer. Pray unceasingly that your child will mirror God's heart for the world and be ready to go when divinely summoned.

"We must be global Christians with a global vision because our God is a global God."
John Stott

August 1

The Stone Was Rolled Away (Part One)

"And they found the stone rolled away" (Luke 24:2).

The resurrection of Jesus rolled away the stone of things that block man's faith.

The stone of doubt was rolled away. The resurrection erodes skepticism by establishing and substantiating the truth and authority of Christianity. With Jesus' resurrection, uncertainty about and refutation of His deity and divine mission (the crux of the Christian faith) are removed and doubts about His ability to keep His promises are erased. If He could keep the promise of John 2:19: "Destroy this temple, and in three days I will raise it up," all others will be kept.

The stone was not rolled away to let Jesus out but to let us look in. The case for the resurrection of Christ has over 500 eyewitnesses consisting of believers and unbelievers alike, verifying that Jesus is the Son of God, not a noble martyr or fraud or liar. "The resurrection of Jesus Christ from the dead," states Spurgeon, "is one of the best-attested facts on record. There were so many witnesses to behold it, that if we do in the least degree receive the credibility of men's testimonies, we cannot and we dare not doubt that Jesus rose from the dead."

The stone of despair was rolled away. The resurrection removes the fear and terror of death, replacing it with peace and hope. It is God's pledge that death will not hold the body prisoner (1 Corinthians 15:19–21). Spurgeon said, "The key is taken from the girdle of death and is held in the hand of the Prince of Life. As Peter, when visited by the angel, found his chains fall from him, while iron gates opened to him of their own accord, so shall the saints find ready escape at the resurrection morning."[375] He continues, "This is noble encouragement to all the saints; die they must, but rise they shall, to everlasting life. Christ's resurrection is the cause, the earnest, the guarantee, and the emblem of the rising of all His people."[376] There will be a resurrection "both of the just and unjust" (Acts 24:15)

"There is more evidence that Jesus rose from the dead than there is that Julius Caesar ever lived or that Alexander the Great died at the age of thirty-three."[377]

Billy Graham

August 2

The Stone Was Rolled Away (Part Two)
"And they found the stone rolled away" (Luke 24:2).

The stone of doom was rolled away. Eternal separation from Holy God in Hell was man's just desert and punishment for sin. It was in every man's future. "But," says Paul, "God commendeth His love toward us, in that, while we were yet sinners, Christ died for us" (Romans 5:8). In compassionate love God sent His only son, Jesus, on a redemptive mission to earth to make it possible for man to escape from Hell and gain Heaven through His atoning death at Calvary and triumphant resurrection on Easter (acquittal and justification).

The stone of the Devil's domination was rolled away. Satan and sin's stranglehold on man's soul was destroyed at the cross and empty tomb. Christ is Victor! The resurrection provided deliverance not only from the power and penalty of sin but the chains and shackles of its captivity.

Paul says, "For if we have been united with him in a death like his, we shall certainly be united with him in a resurrection like his. We know that our old self was crucified with him in order that the body of sin might be brought to nothing, so that we would no longer be enslaved to sin. For one who has died has been set free from sin" (Romans 6:5–7 ESV). "He breaks the power of canceled sin; He sets the prisoner free."

The stone of debated Scripture was rolled away. Biblical prophecies about the Messiah's death and subsequent resurrection were fulfilled to the letter in Jesus, giving irrefutable documentation that He is the Messiah and the Bible is the inspired Word of God.

Praise God that when the stone was rolled away from the tomb of Jesus, it simultaneously was rolled away from man's doubt, despair, and doom, the Devil's domination, and debated Scripture.

"The bodily resurrection of Jesus Christ from the dead is the crowning proof of Christianity. If the resurrection did not take place, then Christianity is a false religion. If it did take place, then Christ is God and the Christian faith is absolute truth."

Henry M. Morris

August 3

Readiness to Suffer

"I am ready" (Romans 1:15).

The Holy Spirit testified to Paul that "in every city...imprisonment and persecutions" were waiting for him (Acts 20:23; Acts 9:16 NRSV). (How about hearing that as a young preacher starting out?) Undaunted by the news, Paul said in Romans 1:15, "I am ready" (a statement specifically regarding going to Rome with the Gospel but applicable to every hostile venue). And history proves that he was "ready" in mind and soul.

Girded with the Word of God and the Sword of the Spirit, as well as the rest of the armor of God (Ephesians 6:10–18), he boldly withstood the adversity and affliction that came with the territory as a minister of God. Paul may have used the words "I am ready" as his life's motto; if so, it would have been most fitting. Whether in the synagogue or the palace; among the Pharisees or Sadducees; with Felix or Agrippa; in jail, under house arrest in Rome, or upon a ship, he stood always ready. Paul's readiness (not just expectation of hardship) to suffer kept him in the ministry (2 Timothy 2:3).

What helped Paul be ready to suffer without fainting? Answers Spurgeon, "He belonged to Christ; he was Jesus Christ's branded slave, and he was absolutely at Christ's disposal. Moreover, he had such trust in his Lord that he felt, "whatever He does with me, it will be good and kind, and therefore I will make no condition; I will have no reserve from Him. It is the Lord; let Him do what seemeth him good." He had resolved to serve his Lord; and therefore, if he had to be bound or to die, he would not shrink back."[378]

Likewise, be ye ready to stand firm and immoveable in the faith. "Say 'Yes' before your fears have time to shape 'No.' Say 'No' before your inclinations have time to whisper 'Yes.'"[379]

"It takes away a thousand ills if we are ready for service, ready for suffering, ready to die."[380]

C. H. Spurgeon

August 4

The Bridge That Christ Built

"For there is one God, and one mediator between God and men, the man Christ Jesus" (1 Timothy 2:5).

The Mackinac Bridge, spanning five miles, connects the upper and lower peninsulas of Michigan. Its construction required 85,000 blueprints, 3,500 workers, 1,016,600 bolts, and nearly 1,000,000 tons of concrete. Why such undertakings to build bridges like this one? The answer: Getting from point A to point B is worth the pain to gain.

This is why Jesus, with His atoning death at Calvary, built a bridge across the eternal chasm (caused by sin) that separates man from God (Galatians 1:3–4). Christ built the bridge to rightness (justification, reconciliation) with God (Romans 5:10), home in Heaven (John 14:1–4), joy in despair (Psalm 30:11; Psalm 16:11), peace in affliction and adversity (John 14:27; Philippians 4:7), comfort in grief and sorrow (Psalm 73:26), hope in hopelessness and despair (Ephesians 1:18), meaningfulness in emptiness (John 10:10; John 4:13–14), freedom from bondage (John 8:36), strength in weakness (2 Corinthians 12:9), victory in defeat (1 John 5:4; 1 John 1:9), and everlasting life in death (John 11:25–26).

This bridge is invincible and durable (Matthew 7:24–27), always able to withstand the blasts of Hell, the antagonism and attack of man, the storms of life, and death itself. Access to it is totally free, with no hidden tolls (Ephesians 2:18; Romans 5:2), to all that know Christ personally as Lord and Savior (John 3:3). Spurgeon says, "The bridge of grace will bear your weight, brother. Thousands of big sinners have gone across that bridge, yea, tens of thousands have gone over it. Some have been the chief of sinners, and some have come at the very last of their days, but the arch has never yielded beneath their weight."

Travelers upon this bridge of salvation are to be its "connectors" to them that are perishing in sin. The children's book *King Nimrod's Tower* tells the story of a boy watching the building of the Tower of Babel. It closes with these words: "The people didn't realize that the kingdom of Heaven is reached by a bridge, not by a tower." Most people still don't.

"Only by being both deity and humanity could Jesus Christ bridge the gap between where God is."
David Jeremiah

August 5

For Future Generations

"One generation shall praise thy works to another, and shall declare thy mighty acts" (Psalm 145:4).

Each generation amasses "fresh" witnesses (testimony, insight and knowledge) to the glory and honor and goodness of God that must be preserved for future generations. Horne states, "As one generation" drops it, 'another' should take it up and prolong the delightful strain till the sun and the moon shall withdraw their light, and the stars fall extinguished from their orbs."[381]

The passing down from generation to generation the mighty doings of God (miracles, awakenings, and deliverances) is the primary mode cited in Scripture whereby such knowledge continues unabated through the ages.[382] Pope says, "It has pleased God to make every generation a trustee for the generations to come."[383]

The receipt of gospel truth which was handed down to us, granting deliverance from the penalty of sin, places us under divine obligation to pass it on to the next generation. Saith Spurgeon, "Our negligent silence must not deprive our own and our father's offspring of the precious truth of God."[384]

Parents are to instill biblical truth into the hearts of their children and their children's children (Deuteronomy 6:7). Politicians are to insure the continuance of biblical values, policies, principles, and laws, as well as religious freedom. Bible colleges and seminaries are to retain and maintain biblical integrity and evangelistic fervor in the instruction and training of ministers. Religious authors must be theologically accurate in writing about the attributes, Word, and works of God. Multiplied harvest workers must be raised up, trained, and thrust out into the mission fields around the world (Matthew 9:37–38).

All this must be done "so that the death of God's worshippers shall be no diminution of His worship, for a new generation shall rise up in their room to carry on that good work, more or less, to the end of time."[385]

"Time is short, and it behooves each one to be working for his Lord, that when he is called home, he may leave behind him something for the generations following."[386]

C. H. Spurgeon

August 6

Encouragement (Part One)

"But God, who encourages those who are discouraged, encouraged us by the arrival of Titus" (2 Corinthians 7:6 NLT).

By what means does the Lord encourage and comfort?

By His steadfast love. "May your unfailing love be my comfort, according to your promise to your servant" (Psalm 119:76 NIV). The awareness that God's love for us is unchanging despite our circumstances and sins brings solace, calm, cheer, and hope to the soul in the darkest times.

By His inspired writing in the Bible. Myriads of saints have been delivered from the agony of despondency by reflection upon the Psalms of David, the trials and deliverances of the prophets, and the promises and the teachings of the Gospels and epistles. "The worst forms of depression," Spurgeon said, "are cured when Holy Scripture is believed."[387]

By communion with Him. Peter exhorts, "Casting all your care [anxiety, worry] upon him; for he careth for you" (1 Peter 5:7). Spurgeon advises the despondent: "You have heard it said that when a pump is dry, you must pour water down it first of all, and then you will get some up. So, Christian, when thou art dry, go to thy God, ask Him to pour some joy down thee, and then thou wilt get more joy up from thine own heart."[388]

By entering the house of the Lord. David, in the time of deepest sorrow, the death of his child, found comfort in the sanctuary (2 Samuel 12:20). The sermon, song, and sweet fellowship with the saints are rich, soothing medicine for the troubled soul. The distraught testify, "I was glad when they said unto me, let us go into the house of the LORD" (Psalm 122:1).

By the ministry of the Holy Spirit. "But the Comforter, which is the Holy Ghost" (John 14:26). "The Comforter" means literally one who is called to the side of another to render help. The Holy Spirit abides with the believer constantly, providing consolation in times of need.

"A helping word to one in trouble is often like a switch on a railroad track—an inch between wreck and smooth, rolling prosperity."
Henry Ward Beecher

August 7

Encouragement (Part Two)

"But God, who encourages those who are discouraged, encouraged us by the arrival of Titus" (2 Corinthians 7:6 NLT).

By that which His hands hath made. "The heavens declare the glory of God, and the sky above proclaims his handiwork. Day to day pours out speech, and night to night reveals knowledge" (Psalm 19:1–2 ESV). Spurgeon says, "Any part of creation has more instruction in it than the human mind will ever exhaust."[389]

A stroll in the museum of nature observing its magnificent majesty—the birds singing, the butterflies fluttering, the flowers blossoming, the bees buzzing, the stars shining in the dark night, the purple mountains' majesty, the roaring ocean, the magnificent waterfalls, and the babbling brook—speaks peace to the troubled breast, providing tranquility.

By the saints. Paul exhorts: "So encourage each other and build each other up" (1 Thessalonians 5:11 NLT). God encourages the believer through the letters, emails, phone calls, visits, and writings of others. Titus was used as an instrument in God's hand to encourage Paul in the time of his discouragement (2 Corinthians 7:6). He used Jonathan to encourage David in his despondency in the woods (1 Samuel 23:16). He used Barnabas to encourage John Mark following his desertion from the missionary team (Acts 15:39), and later John Mark did the same for Paul, (2 Timothy 4:11).

Be a sensitive instrument in the Lord's hand, like them, to render an uplifting word, pat on the back, a well done and "proud of you" just at the right moment. Speaking a fit word at the right time elevates and invigorates the downcast soul. Solomon says, "A word fitly spoken is like apples of gold in pictures of silver" (Proverbs 25:11). "A well-timed expression of encouragement," says Swindoll, "is seldom forgotten."[390] It might just be what the "doctor" ordered to change the trajectory of another's life.

"If I can put one touch of a rosy sunset into the life of any man or woman, I shall feel that I have worked with God."
George McDonald

August 8

Don't Fall by the Way

"Now unto him that is able to keep you from falling, and to present you faultless" (Jude 24).

What might cause a person to fall by the way after making a commitment to follow Christ?

A false start. The pivotal reason for the abandonment of the faith is professing it without possessing it (1 John 2:19).

A forsaken worship. The great awakening among British college students in the late nineteenth century began with their saying to one another, "Remember the morning watch." Neglect of a quiet time suffocates the flame in the soul.

A foolish friend. Some people are a compass and an influence to another, pointing them away from Christ and the Bible (Proverbs 13:20). Lawson remarks, "A well-chosen friend sweetens the present life and assists us in our progress to a better self. An unworthy friend will bring on us disappointment, vexation, and remorse."[391]

A faulty teaching. Spurgeon said, "False doctrine is a deadly poison that must be identified, labeled, and avoided."

A favorite sin. One sin will undo the Christian's walk (not salvation, but dedication) and witness. It's imperative that *all* the enemy be driven from the land (Numbers 33:51–55). Devotion to and dependence upon Christ enables the righteous to stand immovable and steadfast in the face of temptation and opposition.

"None can deliver us from former guilt or keep us from daily faultiness in the future but the Savior Himself."[392]
　　　　　　　　　　　　　　　C. H. Spurgeon

August 9

Noah's Ark and the Cross

"Come thou and all thy house into the ark" (Genesis 7:1).

The message of the cross is illustrated through Noah's Ark.

August

The cross is like Noah's Ark in its purpose. Both were designed to save man from divine judgment upon sin—the flood (Ark) and eternal separation from God (Cross).

The cross is like Noah's Ark in its planning. Blueprints for both were designed in Heaven. Every nail hammered into the Ark or into Jesus' hands upon the cross was divinely planned (1 Peter 1:18–20).

The cross is like Noah's Ark in its provision. As the needs of everyone in the Ark were met, so all that come to the cross in faith discover sufficiency in the atoning work of Christ, not only to save from the power and penalty of sin, but to sustain the Christian walk.

The cross is like Noah's Ark in its preservation. As no one aboard the Ark was lost, so no one who embraces Christ will be lost (1 Peter 1:5). Passengers aboard the Ark arrived safely on Mount Ararat, and the saved will all arrive safely at the port of Heaven. Spurgeon says, "Nobody fell out of that divinely appointed refuge; nobody was dragged out; nobody died in it; nobody was left to perish in it."[393]

The cross is like Noah's Ark in its uniqueness. There weren't several Arks of rescue available to board to escape death by the flood, only ONE; the Cross is man's only refuge of hope from eternal damnation.

The cross is like Noah's Ark in its entrance. The Ark had only one door. The people and animals had to go through that door to gain entrance. The Bible makes clear that there is but one door to salvation from Hell, and that's not baptism, church membership, good works, or morality, but Jesus Christ alone (John 10:9; Acts 4:12).

The cross is like Noah's Ark in its choice. As none boarded the Ark who didn't choose to do so, there are none that become a Christian unwillingly (Revelation 22:17).

The cross is like Noah's Ark in its faith. Noah entered the Ark by faith, believing God's promise to save him from the flood (Hebrews 11:7). No man is saved apart from faith in the finished work of Christ at Calvary (Ephesians 2:8).

The cross is like Noah's Ark in its fleeting opportunity. As with the Ark, an unknown time will come when the door to salvation will be eternally shut (Genesis 6:17; Matthew 25:10).

"In Jesus Christ on the Cross there is refuge, there is safety, there is shelter; and all the power of sin upon our track cannot reach us when we have taken shelter under the Cross that atones for our sins."
                    A. C. Dixon

August 10

Cast Thy Bread upon the Waters

"Cast thy bread upon the waters: for thou shalt find it after many days" (Ecclesiastes 11:1).

Many saints testify that despite having cast their bread upon the waters, no tangible evidence exists to indicate it bore fruit—no testimony of conversions, church additions, profit from Bibles and tracts distributed, lives changed, etc. Are these to believe their labor was in vain, futile and purposeless? Sowing, saith Solomon, always results in reaping.

Our part in labor, he says, is to use the right seed, "thy bread," the seed of the Gospel (Matthew 13:37); sow diligently, "cast" (throw, plant or send out the seed); in the place divinely assigned, "upon the waters" (wherever duty beckons whether favorable or not); and then patiently trust God for a promised harvest, "shall find it [it's not lost!] after many days."

Spurgeon said, "The reaping time will come. The harvest will come in due season. When it comes it will abundantly repay us."[394] Paul states, "We shall reap, if we faint not" (Galatians 6:9) and it is "God [who] gave the increase" (1 Corinthians 3:6).

No believer is able to manufacture fruit ('give the increase') or cause a single seed to spring up sooner than when God ordains. And the psalmist declared that they that scatter precious (valuable) seed "shall doubtless come again with rejoicing, bringing his sheaves with him" (Psalm 126:6).

Upon the text Spurgeon comments: *"Doubtless* you will gather sheaves from your sowing. Because the Lord has written *doubtless*, take heed that you do not doubt. No reason for doubt can remain after the Lord has spoken."[395]

"The due season for harvest is not the day after the seed-sowing, but we must wait awhile and not be weary. The harvest will come as the Lord appoints."[396]
C. H. Spurgeon

August 11

No Labor Is in Vain

"And let us not be weary in well doing: for in due season we shall reap, if we faint not" (Galatians 6:9).

The effect of the Christian's sowing (preaching, witnessing, teaching, singing) is not always immediate or visible. But we may be confident that the seed (Word of God) sown will 'not return unto God void but it shall accomplish that which He pleases, and it shall prosper in the thing whereto He sent it' (Isaiah 55:11). The power of God's Word assures no man is left untouched or unchanged when he hears the Gospel (Hebrews 4:12).

H. Edwards says, "The published Word, being assimilated into the human mind, fashions thought, molds character, regenerates life; and therefore, it does not return void to its Author. And even though it should be humanly rejected, it still would not return void; individual hearing creates individual responsibility, and hence leaves no one in the same place."[397]

A missionary shared a tract with a young man, urging him to be saved. When the missionary departed, the youth thrust the tract into the fire. As the pages of the tract curled up in the fire, he saw the words: "Heaven and earth shall pass away, but My words shall not pass away." The words ignited a fire in his soul causing him to find no rest until he got saved.[398] Though it was unseen by the missionary, the Word of God accomplished its purpose.

If you have labored for Christ without visible success, let that not infer that your work was futile or unproductive. Your part is to sow; it's the Lord's to reap. "To every man will be allotted a recompense, to every sacrifice a compensation."[399] Saith Spurgeon: "We cannot estimate our success. One child in the Sunday school, converted, may turn out to be worth five hundred others, because he may be the means of bringing ten thousand to Christ. It is not the acreage you sow; it is the multiplication which God gives to the seed which will make up the harvest. You have less to do with being successful than with being faithful. Your main comfort is that, in your labor, you are not alone, for God, the eternal One, who guides the marches of the stars, is with you."[400]

The Bible says, "For God is not unjust; he will not forget your work and the love you demonstrated for his name by serving the saints—and by continuing to serve them" (Hebrews 6:10 CSB).

"And when at the last those who have gladly spent and been spent in the service of God, and whose toils and sacrifices have never been sweetened by the knowledge that they were effectual in accomplishing the ends for which they were endured—when these men shall receive their portion from their Judge, there will be given the most effectual demonstration that 'God is not unrighteous to forget their work of labor and love.'"[401]

Henry Melvill

August 12

The Right Measuring Stick in Sowing

"Those who sow with tears will reap with songs of joy. Those who go out weeping, carrying seed to sow, will return with songs of joy, carrying sheaves with them" (Psalm 126:5–6 NIV).

Use the right measuring stick to evaluate success in laboring for the Master—not man's perception, but God's promise. Seed sown will now or later bear fruit. So keep sowing despite the nonvisible result.

Spurgeon said: "Be it ours to sow, not only on the honest and good soil, but on the rock and on the highway, and at the last great day to reap a glad harvest. May the bread which we cast upon the waters in odd times and strange occasions be found again after many days."[402] Keep preaching. Keep teaching. Keep witnessing. Keep singing. Keep playing the piano or organ. Keep writing. Keep mentoring. In time ("due season") that which is sown will bear profitability for others, the kingdom, and yourself.

"The reaping time will come; therefore thrust in the plough."[403] Hold fast to the Sower's promise: "He which soweth bountifully shall reap also bountifully" (2 Corinthians 9:6). Spurgeon comments: "We must sow. We may have to sow in the wet weather of sorrow; but we shall reap and reap in the bright summer season of joy. Let us keep to the work of this present sowing time and find strength in the promise which is here so positively given us. Here is one of the Lord's *shall*s and *will*s; it is freely given both to workers, waiters, and weepers, and they may rest assured that it will not fail: 'in due season we shall reap.'"[404]

He who patiently trusts God for the increase to the seed which is sown thwarts despair and discouragement over what could be misconstrued as failure, defeat and wasted time and effort.

August

"Don't judge each day by the harvest you reap but by the seeds that you plant."
Robert Louis Stevenson

August 13

The Potter and the Clay

"Arise, and go down to the potter's house, and there I will cause thee to hear my words" (Jeremiah 18:2).

In the metaphor the potter is God; man is the clay; and the wheel, the events of life (good and bad) that God tenderly uses with His hands to shape man into His design.

A vessel conceived. The potter has a masterful plan for the shapeless clay. He makes some jars, some pitchers, some cups, and some bowls (1 Corinthians 12:15–18).

A vessel constructed. "I went down to the potter's house and saw him working with clay at the wheel" (Jeremiah 18:3 ERV). With the use of the wheel and his tender hands, the potter molds the pliable clay into the designed vessel (minister, teacher, musician, singer, etc.).

A vessel corrupted. "And the vessel that he made…was marred in the hand of the potter" (Jeremiah 18:4a). It was skillfully and wondrously made by the potter, but a hidden fault (sin) within the clay and/or its unpliableness spoiled it. F. B. Meyer said, "If there be rebellion and resistance, the work of the potter is marred. Let God have His way with you."[405]

A vessel corrected. "So he made it again…as seemed good to the potter to make it" (Jeremiah 18:4b). The corrupted clay was changed, transformed into something beautiful, good, and profitable. The potter is the giver of second chances. He found Peter marred and mended him. He found Jonah marred and mended him. He found David marred and mended him.

Note, the potter's remake of man is as He deems good. It may not be according to the original plan, but nonetheless it still will be wondrously good. Matthew Henry commented, "If the potter's vessel be marred for one use, it shall serve for another."[406]

A vessel compliant. "Doesn't the potter have the right to make out of the same lump of clay one pot for special use and another for ordinary use?" (Romans 9:21 EHV). Simeon says, "If the clay has no right to complain of the potter who forms of it a vessel such as he himself pleases, much less can 'a living man' have right, under any circumstances, to 'complain' of God. Under every trial, of whatever kind it be, we should say, 'It is the Lord: let him do what seemeth him good.'"[407] Clay doesn't complain, it complies in faith to the potter's plan.

A vessel crushed. Jeremiah is instructed to break a piece of pottery and say on behalf of God to the people, "I'll smash this people and this city like a man who smashes a clay pot into so many pieces it can never be put together again" (Jeremiah 19:11 MSG). The time can arrive when the clay (man's heart) is so hardened (by wickedness, stubbornness, rejection, disobedience) that it cannot be reshaped. He crosses God's deadline of no return.

The bottom line: remain pliable and submissive to the Potter to be an honorable, profitable, and prosperous vessel.

"If only we lie as clay in his hands, we have nothing to fear."[408]
Charles Simeon

August 14

Power of the Pen (Part One)
"Writing books involves endless hard work" (Ecclesiastes 12:12 TJB).

Christian writing is a divine calling compelled and enabled by the Holy Spirit to communicate spiritual truth. It travels with little restraint and almost without bounds; works tirelessly and continuously; impacts kings and peasants; never wavers, cowers or retreats; sow's gospel seed silently and privately; and outlives its author by a long time (sometimes hundreds of years). Addressing the impact of Christian books, Oswald Smith stated that it wasn't Luther's preaching but his nearly one hundred books circulated throughout Western Europe that gave us the Reformation.[409]

D. L. Moody said of the impact of Paul's writings: "Think of Paul up yonder. People are going up every day and every hour, men and women brought to Christ through his writings. He set streams in motion that have flowed on for more than a thousand years. I can imagine people going up to him and saying, 'Paul, thank you for writing that letter to the

Ephesians; I found Christ in that.' 'Paul, thank you for writing that epistle to the Corinthians.' 'Paul, I found Christ in that epistle to the Philippians.' 'Thank you, Paul, for that epistle to the Galatians; I found Christ in that.' When Paul was in prison, he didn't fold his hands and sit down in idleness! No, he began to write. And his epistles have come down through the ages and brought thousands upon thousands to a knowledge of Christ crucified."[410]

Through Spurgeon's more than three thousand five hundred fifty printed sermons, hundreds of letters, and nearly one hundred fifty books, he, though long dead, yet preaches the Gospel and trains ministers around the world.

"There are a thousand thoughts lying within a man that he does not know till he takes up a pen to write."
William Makepeace Thackeray

August 15

Power of the Pen (Part Two)
"Writing books involves endless hard work" (Ecclesiastes 12:12 TJB).

When governed by the Holy Spirit, the pen has the potential to edify believers, build the church, expose heresy, spread the Gospel, change lives, convert the lost, and alter the course of nations for the good. Such has happened over the ages.

Luther said, "If you want to change the world, pick up your pen and write." Dewitt Talmage remarked, "The pen is the lever that moves the world." Saith Edward Bulwer-Lytton, "The pen is mightier than the sword." The pen is the tongue that reaches the soul when that which is spoken cannot. Understanding the power of the pen prompted Samuel Johnson to say of Oliver Goldsmith, "No man was more foolish when he had not a pen in his hand, or more wise when he had."[411]

The day will come when the tongue is silenced in death, but not that which is written with a pen. All who are called to write ought to write passionately and prayerfully, regardless of experience or education (like John Bunyan) and to write that which the Holy Spirit prompts and dictates. Remember, as Lord Byron said, "A drop of ink may make a million think!"[412]

"A divine calling to write is a calling from God, through God, and for God. Until the writing is for God, it is not a calling from God."[413]
John Piper

August 16

What Will You Leave Behind?

"They showed him the coats and clothes that Dorcas had made while she was still alive" (Acts 9:39 CEV).

Dorcas in death was remembered for what she left behind—charitableness, godliness, and dresses and cloaks made for the widows. At death what will you leave behind to benefit others and the cause of Christ (Revelation 14:13)? For what will you be remembered? What might be left behind for the next generation to enhance the cause of Christ?

Leave godly footprints. Your life and death will affect others for "none of us lives to himself, and no one dies to himself" (Romans 14:7 NKJV). "In our faith," writes Lucado, "we leave footprints to guide others." Make sure the footprints left point in the right direction (Philippians 3:10–11).

Leave written testimony and exhortation. Jessamyn West said, "People who journal live twice."[414] It affords a second opportunity to make an impact for Christ (Psalm 66:16).

Leave religious books. Books continue to flood out spiritual light long after the author's departure, providing guidance, edification and encouragement.

Leave converts. Moody stated, "If we only lead one soul to Christ, we may set a stream in motion that will flow on when we are dead and gone."

Leave disciples. Make disciples, not clones. Help others be more like Jesus, not yourself.

Leave endowments. Endowments or willed gifts help perpetuate the continuing life of a ministry, church, or religious institution.

Leave laborers. Stay alert to opportunities to help others discern and comply with their call to Christian work.

Leave ministries. Establish ministries that will live on upon your death.

Leave holes in the darkness. Leave the world a little less decadent and deplorable.

Leave a good memory. Your legacy—positive or negative, beneficial or detrimental for Christ and His cause—is how you lived life (priorities, pursuits, passion, performance), and it will bear a lasting effect accordingly.

"Time is short, and it behooves each one to be working for his Lord, that when he is called home, he may leave behind him something for the generations following."[415]
C. H. Spurgeon

August 17

An Ear to Hear God

"My soul waits in silence for God only" (Psalm 62:1 NASB).

A Ph.D. in Entomology, while visiting in the home of Peter Lord, detected sixteen different species of crickets in his yard. This young man's life was dedicated to the study of insects, so the discovery was exciting to him, but not to Peter Lord, who had lived in the home for years. Not only did he not know of the crickets' presence, but he didn't care. Lord uses the story to make the point that one will only hear God when hearing from Him is absolutely vital to life. The more vital listening to God is, the more sensitive the believer will be to hearing Him speak.

Train the ear to recognize Christ's voice. Tozer says, "Listen for the inward voice till you learn to recognize it."[416] Blind snow skiers have to train their "ears" to hear commands (like go left, right, slow down, or crash) of their seeing companion to traverse the slopes safely. Believers must likewise learn to hear God's voice at every turn in the journey of life to navigate it happily and safely.

Take time to let Christ speak. "Gaze on Christ with the eyes of your soul. Practice spiritual concentration."[417] Think through what Christ speaks (jot down notes about what He says). Test what Christ speaks (what you think He says) against the truth of the Scriptures. Take what Christ speaks and apply it to your life.

"If you have trouble hearing God speak, you are in trouble at the very heart of your Christian experience."[418]
Henry Blackaby

August 18

To Die in the Lord

"Blessed are the dead which die in the Lord from henceforth: Yea, saith the Spirit, that they may rest from their labors; and their works do follow them" (Revelation 14:13).

The noblest thing that may be said of a man at death is that he "died in the Lord." What is it to "die in the Lord?"

To die in the Lord is to die knowing the Lord. To die in the Lord is to meet death having a personal relationship with Christ, to know Him personally and intimately as Lord and Savior. It is to possess not only head knowledge of Christ but heart experience with Him.

To die in the Lord is to die testifying of union with the Lord. It's not what the minister or others may say of a man at death that counts. It's the testimony of his own mouth of personal salvation that makes the eternal difference (Matthew 10:32–33).

To die in the Lord is to renounce all other means of salvation. It is to trust wholeheartedly in the finished work at Calvary by Christ as the only means for forgiveness of sins and reconciliation to God (Ephesians 2:8–9; Acts 4:12).

To die in the Lord is to hold fast the promises of Christ. It is in death to say, "For to me to live is Christ, and to die is gain" (Philippians 1:21). It is to die confidently believing the promise of Jesus in John 14:3: "I go and prepare a place for you, I will come again, and receive you unto myself; that where I am, there ye may be also."

To die in the Lord is to have earth's "good works" continue. There is much about a man that cannot be put into a coffin. His influence cannot. His works for Christ cannot. The good that a man does isn't buried with him but remains yet to minister guidance and comfort to family members and point all to the Cross for hope and salvation. "Deeds done in the power of the Spirit are eternal."[419]

To die in the Lord is to die happily. Spurgeon asserts, "The best moment of a Christian's life is his last one, because it is the one that is nearest Heaven."

"I am not tired of my work, neither am I tired of the world; yet, when Christ calls me home, I shall go with gladness."
                    Adoniram Judson

August 19

Demonstrate Gratitude

"She did what she could" (Mark 14:8 NIV).

In Bethany, at the house of Simon the Leper, a woman (we know her to be Mary, the sister of Martha and brother of Lazarus from John 12:3) entered with an alabaster box (vase that held perfume) of ointment (genuine perfume made in India that was extremely costly) and poured it upon Jesus' head. John adds, "And wiped his feet with her hair: and the house was filled with the odor of the ointment" (John 12:3 ASV).

Both Christ's head and feet were anointed. An uproar developed from some that counted the act a grave waste of "money" (the perfume "might have been sold" for more than a year's wages). As they murmured (got vehement) against her, Jesus sternly said to Judas (John 12:4–7), "Let her alone" (Mark 14:6).

He vindicates Mary's gracious act of generosity, saying, "She hath wrought a good work [worthy of praise and honor] on me" (Mark 14:6). (That good work is cited in Mark 14:8, the anointing of His body "aforehand" for burial, the symbol of Christ's forthcoming death). And then He chided the complainers for even suggesting that the perfume might have been sold. Jesus was so honored and blessed by the act of Mary that He said that wherever the Gospel would be preached, what she did would be memorialized.

The expression of sincerest and deepest gratitude, sympathy, generosity, and love flows only from the heart touched profoundly by the caring action of another. It cannot be manipulated, compelled, or demanded. It must be spontaneous from the heart, as was Mary's prompted by Jesus' acts of kindness and goodness toward her.

"He is ungrateful who denies that he has received a kindness which has been bestowed upon him; he is ungrateful who conceals it; he is ungrateful who makes no return for it; most ungrateful of all is he who forgets it."
Seneca the Younger

August 20

"Remember Them That Are in Bonds"

"Remember them that are in bonds, as bound with them; and them which suffer adversity, as being yourselves also in the body" (Hebrews 13:3).

How is it that we are to treat fellow believers in persecution?

With contemplation. "Remember them." The implication is that saints are prone to forget the persecuted for Christ's sake (imprisoned and oppressed). To remember is "to remind oneself" or intentionally recall the estate of the persecuted one and "as a result, respond in an appropriate manner." It means "to give careful consideration to, think of, care for, be concerned about, keep in mind." It's not to be a passive remembrance void of action.

With identification. "As bound with them"; that is, as shackled to them, bearing the same affliction; be identical to them; put yourself in their shoes. Douglas Bazi, a minister in Northern Iraq, said, "Suffering is not killing us, but to suffer alone is killing us." Brothers and sisters in the furnace of affliction must know that they are not forgotten, that they do not stand alone in their resistance to hostile forces of the faith.

With obligation. "Yourselves also in the body"; that is, as being them. "Bear ye one another's burdens" (Galatians 6:2). How?

First, by exhibiting hearty sympathy for them. "Weep with them that weep" (Romans 12:15). Burke says, "Sympathy may be considered as a sort of substitution, by which we are put into the place of another man and affected in many respects as he is affected." Sympathize heartily with them, as you would want others to do for you in the similar circumstance. It is said of Origen, "Not only was he at the side of the holy martyrs in their imprisonment and until their final condemnation, but when they were led to death, he boldly accompanied them into danger."

Second, we help bear the burden of the oppressed through relieving or lessening their pain, discomfort and need.

Third, the believer eases the burden of the persecuted through various means of encouragement (Philippians 4:18).

Fourth, and most importantly, we assist the persecuted with their burden by providing prayer *for* them (Romans 15:30–31; Philippians 1:19, 22) and provision *to* them (Philippians 4:10).

August

"While Christians in America have worshipped without the fear or threat of physical abuse for their beliefs, thousands of their brothers in Christ throughout the world have been tortured and martyred for confessing the name of Christ."
Billy Graham

August 21

Examples of Gratitude

"Warriors from that town traveled all night to Beth-shan and took down the bodies of Saul and his sons from the wall and brought them to Jabesh, where they cremated them" (1 Samuel 31:12 TLB).

Consider the gratitude of the Gileadites to Saul. Upon hearing that the Philistines had beheaded Saul and hung his body on a wall in Beth-shan, the Gileadites retrieved it for a decent burial in Jabesh-gilead (1 Samuel 31:11–13). And then, they fasted for seven days (fasting was associated with mourning and grief). All this was done to display gratitude for that which Saul and his sons did in saving Jabesh-gilead from the Ammonites shortly after becoming king of Israel (1 Samuel 11:9–12). May their tribe increase in today's culture where gratitude is seldom expressed and demonstrated.

Consider the gratitude of Paul to Onesiphorus. Onesiphorus provided Paul shelter, bedding, food, fellowship, and financial help when he was in Ephesus (2 Timothy 1:16). Likely, it was during that time he became Paul's encourager, uplifter and gift-giver unto his death. Barclay states, "Onesiphorus goes down to history as the friend who stuck closer than a brother."[420]

Divine grace connections that last a lifetime like that of Paul and Onesiphorus still happen, quickened by the Holy Spirit, impacting the lives of both for the better. Paul expressed gratitude to Onesiphorus by praying for him and his family. He repaid him with prayers requesting God to grant mercy and favor to his household and to him at the Judgment (2 Timothy 1:16, 18).

Spurgeon says, "Paul felt bound to Onesiphorus and to his family in perpetual thankfulness. Let none of us ever be accused of ingratitude; it is one of the worst of sins. Paul, no doubt, would have done all he could for Onesiphorus in other ways, but he added to all other ways of showing his gratitude, that of praying for him—praying the prayer which we have here put on record in the Book of Inspiration. Learn hence that if we can do nothing else for our benefactors, we can bless them by our prayers. Let us be abundant in pouring out supplications before God for all those who in any way have done us a service."[421]

The danger of ingratitude. Havner said, "We grow up taking things for granted and saving our flowers for the dead. All along the way, countless hands minister to our good, but rarely do we acknowledge them."[422]

And ingratitude crushes the spirit of the giver of the gift, or good deed. Spurgeon says, "Some have a wounded spirit through…the ingratitude of those whom they have helped, and for whom they have had such affection that they would almost have been willing to sacrifice their own lives." Insincere gratitude is easily spotted and most distasteful to its recipient. But genuine gratitude that flows like a gusher from the soul enriches, enlivens, and endears.

"Feeling gratitude and not expressing it is like wrapping a present and not giving it."[423]
William A. Ward

August 22

Step by Step

"The steps of a good man are ordered by the LORD: and he delighteth in his way" (Psalm 37:23).

Its cause. The frailty of the flesh is not equal to the task of life's navigation; that is God's work (Jeremiah 10:23).

Its concept. The believer, when he delights in God's way, doesn't walk randomly, but in an established or prepared manner. Spurgeon said, "All his course of life is graciously ordained, and in lovingkindness all is fixed. No fickle chance rules us; every step is the subject of divine decree."[424]

Its contingency. God orders or directs the steps only of the righteous ("the man who lives in fellowship with Him."[425])—and of these only those that request and submit to it. It is not automatic. Man cannot flippantly live contrary to God's law and will and expect to be led in the path that is most beneficial and blessed.

Its comprehensiveness. The steps of a devoted believer are divinely ordered from the rising of the sun to the going down of the same and all the night through to the time of death. "God is in control. He may not take away our trials or make detours for us, but He strengthens us through them."[426]

Its consequence. A single "step" can bring blessing or cursing, success or failure, life or death, happiness or heartache, victory or moral failure, salvation or eternal damnation. Acting independently of the Lord leads to mistakes, sorrow and woe (Proverbs 8:34; Proverbs 14:12).

Its constraint. He whose steps are ordered by the Lord will be kept on track by the Holy Spirit (Isaiah 30:21).

Its confidence. To have each step ordered by the Lord is faith walking (reliance upon Him for that which is beneficial and best), trusting Him with the unseen and unknown. Note, divine guidance is by "steps." He leads "step by step," not always showing man his way at a distance.

Its comfort.

1. Steps ordered by God control what happens (Romans 8:28).

2. "Falls" caused by missteps in sin are temporary and always recoverable (Psalm 37:24).

"God will never make you take even one step beyond what your feet are able to endure. Never mind if you think you are unable to take another step, for either He will strengthen you to make you able, or He will call a sudden halt, and you will not have to take it at all."[427]
Frances Ridley Havergal

August 23

A Divine Disturbance
"As an eagle stirreth up her nest, fluttereth over her young, spreadeth abroad her wings, taketh them, beareth them on her wings" (Deuteronomy 32:11).

The eagle disturbs its own nest (either demolishes it or changes its design to make it uncomfortable to the eaglet) to force its young to try their wings. That which seems harsh and severe to the eaglet is designed to help them become the free and magnificent bird for which they were born. Eagles are born to fly, not perch in a nest for their lifetime.

The Lord, at times, stirs the believer's nest to move him from a place of complacency, comfort, and contentment to a higher plane of divine dependence, spiritual development, designed duty, and greater productivity. God doesn't want His children to be subpar eaglet-nest dwellers, but eagles that soar. Only with their broad wings fully expanded soaring in the heavenlies of God's will can their dormant energies, untapped giftedness, and fullest potential be realized.

Note, the eagle doesn't give the eaglet new wings, just the means to develop and expand the wings they possess fully. God works likewise with man. He disturbs or stirs his nest by way of sorrows, sermons, suffering, separation (colleagues, friends), setbacks, and restlessness. But He never pushes us out of the nest without a designed purpose, loving affection, and divine protection.

Once we are pushed out of the nest, God's broad sheltering wings are present to bear us up (protection and enablement) in times of trouble, even as the mother eagle bears up the eaglet. Raleigh said, "He protects those who stir themselves when the nest is stirred; those who spread the wing in answer to the outspread wings above them."[428]

Stay in the "nest" until divinely nudged to take flight. To venture into new arenas of ministry, challenges, and pursuits, leaving the comfortable and secure, may be frightening. But He that pushes you out of the nest into them surely will sustain and enable you in the quest. The eagle loves the eaglet too much to let it perish, either in the nest or while exercising its wings in the heavenlies.

"God pushes us out of the nest sometimes, not because He doesn't love us, but because He wants us to learn to fly—He wants us to learn to live for Him."[429]

J. Vernon McGee

August 24

An Uncertain Sound

"For if the trumpet give an uncertain sound, who shall prepare himself to the battle?" (1 Corinthians 14:8).

Some of the failure of modern-day preaching to win the lost is traceable to its "hearers," but often it is due to the "uncertain sound" trumpeted by the preacher.

An uncertain sound is an *unprepared sound*. Saith Spurgeon, "Habitually to come into the pulpit unprepared is unpardonable presumption; nothing can more effectually lower ourselves and our office."[430] Further, he states, "He who no longer sows in the study will no more reap in the pulpit."[431]

An uncertain sound is an *unanointed sound*. Martyn Lloyd-Jones has succinctly asserted, "If there is no power, there is no preaching." Paul preached "in demonstration of the Spirit and of power" (1 Corinthians 2:4).

Ellicott comments, "The Apostle's demonstration of the truth of the Gospel was the result of no human art or skill, but came from the Spirit and power of God, and therefore the Corinthians could glory in no human teacher, but only in the power of God, which was the true source of the success of the Gospel amongst them."[432]

It is an unscriptural sound. Roy Fish stated, "Much preaching has become the theories of men rather than the Word of God. Sermons have become psychological doses of uplift."

Saith Spurgeon, "The Spirit of God bears no witness to Christless sermons. Leave Jesus out of your preaching, and the Holy Spirit will never come upon you." Hold fast to and proclaim "sound words [doctrine]" (2 Timothy 1:13).

It is an incomplete sound. With Paul, the man of God must 'not shun to declare all the counsel of God' (Acts 20:27).

It is an unclear sound. Jettison the language of Zion and use words that connect with the person in the pew.

It is an ineffectual sound. Preaching void of the power of the Holy Spirit and absent of plain scriptural exposition may be eloquent, flowery, and appealing, but will avail nothing.

"The preaching of Christ is the whip that flogs the Devil. The preaching of Christ is the thunderbolt, the sound of which makes all Hell shake."
C. H. Spurgeon

August 25

Adversity Reveals Strength
"If you faint in the day of adversity, your strength is small" (Proverbs 24:10 ESV).

To be slack (discouraged, disheartened, defeated) in the day of distress is to show oneself devoid of sufficient spiritual strength or power to face it successfully.

Adversity eludes no man. Sailing in favorable weather is easy, but everyone, without exception, faces times when boisterous winds and calamitous storms assail, making navigation difficult. Even the godliest are not exempt.

Adversity requires having spiritual muscle to manage and thwart it. "The lighthouse must not only be strong enough to stand in calm weather; it should be able to resist the battering rams of the tempest." Degrees of strength are determined by spiritual walk (exercise of spiritual disciplines). One with little strength may fare okay in the relative calm of minor temptation and tempest, but not in the greater storms. *Guard against delusions of strength.* Don't overestimate the strength you possess to face adversity. Peter boasted that he never would deny the Lord, yet this he did three times (Matthew 26:34–35).

Adversity tests the mettle of perceived strength. Outward appearance, longevity and/or position in the church, or religious activity does not accurately indicate one's strength. The furnace of fire determines the purity of gold, as do seasons of hardship, suffering, and sorrow, the strength of man (1 Peter 1:7).

Spurgeon states, "Trials teach us what we are; they dig up the soil and let us see what we are made of." *Deficient strength in adversity is indicated by tell-tale signs.* Ironside says, "To faint or become disheartened is to show that one has not been truly counting upon God for deliverance."[433]

Store up strength for the time of adversity. The ship must be built for the storm, not just the calm. Strength must be ascertained in fair weather in order to withstand the bad times (Isaiah 40:29).

"A person reveals the degree and extent of his strength by his conduct in crisis."[434]

B. K. Waltke

August 26

Seven Kinds of Church Members
"I know…where thou dwellest" (Revelation 2:13).

August

The seven churches of Asia Minor mirror the kinds of Christians that make up the New Testament church. As in most of them, so in the church today are members that, while exhibiting commendable qualities, possess detrimental traits as well. David Jeremiah says, "The problems that beset the seven churches of Revelation reflect the challenges we face today."[435]

Ephesus Christians, despite sifting out heretical teachers in the church and persevering in their labor for Christ, have drifted away from their first love for and allegiance to Christ (Revelation 2:4).

Smyrna Christians, for Christ's sake, suffer persecution for their convictions and commitments (Revelation 2:10).

Pergamos Christians, while staying firm for Christ, even in the face of death, tolerate heretical teachers in the fellowship (Revelation 2:14–15).

Thyatira Christians maintain a persevering witness to the unsaved (great mission program) but tolerate false teaching (Revelation 2:19–20).

Sardis Christians maintain the reputation of being alive (aflame for God) while they are dead—unregenerate, unredeemed (Revelation 3:1). Chambers says, "We are only what we are in the dark; all the rest is reputation. What God looks at is what we are in the dark—the imaginations of our minds, the thoughts of our heart, the habits of our bodies; these are the things that mark us in God's sight. Character is what you are in the dark."

Philadelphia Christians exhibit faithfulness to the Word of God (Revelation 3:8) and the work of evangelism. David Jeremiah states that the Philadelphia church reached beyond its geographical bounds with the Gospel.[436] Maclaren said, "A church which fails in aggressive evangelistic activity has failed utterly. What is the good of a lamppost if there is no light in it? It is only a nuisance for people to knock their heads against in the dark."[437] F. B. Meyer states, "The church which is not a missionary church will be a missing church when Jesus comes."

Laodicean Christians are lukewarm and manifest an arrogant, overblown view of their status before God (Revelation 3:15–17). Rogers wrote, "Lukewarmness is not weakness; it is wickedness. It is not a small sin; it's a great sin. If the greatest commandment is to love God with all your heart, then the greatest sin is not to do so. Our Lord says that in the last days, lukewarmness will be the condition of the average church."[438]

All seven churches were given a promise conditioned upon their heedful response to the specific message and directives stated to them. The invitation and its promise still stand. Complacent, lukewarm, and carnal saints may return to their first love of Christ, and stagnant and dying churches can be resurrected to their former glory and power if they but repent (Revelation 2:5).

"Many churches are weak because we have members who have turned the meaning of membership upside down. It's time to get it right. It's time to become a church member as God intended. It's time to give instead of being entitled."[439]
Tom Rainer

August 27

Dykes of Courage

"The righteous are bold as a lion" (Proverbs 28:1).

Courage in the midst of fear must be exhibited in times of persecution. Martin Luther King, Jr., said, "We must constantly build dykes of courage to hold back the flood of fear." From whence is courage instilled, these dykes of courage in the heart erected?

The dyke of faith. A confidence in God gives the saint a lion-like courage and boldness to face any danger. Gregory said, "The lion is not afraid in the onset of beasts, because he knows well that he is stronger than them all. Whence the fearlessness of a righteous man is rightly compared to a lion, because, when he beholds any rising against him, he returns to the confidence of his mind and knows that he overcomes all his adversaries because he loves Him alone whom he cannot in any way lose against his will."[440] Pink states, "Faith imparts a steadfastness of purpose, a noble courage, a tranquility of mind, which no human education or fleshly effort can supply. Faith makes the righteous as bold as a lion, refusing to recant though horrible tortures and a martyr's death be the only alternatives." An African proverb says, "The lion does not turn around when a small dog barks."

The dyke of the Spirit. When the Holy Spirit empowers the life, a holy boldness emerges (Acts 4:31). The measure of the Spirit's infilling is largely evidenced in the believer's boldness.

The dyke of the Scriptures. The promises infuse strength and courage to the soul, assuring us of God's abiding presence and power, despite the Goliath we encounter. "Greater is He that is in you, than he that is in the world" (1 John 4:4).

"He is a man of courage who does not run away, but remains at his post and fights against the enemy."[441]
Socrates

August 28

The Knocking Savior

"Behold, I stand at the door, and knock: if any man hear my voice, and open the door, I will come in to him, and will sup with him, and he with me" (Revelation 3:20).

Holman Hunt painted a picture entitled *The Light of the World* in which he depicts Jesus with a lamp in His hand knocking on a door. The door is latched from the inside, and no one opens it. The painting is based upon Revelation 3:20.

The Knocking Person at the door of man's heart seeking entrance is God's only son, Jesus Christ, who died upon a cross and rose from the dead to make possible forgiveness of sin and everlasting life (John 3:16).

The Knocking Purpose is the invitation to receive the free gift of abundant and eternal life (John 10:10).

The Knocking Place is the door to man's heart.

The Knocking Process, modus operandi, to gain entrance into man's heart is multifaceted.

He knocks on the door of a man's heart through church services. It was in a church service that I heard His knock on my heart's door and let Him enter.

He knocks on the door of a man's heart through preachers and Bible teachers.

Jesus may knock on the door of a person's heart through a Sunday school teacher, children's worker or pastor.

He knocks on hearts' doors through friends, prompting one to consider salvation.

He knocks on hearts' doors through the Bible, the most powerful door knocker. Read and listen for God's knocking through its pages (Hebrews 4:12; Romans 10:17).

Jesus knocks on the door of a man's heart through the conscience. The Holy Spirit convicts man of sin, judgment, righteousness, and things to come, stirring his soul unto repentance and faith in the Lord Jesus Christ (John 16:8).

He knocks on hearts' doors through the calamities of life. The psalmist testified, "It is good for me that I have been afflicted; that I might learn thy statutes" (Psalm 119:71).

And Jesus knocks on the doors of hearts through the goodness He extends. Paul says, "Or do you despise the riches of His goodness, forbearance, and longsuffering, not knowing that the goodness of God leads you to repentance?" (Romans 2:4 NKJV).

The Knocking Promise is that Jesus pledges entry into the heart that opens its door. "I will come in"—and He cannot lie (Hebrews 6:18).

"His standing on the outside is of no use to us. A mere outside Christ will profit us nothing. An outside cross will not pacify, nor heal, nor save."[442] Man must open the door to allow Him entry to enrich and save his soul, which is done through confession of sin and repentance and faith (Acts 20:21).

"He never comes empty-handed, but when He enters in, He endows the soul with untold riches."[443]
Alexander Maclaren

August 29

The Church Is Like the Natural Body

"The human body has many parts, but the many parts make up one whole body. So it is with the body of Christ" (1 Corinthians 12:12 NLT).

How is the human body used as a metaphor for the church?

The church is like the body in its liveliness. The church is a living organism, just like the body. It takes its life from Christ, not its organizations, programs, bank account, officers, and meetings.

The church is like the body in its organization. The body, without the defined structure of its parts (designated responsibilities), couldn't survive, and neither can the church apart from the organization of its members (pastor, deacons, elders, teachers, officers).

The church is like the body in its function. The body of Christ needs many parts—many gifts—to function, as does the physical body.

The church is like the body in its unity. Body parts don't battle for one another's jobs. They cooperate with the other members for the good of the body. Can you imagine the outcome in the body if the liver insisted on being the kidneys, or the gall bladder, the lungs? To fulfill its purpose on earth, the church, the body of Christ, must exhibit unison and harmony among its many members in the use of their spiritual gift or gifts (Ephesians 4:16). No member of the body of Christ is to feel inferior to the other parts or be treated as inferior by the other parts.

The church is like the body in its growth. To flourish in health, the body must grow. A seventy-year-old man no longer has the same appetite, appearance, or behavior that he did at age five. The body of Christ is to progressively undergo change to be conformed more to His perfect image and to fulfill His glorious mission. The church that remains static dies.

The church is like the body in its sympathy. The pain of one part of the natural body is felt by the whole. Within the body of Christ, believers share sympathy with the member that suffers (1 Corinthians 12:26; Romans 12:15). Members of the church ought not to be insensitive toward the hurts of others in the body nor jealous or envious of the honor or position another receives.

All that are saved are part of the body of Christ, the church. To extricate oneself from it is harmful both to the body and to the person— to the person by the body's inability to minister the Word of God and loving and caring fellowship, and to the body of Christ by the failure to minister to them and undergird their divine mission (Hebrews 10:25).

"We do not want a church that will move with the world. We want a church that will move the world."
G. K. Chesterton

August 30

Two Burning Questions

"From that time many of his disciples went back, and walked no more with him" (John 6:66).

Morning by Morning

Two burning questions are suggested. The first question: *Why do people walk away from Jesus?*

Some walk away due to misunderstanding. A fourteen-year-old student was saved following the presentation of the Gospel. Afterward, he said, "That was simple. I just needed someone to explain it to me." Many would be saved if presented with the clear, simple gospel message.

Some walk away due to distraction. The magnets of pleasure, popularity, and possessions pull man away from Christ (2 Timothy 3:4). But Jesus warns, "What shall it profit a man, if he shall gain the whole world, and lose his own soul?" (Mark 8:36).

Some walk away due to doubt. Doubts and questions about Christ and the Bible hold some back. These, however, could be resolved if probed to their very depth. God promises to give the necessary light to clarify man's religious questions and difficulties if sought honestly and earnestly (John 7:17).

Some walk away due to discouragement. The hypocritical lifestyle of believers, the godless influence of companions, the misrepresentation of what it means to be saved, and the high cost of being a disciple of Christ keep people back from being saved.

Some walk away due to misinformation. Distorted truth about Christ keeps people back from the faith (Matthew 24:11). The real Christ must be put on display before the world (John 12:32).

Some walk away due to deception. A man blinded by Satan perceives not the danger of his soul and need for the salvation Christ affords (2 Corinthians 4:4).

Some walk away due to delay. Procrastination is not only the thief of time but of the soul. "Behold, now is the day of salvation!" (2 Corinthians 6:2).

The second question: *Where do those that walk away from Christ go?* They that walk away from Christ go to a cistern that cannot remedy the problem of sin, satisfy the deep thirst and hunger of the soul, provide comfort and consolation in the time of storm, grant meaning and happiness to life, and hope for Heaven at death (Jeremiah 2:13). To these, Jesus compassionately says, "Ye will not come to me, that ye might have life" (John 5:40).

"If a man is saved, it is because God has saved him. But if a man is lost, that is to be attributed to his own rejection of the Gospel and his own rebellion against God's way of salvation."
Martyn Lloyd-Jones

August 31

A Name Above Every Other Name
"Thou shalt call His name JESUS" (Matthew 1:21).

Of all the names given to our Lord, that of Jesus is used most by scripture writers, believers, and hymnists. Presently the name of Jesus is found in over six thousand languages. Charles Wesley wrote, "Blessed be the Name of the Lord," and Edward Perronet, "All hail the power of Jesus' name!" And the Gaithers further memorialized the name in song, "There's just something about that name."

Jesus—It is a Simple Name. Wondrous it is that God did not tell Mary to name the child, Maher-shalal-hash-baz (the name of Isaiah's son, the longest in the Bible). The name Jesus is simple enough for the littlest child to say and sing.

Jesus—It is a Sacred Name. The name of Jesus was not humanly selected but supernaturally announced. "Thou shalt call His name JESUS." It's a holy name worthy of the highest honor, praise, and reverence. What blasphemy it is to profane and abuse it (Exodus 20:7).

Jesus—It is a Saving Name. The name itself means "Savior." D. A. Carson says the name "identifies Mary's Son as the one who brings Yahweh's promised eschatological salvation."[444] The mission of Jesus to earth was to save man from the penalty and power of sin. Luke says, "Neither is there salvation in any other: for there is none other name under heaven given among men, whereby we must be saved" (Acts 4:12). And Paul says, "For whosoever shall call upon the name of the Lord shall be saved" (Romans 10:13).

Jesus—It is a Staying Name. Jesus was born in obscurity over 2,000 years ago and horribly crucified. Yet His name lives on and is the most renowned among men. Warren Wiersbe states, "Great names come and go, but the name of Jesus remains. The Devil still hates it, the world still opposes it, but God still blesses it, and we can still claim it!"[445] There's still power in the name of Jesus to resolve man's every need.

Jesus—It is a Soul-Nourishing Name. "The sweet Name of Jesus produces in us holy thoughts, fills the soul with noble sentiments, strengthens virtue, begets good works, and nourishes pure affection. All spiritual food leaves the soul dry, if it contains not that penetrating oil, the Name Jesus," said St. Bernard of Clairvaux.

Morning by Morning

Jesus—It is a Succoring Name. "Soothly," states Richard Rolle in the 14th century, "the Name of Jesus is in my mind a joyous song, in my ear a heavenly sound, in my mouth honey-full sweetness. Therefore, it is no wonder if I love that Name which gives me comfort in every anguish. I cannot pray; I cannot meditate but in sounding the Name of Jesus." The name of Jesus "charms our fears and bids our sorrows cease; 'tis music in the sinner's ears; 'tis life and health and peace."

Jesus—It is a Splendorous Name. "Wherefore God also hath highly exalted him, and given him a name which is above every name: That at the name of Jesus every knee should bow, of things in heaven, and things in earth, and things under the earth" (Philippians 2:9–10). The longest sentence in the Bible exalts the splendor of the name Jesus (Ephesians 1:19–23). "Oh, what a lovely name, this name called Jesus. Let the world proclaim, what a lovely name."

"There are two hundred and fifty-six names[446] given in the Bible for the Lord Jesus Christ, and I suppose this was because He was infinitely beyond all that any one name could express."
                    Billy Sunday

September 1

The Mission of the Church

"And Jesus came and spake unto them, saying, All power is given unto me in heaven and in earth. Go ye therefore, and teach all nations, baptizing them in the name of the Father, and of the Son, and of the Holy Ghost: Teaching them to observe all things whatsoever I have commanded you: and, lo, I am with you alway, even unto the end of the world" (Matthew 28:18–20).

The mission of the church can be summed up in four words.

Introduction. "Go ye into all the world." The church's work is spiritual enlightenment and revelation to them that sit in darkness far and wide, locally and globally, without discrimination.

Invitation. "Teach all nations"; i.e., make disciples. Coupled with the introduction must be an invitation. It's not enough to tell man of Christ and man's need for salvation. A way must be opened in the pulpit and personal witnessing for man to respond to His offer of forgiveness of sin and reconciliation with God. We must call for a "verdict."

Induction. "Baptizing [*baptizo*—to immerse] them in the name of the Father, and of the Son, and of the the Holy Ghost." All that are saved must be inducted into the church (membership) through the ordinance of believers' baptism. Some churches are omitting this part of Christ's orders, but it stands unalterable.

Instruction. "Teaching them to observe all things." The Church is to be a training, instructional school for the new believer. The curriculum? Not theories, philosophies, and opinions, but "Whatsoever I have commanded you." That covers the whole of the Bible—biblical doctrines, disciplines, and duties.

"*I am with you alway, even unto the end of the world.*" Christ's promise of His presence and power ("All power is given unto me") for the church's task ensures its final success.

"How little chance the Holy Ghost has nowadays. The churches and missionary societies have so bound Him in red tape that they practically ask Him to sit in a corner while they do the work themselves."
                              C. T. Studd

September 2

What's So Great About Salvation?

"How shall we escape, if we neglect so great salvation?" (Hebrews 2:3).

What makes salvation so great?

Salvation is great in its provider. The Bible says, "He became the source of eternal salvation" (Hebrews 5:9 NLT). Spurgeon says, "He is the cause of salvation; the originator, the worker, the producer of salvation."[447] Ryle states, "In Christ alone God's rich provision of salvation for sinners is treasured up; by Christ alone God's abundant mercies come down from Heaven to earth. Christ's blood alone can cleanse us; Christ's righteousness alone can cleanse us; Christ's merit alone can give us a title to Heaven. Jews and Gentiles, learned and unlearned, kings and poor men—all alike must either be saved by the Lord Jesus, or lost forever."

Salvation is great in its power. It delivers from sin's captivity and penalty (the everlasting damnation of the soul). "He breaks the power of canceled sin; He sets the prisoner free."

Salvation is great in its promise. The Bible states, "If you confess with your mouth that Jesus is Lord and believe in your heart that God raised him from the dead, you will be saved" (Romans 10:9 ESV). This and other such promises anchor the soul in confidence to the providing of salvation by faith, not feeling.

Salvation is great in its price. It is provided freely to all through the finished work of Jesus at Calvary (substitutionary death and atoning work). Saith Graham, "Salvation is free! God puts no price tag on the Gift of gifts."[448]

Salvation is great in its plainness. Salvation's message is so simple to understand and claim that children may embrace it. 'Forbid not the little ones to come unto me.'

Salvation is great in its permanence. The salvation Jesus procured is an eternal one. He says, "And I give to them eternal life, and they shall by no means perish forever, and no one shall snatch them out of My hand" (John 10:28 RV). Absolutely nothing—sin, Satan, the world, demons, or man himself—can snatch a born-again person from the Father's hand. Spurgeon says, "Jesus does not save us today and leave us to perish tomorrow; He knows what is in man, and so He has prepared nothing less than eternal salvation for man."[449]

"You are not saved by the plan of salvation. You are saved by the man of salvation."
Adrian Rogers

September 3

Care and Cultivation of the New Convert

"We use all wisdom to counsel every person and teach every person. We are trying to bring everyone before God as people who have grown to be spiritually mature in Christ" (Colossians 1:28 ERV).

Dawson Trotman said, "You can lead a soul to Christ in anywhere from twenty minutes to a couple of hours. But it takes from twenty weeks to a couple of years to get him on the road to maturity."[450] To develop disciples requires four essentials.

Mentorship. The spiritually immature require the coaching of the mature saint to be firmly established in the faith, specifically its doctrine, teaching, privileges, and practice. "Disciples," wrote J. Oswald Sanders, "are not manufactured wholesale. They are produced one by one because someone has taken the pains to discipline, to instruct and enlighten, to nurture and train one that is younger."[451] Mentorship is individualized attention and instruction—"teaching every man." The believer, at conversion, is like the clay in the hands of the sculptor. He must be tediously molded into a wondrous design. Questions need answering, and doubts and temptations need spiritual advice and resolution.

Membership. Every new believer needs to be a part of the New Testament church, the body of Christ, to be spurred on and to spur others on in the faith, and to feed upon the Word of God provided by the pastor in Worship and Bible Study times and through the Sunday school. Saith Calvin, "The church is the gathering of God's children, where they can be helped and fed like babies and then, guided by her motherly care, grow up to manhood in maturity of faith."

Companionship. Different from mentorship, companionship is guardianship and fellowship, whereby the mature saint provides protection and care for the new believer, lest "the care of this world, and the deceitfulness of riches, choke the word, and he becometh unfruitful"

(Matthew 13:22). Jonathan strengthened David's grip on God in a difficult time by sharing words of encouragement (1 Samuel 23:16–17). "So support one another. Keep building each other up as you have been doing" (1 Thessalonians 5:11 VOICE). The giant redwoods of Northern California (the tallest trees on earth), which have shallow root systems of less than twelve feet, withstand the force of mighty storms by intertwining their roots with those of other trees in their grouping (they grow in groups). Mature, strong Christians intertwine their roots with immature, weak Christians to enable them to stand firm in the faith. The wisest man that ever lived, Solomon, said, "Two are better than one" (Ecclesiastes 4:9).

Apprenticeship. Spiritual exemplary leaders and workers (ministers, teachers, musicians, and soul-winners) within the church must reproduce their kind. People learn what to do and how to do it by the example and instruction of those that do it. The church's job is to equip the saints for the work of the ministry.

"The conversion of a soul is the miracle of a moment, but the manufacture of a saint is the task of a lifetime."
                                      Alan Redpath

September 4

Preaching to Dry Bones (Part One)

"Prophesy upon these bones, and say unto them, O ye dry bones, hear the word of the Lord" (Ezekiel 37:4).

This preacher's summons. Ezekiel was expressly assigned by God to preach the message of restoration to a congregation of dry bones (Ezekiel 37:1–4). Note the wording, that the Lord literally "carried" the prophet to the valley of dry bones (that's what He does spiritually with every minister who is submitted to Him to preach wherever He assigns). A preacher should not choose his post but have it divinely chosen, even if the post is at Dry Bones Baptist Church, Death Valley, USA, where the prospects of success seem unlikely. "We must discharge our trust," says Matthew Henry, "must prophesy as we are commanded, in the name of Him who raises the dead and is the fountain of life."[452]

This preacher's surety. To the question, "Son of man, can these bones live?" Ezekiel replied, "O Lord God, thou knowest" (Ezekiel 37:3).

September

Note that he does not say they cannot live. Ezekiel had no confidence in his prowess (eloquence of speech, expertise, or seminary degrees) to make the bones live, but He did in God's ability. "For with God all things are possible." And this confidence (faith) in God prompted unquestionable obedience to the mission.

To the preacher or Christian worker, the Lord asks upon every assignment, "Do you believe that I am able to do this?" (Matthew 9:28 ESV). Why? For "without faith it is impossible to please Him" (Hebrews 11:6). Maclaren states, "Faith has the prerogative of seeing possibilities of life in what looks to sense hopeless death."[453]

This preacher's sermon. It was a message received from God, not one of Ezekiel's own making. Watchman Nee asserts, "The Gospel we preach must not be just something we hear from men or read from books or even conceived through our meditation. Unless it is delivered to us by God, it can serve no spiritual utility."

"I discovered that no revival comes if we don't preach the Word of God under the anointing of the Holy Spirit."
Reinhard Bonnke

September 5

Preaching to Dry Bones (Part Two)

"Prophesy upon these bones, and say unto them, O ye dry bones, hear the word of the LORD" (Ezekiel 37:4).

This preacher's supplication. The Word proclaimed caused an awakening and shaking. But there was no life to the bones until the Holy Spirit's power was invoked upon that which was preached. The preacher's words are powerless until made powerful by the Holy Spirit. He must pray, "Come from the four winds, O breath, and breathe upon these slain, that they may live" (Ezekiel 37:9). Henry says, "See the efficacy of the Word and prayer, and the necessity of both, for the raising of dead souls."[454]

This preacher's success. The aim in the sermon was accomplished. The dead bones were resuscitated and stood to their feet as a mighty and effective army (Ezekiel 37:10). The "impossible" became possible. Yates writes, "The coming of God's Spirit brings life. The same thrilling truth is still needed in a world that has dry bones everywhere. What we need is to have the Holy Spirit come with His quickening power that a genuine revival may sweep the earth."[455]

The bottom line. With a divinely assigned preacher, the authoritative Word of God, and the anointing of the Holy Spirit, dry and dead bones (congregations, churches) can be resuscitated and the unregenerate resurrected. What encouragement this is to the worker of God.

Note, the vision of Ezekiel not only pictures the spiritual resurrection of congregations and the lost by the means of preaching, but that of the saints at the great resurrection day. Hallelujah! With regard to the dead in Christ whose bones lie buried in the earth, the Lord asks, "Can these bones live?"

And we by faith exclaim, "Thou knowest. And you, O Lord, say, 'I am the resurrection and the life. He who believes in Me, though he may die, he shall live'" (John 11:25).

"Be resurrection preachers to dead churches."
L. R. Scarborough

September 6

The Prodigal's Reception Home (Part One)

"But while he was still a long way off, his father saw him and felt compassion, and ran and embraced him and kissed him" (Luke 15:20 ESV).

Christ welcomes the prodigal home despite how far into the far country he has gone, how long he has been there, and the sins committed while there.

The reception home will not be gradual. Acceptance by the Lord is not progressive. The prodigal is not required to jump through a series of hoops to attain full restoration and acceptance. All that is required is godly sorrow, repentance, and confession of the sin committed, saying, "Father, I have sinned against heaven, and in thy sight, and am no more worthy to be called thy son" (Luke 15:21). See 1 John 1:9.

The reception home will not be partial. The returning prodigal receives the same benefits afforded to others in the father's house. None are withholden because of his departure to the far country. He is not forced to sleep in the barn and eat in the kitchen but dines and resides with all the family in the father's house. He is allowed to wear the father's ring and shoes coat and eat his fatted calf. Lincoln, being asked how he would treat the returning rebellious southerners to the Union of the United States, replied, "I will treat them as if they had never been away." Out of mercy and grace, that's how the Father treats every prodigal that returns home.

The reception home will not be with chiding. Without a word of rebuke over the prodigal's departure and sin, the father with open arms receives him into His arms (Luke 15:22). Without reprimand or castigation about the past, Christ lovingly and compassionately receives the erring child home.

"The man who has received this great deliverance is no longer a convict, painfully observing all prison rules with the hope of shortening his sentence, but a child in the home of God."
                                                    Robert William Dale

September 7

The Prodigal's Reception Home (Part Two)

"But while he was still a long way off, his father saw him and felt compassion, and ran and embraced him and kissed him" (Luke 15:20 ESV).

The reception home will not be temporary. The father didn't kiss and embrace him only to disown him. In saying, 'Put a ring upon his hand,' the father vowed to always love his son and include him in the family. Christ receives the prodigal home with irrevocable love and affection. The only one to depart from the fellowship of father's house is he that of his own accord chooses to leave.

The reception home will not be delayed. Of old, prodigals at the altar would moan, cry, and pray hours and days awaiting restoration to the Father. But sincere and pious as they were, they erred in theology. The Luke 15 narrative teaches that reception and restoration happen instantly at the moment of repentance and confession (Luke 15:21–24).

The reception home will not be unchallenged. The prodigal's delight in returning to the father's house met with his brother's dismay ("and he was angry", Luke 15:28). The reason was possibly that it could alter his inheritance. But the father immediately silenced it (Luke 15:31–32). Regrettably, there are "elder brothers" in the father's house who snub and criticize returning prodigals to the dismay of the Father.

The reception home will not be denied. The prodigal feared the father's refusal to allow his return (Luke 15:19). But he was mistaken. And, oh, how he was mistaken, for the father, in seeing him, ran to meet him and embraced and kissed him and threw a huge welcome home party for him (Luke 15:20). Simeon states, "Some perhaps may fear to return, because they have been so exceeding vile, but let none imagine that they have gone beyond the reach of mercy. The promise of acceptance extends to all without exception. 'There is bread enough and to spare' for all that will go to God."[456] "Christ receiveth sinful men, even me with all my sin."

What compelled the prodigal to return home? The goodness of the father. He said, "How many hired servants of my father's have bread enough and to spare, and I perish with hunger!" (Luke 15:17). It is the goodness of God that is intended to turn man from sin and bring him home to the Lord (Romans 2:4).

"One of the hardest things in the world is to stop being the prodigal son without turning into the elder brother."
John Ortberg

September 8

The Biblical Role of Grandparents

"Since my youth, God, you have taught me, and to this day I declare your marvelous deeds" (Psalm 71:17 NIV).

The role of grandparents:

God wants you to be a Blessing Giver. "The memory of the righteous is a blessing" (Proverbs 10:7 ESV). Matthew Henry is correct to say, "Blessed men leave behind them blessed memories."[457] The memory of the righteous (the grandparents' reputation of godliness, saintliness, holiness, fairness, uprightness, honesty) will be a blessing to their grandchildren long after their death.

God wants you to be a Pattern Setter. "The righteous lead blameless lives; blessed are their children after them" (Proverbs 20:7 NIV). God wants you to be a track setter for your grandchildren by exhibiting a godly example in every facet.

God wants you to be a Message Bearer. "Even when I am old and gray, do not forsake me, my God, till I declare your power to the next generation, your mighty acts to all who are to come" (Psalm 71:18). Grandparents instill the seed of the Word in their grandchildren. They assist in their at-home theological schooling and discipleship.

God wants you to be a Prayer Intercessor. "I exhort therefore, that, first of all, supplications, prayers, intercessions, and giving of thanks, be made for all men" (1 Timothy 2:1). Martyn Lloyd-Jones stated, "Always respond to every impulse to pray"—especially for your grandchildren. Stand in the gap for them regarding their schooling, home life, relationships, dating, health, and outside influences. Every day I pray a hedge of protection about our three grandchildren (Madison Clark, Jude, and Hudson) that Satan in no wise will be able to 'steal, kill, or destroy.' Little may it be realized how often the intercessory prayers of grandparents was the very thing that protected their grandchildren from harm.

"Grandparents have always played an important role in providing stability and support for families."
Jay Kesler

September 9

The Profit of the Revival Meeting
"Wilt thou not revive us again?" (Psalm 85:6).

Nothing is better than an old-fashioned revival where powerful preaching is heard, soul-stirring music is sung, saints get right with God and each other, sinners are born into the family of God, passion for the lost is rekindled, prayers at the altar are answered, excitement and joy are experienced, and the church is faithfully attended. A revival meeting is profitable for the church for seven reasons.

1. It is profitable with regard to the souls that are saved. Revival is still one of the most effective means to reach the lost. Millions would be in Hell right now had they not been saved in a revival/crusade.

2. It is profitable with regard to baptisms.

3. Revival is profitable with regard to the renewal of the saved. It points the carnal to a higher spiritual plane and to a return to their "first love" for God. It produces harmony and unity among the brethren. Revival refreshes and energizes the saint.

4. Revival ignites spiritual passion for the lost. In this alone the value of revival is priceless.

5. Revival is profitable with regard to the pastor. It rekindles his fire, restores his hope, refreshes his soul, renews his ministry/personal disciplines [study, prayer, preaching, soul winning].

6. Revival brings the church back to its evangelistic roots. Many churches have lost the "seeking note" in the purpose for their existence ["to seek and to save"]. The farmer who builds a barn must not forget why he built it; the same is true for the church. A return to an evangelistic mind-set is imperative in preaching, teaching, and worship; and a revival can be the spiritual catalyst for this to happen.

7. Genuine revival always brings renewed joy, excitement, and expectation. Why not have an old fashioned revival?

"A church that needs to be revived is a church that is living below the norm of the New Testament pattern....It is a tragic fact that the vast majority of Christians today are living a subnormal Christian life....The church will never become normal until she sees revival."[458]
James Stewart

September 10

Wonderful Peace

"Then, because you belong to Christ Jesus, God will bless you with peace that no one can completely understand. And this peace will control the way you think and feel" (Philippians 4:7 CEV).

The Subject of Peace. It's a possession of the redeemed. "To be spiritually minded is life and peace" (Romans 8:6).

The Source of Peace. Barnes says, "Nothing else will furnish it but *Christ.* No confidence that a man can have in his own powers; no reliance which he can repose on his own plans or on the promises or fidelity of his fellowmen, and no calculations which he can make on the course of events can impart such peace to the soul as simple confidence in God."[459] To know the fullness of peace, fixate upon God (Isaiah 26:3) and trust (rely upon) His promises (Romans 8:28). MacArthur states, "Inner calm or tranquility is promised to the believer who has a thankful attitude based on unwavering confidence that God is able and willing to do what is best for His children."[460]

The Scope of Peace. It silences all that seeks to disturb the rest of the soul (doubt, worry, anxiety, fear, the unexplainable).

The Supply of Peace. It's inexhaustible. Its fountains are full and flourishing, and though used billions of times it has not diminished the slightest.

The Strangeness of Peace. It "surpasses all understanding," defying comprehension and explanation. Courson says, "We have been given the peace of Jesus Christ. Even though I might not understand what's going on, I have a peace that bypasses my brain and permeates my heart. I might not know why things aren't working out or why things are coming down. But in the midst of it all, Jesus offers me His peace."[461]

The Sentinel of Peace. 'It keeps the heart and mind in Christ Jesus' (Philippians 4:7). Wuest says, "The words 'shall keep' are from a military word which means, "shall mount guard." God's peace, like a sentinel, mounts guard and patrols before the heart's door, keeping worry out."[462] "It is a pledge," Bradley says, "of the special love of God to the soul, and as such it begets confidence in Him. Let a worldly man lose his earthly comforts and he has lost all; but let a man of God lose what he may, his chief treasure is safe."[463]

True faith, by a mighty effort of the will, fixes its gaze on our Divine Helper, and there finds it possible and wise to lose its fears. It is madness to say, 'I will not be afraid'; it is wisdom and peace to say, 'I will trust and not be afraid.'"
Alexander MacLaren

September 11

Gracious Giving

"Give, and it shall be given unto you; good measure, pressed down, and shaken together, and running over" (Luke 6:38).

The Macedonian saints serve as a pattern of New Testament stewardship (2 Corinthians 8:1–15).

They gave themselves. "But first they gave their own selves to the Lord" (2 Corinthians 8: 5 ASV). The priority of these early saints was to make a total presentation of body, mind and soul unto God (Romans 12: 1–2). Herein lies the foundation of biblical stewardship from which the *grace* of giving springs.

They gave eagerly. "They begged us again and again for the privilege of sharing in the gift for the believers in Jerusalem" (2 Corinthians 8:4 NLT). They were not beggars not for help, but to help. Remarkable!

They gave sacrificially. "They are being tested by many troubles, and they are very poor. But they are also filled with abundant joy, which has overflowed in rich generosity" (2 Corinthians 8:2 NLT). In deprivation they gave bountifully.

They gave joyously. "The abundance of their joy" (2 Corinthians 8:2). Saints are to contribute to the cause of Christ not grudgingly but cheerfully (2 Corinthians 9:7).

They gave willingly. "They were willing of themselves" (2 Corinthians 8:3). The maxim in giving is to give without compulsion of man, but in willingness of heart.

They gave systematically. The manner of giving, though unstated in the text, was the same as specified for the churches of Galatia (systematically on the first day of the week based upon ability; how God "had prospered him"). The tithe is the *floor* level of giving, not the *ceiling* (Haggai 2:8; Malachi 3:10).

"Giving is more than a responsibility—it is a privilege; more than an act of obedience—it is evidence of our faith."
William Arthur Ward

September 12

Arrogance and Conceit

"Don't cherish exaggerated ideas of yourself or your importance" (Romans 12:3 PHILLIPS).

Arrogance is like kudzu. It quickly takes root in the heart, grows with unimaginable speed, and hangs on insidiously. Success, achievement,

September

status, and flattery feed it. It is so ugly and detestable that it is included among the seven deadly sins that God hates (Proverbs 6:17).

Arrogance and conceit have brought down kings, rulers, politicians, and preachers. They defile the soul with their ugliness and wantonness, distress God, and disparage others. Colton says, "Pride, like the magnet, constantly points to one object—self; but, unlike the magnet, it has no attractive pole, but at all points repels."[464]

Bonar asserts, "The believing man will be a humble man. He will...refrain from giving prominence to self in any of his proceedings. His great object will be to hide self; and not only to forget it himself, but to make others forget it too. The man that is still proud, boastful, vainglorious, self-confident has good reason to suppose that he has never yet believed."[465] Saith C. S. Lewis, "If anyone would like to acquire humility, I can, I think, tell him the first step. The first step is to realize one is proud—and a biggish step, too. At least nothing whatever can be done before it. If you think you are not conceited, it means you are very conceited indeed."[466]

"'Bad pride' is the deadly sin of superiority that reeks of conceit and arrogance."
John C. Maxwell

September 13

The Power of Reading (Part One)

"Give attendance to reading" (1 Timothy 4:13).

Saith Spurgeon, "Personally, I have to bless God for many good books."[467] *Why read?*

1. Read to be changed. Thoreau said, "How many a man has dated a new era in his life from the reading of a book."[468]

2. Read to be connected. Books afford the privilege to connect with noble, sanctified, and wise minds (Proverbs 1:5).

3. Read to be challenged. Good religious books raise the bar for spiritual excellence in every facet of life, making us better ministers, servants, and followers of Christ. Emerson stated, "I cannot remember the books I've read any more than the meals I have eaten; even so, they have made me."[469] Don't devalue the role of books in God's plan to "make" you into a vessel of honor and profit.

4. Read to be comforted. C. S. Lewis wrote, "We read to know we are not alone."[470] Books are friends that sit up with us during the bitter and dark night when others don't, to provide compassion and hope in our time of dilemma, despair, and defeat. Oliver Wendell Holmes, Sr., advises, "The books we read should be chosen with great care, that they may be, as an Egyptian king wrote over his library, 'The medicines of the soul.'" And the books whose foundation is exclusively the Holy Scriptures provide such medicines for the wounded heart. Oswald Chambers said, "Books are the blessed chloroform of the mind."[471] Spurgeon's sufferings were assuaged by the reading of six books a week.

"Books are like imprisoned souls till someone takes them down from a shelf and frees them."[472]
Samuel Butler

September 14

The Power of Reading (Part Two)
"Give attendance to reading" (1 Timothy 4:13).

5. Read to be cultivated. Books are ladders to knowledge unknown to the reader and bridges to spiritual understanding and maturity.

6. Read to be combatant. Saith Spurgeon: "You may get much instruction from books which afterwards you may use as a true weapon in your Lord and Master's service."[473] See 2 Timothy 4:13.

7. Read to be counseled. Saith Charles Baudelaire, French poet (1821–1867), "A book is…a counselor, a multitude of counselors."[474] Solomon says, "Without guidance people fall, with many counselors there is deliverance" (Proverbs 11:14 TLV). Charles William Eliot, president of Harvard University (1869), said, "Books are the quietest and most constant of friends; they are the most accessible and wisest of counselors, and the most patient of teachers."[475] Saith Elizabeth Barrett Browning, "No man can be called friendless who has God and the companionship of good books."[476] Books provide access to and spiritual advice by the church's most knowledgeable, trustworthy, and gifted ministers over the centuries (Spurgeon, Adrian Rogers, James Dobson, W. A. Criswell, Billy Graham).

September

"If you cannot read all your books...fondle them—peer into them; let them fall open where they will; read from the first sentence that arrests the eye; set them back on the shelves with your own hands; arrange them on your own plan so that you at least know where they are. Let them be your friends; let them, at any rate, be your acquaintances."[477]
Winston Churchill

September 15

The Watchman over Souls

"They watch for your souls, as they that must give account" (Hebrews 13:17).

Foremost in the pastor's job authorized by the Holy Spirit is to keep watch over the souls of the flock, a task for which "God will judge them on how well they do" (Hebrews 13:17B TLB).

The pastor's watch is that of an observer and admonisher. Paul kept an eye on Timothy's flame, and when it began waning said to him, "Stir up (rekindle the embers of, fan the flame of, and keep burning) the [gracious] gift of God, [the inner fire] that is in you" (2 Timothy 1:6 AMPC). That's part of the pastoral job—to watch for members whose fire is waning and exhort them to restore it to full flame.

The pastor's watch is that of a protector and defender. He vigilantly guards the sheep against vicious wolves in sheep's clothing who seek to smother their flame through doctrinal heresy and conformity to the world. It is said that a good shepherd doesn't coddle wolves; he shoots them. He doesn't condone them; he combats them. When the world seeks to quench the flame of a saint, as it did the faith of Demas, the pastor combats it tooth and nail through prayer, warning, and exhortation. Note, this is one of the numerous reasons why Christians ought to be a part of the local church—and one of its utmost benefits.

The pastor's watch is that of a feeder and nourisher. John Owen said, "The first and principal duty of a pastor is to feed the flock by diligent preaching of the word."[478] And even more emphatically he said, "He is no pastor who doth not feed his flock."[479] The reason the sheep are famished in many folds (churches) is the absence of the proclamation of the unadulterated Word of God. To this Solomon attests, "Where there is no vision [feeding of the Word], the people perish" (Proverbs 29:18). John Milton observed, "The hungry sheep look up and are not fed."

"They [pastors] are to watch against everything that may be hurtful to the souls of men, and to give them warning of dangerous errors, of the devices of Satan, of approaching judgments; they are to watch for all opportunities of helping the souls of men forward in the way to heaven."[480]
Matthew Henry

September 16

A Neglected Vineyard

"They made me the keeper of the vineyards; but mine own vineyard have I not kept" (Song of Solomon 1:6).

The Shulamite woman was entrusted with the care of the vineyards of others, which she managed well, howbeit, to the neglect of her own. She enabled the vineyards of others to stay pruned and thus bear much fruit, while her own was overtaken with weeds and thorns, yielding little or no fruit.

Regrettably, her fault is the fault of many in the ministry. While busily caring for the spiritual welfare of others, they are negligent of the work needed in their own vineyard. They promote the growth of others spiritually, while they remain stunted. They fuel the fire of others, while their own fire, perhaps unknown to them, dies out.

In a lecture to the students at his Pastor's College, Spurgeon gave advice worthy of heeding by every pastor: "Feed the flame, my brother; feed it frequently. Feed it with holy thought and contemplation, especially with thought about your work, your motives in pursuing it, the design of it, the helps that are waiting for you, and the grand results of it if the Lord be with you."[481]

"Jesus taught that your highest priority must be your relationship with Him. If anything detracts you from that relationship, that activity is not from God. God will not ask you to do something that hinders your relationship with Christ."
Henry Blackaby

September 17

Help Them Hear the Call

"As they ministered to the Lord, and fasted, the Holy Ghost said, separate me Barnabas and Saul for the work whereunto I have called them" (Acts 13:2).

While praying and fasting, the saints at the Antioch church were told by the Spirit to inform Paul and Barnabas of their call to missionary service and commission them to it. Sometimes help is needed to identify God's call, and encouragement to surrender to it is required.

George W. Truett aimed to be a lawyer, but the members of Whitewright Baptist Church, where he taught Sunday school and often filled in for the pastor, discerned his giftedness and call to the ministry. To his shocking surprise, during a Saturday church meeting in 1890, the members voted to ordain him to the ministry. That changed the trajectory of his life. He would become one of the greatest preachers of the Twentieth Century and pastor the First Baptist Church, Dallas, Texas, for 41 years, where the church grew from 715 members to more than 7,000. God used the members of Whitewright Baptist Church to help Truett recognize the call to vocational ministry.

With regard to a divine call, Spurgeon said, "Considerable weight is to be given to the judgment of men and women who live near to God, and in most instances their verdict will not be a mistaken one."[482] Saints in general, and churches at large that discern the divine call in a person mustn't hesitate to share that insight with him, and once the call is confirmed by the Holy Spirit and the Word, they must give him encouragement to engage in it.

"God's call is an inner conviction given by the Holy Spirit and confirmed by the Word of God and the body of Christ."[483]
Erwin Lutzer

September 18

Pray for Laborers

"Pray ye therefore the Lord of the harvest, that He will send forth laborers into His harvest" (Matthew 9:38).

How might the right laborer get to the right field at the right time? Jesus reveals the answer in two Greek words.

Jesus says, "Pray ye." The Greek word for "pray," *deomai,* means "to entreat, to plead earnestly, and to beg" with urgency. It's the word used by the father that sought the expulsion of demonic spirits from his son (Luke 9:38) and the leper that fell to the ground pleading for healing (Luke 5:12).

The second Greek word is *ekballo,* translated as "send forth" (Luke 10:2). It means "to drive or thrust forth," indicating the urgency of the mission (Vincent). It is used also for casting out demons (Matthew 8:16) and for expelling the money changers in the temple (John 2:15).

In Jesus' use of the words (*deomai* and *ekballo*) it's clear that believers are to pray, cry out to God to thrust out or dispatch laborers into the harvest with the same tenacity and fervency as they would for the exorcism of a demon and the healing of an incurable disease. Note, the same supernatural power that was required to cast out demons, heal the leper, and drive out the money changers is necessary for God to thrust laborers into the harvest.

"Lord, breathe Thine own Spirit on all Thy children, that they may learn to live for this one thing alone—the Kingdom and glory of their Lord—and become fully awake to the faith of what their prayer can accomplish."[484]
Andrew Murray

September 19

The Believer's Hope

"My flesh shall rest in hope" (Acts 2:26).

Biblical hope, unlike secular hope, means certainty, confidence, and assurance of something happening. It's not wishful thinking but undoubtable reality. John Bunyan clarifies the difference yet affinity between faith and hope: "Faith says to hope, 'Look for what is promised'; hope says to faith, 'So I do, and will wait for it too.'"[485] What is the believer's hope?

1. *It consists of the resurrection of the body.* Paul said, "If in this life only we have hope in Christ, we are of all men most miserable (1 Corinthians 15:19). Jesus is proof as well as the preview of the

September

resurrection. He rose bodily and was recognizable, just as will be the case with every believer (Luke 24:39). Paul says, "Just as we have borne the image of the man of dust, we shall also bear the image of the man of heaven" (1 Corinthians 15:49 ESV).

Jesus gives promise of the resurrection in John 11:25: "I am the resurrection and the life. He who believes in Me, though he may die, he shall live" (NKJV). J. C. Ryle writes, "There is a resurrection after death. Let this never be forgotten. The life that we live here in the flesh is not all. The visible world around us is not the only world with which we have to do. All is not over when the last breath is drawn and men and women are carried to their long home in the grave. The trumpet shall one day sound, and the dead shall be raised incorruptible. Let us cling to it [this hope] firmly and never let it go."[486]

2. *It consists of future life in Heaven.* Billy Graham says, "Because Heaven is real, we have hope—hope for the future and hope for our lives right now. No matter what happens to us now, we know it won't last forever, and ahead of us is the joy of Heaven."[487] In Heaven there will be the absence of sickness, sorrow, and suffering that bring tears to our eyes and heart (Revelation 21:4).

3. *It consists of Christ's return.* Paul writes, "Looking for that blessed hope, and the glorious appearing of the great God and our Savior Jesus Christ (Titus 2:13). Fear, anxiety, despair, and misery are dispelled in the hope of Christ's soon return. Confidence for the hope of His return is undergirded by the fact that He initially appeared as promised by Old Testament prophets[488] and His personal promise to return in John 14:3.

4. *It consists of reunion with loved ones beyond this life.* The Bible says, "Then we which are alive and remain shall be caught up together with them in the clouds, to meet the Lord in the air: and so shall *we* ever be with the Lord" (1 Thessalonians 4:17). A grand reunion day of unending fellowship with loved ones and saints of all ages awaits the redeemed at death or the Lord's coming. To know that we will see loved ones and friends again beyond the veil of this life grants unspeakable peace and calm in the midst of grave sorrow. What a glorious Hope we have in Christ Jesus!

"Without Christ there is no hope."
C. H. Spurgeon

September 20

Real Evangelism

"We are Christ's ambassadors. God is using us to speak to you: we beg you, as though Christ himself were here pleading with you, receive the love he offers you—be reconciled to God" (2 Corinthians 5:20 TLB).

Paul understood real evangelism. His preaching and personal work in soul winning was framed around the death, burial and resurrection of Christ Jesus for man's redemption (1 Timothy 1:15; Galatians 3:13; 1 Thessalonians 1:10; Romans 14:9).

Peter understood real evangelism. To the diverse ethnic and racial crowd (Acts 2:5) at Pentecost, he boldly declared the crucifixion and resurrection of Jesus, urging them to believe and be saved (Acts 2:36–38).

It is evident that *Timothy understood real evangelism*, for he did the "work of an evangelist" (2 Timothy 4:5).

Others in Paul's company (Epaphras, Tychicus, Onesimus, Barnabas, etc.) understood real evangelism, for they too presented the central message of the cross to those confronted (Colossians 1:20).

Great preachers of yesterday such as Finney, Moody, Sunday, Whitefield, Rice, Scarborough, Torrey, Chapman, and Graham understood *pure* and *undefiled* evangelism in the same manner. "In our work of evangelism," states J. I. Packer, "Christians are sent to convert, and they should not allow themselves, as Christ's representatives in the world, to aim at anything less. Evangelizing includes the endeavor to elicit a response to the truth taught. It is communication with a view to conversion. It is a matter not merely of informing, but also of inviting. It is an attempt to *gain* or *win* or *catch* our fellow men for Christ (1 Corinthians 9:19–23; 1 Peter 3:1; Luke 5:10). Our Lord depicts it as fishermen's work (Matthew 4:19; 13:47)."[489]

"A proper theology of evangelism...will result in a profound zeal to win the lost."[490]

Lewis Drummond

September 21

The Modernistic Sermon

"Woe is unto me, if I preach not the gospel" (1 Corinthians 9:16).

September

It is with sacred memory that it is recalled that the preacher of yesterday (pioneer or old-fashioned gospel preacher) actually "preached." They were men full of zeal and passion for the heavenly assigned task. Their manner of speaking was not dull monotone or mere script reading from a staled manuscript filled with another's words and thoughts. They preached Jesus and Him crucified, buried and raised, with pathos in their bones, fervency in their soul and a glowing sincerity upon their face.

Stewart asserts, "There is something wrong if a man, charged with the greatest news in the world, can be listless and frigid and feckless and dull. Who is going to believe that the tidings brought by the preacher matter literally more than anything else on earth if they are presented with no sort of verve or fire or attack, and if the man himself is apathetic and uninspired, afflicted with spiritual coma and unsaying by his attitude what he says in words?"[491]

The mainline (or modernistic) sermon at present has drifted far afield from its biblical predecessor in content, delivery, and invitational appeal. With regard to delivery, it has more of a ring of a lecturer or teacher (certainly not like the old-time preacher that started low, aimed high and caught fire as he preached). With regard to its content, it consists more of good advice than the Good News with its subject matter perhaps framed from the Bible, but not upon the Bible. The sermon itself deals more with personal relevance than with God's revelation,[492] self-improvement than rightness with God, and more with "feel good" psychological doses of uplift than sound theological exhortation.

The tenets of "the old-time religion" have little or no place in its theology and preaching. And it, unlike its New Testament standard, rests on human intellectualism, persona, and charisma, not the power of the Holy Spirit (1 Corinthians 2:4). Whitesell said it best: "Our day needs New Testament evangelistic preaching—Spirit-empowered preaching, bold preaching, doctrinal preaching, Biblical preaching, relevant preaching, persuasive preaching, pungent preaching, preaching full of the love of Christ supported by transformed lives."[493]

Brethren, may we beg God for a return to such preaching for the church's sake, our family's sake, and the sake of the eternally damned.

"There is no Gospel if the atoning blood of Christ is omitted, the virgin birth denied, Christ's resurrection eliminated and justification by faith not proclaimed."
R. G. Lee

September 22

The Coming Sermon

"Remove not the ancient landmark, which thy fathers have set" (Proverbs 22:28).

One can only fear the makeup of *the coming sermon*. How much more can God's Word be adulterated, abandoned and abused in preaching? How much further will the church drift from its foundational roots of preaching paved by the likes of men like C. H. Spurgeon, R. G. Lee, G. Campbell Morgan, John R. Rice, W. A. Criswell, John Wesley, Billy Graham, A. C. Dixon, E. J. Daniels, Adrian Rogers and lesser knowns, but nonetheless just as bold and powerful in their preaching?

We must return to our spiritual roots of New Testament preaching lest the coming sermon become nothing more than mere platitudes that scratch "itching ears" (2 Timothy 4:3). God forbid, but unless things change, the coming sermon that soon will be heard will be one about a Christ without a Cross, a God without wrath, a Heaven without a Hell, sin without consequence, a manger without the virgin birth, a Christian without commitment, and a salvation without the blood atonement of Christ.

And such forces tears to my eyes and pain to my heart as I but ponder such a woeful and devastating possibility in the not too far future. At present, sound biblical theological sermons are thundered by a faithful few in country, rural and city venues. But they are becoming scarcer.

Honor such men, uphold them, encourage them, defend them, pray for them, and USE them. Don't wait until they're gone to realize their invaluable contribution to the kingdom. The last sermon the famous pastor, W. A. Criswell of the First Baptist Church, Dallas, Texas, preached was entitled, "The Old-Time Religion." Such a sermon is timely for this hour of the church.

"If we are to see the church of God really restored to her pristine glory, we must have back this plain, simple, gospel preaching."[494]
C. H. Spurgeon

September 23

Seven Robbers of Peace

"And the peace of God, which passeth all understanding, shall keep your hearts and minds through Christ Jesus" (Philippians 4:7).

Peace divinely afforded to the child of God may be stolen suddenly by one of seven thieves of darkness (1 Peter 5:8).

Worry and anxiety. The main cause for worry is uncontrolled futile, frivolous, and foolish imaginations. Wrong thinking leads to wrong feelings, instilling anxiety and worry. Dr. Walter Cavert states that only 8 percent of things that we worry about are legitimate matters of concern. The remaining 92 percent of things that cause worry either are imaginary, never happened or involve matters over which we have no control. The thief of worry is capturable and conquerable by allowing Christ to rule the domain of your mind (2 Corinthians 10:3–5) and by exhibiting trusting confidence in His ability to care for you (Philippians 4:6–7).

Unconfessed sin. David's unconfessed sin caused him despair and misery. When it was resolved through confession, peace and joy were restored (Psalm 51:12). Matthew Henry says, "What peace can they have who are not at peace with God?"

Flight from God's plan. Jonah fled from God's plan but experienced heartache and havoc in the process.

Wrong expectations. Unrealistic expectations personally and for others (spouse, friend, employer, minister) lead to emotional shipwreck (bitter disappointment and frustration). Wrong expectation accounts for multitudes of suicides and barbiturate addicts.

Suffering, pain, and sorrow. Apart from the grace of God to bear adversity and affliction, peace is elusive. "My grace is sufficient for you" (2 Corinthians 12:9 ESV).

Grieving the Holy Spirit. Sin grieves the Holy Spirit, quenching His peace.

Hopelessness. "Hopelessness constricts and withers the heart, rendering it unable to sense God's blessings and grace."[495] "Hope thou in God" (Psalm 42:11).

"God cannot give us a happiness and peace apart from Himself, because it is not there. There is no such thing."
                                  C. S. Lewis

September 24

Hopelessness

"Why are you so depressed, O my soul? Why so disturbed within me? Hope in God" (Psalm 42:5 EHV).

The Psalmist, in a state of mental anguish and gloom, arouses himself through self-interrogation not to lose hope but trust God for consolation. Boice says, "It is a case of the mind speaking to the emotions rather than the emotions dictating to the mind." [496] D. Martyn Lloyd-Jones similarly states, "You have to take yourself in hand; you have to address yourself, preach to yourself, question yourself. You must say to your soul, 'Why art thou cast down'—what business have you to be disquieted? You must turn on yourself, upbraid yourself, condemn yourself, exhort yourself, and say to yourself, 'Hope thou in God'—instead of muttering in this depressed, unhappy way."[497]

The Psalmist had to chide himself three times about hopelessness, fretting and grieving before finally victory came (Psalm 42:5; Psalm 42:11; Psalm 43:5). In saying the right thing to one's soul, repetition is at times needed for the sun to burst out upon the darkness of the soul. "Hope thou in God" is healthy to repeat again and again until the soul soars out of its captivity.

"Emotion varies, but God is the same. The secret of calm is to dwell in that inner chamber of the secret place of the Most High."[498]
Alexander Maclaren

September 25

And All the Night Through

"In the daytime also, he led them with a cloud, and all the night with a light of fire" (Psalm 78:14).

God led the Israelites when it was light all around and when all was enveloped in deep darkness. Not for a moment were they ever out of His protective custody and care. In the nighttime, times of deepest darkness and despair (whatever their cause), clutch five eternal certainties for calm and comfort.

September

God's care is undoubted. Doubt not, deny not, question not God's care for you, for it hath been documented in Scripture: "He cares for you" (1 Peter 5:7 ESV), and substantiated experientially by untold millions innumerable times.

God's care is unchanging. The God of the mountain (daytime when all is well) is the God of the valley (night when all is dreadful). As God cares for and maintains our cause in the day tenderly and lovingly, just so He does in the night.

God's care is unceasing. "God's watch is an undivided one."[499] It is comprehensive, complete and continuous. God isn't on "shift-duty"; He doesn't rotate on and off providing the custodial care summoned.

God's care is unwearying. Unwearyingly and patiently, God manifests loving care. Friends and family wearied with our nighttime episodes gradually faint and fade away—but not God. Unrelentingly ("shall neither slumber nor sleep") He holds our hand, cools our fevered brow, and calms our disturbed soul, all through the night.

God's care is unfailing. It is efficacious. The Bible says, "The LORD *shall* preserve thee from all evil: he *shall* preserve thy soul" (Psalm 121:7). God's loving-kindness and tender mercies always provide the medication (grace) necessary to enable us make it through the night. "We never can enjoy any real repose of soul unless it be in the consciousness that God is near us, above us, manifesting Himself for us. A watchful and a watching God is the believer's warrant for repose (rest; peace); we repose beneath, when we are sure that He watches above."[500]

"If God cares for you, why need you care too? Can you trust Him for your soul, and not for your body? He has never refused to bear your burdens; He has never fainted under their weight. Come, then, soul! have done with fretful care and leave all thy concerns in the hand of a gracious God." [501]

C. H. Spurgeon

September 26

Ways the Holy Spirit Comforts

"Nevertheless, I tell you the truth; It is expedient for you that I go away: for if I go not away, the Comforter will not come unto you; but if I depart, I will send him unto you" (John 16:7).

The Holy Spirit ministers comfort to the saint in the storms of life by several means.

He comforts by His awesome presence (1 Corinthians 3:16).

He comforts through divine promises (Psalm 119:92).

He comforts through whispers of sweet and uplifting consolation (Hebrews 3:7).

He comforts through the reminder of Christ's teachings and past interventions (John 14:26).

He comforts through the manifestation of the fulness and sufficiency of Christ for every need (2 Corinthians 12:9).

He comforts through making God's Word understandable and applicable to the circumstance (Psalm 119:50).

He comforts through believers that He comforted (2 Corinthians 1:4).

He comforts through intercession for the believer (Romans 8:27).

He comforts through the impartation of hope (Romans 15:13).

He comforts through being a reservoir of God's love (Romans 5:5).

"Whenever peace enters your heart in the midst of grief...Whenever joy enters your heart in the midst of a trial...Whenever you see evidence of His life in yours...you can be sure the Holy Spirit is flowing through your life."[502]
Adrian Rogers

September 27

The Promises

"Thereby are given unto us exceeding great and precious promises" (2 Peter 1:4a KJ21).

Phil Pringle states, "The promises of God become the power of God when they are believed and acted upon."[503] Corrie ten Boom said, "Let God's promises shine on your problems."[504] Chan says, "True faith means holding nothing back. It means putting every hope in God's fidelity to His Promises."[505] Spurgeon remarked, "Every promise of Scripture is a writing of God, which may be pleaded before Him with this reasonable request: 'Do as Thou hast said.' The Heavenly Father will not break His Word to His own child."[506]

September

They are prodigious promises. They are not just great, but exceedingly great—great in scope, strength, suitability, stability, sufficiency, and supply. Their value is due to the hand from which they come, that of a great and mighty God.

They are precious promises. The word "precious" means of great value or worth, to be honored and highly esteemed. Ponder what the absence of any of them would mean and their preciousness is revealed to be that of pearls beyond price.

They are present promises. Each one is a gift to the saints.

They are pledged promises. They are signed with God's hand and assured with an oath. Pink says, "The permanence of God's character guarantees the fulfillment of his promises."

They are purposed promises. The promises are designed to nourish, strengthen, console, encourage, edify, inspire hope, assure, and embolden (2 Peter 1:4b). Claim them, apply them, and be blessed by them.

"God has given no pledge that He will not redeem, and encouraged no hope that He will not fulfill."
Charles Spurgeon

September 28

Arguments for Assurance (Part One)

"Don't be afraid. I am with you. Don't tremble with fear. I am your God. I will make you strong, as I protect you with my arm and give you victories" (Isaiah 41:10 CEV).

Note three arguments for the saint's unflinching assurance of God's faithfulness to help in the hour of need.

The Power of God. God is omnipotent, without limit or restriction in His power or authority. His power surpasses every hardship and hurt, conflict and concern, challenge and crisis. The "immeasurable greatness of his power" (Ephesians 1:19 ESV) provides a firm foundation upon which the believer can rest secure despite the circumstance.

Pompey boasted that with one stamp of his foot he could marshal all Italy to battle. But God, by one word, yea even a thought, can elicit all the powers of Heaven and earth to the aid of His children in distress. Tozer remarks, "With the goodness of God to desire our highest welfare, the wisdom of God to plan it, and the power of God to achieve it, what do we lack? Surely, we are the most favored of all creatures."[507]

The Past Performances of God. The past performances of God give proof to His faithfulness and ability to help today. The psalmist said, "I recall the many miracles he did for me so long ago" (Psalm 77:11 TLB). Newton says, "Assurance grows by repeated conflict, by our repeated experimental proof of the Lord's power and goodness to save; when we have been brought very low and helped, sorely wounded and healed, cast down and raised again, have given up all hope and been suddenly snatched from danger and placed in safety; and when these things have been repeated to us and in us a thousand times over, we begin to learn to trust simply to the word and power of God, beyond and against appearances. And this trust, when habitual and strong, bears the name of assurance; for even assurance has degrees."[508]

"Everything about God is great, vast, incomparable. He never forgets, never fails, never falters, never forfeits His word. To every declaration of promise or prophecy the Lord has exactly adhered; every engagement of covenant or threatening He will make good."[509]
A. W. Pink

September 29

Arguments for Assurance (Part Two)

"Don't be afraid. I am with you. Don't tremble with fear. I am your God. I will make you strong, as I protect you with my arm and give you victories" (Isaiah 41:10 CEV).

The Promises of God. "Let us hold fast the confession of our hope without wavering, for he who promised is faithful" (Hebrews 10:23 ESV). A. W. Pink argues, "But why should we not place implicit confidence in God and rely upon His word of promise? Is anything too hard for the Lord? Has His word of promise ever failed? Then let us not entertain any unbelieving suspicions of His future care of us. Heaven and earth shall pass away, but not so His promises."

God will do that which He said. J. C. Ryle asserts, "Let us learn to rest on promises and embrace them. Let us not doubt that every word of God about His people concerning things future shall as surely be fulfilled as every word about them has been fulfilled concerning things past. Their safety is secured by promise.

The world, the flesh, and the Devil shall never prevail against any believers. Their acquittal at the last day is secured by promise. They shall not come into condemnation but shall be presented spotless before the Father's throne. Their final glory is secured by promise.

Their Savior shall come again the second time, as surely as He came the first time—to gather His saints together and to give them a crown of righteousness. Let us be persuaded of these promises. They will never fail us. God's word is never broken. He is not a man that He should lie."[510]

"God writes with a pen that never blots, speaks with a tongue that never slips, acts with a hand that never fails."
C. H. Spurgeon

September 30

Proof of the Call to Ministry

"Unto me...is this grace GIVEN, that I should preach" (Ephesians 3:8).

Paul testified to Agrippa of the surety of his call (Acts 26:16–19), declaring that he was not "disobedient unto [that] heavenly vision" (Acts 26:19). And Spurgeon said, "It would have been a fearful thing for me to have occupied the watchman's place without having received the watchman's commission."[511]

Let him who contemplates entrance into the ministry make proof of the calling, for without it *fainting* will result when trials and suffering arise. "It will be a lamentable thing for us," saith Spurgeon, "to start in our course without due examination, for if so, we may have to leave it in disgrace....When I think upon the all but infinite mischief which may result from a mistake as in our vocation for the Christian pastorate, I feel overwhelmed with fear lest any of us should be slack in examining our credentials; and I had rather that we stood too much in doubt, and examined too frequently, than that we should become cumberers of the ground"[512]

Bridges states, "To labor in the dark without an assured commission greatly obscures the warrant of faith in the Divine engagements; and the

Minister, unable to avail himself of heavenly support, feels his 'hands hang down, and his knees feeble' in his work. On the other hand, the confidence that he is acting in obedience to the call of God—that he is in His work, and in His way—nerves him in the midst of all difficulty, and under a sense of his responsible obligations, with almighty strength."[513]

Upon confirmation of the call, "go forth armed from head to foot with armor of proof."[514] George Kulp states, "There will be a time come in the ministry of every preacher when he will be glad 'that God put him in the ministry,' that he did not seek the office, for with the knowledge that it was God who called him there will come the assurance that He who called will also equip, defend, accompany, and energize His servant, rendering him effective wherever his lot may be cast."[515]

"I don't see how anyone could survive in the ministry if he felt it was just his own choice. Some ministers scarcely have two good days back-to-back. They are sustained by the knowledge that God has placed them where they are. Ministers without such a conviction often lack courage and carry their resignation letter in their coat pocket. At the slightest hint of difficulty, they're gone."[516]

Edwin Lutzer

October 1

Down in the Dumps

"We were pressed beyond measure, beyond strength" (2 Corinthians 1:8 KJ21).

The picture is of an overloaded ship weighed down deep into the water, unable to rise. Paul's despair was so crushing and acute he felt there was no way out of it, no way of escape or hope of recovery from it. The cause is not revealed, but it exceeded in hardship the five beatings, shipwrecks, stoning, slander, and imprisonments he endured (2 Corinthians 11:25–28).

If one as spiritual as Paul battled hopelessness and utter despair, certainly no believer is exempt from its snare. Jonah faced it, as did Elijah. The great London pastor C. H. Spurgeon combatted deep depression for most of his ministry. Note, to assume certain men are exempt from deep crushing discouragement or despair based on their godliness or ministerial position is to err greatly. All men have feet of clay.

By the intervention of God, the result of the prayers of the saints (2 Corinthians 1:11), Paul survived the trial and said, "Praise be to the God and Father of our Lord Jesus Christ, the Father of compassion and the God of all comfort, who comforts us in all our troubles" (2 Corinthians 1:3–4 NIV). The sovereign God of the universe, saith Paul, is a comforter and encourager and the lifter of the head. To this David testified, as have all saints that have been in the miry pit of despair: "But thou, O LORD, art a shield for me; my glory, and the lifter up of mine head" (Psalm 3:3).

"I find myself frequently depressed—perhaps more so than any other person here. And I find no better cure for that depression than to trust in the Lord with all my heart and seek to realize afresh the power of the peace-speaking blood of Jesus and His infinite love in dying upon the cross to put away all my transgressions."
C. H. Spurgeon

October 2

Such a Worm As I

"Fear not, thou worm Jacob" (Isaiah 41:14).

The characterization of man as a "worm" depicts his utter weakness and impotency to handle life's issues without the help of God. A haughty spirit, however, prompts him to try. It keeps him from trusting God and brings havoc and heartache (Proverbs 16:18).

Spurgeon says, "When God's warrior marches forth to battle...saying, 'I shall conquer; my own right arm and my mighty sword shall get unto me the victory,' defeat is not far distant. God will not go forth with that man who goeth forth in his own strength."[517]

The way Up is Down. Humility is the foundation to help. Packer said, "Not until we have become humble and teachable, standing in awe of God's holiness and sovereignty, acknowledging our own littleness, distrusting our own thoughts, and willing to have our minds turned upside down, can divine wisdom [and help] become ours." "But I am poor and needy;...thou art my help and my deliverer; make no tarrying, O my God." (Psalm 40:17).

Oh, to be saved from self-trust, dear Lord;
   Oh, to trust wholly in thee;
Oh, to depend upon Thee in all weather
   Will be far better for me.
Frank Shivers (2021)

"Every now and again, Our Lord lets us see what we would be like if it were not for Himself; it is a justification of what He said—'Without Me you can do nothing.' That is why the bedrock of Christianity is personal, passionate devotion to the Lord Jesus."
Oswald Chambers

October 3

A Promise to Help

"Don't be afraid, people of Israel, for I will help you" (Isaiah 41:14 NLT).

Its Pledge. "I will help you." Henry states, "It is the honor of God to help the weak. He will help them, for he is their Redeemer."[518]

Its Provision. No limitations or exception clauses are included in the promise "I will help thee." It is all inclusive to the child of God whether the help needed is in regard to livelihood, infirmity, imprisonment, addiction, adversity, or sorrow. To all cares that possess you, the Sovereign God of the Universe says, "I will help thee."

Its Power. J. D. Watts says, "There can be no doubt about the effectiveness of this help. It is The Holy One of Israel, Yahweh himself, who has promised it."[519]

Its Proof. The proof of God's ability and willingness to come to our rescue in times of trouble is firmly established by divine aid in the past. The psalmist says, 'As I remember what you did yesterday for me, I stretch out my hands in trust for your help today' (Psalm 143:5–6, paraphrase). Spurgeon comments, "We ourselves have a rich past to look back upon. We have sunny memories, sacred memories, satisfactory memories; and these are as flowers for the bees of faith to visit, from whence they may make honey for present use."[520]

"Give not way then to dejection or sloth, but go forth in the strength of the Lord Jesus, and when difficulties appear to be absolutely insurmountable, then go to Him, and remind Him of His promise: 'I will strengthen thee, yea I will help thee.'"[521]
Charles Simeon

October 4

Preserving Power of God's Word

"Unless thy law had been my delights, I should then have perished in mine affliction" (Psalm 119:92).

David appropriated God's Word to his troublesome circumstance and was rejuvenated. Matthew Henry says, "It was so now in his affliction; it [God's Word] afforded him an abundant matter of comfort, and from these fountains of life he drew living waters when the cisterns of the creature were broken or dried up. His converse with God's law, and his meditations on it, were his delightful entertainment in solitude and sorrow."[522]

It is said there are 7,487 divine promises God has made payable to His children.[523] And each is exceedingly great and precious (2 Peter 1:4). "There may be a promise in the Word," Spurgeon says, "which would exactly fit your case, but you may not know of it, and therefore you miss its comfort. You are like prisoners in a dungeon, and there may be one key in the bunch which would unlock the door, and you might be free; but if you will not look for it, you may remain a prisoner still, though liberty is so near at hand. There may be a potent medicine in the great pharmacopeia of Scripture, and you may yet continue sick unless you will examine and search the Scriptures to discover what He hath said."[524] The Word must be applied for it to provide.

"It is impossible to delight in God's Word, containing as it does rich promises and the revelation of a glorious future, without having resignation, fortitude, hope, etc."[525]
The Homilist

October 5

Hide God's Word in the Heart

"Thy word have I hid in mine heart, that I might not sin against Thee" (Psalm 119:11).

David treasured God's Word to the degree that he 'hid it in his heart' (Psalm 119:11). He never wanted to be a moment without it. The Word of God in the coffin of his heart, though unseen, "constituted the secret power by which he was governed; it was permanently deposited there, as the most valuable of his treasures."[526]

Memorization of Holy Scripture enhances our comprehension, application, and utilization of it. Spurgeon said, "The Bible in the memory is better than the Bible in the bookcase." "Gather the riches," says Corrie ten Boom, "of God's promises. Nobody can take away from you those texts from the Bible which you have learned by heart."

Note, a day may be forthcoming when the Bible in your heart may be the only one upon which you may lean (grave illness, loss of eyesight, or censorship by persecution). Memorize it so you will not be deprived of it when it perhaps is needed the most. Fanny Crosby, though blind, memorized five chapters of the Bible each week.

"The word of God is a most powerful antidote against sin when it has a place in the heart; not only the precepts of it forbid sin, but the promises of it influence and engage to purity of heart and life."[527]
John Gill

October

October 6

Treatment of the Bible

"All Scripture is given by inspiration of God, and is profitable for doctrine, for reproof, for correction, for instruction in righteousness" (2 Timothy 3:16).

Do five things with the Word of God.

Possess it. That is, know it; don't simply tote it. Master the Bible as a lawyer would master a law manual; or a doctor, a medical book. Bonar said, "We must study the Bible more. We must not only lay it up within us but transfuse it through the whole texture of the soul."

Prize it. Treat it as a rare treasure. Prize it above the riches and honor of the world.

Protect it. Stand ready to defend it from the gainsayers (1 Peter 3:15; Jude 3).

Proclaim it. "Proclaim the Word of God and stand upon it no matter what!" (2 Timothy 4:2 TPT).

Practice it. Flesh the Word out into conduct. "Be ye doers of the word, and not hearers only" (James 1:22).

"Knowledge of the Bible never comes by intuition. It can only be obtained by diligent, regular, daily, attentive reading."
J. C. Ryle

October 7

What Is Truth?

"Pilate said unto Him, 'What is truth?'" (John 18:38 KJ21).

To the question, Pilate waited not for an answer, nor did he seemingly want it. He spoke as a scoffer, not as a seeker. There are many Pilates who ask the question lightheartedly but are undeserving of an answer.

The prejudicial inquirer. He is biased against the source and meaning of truth (closeminded)—and he rejects it.

The pompous inquirer. Truth about himself as revealed in Christ is too humbling to embrace—and he evades it.

The petty inquirer. Truth to him is that which is too frivolous and trivial to seriously consider—and he scorns it.

The profligate inquirer. Truth is the enemy to his licentious pursuits and pleasures—and he fights it.

The serious inquirer. Truth to him must be known at all cost and consequence—and he receives it.

Application:

1. "Answer not a fool according to his folly" (Proverbs 26:4). Don't cast your pearls before swine (Matthew 7:6). Matthew Henry says, "Wise men have need to be directed how to deal with fools; and they have never more need of wisdom than in dealing with such, to know when to keep silence and when to speak, for there may be a time for both." Bridges asserts, "Silence may sometimes be mistaken as defeat. Unanswered words may be deemed unanswerable, and the fool become arrogant, more and more wise in his own conceit. An answer therefore may be called for."[528]

2. The person that seeks the truth about Christ and the need of salvation will certainly find it. "And ye shall seek Me, and find Me, when ye shall search for Me with all your heart" (Jeremiah 29:13).

"Searching for God with one's heart is the way to find Him out; for God is discerned by the heart."[529]

Henry Ward Beecher

October 8

Healing for Hurt

"Who…walketh in darkness and hath no light? Let him trust in the name of the Lord, and stay upon his God" (Isaiah 50:10 KJ21).

Healing is found in the presence of God. "The Lord is nigh unto them that are of a broken heart" (Psalm 34:18). Fixate on Christ's loving care and sympathy *with* you. He that promised never to leave or forsake you is with you to bear you up on wings of eagles. "From the highest throne in glory to the place of deepest woe," the Lord hath come to assist you.

Healing is found in the promises of God. The promises are a "strong and trustworthy anchor for our souls" (Hebrews 6:19 NLT). It is an anchor that will hold the ship steady and secure in the worst of turbulent seas. In that "medicine cabinet" there is a healing salve to mend every broken heart (Lamentations 3:22–23).

Healing is found in the people of God. It was when David was weak and troubled that Jonathan strengthened and encouraged him (23:16).

Healing is found in the praise of God. Emotional heaviness zaps one of spiritual vitality, robs joy and peace, crushes faith and diminishes hope. God promises a great exchange: "the garment of praise for the spirit of heaviness" (Isaiah 61:3). The "garment of praise" literally means to be "wrapped up in praise." Wrap or envelop your soul in continual praise to God, and the depressing and oppressing spirit of heaviness will vanish.

"Safety and peace come only after we have been forced to our knees."
A. W. Tozer

October 9

The Land of Beginning Again

"Behold, I make all things new" (Revelation 21:5).

Alice Chase Chin wrote, "For each of us that have traveled the road of sorrow, misfortune, and sin, there's a wonderful place of courage and hope called the Land of Beginning Again!" Chin sighed for a land where she could lay aside the past, much the same way a man puts aside soiled clothes and starts life afresh.

This "Land of Beginning Again" is found in a relationship with Christ called "The New Birth" (John 3:3). With the New Birth the sinner's soiled garments of the flesh (sinfulness, wretchedness) are supernaturally replaced with the clean and righteous garments of Christ, resulting in a miraculous change, "a new creation" (2 Corinthians 5:17). Of it, Spurgeon remarked, "This great work is supernatural. It is not an operation which a man performs for himself; a new principle is infused, which works in the heart, renews the soul, and affects the entire man. It is not a change of my name, but a renewal of my nature, so that I am not the man I used to be, but a new man in Christ Jesus."[530]

Characteristics of the change:

A change of spiritual state—no longer a slave to sin, but a son of God.

A change of heart about Christ. The indifference or enmity toward Christ changes to reverence, allegiance, honor, admiration, and gratitude.

A change of conduct. The things of Christ once despised or loathed now are loved and cherished.

A change of feeling about the church. It once was neglected and avoided; now it is attended and supported.

A change of attitude about the world. It ceases to be the dominating object of life; living for Christ and eternity are instead.

A change of temperament toward people. Enmity toward others is replaced with the love of Christ.

A change of destination. The saved man is now bound for Heaven, not Hell.

Note, to experience this change, this "Land of Beginning Again," the sinner must be "born again"—not a mere modification or alteration of life, but a complete transformation that Jesus only can produce. And this He will do for any man that places faith in Him as Lord and Savior and gives evidence of that faith by repentance of sin.

"The new birth is inexplicable. One can only observe the results."[531]
Ed Hindson

October 10

"Fresh Oil"

"I shall be anointed with fresh oil" (Psalm 92:10).

The infilling of the Holy Spirit is the surrender of self anew to the Holy Spirit's control, authority, and supremacy in the heart. It is the requisite for spiritual gianthood.

Watchman Nee says, "Just as the right relationship with Christ generates a Christian, so the proper relationship with the Holy Spirit breeds a spiritual man." It is essential for victory in warfare (Zechariah 4:6) and success in service (Acts 1:8). Meyer said, "We shall stand powerless and abashed in the presence of our difficulties and our foes until we learn what He [the Holy Spirit] can be as a mighty tide of love and power in the hearts of His saints."[532] Duncan Campbell said, "It is the signature of the Holy Ghost upon our work and witness that makes all the difference."

"Fresh oil" is needed in times of physical and spiritual taxation; spiritual complacency, apathy, and staleness; and following sin and compromise. Infilling or control of the Holy Spirit is acquired by confession of sin, surrender of self, and request of God (Luke 11:11–13).

"We cannot expect to have the Holy Spirit's fullness in our lives if we are quite content to live without it. Our Father is not likely to entrust this priceless gift to those who are indifferent to its possession. We must, therefore, stir up the gift that is within us by a quiet consideration of all that is meant by becoming Spirit-filled."[533]

F. B. Meyer

October 11

Marks of the Spirit-Filled

"And be not drunk with wine, wherein is excess; but be filled with the Spirit" (Ephesians 5:18).

The spirit-filled man resembles a drunkard in five respects.[534]

In ecstatic singing. The drunkard sings bawdy, raucous songs; the infilled saint sings songs of praise from the heart to the Lord. MacArthur states, "The first consequence of the Spirit-filled life that Paul mentioned was not mountain-moving faith, an ecstatic spiritual experience, dynamic speaking ability, or any other such thing. It was simply a heart that sings."[535]

In talkativeness. The drunkard can't shut up; the man infilled with the Holy Spirit can't be silenced in talking about Christ and that which He has done for him.

In invincibility. The drunkard thinks he can fight any man and win; the infilled man is conscious of the power of the Holy Spirit residing in him to thwart the efforts of Satan and the workers of darkness (Micah 3:8).

In fearlessness. The drunkard is the bravest man in the bar; the man infilled with the Spirit is bold as a lion (Proverbs 28:1). A pivotal sign of the infilling of the Holy Spirit is dauntless boldness and courage to stand up and speak up for Christ without regard of the consequence. It is recorded of the disciples that "when they had prayed, the place was shaken where they were assembled together; and they were all filled with the Holy Ghost, and they spake the word of God with boldness" (Acts 4:31). The Holy Spirit banishes the fear of man in witnessing and other Christian work.

In comportment. The drunkard walks staggering, unnaturally; the infilled man walks more godly, naturally. "What I am saying is this: run your lives by the Spirit. Then you will not do what your old nature wants" (Galatians 5:16 CJB).

"We need men so possessed by the Spirit of God that God can think His thoughts through our minds, that He can plan His will through our actions, that He can direct His strategy of world evangelization through His Church."
Alan Redpath

October 12

Rest for the Weary Saint

"Come unto me, all ye that labor and are heavy laden, and I will give you rest" (Matthew 11:28).

Christ invites the saint that is taxed heavily with physical burdens, emotional turmoil, grief, fright, guilt and hopelessness to come to Him for rest, and restoration. Bradley says, "There is more power in Christ to comfort than in the world to disquiet."[536]

Of this promised rest Brooks says, "'Come,' saith Christ, 'and I will give you rest.' I will not *show* you rest, nor barely *tell* you of rest, but I will *give* you rest. I am faithfulness itself, and cannot lie, I will give you rest. I that have the greatest power to give it, the greatest will to give it, the greatest right to give it. Come, laden sinners, and I will give you rest. Rest is the most desirable good, the most suitable good, and to you the greatest good."[537]

The offer is available to all that need it, and it will be given immediately to all who by faith request it. Saith Spurgeon, "It is present. 'Come' now; do not wait. So sweet an invitation demands a spontaneous acceptance. Do nothing else but come to Him."[538]

October

"There are many heads resting on Christ's bosom, but there's room for yours there."[539]
Rutherford

October 13

Rest for the Weary Sinner

"Come unto me, all ye that labor and are heavy laden, and I will give you rest" (Matthew 11:28).

It is an invitation to rest extended to the unsaved who are "heavy laden" (exhausted, frustrated) in the quest of salvation through religious works, rites and ordinances, and obedience to rules. It is extended to the man weary of the addiction to alcohol, drugs, gambling, or pornography. It is extended to the man weary and worried about eternal damnation and separation from God and saved loved ones at death. It is extended to the man tired and weary of working hard to earn God's approval. It is extended to the man that is distraught, dismayed and unhappy over the life that he lives and the impact it bears upon himself and others. It is extended to the man plagued with fear over the uncertainty of tomorrow.

There is no rest to be found in worldly pleasures, possessions, religion, medicine, philosophy, or an empty Christian profession. But in Christ there is promised rest. It's a satisfying rest. It's a confident rest about tomorrow. But most of all, it's a rest from sin—its guilt, torment, misery, power, consequence, eternal judgment.

And this rest is afforded freely to all who come to Christ by faith and repentance. There is no justification for delay. It's time for the prisoner to be set free and to come Home where he belongs in Christ Jesus.

Why go another moment wracked with inner turmoil when real soul rest can be known immediately? Augustine said, "Lord, Thou madest us for Thyself, and we can find no rest till we find rest in Thee!"[540] "I *will* give you rest" (Matthew 11:28). See Romans 10:9–13.

"You may be ready to fear that your burdens are too heavy to be removed, and your sins too great to be forgiven, but the persons whom Christ invites are the heavy-laden, yea, all of them without exception, whatever be their burdens, and whatever be their sins."[541]
Charles Simeon

October 14

The Forsaken Church

"Why is the house of God forsaken?" (Nehemiah 13:11).

1. The church declines because of being displaced by virtual worship. Virtual worship can never replace the need for what in-house worship affords (Hebrews 10:25).

2. It declines because of dissension among the members. Members and outsiders alike are repelled by the faction, fussing, and feuding that is witnessed within the doors of the church.

3. It declines because of departure from the Bible being preached and taught soundly as the authoritative Word of God (Proverbs 29:18). The power and blessing of God are withheld from the church that minimizes the Word of God (1 Corinthians 2:4).

4. It declines because of dullness in its services fueled by cold formality and ritualism. When the Holy Spirit's fire is quenched, the church becomes a valley of dry bones.

5. It declines because of the negative impression among the unsaved due to inconsistent churchgoers (Leviticus 19:14). Hypocritical behavior turns the unsaved away from the church.

6. It declines because of a deficit of funds (Haggai 1:4). Financial struggles force church closures.

7. It declines because of a disconnect between pulpit and pew (Jeremiah 3:15). Preaching and teaching that fail to connect with the needs of the man in the pew discourage attendance.

8. It declines because of a lack of desire by members to attend (Psalm 122:1). Aughey rightly says, "A little thing will keep them from the house of God who have no desire to go to it."[542]

9. It declines primarily because of the darkness that encompasses the unregenerate, blinding them as to the need of Christ, and therefore His church (2 Corinthians 4:4; 2 Timothy 3:1–5).

"Churches should evaluate everything they do to determine how it can be done better."
Thom S. Rainer

October 15

Three *R*s of Revival

"Remember therefore from where you have fallen; repent and do the first works" (Revelation 2:5 NKJV).

What might be done to cause the church that is in a state of decline to prosper? There's but one cure: revival.

Jesus gave the church at Ephesus the three *R*s of revival. He said, they were to remember, repent and return.

Remember the spiritual healthy estate from which you have fallen. "Let's examine and probe our ways, and turn back to the LORD" (Lamentations 3:40 CSB). With desperation, cry out to God with Job, "Oh that I were as in months past" (Job 29:2).

Repent, turn away not just from the sins that caused the fall but all sin. Jesus said, "If we confess our sins, he is faithful and just to forgive us our sins, and to cleanse us from all unrighteousness" (1 John 1:9).

And then, *Return,* "do the first works." Get back to communion with God, back to the Bible, back to the prayer closet, back to your "first love," back to working for God as you formerly did, back to giving, back to witnessing, and back to faithfulness to the church.

Revival fire is flamed in the believer's heart personally prior to spreading to the church body corporately. Lord, send a revival! "O Lord, send a revival, and let it begin in me!"

"A revival is nothing else than a new beginning of obedience to God."
Charles G. Finney

October 16

If God Was Not on Our Side (Part One)

"If it had not been the Lord who was on our side" (Psalm 124:1).

What "if" God had not intervened for us in times of affliction, trouble, assault by adversaries, false accusations, and suffering?

But He did. Davies said, "If we had stood alone, if God had not been round about us, if unerring wisdom had not thought for us and worked for us when the calamity threatened, then had we been as the bird in the snare of the fowler; then had we been overwhelmed!"[543]

What "if" He had not intervened on our behalf with regard to sin and its eternal penalty?

But He did. "There is no doubt," Spurgeon says, "as to our deliverer, we cannot ascribe our salvation to any second cause, for it would not have been equal to the emergency; nothing less than omnipotence and omniscience could have wrought our rescue. We set every other claimant on one side and rejoice because the Lord was on our side."[544]

What "if" God had not intervened in giving us second chances?

But He did. God doesn't desert us when we stumble.

What "if" God had not intervened in our ministry, immersing it in His power to accomplish His purposes?

But He did. Apart from His power infused into our preaching and teaching it would have been as tinkling cymbals and sounding brass, void of any spiritual or lasting profit.

What "if" God had not intervened in preservation of accomplishments attained in our labor?

But He did. It's uplifting to realize that fruit borne in labor for Christ will outlast time. He has established it to be so.

C. T. Studd said, "Only one life, 'twill soon be past; only what's done for Christ will last."[545] Hallelujahs to our great and enabling God. If God had not been with and for us, even in the worst of circumstances, our lot would have been multiple times worse (Habakkuk 3:17–19).

"The stamp of "impossible" cannot rest upon anything if we are able to say concerning it, "It has been done." And that we are able to say concerning every kind of strain or calamity that "turns up" in a religious experience."[546]
R. Tuck

October 17

If God Was Not on Our Side (Part Two)
"If it had not been the Lord who was on our side" (Psalm 124:1).

October

What "if" God had not intervened for us in the time of bereavement?

But He did. The Bible says, "He healeth the broken in heart, and bindeth up their wounds" (Psalm 147:3).

What "if" God had not granted the believer the promise of everlasting life at death?

But He did. Paul exclaims, "'Where, O death, is your victory? Where, O death, is your sting?' The sting of death is sin, and the power of sin is the law. But thanks be to God! He gives us the victory through our Lord Jesus Christ" (1 Cor. 15:55–57).

What "if" God never promised that He would never leave us or forsake us?

But He did. To know that He is with us in our troubles and trials, granting comfort and hope, makes the unbearable bearable.

What "if" God had not intervened on behalf of our nation in the past?

But He did. "It is thou, O Lord Jesus, who hast wrought for us this great salvation; it is Thou who from the beginning hast preserved Thy church in the world, amidst the persecutions which must otherwise have put an end to its very existence."[547]

Yea, in all these challenges, calamities, and crises of life, "God was on our side; He took our part, espoused our cause, and appeared for us. He was our helper, and a very present help, a help on our side, nigh at hand. He was with us, not only for us, but among us, and commander-in-chief of our forces. If it had not been Jehovah himself, a God of infinite power and perfection, that had undertaken our deliverance, our enemies would have overpowered us."[548]

The "if" is the believer's eternal promise and stronghold in the time of trial. Spurgeon says, "The glorious Lord became our ally; He took our part and entered into treaty with us. If Jehovah were not our protector, where should we be? Nothing but His power and wisdom could have guarded us. The Lord was on our side, and He is still our defender, and will be so from henceforth, even forever. Let us with holy confidence exult in this joyful fact."[549]

"The presence of God results in His blessing, which includes protection from enemies and dangers, even as He had promised."[550]
W. A. VanGemeren

October 18

The Preacher's Mandate

"I am ready to preach the Gospel" (Romans 1:15).

The preacher's charge. "Preach the word; be instant in season, out of season; reprove, rebuke, exhort with all long suffering and doctrine" (2 Timothy 4:2).

The preacher's compulsion: "For though I preach the Gospel, I have nothing to glory about, for necessity is laid upon me. Yea, woe is unto me if I preach not the Gospel!" (1 Corinthians 9:16 KJ21).

The preacher's confidence: "Now therefore go, and I will be with thy mouth, and teach thee what thou shalt say" (Exodus 4:12).

The preacher's consolation: "And they, whether they will hear, or whether they will forbear, (for they are a rebellious house,) yet shall know that there hath been a prophet among them" (Ezekiel 2:5).

"Other men may preach the Gospel better than I, but no man can preach a better Gospel."
George Whitfield

October 19

What Prayer Can Do

"And when they had prayed" (Acts 4:31).

Upon the release of Peter and John from jail, a spontaneous prayer meeting developed with other believers (Acts 4:23). Examination of the effects of that time spent in prayer reveals what sincere and believing prayer accomplishes (Acts 4:31–33).

Prayer shakes things up. "And when they had prayed, the place was shaken where they were assembled together" (Acts 4:31). A physical phenomenon happened as they prayed. The place literally was shaken (to rock, or oscillate, like a ship in turbulent waters). Prayer possesses the supernatural power of God and therefore ought always to shake and shape "things" when engaged in biblically.

October

Prayer fills the believer up. "And they were all filled with the Holy Spirit" (Acts 4:31). Criswell says, "Special fillings occur in times of need for particular spiritual prowess."[551]

Prayer loosens the tongue to speak of Christ. Rising from their knees, the believers immediately began to speak the "Word of God" (Acts 4:31). In prayer, their hearts were inflamed to testify to the unsaved.

Prayer emboldens the believer to stand for Christ. Needing boldness, they requested and received it to face the fierce persecution (Acts 4:31). Pray for the courage to respond to persecution.

Prayer unites the brethren. Prayer bonded them together as one (Acts 4:32). Prayer has a way of diffusing differences and uniting the divided.

Prayer empowers the believer. Rising from their knees, these saints possessed "great power" (Acts 4:33). Kroll says, "Fervent prayers produce phenomenal results."[552]

"Our praying needs to be pressed and pursued with an energy that never tires, a persistency which will not be denied, and a courage that never fails."[553]
E. M. Bounds

October 20

The Giant Cedar Has Fallen

"Howl [moan, distraught, wail], fir tree [those left without them]; for the cedar [the close and dearest companions] is fallen" (Zechariah 11:2).

Learn from the fallen cedar.

Even the biggest tree in the forest will fall. When they that are spiritually strong, healthy, mighty, and exceptionally useful fall, let the fir tree take notice that their own death is forthcoming. Death is no respecter of persons. That which was the cedar's lot will also be the fir's. Make preparation to be ready for it. Don't become callous to the news of death and that of its personal eventuality. Spurgeon says, "When the voice of God is heard among the trees of the garden, let fig tree and sycamore, and elm and cedar alike hear the sound thereof."[554]

When the giant cedar falls, the impact will be great. Family, friends, churches, ministries, and nations "howl" when their giant cedar falls in death. It is right to be saddened and distraught. The majestic cedar of godliness, boldness, integrity, dependability, influence, leadership, mentorship, wisdom, and defense is fallen—how could they not be missed?

Cedars leave behind a sweet-smelling aroma. Cedars transfer an unending sweet aroma into the objects around them (as in cedar chests). The aroma of a fallen cedar ever abides with the fir it richly benefited.

Fir trees can become giant cedars. That which is unnatural in nature is possible with man. The fir tree can become a giant cedar to a friend, spouse, ministry, or church. And through disciplined spiritual cultivation they may, if ordained by God, become giant cedars to the kingdom, nation and/or world, as with Spurgeon and Graham.

The fir tree is sovereignly sustained when the giant cedar falls. At the fall of the cedar, the cry is heard, "How can the fir tree stand when the cedar is fallen?" How can those who lose their cedar be strong enough to live life or continue in ministry without them? The Lord gives answer: "My grace is sufficient for thee." Remember, the saint's dependency on a cedar is only secondary. God is first and foremost, and He promises never to forsake or abandon us. With Him to strengthen, succor, and secure, the fir tree, despite the absence of the cedar, will be sustained and will flourish.

"This is our comfort. We are 'immortal until our work is done'; mortal still, but immortal also. Let us never fear death, then, but rather rejoice at the approach of it, since it comes at our dear Bridegroom's bidding!"
C. H. Spurgeon

October 21

Wait for the Answer

"Wait, I say, on the LORD" (Psalm 27: 14).

Wait on the Lord that He may "strengthen" thy heart to grow firm and strong, to be fortified against that which oppresses, opposes, obstructs, or overwhelms. Paul, through waiting, was granted strength (supernatural enabling) with regard to the thorn in his flesh that afflicted him sorely (2 Corinthians 12:9), and its pain (and that of other afflictions) turned into pleasure (2 Corinthians 12:10). Now that's worth waiting upon the Lord to attain!

Waiting dispels despondency, dread, despair and defeat. Waiting comforts (instills peace), enables (empowers), clarifies (illuminates the mind about the will of God), emboldens (infuses bravery sufficient for the challenge) and awakens the soul to God's perspective and purpose.

Blackaby and King offer great advice on what to do while you wait: "Let God use times of waiting to mold and shape your character. Let God use those times to purify your life and make you into a clean vessel for His service."[555] Swindoll states, "We don't like waiting, but that's when God does some of His best work on our souls."[556]

A minister, often interrupted by annoying knocks on his door by fleeing children, hung under the knocker the polite request, "Please don't knock unless you wait for an answer." Let's not "trouble" God with our requests (knocks at His door) unless we are willing to wait for Him to answer.[557] Bring your troubles to the Lord, and then wait upon Him to grant rescue, relief, or remedy. Rest assured He will answer the knock.

"It may seem an easy thing to wait, but it is one of the postures which a Christian soldier learns not without years of teaching."[558]
C. H. Spurgeon

October 22

Failure Is Not Final

"If you return to me, I will restore you so you can continue to serve me" (Jeremiah 15:19 NLT).

Christians, even the godliest of them, falter. Peter did in denying the Lord thrice. Elijah did in fleeing from Jezebel in cowardice. King David did in the adulterous affair with Bathsheba and the murder of her husband. John Mark did in abandoning Paul and Barnabas. And Jonah did in running from God's call.

No Christian, despite the sin, is beyond restoration. Epps states, "When God forgives, He at once restores."[559] As God restored these men following failure, He stands eagerly ready to restore you. What should the believer that stumbles into sin do to be restored?

Recognize it. (Own it.) Accept responsibility for the sin done (Proverbs 28:13).

Repent of it. (Confess it.) Henry Ward Beecher said, "God pardons like a mother, who kisses the offense into everlasting forgiveness."[560]

Release it. (Forget it.) Saith Kroll, "God forgets your confessed sins; so should you."[561] Refuse to allow Satan to intimidate you over a forgiven past sin. Unless we let go of the failures (sins) placed under the blood of Christ Jesus (1 John 1:7b), we will be spiritual and emotional cripples until death (Romans 5:20).

Rebound from it. (Snap back from it.) "The godly may trip seven times, but they will get up again." (Proverbs 24:16 NLT). Chambers wrote, "Never let the sense of failure corrupt your new action." Failure doesn't have to be fatal or final, not with God in the equation. Enter into the restoration He provides through Christ Jesus (1 John 1:9). A paralyzing past or a magnificent future is your choice.

"When we set sin before our face (as David did, 'My sin is ever before me') God casts it behind his back."[562]
Matthew Henry

October 23

Holding Up a Friend's Hands

"They stood on each side of Moses, holding up his hands. So his hands held steady until sunset" (Exodus 17:12 NLT).

The narrative of Aaron and Hur holding up Moses' hands suggests several traits of true friendship that were manifested by them.

Friends seize the opportunity to help. A friend in need is a friend indeed. "A friend loveth at all times, and a brother is born for adversity" (Proverbs 17:17).

Friends help without being asked. When a friend is in need, there is no tomorrow. Someone said, "Friendship isn't about whom you've known the longest. It's about who walked into your life, said, "I'm here for you," and proved it."[563]

Friends do what they can do to help. "To please a friend is a welcome bonus; to help him is the great reward."[564] Jonathan strengthened David's grip on God. An old proverb says, "Hold a true friend with both your hands." Friends live to make life less difficult for their friends.

October

Friends stay the course to the end. A note in Moody's Bible says, "A true friend is like ivy—the greater the ruin, the closer he clings."⁵⁶⁵

Friends are difference makers. "Ointment and perfume rejoice the heart: so doth the sweetness of a man's friend by hearty counsel" (Proverbs 27:9). He that holds a friend's hands up faithfully will make his bed of sickness softer, affliction bearable, disposition enjoyable, suffering manageable, and impending death easier. They make their journey of life sweeter and more enjoyable.

*"Friends voluntarily tie their hearts to one another. They put their happiness into their friends' happiness, so they can't emotionally flourish unless their friends are flourishing too."*⁵⁶⁶
Timothy Keller

October 24

Miracles Happen

"Listen to these words, fellow Israelites! Jesus of Nazareth was a man whose divine authority was clearly proven to you by all the miracles and wonders which God performed through him. You yourselves know this, for it happened here among you" (Acts 2:22 GNT).

Miracles are God-ordained supernatural interventions. Scripture records only thirty-seven of the many miracles of Jesus (John 20:30–31).

Some of the miracles were natural occurrences whose timing was supernaturally set. It is no miracle to catch a net full of fish. But to catch them after fishing futilely all night immediately upon doing what Christ instructed is a miracle. Other miracles He did were unnatural occurrences. It's not according to natural law for a man to walk on water, yet Peter miraculously did at the word of Jesus.

Michael Green explains the purpose for the miracles. "The miracles are pictures of what Jesus offers to do in the human heart. His opening the eyes of a blind beggar, Bartimaeus, is a picture of the new vision He offers too all. His healing of paralyzed people is a picture of the new power He makes available to those who put their lives in His hand. His turning of water to wine shows how He can change the ordinary drudgery of life into high-octane living. His feeding of the multitude shows how He longs to be the bread that satisfies the believers' heart. His raising of Lazarus from the grave points to His ultimate offer: to give new and eternal life to all who trust themselves to Him. That is one of the main reasons why Jesus worked miracles."⁵⁶⁷ But the foundational reason for the miracles of Christ was to substantiate His claim of deity (John 14:11; Matthew 9:6–8; Acts 2:22).

Do miracles continue? Saith Spurgeon, "The greatest, strongest, mightiest plea for the church of God in the world is the existence of the Spirit of God in its midst, and the works of the Spirit of God are the true evidences of Christianity. They say miracles are withdrawn, but the Holy Spirit is the standing miracle of the church of God today." "Jesus Christ the same yesterday, and today, and forever" (Hebrews 13:8). Open your eyes. All around you are evidences of miracles.

"Miracles are not meant to be understood; they are meant to be believed."
D. Martyn Lloyd-Jones

October 25

Void If Detached

"Without me ye can do nothing" (John 15:5).

A bus ticket read, "Void if Detached." This meant that the stub of the ticket was of no value by itself. Its value and power were linked to its attachment to the ticket.

The same is true for the believer in the spiritual walk. Attached to Christ ("abide in me"), he possesses the power to pray, witness, work, thwart temptation, grow, bear fruit, and live victoriously. Detached from Him, however, the believer can do nothing [not detachment regarding salvation, but communion].

Stay connected to the power source by walking in unison with Christ 24/7. The stub is no good apart from its attachment to the ticket.

"The believer must keep on looking to Christ, day by day, for his spiritual life; must keep in constant hourly touch with Him; must by a life of prayer, communion, and trust keep momentarily drawing upon Him 'in whom dwelleth all the fullness of the Godhead bodily.'"⁵⁶⁸
James McConkey

October 26

A Word Did It!

"Let there be light: And there was light" (Genesis 1:3).

At God's word the Red Sea dried up to permit the Israelites passage of escape from the Egyptian army. "He rebuked the Red Sea also, and it was dried up" (Psalm 106:9a). *A word did it.* To escape the clutches of satanic bondage, it only takes the right word.

Crossing the sea of Galilee, the disciples and Jesus encountered a furious storm. To the boisterous winds and raging sea Jesus said, "Peace, be still," and at once it obeyed (Mark 4:39–41). *A word did it.* Whatever storm threatens life, a word from Christ grants calm and peace.

A nobleman besought Jesus to heal his dying son. "Jesus saith unto him, Go thy way; thy son liveth. And the man believed the *word* that Jesus had spoken" (John 4:50–53). And the son was healed at that moment (John 4:51). *A word did it.*

Upon Hezekiah's request of God for healing, fifteen years were added to his life (2 Kings 20:5–6). *A word did it.* In grave illness, with no hope of recovery, a word from Christ can heal.

The penitent thief said to Jesus, "'Lord, remember me.' And Jesus said, 'Today you will be with Me in paradise'" (Luke 23:43 MEV). *A word did it.* A word from Christ infuses hope in dying.

Paul, in battling a relentless "thorn in the flesh," found relief in Jesus' word, "My grace is sufficient for thee" (2 Corinthians 12:9–10). *A word did it.* Agonizing suffering becomes endurable at the word of Christ.

Martha's sorrow in Lazarus' death was consoled with a word from Christ. "Jesus said to her, 'I am the resurrection and the life'" (John 11:25 ESV). *A word did it.* In bereavement but a word from Christ brings comfort.

Zacchaeus sought Christ. "Jesus said unto him, this day is salvation come to this house" (Luke 19:9). He was saved. *A word did it.*

"The work begins with light. God said, 'Let there be light,' and at once light shone where all before was dark. God says, 'Repent ye—the kingdom of heaven is at hand'; then our darkness displeases us, and we are turned to light."[569]

Whatever the need, bring it to Jesus. At His word the impossible becomes possible. Saith Delitzsch, "He speaks, and it is done; He commands, and it stands fast."[570] Don't deprive yourself of its incomparable potent medicine. Receive by faith the word spoken unto you from the heart of Christ.

A word did it for the Israelites, the nobleman, the thief on the Cross, Hezekiah, Paul, Martha, and Zacchaeus. Let it do it for you. And in doing so, may you testify with them regarding the mighty change that takes place, saying, *A word did it*. It took only a word from Christ.

"Oh, the power of the word of God! He spoke, and it was done, done really, effectually, and for perpetuity."[571]
Matthew Henry

October 27

Jesus Prepared a Place

"I go to prepare a place for you" (John 14:2).

The imagery of Jesus returning to His carpentry skills, pounding nails into boards and constructing houses for believers is spurious. Rather, it surely describes his death, resurrection, ascension, and princely role at the Father's right hand. His return to Heaven completed the divinely assigned redemptive mission (the final "nail" to be hammered) to make saints ready for Heaven and Heaven ready for them.

D. A. Carson agrees, saying the words "presuppose that the 'place' exists before Jesus gets there. It is not that He arrives on the scene and then begins to prepare the place; rather, in the context of Johannine theology, it is the going itself, via the cross and resurrection, [and I add ascension] that prepares the place for Jesus' disciples." Pink further unravels the words, *I go to prepare a place for you*. He said [my paraphrase]: It means that Jesus has procured the right for every regenerated sinner to enter Heaven by His death on the Cross. He has "prepared" us a place there as our Representative (Forerunner) by planting His royal banner in its soil and procuring it on our behalf.

Further, Jesus has "prepared" for us a place there by entering the "holy of holies" on High as our great High Priest, carrying our names in with Him." Christ did all that was necessary to secure a permanent place in Heaven for His children.

Christ prepares the place in Heaven for His own, and the Holy Spirit prepares the redeemed on earth for their place in Heaven. After all, Heaven is a prepared place for a prepared people. Apart from Christ's cross, triumphant resurrection and exaltation (redemptive work), no place in Heaven could have been prepared for the sinner.

"Heaven would be an unready place for a Christian if Christ were not there."[572]

Matthew Henry

October 28

Make Every Day Count

"Teach us to number our days" (Psalm 90:12).

Moses likens man's lifetime to seven things.

1. To a small speck of the day (Psalm 90:4).

2. To a small portion of a night (Psalm 90:4).

3. To a dream that quickly disappears (Psalm 90:5).

4. To a blade of grass that blossoms in the morning only to wither and die in the evening (Psalm 90:6).

5. To a mere passing thought (Psalm 90:9).

6. To a mighty gale force wind that blows it away quickly like a piece of straw (Psalm 90:9).

7. To a bird that swiftly flies away (Psalm 90:10).

They all are intended to awaken man to the brevity and frailty of life, to its sudden, unexpected end, so that he may make every day count for God. Saith Spurgeon, "A short life should be wisely spent. We have not enough time at our disposal to justify us in misspending a single quarter of an hour. Neither are we sure of enough of life to justify us in procrastinating for a moment. If we were wise in heart, we should see this, but mere head wisdom will not guide us aright."[573]

Why are we slow to number our days? We don't like how they add up. We don't see the paramount need. We foolishly think that old age is the time to ponder death, not the springtime of youth and middle-age. Therefore, we must do as Moses instructs and beg God to help us number our days, for if He doesn't, we will not.

How to number our days? Number them as you might number the last days to be spent with a close friend, so you can cram each day full with the things that matter most.

"It is an excellent art rightly to number our days, so as not to be out in our calculation, as he was who counted upon many years to come when, that night, his soul was required of him. We must live under a constant apprehension of the shortness and uncertainty of life and the near approach of death and eternity."[574]
Matthew Henry

October 29

Divine *Unshakable*s
"Those things which cannot be shaken" (Hebrews 12:27).

God's presence with you is unshakable. In the darkest night when God appears nowhere to be found, He faithfully abides with you. "My unfailing love for you *will not be shaken* nor my covenant of peace be removed,' says the Lord, who has compassion on you" (Isaiah 54:10 NIV).

God's promises to you are unshakable. Heaven and earth may pass away but His Word stands sure forever (Matthew 24:35). Not one promise has failed or ever will.

God's power in you is unshakable. The "immeasurable greatness of his power" abides in you (Ephesians 1:19 ESV). It enables calm in tempest, comfort in trials and courage in terror.

God's purpose for you is unshakable. Paul says, "God began doing a good work in you, and I am sure he will continue it until it is finished when Jesus Christ comes again" (Philippians 1:6 NCV). Jeremiah says, "'For I know the plans and thoughts that I have for you,' says the Lord, 'plans for peace and well-being and not for disaster, to give you a future and a hope'" (Jeremiah 29:11 AMP).

Regardless of the form, severity or duration of the trial, God's plan for you remains unshakable and unalterable. "So we will not be afraid, even if the earth is shaken and mountains fall into the ocean depths; even if the seas roar and rage, and the hills are shaken by the violence"

October

(Psalm 46:2–3 GNT). Though all about the saint is shaken, he rests upon an unshakeable and sure foundation in Christ.

"We will all acknowledge, I think, that if our souls are to rest in peace and comfort, it can only be on unshakable foundations. It is no more possible for the soul to be comfortable when it is trying to rest on 'things that can be shaken' than it is for the body. No one can rest comfortably in a shaking bed or sit in comfort on a rickety chair. Foundations, to be reliable, must always be unshakable."[575]
Hannah Whitall Smith

October 30

Attitude in Suffering

"Endure suffering…as a good soldier of Christ Jesus" (2 Timothy 2:3 NLT).

The saint's response to suffering is prescribed in the Scripture.[576]

1. Bear it. Jeremiah said, "Surely this sickness and suffering and grief are mine, And I must bear it" (Jeremiah 10:19 AMP). God never places upon His child a load too heavy to carry.

2. Be content in it. Paul testified, "Whatsoever state I am, therewith to be content" (Philippians 4:11).

3. Glory in it. "Most gladly therefore will I rather glory [boast] in my infirmities, that the power of Christ may rest upon me" (2 Corinthians 12:9). Beecher said, "We are always in the forge, or on the anvil; by trials God is shaping us for higher things."[577] And it is for this reason the Christian glories in suffering and trouble.

4. Joy in it. "Instead, be really glad—because these trials will make you partners with Christ in his suffering, and afterwards you will have the wonderful joy of sharing his glory in that coming day when it will be displayed" (1 Peter 4:13 TLB). Jerry Bridges said, "God does not ask us to rejoice because we have lost our job, or a loved one has been stricken with cancer, or a child has been born with an incurable birth defect. But He does tell us to rejoice because we believe He is in control of those circumstances and is at work through them for our ultimate good."[578]

5. Be patient in it. "When trials come endure them patiently" (Romans 12:12 PHILLIPS).

6. Be steadfast in it. "But none of these things move me" (Acts 20:24). Graham said, "Christians are not to be moved away from their faith by suffering and trial, but rather strengthened and fortified."[579]

7. Be prayerful in it. "In my distress I cried unto the Lord, and he heard me" (Psalm 120:1). Man prays best in adversity.

8. Be still in it. "Be still, and know that I am God" (Psalm 46:10). Be still, exhibit trust in God, and He will quiet the angry sea, giving peace and calm. Note, these traits in suffering not only will glorify Christ but infuse hope, patience, happiness, and peace hitherto unknown.

"If I had not felt certain that every additional trial was ordered by infinite love and mercy, I could not have survived my accumulated sufferings."
Adoniram Judson

October 31

Divine Healing

"The Lord sustains him on his sickbed; in his illness you restore him to full health" (Psalm 41:3 ESV).

All healing is divine healing. The most brilliant medical specialist or successful surgeon cannot heal. Wherever healing takes place, its foundational cause is the hand of God. We are not guaranteed a pain-free or illness-free life. Neither are we promised healing in every case. But we as believers do have every biblical right to look to God for healing in time of sickness.

1. Because of His divine goodness. The benevolent character or nature of God is to heal. That's who He is. That's His "DNA." All healing flows ultimately from His goodness toward man. Spurgeon said, "The sweetest prayers God ever hears are the groans and sighs of those who have no hope in anything but his love."[580]

2. Because of His divine attestation. "I am the Lord that healeth thee" (Exodus 15:26).

3. Because of divine documentation. Numerous accounts of healings in the Bible affirm God's practice of healing the sick. Jesus healed Bartimaeus (Mark 10:46–52). He healed Jairus' daughter (Matthew 9:18–26). And since Jesus remains "the same yesterday, today, and forever"

October

(Hebrews 13:8 CSB), we may be confident that He stands ready to heal infirmities today.

4. Because of His omnipotent power. No disease or sickness is beyond His ability to heal. No timetable is too soon or too late for Him to heal. God reversed Hezekiah's illness while he was upon the death bed (2 Kings 20:1, 5).

5. Because of His overriding plan. God's eternal plan for our life vetoes any illness that might impede it. Henry Martyn said, "I am immortal until God's work for me to do is done."

6. Because of the substantiation of the Holy Scripture. The psalmist proclaims that it is the Lord "who heals all your diseases" (Psalm 103:2–3 ESV).

"He [Christ] is the only universal doctor, and the medicine He gives is the only true catholicon [a cure-all], healing in every instance."[581]
C. H. Spurgeon

November 1

The Proof That Prayer Works

"Call unto me, and I will answer thee, and shew thee great and mighty things, which thou knowest not" (Jeremiah 33:3).

"The proof that God answers prayer," saith Chadwick, "is in praying."[582] Prayers in Jesus name based upon Scripture and God's will are accompanied with answers.

S. D. Gordon writes, "True prayer never fails. It cannot, because it depends on God and on His pledged Word."[583] "It is not a matter of doubt," saith Spurgeon, "as to whether God hears and answers prayer—if there is any fact in the world that is proved by the testimony of honest men, this is that fact!"[584] Multiplied testimonies attest to diseases cured, monetary needs supplied, marriages restored, lives transformed, accidents averted, jobs provided, protection from harm granted, laborers raised up, doors to ministry opened, great works done, and revival fires ignited through the efficacy of prayer.

Jehoshaphat, king of Judah, received a frightening report: "A vast army is coming against you!" Alarmed, Jehoshaphat stopped what he was doing and prayed: "O our God, will You not judge them? For we have no power against this great multitude that is coming against us; nor do we know what to do, but our eyes are upon You" (2 Chronicles 20:12 NKJV). Jehoshaphat and the people prayed for divine help. "All Judah, with their little ones, their wives, and their children, stood before the LORD" (2 Chronicles 20:13 NKJV). God responded favorably to their prayer and gave them the victory in the battle.

Hannah prayed that God would give her a son (1 Samuel 1:1–20). And He did, with the birth of Samuel. Peter in prison awaiting execution was prayed for by the church. As they prayed an angel of the Lord came to Peter and escorted him to safety (Acts 12:1–17). Elijah prayed for rain, and it rained. He prayed that the rain would stop. And it stopped (James 5:17–18). After a plague was sent upon Egypt, Pharaoh begged Moses to pray for its removal (Exodus 10:17). The record states that God answered Moses' prayer miraculously and removed it plague as quickly as it arose. In travel to Rome by ship, the lives of Paul and the crew were in jeopardy amidst a great storm. Paul took a long absence from others to pray and all aboard were saved (Acts 27:21).

All through the sacred pages of God's Word miracle after miracle is recorded in response to the prayer of faith. E. M. Bounds says, "Miracles and faith went hand in hand. They were companions. The one was the cause; the other was the effect. The miracle was the proof that God heard and answered prayer."[585] Miracles, happenings that defy human comprehension or explanation and transcend the laws of nature yet happen today when God's people dare exhibit faith in their asking, even as these events of olden days. The proof of the power of prayer is in its answer.

"Thousands and tens of thousands of times have my prayers been answered. When once I am persuaded that a thing is right and for the glory of God, I go on praying for it until the answer comes."[586]
George Müller

November 2

A Thorn in the Flesh

"There was given to me a thorn in the flesh" (2 Corinthians 12:7).

"A thorn in the flesh." It was divinely allowed to counteract the uprising of pride in Paul. A thorn permitted is for a divine purpose intended. "A thorn in the flesh."

It is unforgettable. Its incessant pain makes it impossible to ignore.

It is unpleasurable. Nowhere is the saint told he must enjoy a thorn (suffering); we are just called upon to endure it as good soldiers.

It is undetectable. It is secretive to most outside the sufferer. Many bear a thorn unseen to others. Just because another seems blessed, says Spurgeon, don't suppose his path is smooth. "His roses have their thorns; his bees, their stings."[587]

It is unavoidable. Paul couldn't, nor can anyone else. It is not delivered by man, but by God.

But it is bearable and tolerable. "My grace is sufficient for thee." Grace sustained Paul, and it will also sustain you. Philip Hughes is surely correct when he writes: "Is there a single servant of Christ who cannot point to some 'thorn in the flesh,' visible or private, physical or psychological, from which he has prayed to be released, but that has been given him by God to keep him humble, and therefore fruitful? Paul's 'thorn in the flesh' is, by its very lack of definition, a type of every Christian's 'thorn in the flesh.'"[588]

November

"He who sent Paul thorns for his good once wore a thorn-crown Himself for the salvation of sinners."[589]
C. H. Spurgeon

November 3

Remember the Chains

"Remember my chains" (Colossians 4:18 ESV).

Many saints are shackled to a chain that hinders greater work for Christ. For some, it is the chain of sickness and suffering. The medically chained desire to do more for Christ, but infirmities hinder.

For some, it is the chain of financial inadequacy and hardship. Monetary limitation and strain prevent saints from giving more to the cause of Christ. The heart wants to, but the pocketbook prohibits.

For some, it is the chain of work. Secular work, a necessity for livelihood, impedes Christian service. The bivocational pastor is hampered by such a chain ("tentmaking").

For some, it is the chain of frailty. As the body grows older, its members become frail and worn, hindering them from doing that which was done in younger years.

For some, it is the chain of being a caretaker. The task of caring for a chronically ill spouse, child or parent 24/7 hampers and impedes much of what one desires to do for Christ.

For some, it is the chain of parenthood. Children limit that which mom and dad can do for the Lord. The cries of the cradle hold them back.

For some, it is the chain of school. Class attendance and studies hinder Christian work.

For many, it is the chain of marriage. Loyalty to one's spouse places limitations on service to Christ. This is why Paul advised, if possible, not to marry.

For some, it is the chain of immobility. The wheelchair, a cane or crutches prohibit ease of mobility from place to place, hampering what might be done for Christ.

And yet for others, it is the chain of incarceration. The confinement of prison limits Christian service as it did for Paul.

Many are strapped to such chains of impediment. Remember the chain of others with discernment. Look deeper at one's life before you hastily jump to the wrong conclusions. Often when we do that, a chain previously unknown to us is discovered and explains the person's actions or lack thereof. "Remember my chains."

"A book cover doesn't always reflect the real story inside its flaps."
Frank Shivers

November 4

The Saint's Reaction to Chains

"Remember my chains" (Colossians 4:18 ESV).

The saint in chains ought to react to them as Paul did.

You do so heartily. Paul is never seen posing the "Why?" question (Why did God allow this chain? Why doesn't He set me free from it?). Rather, he trusted the chain into God's loving and caring hand for His purposes to be fulfilled, whether continued hindrance or deliverance from it.

That's what we ought to do with our chains. We trust God with them, even when we don't understand them or have a revealed reason for them. What we don't do is panic, worry, and fear, become bitter and angry with God or discouraged beyond hope in the despair. What we don't do, if not delivered, is change our theology to say God no longer heals or cares or is compassionate.

You do so happily. Chains bound Paul's hands, not his heart. No extremity of adversity should quench the saint's joy.

You do so helpfully. Paul, despite chained hand-to-hand to a Roman guard, wrote the epistles of Ephesians, Philippians, Colossians, and the letter to Philemon. Alford comments movingly: "When we read of his chains, we should not forget that they moved over the paper as he wrote (his signature). His hand was chained to the soldier that kept him."[590]

Shackled to chains in the Philippi jail, he bore witness to Christ through singing at midnight (and later by preaching to the jailer's household). He refused to allow the chains to inhibit that which was possible. Learn from him. Make the most out of your chain for Christ.

November

That's all expected. The river may flow through a different channel because of obstructions ("chains"), yet it keeps flowing.

You do so hopefully. Paul hoped to be set free from his chains (Philemon 22). Herbert says, "He that lives in hope danceth without music." It is right to hope for and pray to be set free from chains. Whether or not that happens rests in the hands of Sovereign God who always does that which is best for His children (Romans 8:28).

"We don't determine what challenges, what hardships, or what difficulties come our way. All we determine is how we will react to those things when they come."[591]
Greg Laurie

November 5

Ministry in a Cage

"The Lord's word came to Jeremiah when he was still confined to the prison quarters" (Jeremiah 39:15 CEB).

In the cage of confinement (prison, hospital, nursing home, or home) may be found the most useful and effective ministry. John Bunyan seized his confinement as a prisoner in Bedford Gaol to write the classic treasures of *The Pilgrim's Progress*, *The Holy War* and *Grace Abounding to the Chief of Sinners*. Richard Baxter used his confinement as an invalid to write *The Saint's Everlasting Rest*.[592] Joseph used his confinement as a prisoner in Potiphar's jail to magnify God's power to Pharaoh. Paul seized the time spent in prison confinement in writing the epistles of Ephesians, Philippians, Colossians, and the letter to Philemon, witnessing to guards and singing.

Some birds sing in delight in a cage, while other birds scream, beating against its bars in discontent and dismay.[593] When in a cage, don't waste time beating against its bars in protest and despair. Redeem the time.

"Our time is a talent given us by God for some good end, and it is misspent and lost when it is not employed according to his design."[594]
Matthew Henry

November 6

The Blessing of Weakness

"Blessed is the man whose strength is in thee; in whose heart are the ways of them. Who passing through the valley of Baca make it a well....They go from strength to strength, every one of them in Zion appeareth before God" (Psalm 84:5–7).

The valley of Baca, the dry, the parched, the arid, the sun-burnt terrain which lies on the route to Jerusalem (Zion), demanded divine help for the Israelites to endure and survive. Much there is on the highway to heavenly Zion that draws tears from the believer's eyes, requiring divine strength to navigate and sustain. The believer that trusts the arm of flesh to sustain him will falter in despair and misery, a lesson many learn the hard way.

By what means do believers discover their frailty and feebleness to find all-sufficient strength in God? The psalmist said, "He weakened my strength in the way" (Psalm 102:23). Ultimately it is found through defeat and despair in battling temptation, coping with trials, hardships and persecution, and overcoming sorrow and grief. It is our impotence and inability to conquer these afflictions and adversities that reveal the utter weakness of the flesh and need for supernatural strength and power to withstand them.

Weakness to resolve life's trials and troubles is a tool in and of itself that God uses to crush dependence on self so we will trust Him alone. "When we come to the end of ourselves, we come to the beginning of God." Fleshly weakness is the believer's asset and ally in the journey to Heaven, for it compels him to depend upon God's enablement alone for strength and power to cope with and conquer the hardships encountered. It is in this reliance, as Paul learned, that the believer learns that "when I am weak, then am I strong" (2 Corinthians 12:10) and that God's grace is sufficient to sustain despite the magnitude of the trial (2 Corinthians 12:9). "Blessed is the man whose strength is in THEE" (Psalm 84:5).

"So far from being wearied they [believers] gather strength as they proceed. Each individual becomes happier; each holy song, more sweet and full. We grow as we advance if Heaven be our goal. If we spend our strength in God's ways, we shall find it increase."[595]

C. H. Spurgeon

November 7

Why I Believe in God (Part One)
"But there is a God in heaven" (Daniel 2:28).

What arguments are there for believing in the existence of God?

The cosmological argument. For every effect, there has to be a cause. There has to be an explanation for all that exists; nothing is self-existent except God. It follows that if there is a cause for all that exists, there must be a "first cause" to set things in motion. There has to be a beginning "domino." This "first cause" is God. He is the originating "domino" (Creator) who has set the world in motion.

The teleological argument. Where there is "design," there must be a "designer." The possibility of a watch's intrinsic parts just coming together for its formation and accurate function is so far out that it is absurd to consider. The same applies to the intrinsic design and operation of the universe. Where there is a watch, there is a watchmaker, and behind the incredible, complex universe is a master designer, who is God. W. H. Fitchett said, "The absolute proof of God's existence is thus found in the relations in which the mindless elements of the universe are set with each other, producing an order of which they are not only incapable but unconscious."[596]

The anthropological argument. The fact of man and the recognition of moral law points to a Creator and Lawgiver. That is God. The Bible says, "For when Gentiles who do not have the Law do instinctively the things of the Law, these, not having the Law, are a law to themselves, in that they show the work of the Law written in their hearts, their conscience bearing witness and their thoughts alternately accusing or else defending them" (Romans 2:14–15 NASB).

Lewis Chafer states, "There are...moral features in man's constitution which may be traced back to find their origin in God....A blind force...could never produce a man with intellect, sensibility, will, conscience, and inherent belief in a Creator."[597] W. A. Criswell states, "The fact that we are persons leads one to conclude that wherever we came from, whoever did it, must Himself have been a person of mind and intelligence. That is God."[598] The fact of God is divinely stamped in man's mind. Worship of a Supreme Being throughout the world gives credence to the fact of God who created man with that inward thirst and hunger to know and worship Him.

"Thou hast made us for thyself, O Lord, and our heart is restless until it finds its rest in thee."

Augustine

November 8

Why I Believe in God (Part Two)

"But there is a God in heaven" (Daniel 2:28).

The theological argument. "In the beginning was the Word, and the Word was with God, and the Word was God" (John 1:1). Biblical writers did not endeavor to prove the existence of God. To them, that was self-evident. However, the Bible's remarkable unity, historical accuracy, confirmation from archeological finds, and millions of testimonies regarding its trustworthiness prove the existence of its Author, God. Within its inspired sacred pages, God discloses Himself.

The Resurrection Argument. The Resurrection of Jesus is a miracle that only the Supreme Maker and Controller of the cosmos could bring about. That is God. Billy Graham said, "There is more evidence that Jesus rose from the dead than there is that Julius Caesar ever lived or that Alexander the Great died at the age of thirty-three." "There exists such overwhelming evidence…that no intelligent jury in the world could fail to bring a verdict that the resurrection story is true," said Lord Darling, former Chief Justice of England.

The testimonial argument. "One thing I know, that, whereas I was blind, now I see" (John 9:25). Grave proof of the fact of God is found in the miraculous change (intellectual, moral, and spiritual) that happens to the person that embraces Him by faith. No explanation exists for the transformation outside the supernatural intervention of God. "A new heart also will I give you, and a new spirit will I put within you: and I will take away the stony heart out of your flesh, and I will give you an heart of flesh" (Ezekiel 36:26). "What a wonderful change in my heart has been wrought since Jesus came into my heart."

Man's denial of God's existence doth not in one iota alter its fact. Spurgeon says, "If the sinner could by his atheism destroy the God whom he hates, there was some sense, although much wickedness, in his infidelity; but as denying the existence of fire does not prevent its burning a man who is in it, so doubting the existence of God will not stop the Judge of all the earth from destroying the rebel who breaks His laws.

November

Nay, this atheism is a crime which much provokes Heaven and will bring down terrible vengeance on the fool who indulges it."

Wernher von Braun said, "My experiences with science led me to God. They challenge science to prove the existence of God. *But must we really light a candle to see the sun?*" Nobody is blinder than the person who refuses to see. The Scriptures say, "The fool hath said in his heart, There is no God" (Psalm 14:1; Psalm 53:1).

"He who denies the existence of God, has some reason for wishing that God did not exist."
Augustine

November 9

Take This Cup from Me

"O my Father, if it be possible, let this cup pass from me: nevertheless not as I will, but as thou wilt" (Matthew 26:39).

Jesus prays in the Garden of Gethsemane for His father to spare Him from drinking the cup of suffering, if that would be in agreement with His will. In the "cup" was the culmination of every sin committed or that would be committed as well as the divine judgment (wrath of Holy God) that would be poured out on Jesus in fullest measure at Calvary (Isaiah 51:17) with the temporary abandonment of God while He bore the sin of the world (Matthew 27:46).

Spurgeon said, "All Hell was distilled into that cup of which our God and Savior, Jesus Christ, was made to drink! It was not eternal suffering, but since He was Divine, He could, in a short time, offer unto God a vindication of His Justice." Jesus drank the cup to its last drop of God's judgment and wrath that was meant for you and me that we might drink the cup of sweet fellowship with Him now and forever.

We too have bitter cups to drink. When faced with drinking a bitter cup, remember from whose hands it is served. Spurgeon says, "Let the thought of His special love to you be a spiritual painkiller, a dear quietus to your woe." If He gave the cup, you can drink it confident that its purpose is for your highest and best good and His glory, and comes with sufficient grace to drink it and endure victoriously, as the Apostle Paul did.

"Whatever is in the cup that God is offering to me, whether it be pain and sorrow and suffering and grief along with the many more joys, I'm willing to take because I trust Him. Because I know that what God wants for me is the very best."[599]

Elizabeth Elliot

November 10

David and Goliath

"Then said David to the Philistine, Thou comest to me with a sword, and with a spear, and with a shield: but I come to thee in the name of the LORD of hosts, the God of the armies of Israel, whom thou hast defied" (1 Samuel 17:45).

David's battle with the giant Goliath reveals the means of triumph in spiritual endeavors and challenges.

Think Big. Long before David did big, he thought big. Hear him pondering and inquiring, "What shall be done to the man that killeth this Philistine, and taketh away the reproach from Israel?" (1 Samuel 17:26). D. L. Moody advised, "If God is your partner, make your plans BIG!"[600] Dare to think the unimaginable and dream the impossible for God!

Talk Big. David talked big about what he had done and planned to do. Upon the Holy Spirit's confirmation of the work to be done, talk it up (Genesis 37:9), unless there is reason to maintain its secrecy, as in Nehemiah's case in rebuilding the walls in Jerusalem (Nehemiah 2:12).

Believe Big. The narrative is not just about a mere lad conquering a giant but about a Christian daring to believe God against immeasurable odds! What gave David reason to believe that he would triumph over Goliath? His prior experience of God's help in fighting bears and lions (1 Samuel 17:37) and a firm conviction that the battle was the Lord's and He, therefore, would join him in the fight (1 Samuel 17:47; Exodus 14:14).

Stand Big. The Bible says, "Eliab, David's oldest brother, heard David talking to the men. He became angry with David and said, 'What are you doing here? Who is taking care of those sheep of yours out there in the wilderness?'" (1 Samuel 17:28 GNT). David noncontentiously replied to the cruel and vindictive insinuations, saying, "Is there not a cause?" (1 Samuel 17:29). Be nonretaliatory to criticism and opposition, as David was to Eliab's.

Pray Big. Brooks said, "Do not pray for tasks equal to your powers. Pray for powers equal to your tasks."[601] This is what David did (1 Samuel 17:45–46). No work ought to be undertaken apart from fervent prayer beckoning the fullness of the Spirit and God's all-powerful enablement. Saith Spurgeon, "There cannot come out of you what has not been put into you."[602] Defeat and woe await the Christian that battles Goliath with the arm of the flesh.

Do Big. To think big, talk big, believe big, stand big, and pray big are nothing unless one does big. David selects the most appropriate means to accomplish the task and then does it.

Think big about what God wants you to do, talk big about it, believe big about it, stand big against difficulty and opposition to it, pray big to ascertain God's power to do it, but then do big about it. There are many who think big, talk big, believe big, stand big, and pray big but never do big.

There are giants to thwart, evils to defeat, souls to be won, and new works to undertake in Christ's name. What will you do? Will you cower in a foxhole, panic-stricken and paralyzed by fear, in comfort and safety? Or will you get into the fray?

"Faith must trample under foot all reason, sense, and understanding."
Martin Luther

November 11

What's That in Your Hand

"What is that in thy hand?" (Exodus 4:2 ASV).

It may be that your spiritual giftedness is in the use of a small sling and stone, not a huge sword. Let that not dissuade you or detour your service. Be encouraged to know that "God has chosen what the world calls foolish to shame the wise; he has chosen what the world calls weak to shame the strong. He has chosen things of little strength and small repute, yes and even things which have no real existence to explode the pretensions of the things that are—that no man may boast in the presence of God" (1 Corinthians 1:27 PHILLIPS).

All that one can do is bring to the table (battle, work, ministry) the divine giftedness received, the sling or the sword, trusting God by faith to use it to accomplish His purpose. The best-trained and most gifted believer who sits in idleness doing nothing pales in comparison to the weakest believer who utilizes his limited giftedness to the fullest extent. F. B. Meyer states, "The weakest man who knows God is strong to do exploits."[603]

"What is that in thy hand?" (Exodus 4:2 ASV). For David it was a sling; Moses, a rod; Shamgar, an ox goad; Samson, a jawbone of a donkey; and Dorcas, a needle and thread.

What is in your hand? Take it and use it to do exploits for God. William Carey said, "Expect great things from God. Attempt great things for God." The doing will always follow the believing, provided the belief (faith) is sure and steadfast in the Lord.

"God takes the weakest instruments to accomplish His mightiest ends."[604]
A. Nevin

November 12

Promptings of the Spirit

"He that hath an ear, let him hear what the Spirit saith" (Revelation 2:7a).

The Holy Spirit is the saint's counselor, consultant, and conductor, prompting him in the way of righteousness, holiness, effective service, and happiness (Isaiah 11:2). What the clouds were to the Israelites in the wilderness the Holy Spirit is to the believer in the sojourn of life. According to Watchman Nee, the prompting of the Spirit is a sudden touch, an inescapable impression, a lightning flash out of nowhere prodding specific conduct, to do or say something or to remain silent and still, and to teach what is of God and what is not (Isaiah 30:21).

It is sweet to know that in the twists and turns of life we have an infallible guiding polestar, a divine navigator and all-powerful superintendent guiding us in all "truth" (John 16:13; Romans 8:14) preventing our missteps and enabling our sanctification, if we hearken. The Holy Spirit longs to always lead us, but alas, sometimes we are stubborn and indifferent to His guidance. We refuse to be led. And in such times, He will not drive us!

To ignore, repress, or dismiss the inner stirrings of the Spirit is to court heartache and hardship and miss opportunities of ministry. Pray

November

with John Baillie: "Holy Spirit of God, abide with us; inspire all our thoughts; pervade our imaginations; suggest all our decisions; order all our doings. Be with us in our silence and in our speech, in our haste and in our leisure, in company and in solitude, in the freshness of the morning and in the weariness of the evening; and give us grace at all times humbly to rejoice in Thy mysterious companionship."

"Because we have shut out the Holy Spirit in so many ways, we are stumbling along as though we are spiritually blindfolded."
A. W. Tozer

November 13

The Manner of the Spirit's Leading
"Led by the Spirit" (Romans 8:14).

"Led," not dragged, driven, or coerced, but gently guided by the Spirit; led like a mother that walks with her child or a shepherd with his sheep in the sojourn of life to avoid that which is wrong, affirm that which is right, mortify sin, discern that which ought to be done or left undone, pay attention to something or ignore it, persist or desist in a matter, enter into a partnership or business venture or walk away, pray for a person or ministry, invest in a ministry or other charitable cause, and enter a door of ministry or not.

The Spirit's promptings, as revealed in the lives of biblical saints, occurs in usual and unusual ways. Paul was "constrained by the Spirit" to go to Jerusalem despite the persecution that awaited (Acts 20:22 ESV) and "forbidden of the Holy Ghost to preach the Word in Asia" (Acts 16:6). Simeon was "moved by the Spirit" to go into the temple where Joseph and Mary were dedicating Jesus (Luke 2:27 NIV). Jesus was "led by the Spirit" into the desert to be tempted by the Devil (Luke 4:1). Peter was 'told by the Spirit' to go with three men to see Cornelius (Acts 11:12). The Magi were warned in a dream to depart another way for their home to avoid King Herod (Matthew 2:12). The Spirit told the church at Antioch to set apart Barnabas and Paul for the ministry (Acts 13:2). Philip was told by the Spirit to join an Ethiopian in his chariot (Acts 8:29).

As with these believers, the Spirit's prompting (nudges, prods, impressions) may come mentally, through the saints, sermons, dreams, Scripture, prayer, and open and shut doors. Train the inner ear to recognize His voice. Prompt response to His prod is essential. Do that task, say that word, write that letter, make that visit, pray that prayer, write that check, witness to that soul, without delay.

"So live as that it may appear to others that you are led by this Spirit."[605]
J. Jacomb

November 14

Revival Praying

"It is time for thee, LORD, to work" (Psalm 119:126).

Packer says, "Revival is the visitation of God which brings to life Christians who have been sleeping and restores a deep sense of God's near presence and holiness." Revival comes from revival praying in closets and at church altars. Revival praying is to fervently echo the cry of Habakkuk, "O LORD, revive thy work in the midst of the years." It is to echo the cry of David, "Wilt thou not revive us again: that thy people may rejoice in thee?" (Psalm 85:6).

We can't organize revival, but we can agonize at the throne of God in prayer for it. We can't work it up, but we can pray it down. Habakkuk's prayer was founded on faith. Oh, that we had more who prayed like him. Oh, for more to pray like Elijah, by whose faith the windows of heaven opened. Murray writes, "Faith in the promise is the fruit of faith in the promiser. The prayer of faith is rooted in the life of faith."[606] Sanders said, "Faith does not require external confirmation but believes God in spite of appearances."

To pray for revival believingly is to look expectantly for its coming. Pray with the confidence of Spurgeon for revival: "Lord, Thou canst revive us again. We are not so deep in the mire but that Thou canst lift us out. We are not so dead but that Thou canst make us alive. Wilt Thou not revive us again? It is impossible to us, but it is possible to Thee. Lord, one touch of Thy hand, a breath from Thy blessed lips, and it is done. Wilt thou not revive us again?"[607] Spurgeon concluded, "Brothers, sisters, we believe in God, do we not? And if we do, we believe that whatever state a church is in, God can bring it out of it."[608]

"All revival begins and continues in the prayer meeting."
Henry Blackaby

November 15

The Heart's Private Sorrow

"The heart knoweth his own bitterness; and a stranger doth not intermeddle with his joy" (Proverbs 14:10).

Bitterness refers not to its general meaning of resentment, but inner pain and suffering. The Proverb reveals what all have experienced with regard to heart distress ("bitterness")—that emotional trauma (hurt, pain, despair, anxiety) is impossible to fully convey even to choicest and closest friends. "No person stands in such intimate relation to us, or can put himself so entirely in our place, as to feel that which we feel."[609] "There is many a dark spot, many a grief, of which our best friend knows nothing; the skeleton is locked in the cupboard, and no one has the key but ourselves."[610]

Paul states the same, saying, "No one can know a person's thoughts except that person's own spirit" (1 Corinthians 2:11 NLT). John Foster, in the essay "On a Man's Writing Memoirs of Himself," said, "Each mind has an interior apartment of its own, into which none but itself and the Divinity can enter."[611] Then he says, "Unless we have Jesus with us in the darkness, we have no one."[612]

Note, the inner hurt of another is always *heavier* and more *horrendous* than communicated or conceived. "Their stroke perhaps is heavier than their groaning."[613] An unknown author has well said, "Sometimes the prettiest smiles hide the deepest secrets, the prettiest eyes have cried the most tears, and the kindest hearts have felt the most pain." Appearances are deceitful with regard to the crucible of pain others bear. Learn to see through the "I."

The Christian finds great comfort and consolation in knowing that though man is incapable of empathizing with the "bitterness" of soul experienced, Jesus Christ can and will. He is "acquainted with [our deepest] grief" (Isaiah 53:3); "surely he hath borne our griefs, and carried our sorrows" (Isaiah 53:4). "No one knows the troubles I've seen—no one but Jesus. Glory, Hallelujah!"

"The soul that has to wade through deep waters has always to do it alone; for no human sympathy reaches to full knowledge of, or share in, even the best-loved one's grief. We have companions in joy; sorrow we have to face by ourselves."[614]

Alexander Maclaren

November 16

A Defiant and Ungrateful Child

"Children will turn against their parents" (Matthew 10:21 CEV).

Shakespeare says in *King Lear*, "How sharper than a serpent's tooth it is to have a thankless child."[615] The disrespect and ingratitude of a child toward a parent is more venomous than the bite of a rattlesnake.

A young man was just this to his mother, ungrateful and defiant. One night when he arrived home past curfew again, his dad waited with a shotgun in hand. As the boy entered the house, he tossed the gun to him saying, "Go upstairs, put the barrel to your mother's head, and pull the trigger."

The boy, set back by the instruction, replied, "Dad, what are you asking me to do?" The father repeated the instructions, to which the son asked, "Why?" The father told him that to shoot his mother would be the merciful way to kill her instead of the gradual, slow way he was killing her with rebellious behavior.

Shakespeare is so right; disrespectful, deviant and disobedient behavior to one's parents is like sharp fangs mightier than those of a serpent, gradually killing them. Pillows are wet continuously with the tears of hurting parents over the defiance and disrespect of their children.

Says Harriet Beecher Stowe, "The bitterest tears shed over graves are for words left unsaid and deeds left undone." What words yet need to be said and deeds yet need to be done to show honor and love to your parents?

"A wretched child Is he who does not return his parents' care."
                            Euripides

November 17

When Your Elijah Dies

"As the LORD liveth, and as thy soul liveth, I will not leave thee" (2 Kings 2:2).

The Elisha-Elijah relationship is similar to that of David and Jonathan (2 Kings 2:1–12). It is a close-knit holy connection that instills love and support in every trial.

November

When the day arrives when our Elijah must depart to Heaven, how do we say goodbye? What might be done at the word of his approaching death? This biblical narrative citing Elisha's long goodbye to Elijah gives answer.

Stay close to him. The record indicates that fifty ministerial students or disciples "viewed from afar off" Elijah's exodus (2 Kings 2:7). But it was Elisha that walked step by step with him to the place it happened, despite being told three times to remain behind. Most Elijahs welcome their Elishas to be by their side at the crossing of Jordan, as Paul welcomed Timothy's (2 Timothy 4:9).

Redeem the time left with him. As Elisha walked with Elijah in those last hours of life, much was communicated. It's most solemn, wondrous, memorable, and yet grievous to sit by the bed of a dying Elijah who speaks for the final time. Don't squander the opportunity. Sit at his feet as often as possible to be benefited from rich counsel and insight.

Walk with him until God takes him Home. Witness your Elijah's translation to Heaven as Elisha saw Elijah's (2 Kings 2:11). What comfort and consolation to Elijah it was to have had Elisha walk with him to the banks of Jordan. It is so for any Elijah. Matthew Henry comments, "Elisha desired to be satisfied concerning Elijah's departure, and to see him when he was taken up, that his faith might be confirmed and his acquaintance with the invisible world increased."[616]

The dearest friend and mentor (Elijah) must depart. It may happen expectedly or suddenly and without warning. Ready yourself for it. And embrace your Elijah in and through it, ensuring a comfortable and glorious transition.

"How great is the loss of one who has opened our eyes to eternal things, and by his watchful care and salutary advice has led us forward toward the possession of everlasting bliss!"[617]
Charles Simeon

November 18

Reaction to an Elijah's Death

"My father, my father [a term of endearment], the chariot of Israel, and the horsemen thereof" (2 Kings 2:12).

How might we respond to our Elijah's death?

Express grief. Elisha grieves over the nation's loss of Elijah as well as his own—so much so that he rips his clothing *into two pieces*. It's natural and healthy to mourn the death of an Elijah. "Respond in grief," advises Jim Henry, "until you find relief. If we bury our grief, it is like toxic waste. It will surface again, and the contamination makes for more trouble."

Stay on track with God's plan. Elisha could have panicked and allowed Elijah's departure to result in bitterness toward God and lifelong despair. Instead, it was allowed to turn him Godward and to the task that Elijah prepared him to accomplish for the Lord. At Elijah's exodus, Elisha received the mantle of Elijah (cloak that symbolized the prophet's office and authority) and continued in devotion and ministry to God (2 Kings 2:8, 13). Your Elijah though dead, yet speaketh (Hebrews 11:4). He lives on through the work he wrought in and through you and others.

Anticipate reunion with him. A goodbye to Elijah here will soon turn to hello to him up there. Consolation is found in the promise of a reunion day in Heaven with our Elijah (1 Thessalonians 4:13–18).

"There is going to be a meeting in the air, in the sweet, sweet bye and bye. I am going to meet you, meet you over there, in that home beyond the sky."
May Taylor Roberts

November 19

Retired Daniels (Part One)

"There is a man in thy kingdom, in whom lives the spirit of the holy God; and in the days of thy father light and intelligence and wisdom, like the knowledge of God, was found in him." (Daniel 5:11 JUB).

Daniel served the Lord for over 70 years and was in his eighties when summoned out of retirement by Belshazzar to interpret the meaning of the mysterious handwriting on the wall (Daniel 5:13–14). Daniel hastily responded.

1. The story illustrates in part how godly ministers in retirement are often forgotten and overlooked, despite their rich experience, vast knowledge, and holiness of life. Matthew Henry observes: "There are a great many valuable men, and such as might be made very useful, that lie

long buried in obscurity, and some that have done eminent services that live to be overlooked and taken no notice of. But whatever men are, God is not unrighteous to forget the services done to His kingdom. Daniel, being turned out of his place, lived privately and sought not any opportunity to come into notice again; yet he lived near the court and within call."[618]

2. The story illustrates that a day will come when a Belshazzar will summon the retired Daniel for help. As a retired Daniel, live in expectation and readiness for that day. You might be ignored and snubbed now. Just bide your time. The hour will come when coldness or conflict in the church, crisis in a person's life, or chaos in the world will prompt a summons for your help. Belshazzar will turn to the man in touch with God when a pressing need arises or when reminded of him by another that knows of his life and work (Daniel 5:15–16).

"You will be wanted someday by Belshazzar."
Joseph Parker

November 20

Retired Daniels (Part Two)
"There is a man in thy kingdom, in whom lives the spirit of the holy God; and in the days of thy father light and intelligence and wisdom, like the knowledge of God, was found in him." (Daniel 5:11 JUB).

3. The story illustrates that the retired Daniel must stay ready for the summons to serve. Until the call comes to serve, the retired Daniel must resolve to "live near the court and within call" (available, prepared, and willing to utilize their giftedness and experience to assist the church or believer whenever, wherever, and however possible).

4. It illustrates the invaluable benefit of utilizing the retired Daniel. Daniel profited the kingdom of God not only in the interpretation of the handwriting he made, but in the role he played under Darius. Despite years of distinguished and faithful ministry, a retired Daniel lives in large part in comparative obscurity near your church. They live "near the court and within call" but are often ignored and overlooked. What a tragedy. What a waste. What a shame. And the church and kingdom of God are the poorer for it. Let him that possesses the influence and platform to encourage churches, colleges, camps, and schools, to use the theological

knowledge (Daniel 5:11–12), spiritual wisdom (Daniel 5:11), and practical experience (Daniel 5:12) of a retired Daniel, do so!

"There are a great many valuable men, and such as might be made very useful, that lie long buried in obscurity, and some that have done eminent services that live to be overlooked and taken no notice of. But whatever men are, God is not unrighteous to forget the services done to his kingdom."[619]
Matthew Henry

November 21

Characteristics of Kingdom Citizens (Part One)
"And he opened his mouth, and taught them" (Matthew 5:2).

Kingdom citizens manifest characteristics that differ vastly from those of the world.

They are poor in spirit. To be poor in the material sense, like Lazarus, is to be completely dependent upon the gifts of another. The Christian acknowledges the poverty or bankruptcy of his soul ("in me…dwelleth no good thing"; "I am poor and needy") and relies upon God for salvation and grace to supply every need.

They mourn. Man mourns or expresses grief either for loss of what is desired or for sin. Here the latter is meant. David groaned in godly sorrow over his sin (Psalm 32:3–4). The Christian takes all sin seriously, not casually, and expresses brokenness over it and sorrow for it unto God. Not only is he grieved over personal sin, but that of others (Psalm 119:158).

They are meek. The meek possess the spirit of Christ—gentleness and self-control toward all men. MacDonald asserts, "Meekness implies acceptance of one's lowly position. The meek person is gentle and mild in his own cause, though he may be a lion in God's cause or in defending others."[620]

They hunger and thirst after righteousness. The happy are they that ardently pursue personal holiness, honesty, and integrity. J. N. Darby said, "To be hungry is not enough; I must be really starving to know what is in [God's] heart towards me. When the prodigal son was hungry, he went to feed upon husks; but when he was starving, he turned to his father."[621] Gamaliel Bradford wrote that Christians manifest "a thirst no earthly stream can satisfy, a hunger that must feed on Christ or die."[622]

November

"If we were to set out to establish a religion in polar opposition to the Beatitudes Jesus taught, it would look strikingly similar to the pop Christianity that has taken over the airwaves of North America."
Tony Campolo

November 22

Characteristics of Kingdom Citizens (Part Two)

"And he opened his mouth, and taught them" (Matthew 5:2).

They are merciful. To be merciful is to exhibit undeserved compassion and sympathy. God showed mercy to man in sparing him deserved judgment for his sin, eternal damnation, through the work of Christ at Calvary. "But God is so rich in mercy; he loved us so much that even though we were spiritually dead and doomed by our sins, he gave us back our lives again" (Ephesians 2:4–5 TLB). Recipients of that mercy are to express mercy to others.

They are pure in heart. In New Testament times, the Greeks used the word *purity* to refer to something physically clean, like a cloth free of dirt. To them, something was pure when it was free from additives, things that would hinder it from being used for its designed purpose. For example, a surgical cloth was pure when separated from deadly bacteria. A man is pure when sinful additives (unchaste thoughts and ungodly conduct) are removed from the life through divine forgiveness and cleansing, allowing it to be lived as God designed (the process of sanctification).

They are peacemakers. A peacemaker promotes peace and, if possible, restores it among the factious. However, it never ought to come at the expense of doctrinal, ethical, and moral compromise. The peacemaker also seeks to bring the unsaved to peace with God through His Son, the Lord Jesus Christ. Saith Spurgeon, "There is no peace out of Him. He is our peace."

They are persecuted. Billy Graham stated, "Persecution is one of the natural consequences of living the Christian life." J. C. Ryle said, "Let it never surprise us, if we have to endure mockery and ridicule and false reports because we belong to Christ. The disciple is not greater than His

Master, nor the servant than His Lord." Adrian Rogers says, "The new whipping boy in the world today is the Bible-believing Christian. He may be the most hated, persecuted person on earth. Bible Christians today endure everything from the limitations of their freedoms and civil rights to scorn and ridicule in the media. Many are going through prison, and many through death."

"The glory of the gospel is that when the Church is absolutely different from the world, she invariably attracts it. It is then that the world is made to listen to her message, though it may hate it at first."[623]
D. Martyn Lloyd-Jones

November 23

A Reason to Sing Praise

"Now may Israel say; If it had not been the Lord who was on our side" (Psalm 124:1–2).

As with David and the Israelites, we have great reason to praise the Lord for His hand of goodness upon us. The *what ifs* of David were faith builders, as they must be for every believer. If God intervened in the past for us, He will certainly be faithful to do so again.

In 1582, upon the release from prison of John Durie, a minister, two thousand friends gathered on High Street to celebrate. Andrew Bonar states that the great crowd sang Psalm 94, "Now Israel May Say," in four parts with such deep sincerity and joy that it alarmed one of the chief persecutors more than anything he had ever experienced in Scotland.[624]

Let's join their song, singing, "Blessed be the Lord, who hath not given us as a prey to their teeth. Our soul is escaped as a bird out of the snare of the fowlers: the snare is broken, and we are escaped. Our help is in the name of the Lord, who made heaven and earth" (Psalm 124:6–8). Spurgeon observes, "We are far too slow in declaring our gratitude, hence the exclamation which should be rendered, 'Oh, let Israel say.' We murmur without being stirred up to it, but our thanksgiving needs a spur, and it is well when some warmhearted friend bids us say what we feel. Imagine what would have happened if the Lord had left us, and then see what has happened because He has been faithful to us. Are not all the materials of a song spread before us? Let us sing unto the Lord."[625]

November

"Nothing calls out so deep and strong a sense of indebtedness to God (or to man) as a consciousness that we owe to Him an escape from a great calamity. We bless the Lord with the most fervent gratitude as we realize that he has healed our disease and redeemed our life from destruction."[626]

November 24

The Turning of Job's Captivity

"And the Lord turned the captivity of Job" (Job 42:10).

Job's afflicted state was like a state of forced exile or captivity from his life of prosperity and health. All taken into such exile know its bitter heartache and havoc. The expression "turned the captivity of Job" means a time came when Job's health, friends, possessions and happy state (peace and calm of mind) were restored (Job 42:12).

Zuck says, "Since Job had (unknowingly) silenced Satan by not cursing God, and since he had repented of his pride, his suffering did not need to continue."[627] Job's restoration (turn-about) set him free—free from the conflict that embroiled his life, free from the pain and suffering inflicted by the boils, free from the mental torment that ravaged his mind, free from the domination of grief and sorrow that plagued his heart over the death of his children. Job is free from allowing the hardships, sorrows, illnesses and losses of life to dictate his future. He is free from Satan's unrestricted harassment and havoc upon his life.

Job's restoration provides hope and encouragement to all in the 'strange land' of suffering and sorrow by testifying that "weeping may endure for a night, but joy cometh in the morning" (Psalm 30:5), bearing witness to the truth that God will "restore to you the years that the locust hath eaten" (Joel 2:25) and verifying that God is able to 'turn again their captivity' to former happier and prosperous days. Your predicament and pain may differ from that of Job. The when and form of your deliverance may differ. But there is no difference in the God that delivers.

"Suffering is unbearable if you aren't certain that God is for you and with you."[628]

Martin Luther

November 25

Why Is Death's Time Unknown?

"Man knoweth not his time [to die]" (Ecclesiastics 9:12 YLT).

Why is man's time of death an unknown?

1. To prevent trepidation over that which surrounds one's death (and that of family and friends).

2. To prevent one from putting off until the end doing things that ought to be done at present, especially with regard to salvation, stewardship, and service. Augustine said, "The last day is kept secret that every day may be watched."

3. So the discouragement and disheartenment the knowledge might bring will not cause us to be resigned to failure in life's duties and responsibilities.

4. To prevent devastation of happiness. To live knowing the hour of our death and that of our family members and friends would be most chilling in effect.

5. To prevent ruination of life. To know the time of death certainly would incite some to eat, drink, and be merry (live wantonly and wastefully) up to their final moments of life, and then repent.

The bottom-line? God has kept the time of death concealed knowing its revelation would prove more injurious than advantageous (would be a curse instead of a blessing) to us.

"Because life is fragile and death inevitable, we must make the most of each day."
Thomas S. Monson

November 26

The Place Called Calvary

"And when they were come to the place, which is called Calvary, there they crucified him" (Luke 23:33).

What is the place called Calvary?

A planned place. Calvary was not "Plan B" of God to save the world; it was the plan from the beginning. It was not an afterthought of

November

God (1 Peter 1:19–21). And since the Cross was divinely orchestrated, neither the power of man nor Hell could avert it.

A prophetic place. Multiple Old Testament passages prophesied the crucifixion of Christ with explicit details hundreds of years before it took place. Soldiers would pierce His hands and feet (Psalm 22:16; Zechariah 12:10), cast lots for His clothing (Psalm 22:18), and hurl insults at Him (Psalm 22:17). None of His bones would be broken (Psalms 34:20); vinegar would be provided to Him to drink (Psalm 69:21); He would be crucified between two criminals (Isaiah 53:12); He would experience agony and suffering (Psalm 69:20–21).

A painful place. Frederic Farrar describes the agony and torment of crucifixion. "Dizziness, cramps, thirst, starvation, sleeplessness, publicity of shame, the long continuance of torment, horror of anticipation, mortification of untended wounds—all intensified just up to the point at which they can be endured at all, but all stopping just short of the point which would give the sufferer the relief of unconsciousness. The unnatural position made every movement painful; the lacerated veins and crushed tendons throbbed with incessant anguish; the wounds, inflamed by exposure, gradually gangrened; the arteries—especially of the head and stomach—became swollen and oppressed with surcharged blood; and while each variety of misery went on gradually increasing, there was added to them the intolerable pain of a burning and raging thirst; and all these physical complications caused an internal excitement and anxiety, which made the prospect of death itself—of death, the awful unknown enemy, at whose approach man usually shudders most—bear the aspect of a delicious and exquisite release." He concludes, "Such was the death to which Christ was doomed."

A propitiatory place. Paul says, "God wiped out the charges that were against us for disobeying the Law of Moses. He took them away and nailed them to the cross" (Colossians 2:14 CEV). The indebtedness of man to God for violating His law is unpayable, and its payment of eternal death is unavoidable in and of man himself. But God did for man that which he could not do. He put man's sin debt to Christ's account at Calvary, allowing Him in their place to pay its penalty, satisfying or appeasing His righteous wrath. John states, "He is the payment for our sins, and not only for our sins, but also for the sins of the whole world" (1 John 2:2 GW). Paul says, "For He hath made Him who knew no sin to be sin for us, that we might be made the righteousness of God in Him" (2 Corinthians 5:21 KJ21). Barclay asserts, "The sacrifice of Jesus was not only the paying of a debt; it was the giving of a victory. What Jesus did puts a man right with God, and what He does enables a man to stay right with God. The act of the cross brings to men the love of God in a way that takes their terror of Him away; the presence of the living Christ brings to them the power of God so that they can win a daily victory over sin."

A permanent place. "For Christ died for sins once and for all, a good man on behalf of sinners, in order to lead you to God" (1 Peter 3:18 GNT). MacArthur asserts, "Christ's one sacrifice for sins was of such perpetual validity that it was sufficient for all and would never need to be repeated." "There remaineth no more sacrifice for sins" (Hebrews 10:26).

A procuring place. "Today shalt thou be with me in paradise" (Luke 23:43). The dying thief found salvation at Calvary by exhibiting a belief in Christ. All men may do the same, and it is the only place where they can. Stephen Charnock said, "Let us look upon a crucified Christ, the remedy of all our miseries. His cross hath procured a crown; His passion hath expiated our transgression. His death hath disarmed the law; His blood hath washed a believer's soul. This death is the destruction of our enemies, the spring of our happiness, and the eternal testimony of divine love." A person may reject the atoning work of Christ (salvation), accepting condemnation instead.

"Come and see the victories of the cross. Christ's wounds are thy healings, His agonies thy repose, His conflicts thy conquests, His groans thy songs, His pains thine ease, His shame thy glory, His death thy life, His sufferings thy salvation."

Matthew Henry

November 27

Spiritual Gifts

"Christ has given each of us special abilities—whatever he wants us to have out of his rich storehouse of gifts" (Ephesians 4:7 TLB).

I read of the story of a duck, squirrel, eagle, and rabbit that all attended the same training school. The duck was the head of the class in swimming, but slowest in running. The squirrel excelled in climbing, but poor in flying. The eagle soared in flying but floundered in climbing. The rabbit was terrific in running but poor in climbing.

November

The lessons drawn from the story: be content with the gift(s) conferred by Christ. Minister in your element (giftedness) for chiefest success and greatest fruit. Don't covet or be envious of another's gift. "The amount and character of 'grace' possessed by others ought surely to create no uneasiness nor jealousy, for it is of Christ's measurement as well as of His bestowment, and every form and quantity of it as it descends from the one source is indispensable to the harmony of the Church."[629]

Recruit or rely upon others to do that which falls outside your giftedness—be a team player. Whatever you are—duck, or squirrel, or eagle, or rabbit—be the best one possible. Give credit to whom it is due, the Lord Jesus Christ, for the giftedness possessed.

"Not to use our gift is an affront to God's wisdom, a rebuff of His love and grace, and a loss to His church. We did not determine our gift, deserve it, or earn it. But we all have a gift from the Lord, and if we do not use it, His work is weakened and His heart is grieved."[630]
John MacArthur

November 28

Iron Sharpens Iron

"As iron sharpens iron, so one person sharpens another" (Proverbs 27:17 NIV).

Soul sharpening can work in two ways with two opposite results. The Bible says, "He that walketh with wise men shall be wise: but a companion of fools shall be destroyed" (Proverbs 13:20). Friends sharpen and shape toward their bent. A Dutch proverb says, "He that lives with cripples learns to limp"; and the Spanish say, "He that goes with wolves learns to howl." The example and instruction (iron sharpening) of the wise (the godly and righteous) enhance the pursuit of godliness, whereas that of the foolish (the unspiritual, ungodly) spur carnality and wickedness.

Godly iron sharpeners and shapers, prompted by caring concern and love, make others better (more perceptive, prudent, proficient, and pious) through their encouragement, dialog, advice, guidance, insight, instruction, warning, and association. They bear burdens, awaken and unlock potential; help with defects and failure; instruct in godliness with lip and life; equip for spiritual walk, work and warfare; undergird; and infuse hope and joy in times of melancholy, dispelling the gloom and enlivening the soul, leaving their indelible footprint.

Isaac Newton testified, "If I have seen further, it is by standing on the shoulders of giants." If Paul needed the shoulders of a Barnabas, Timothy the shoulders of a Paul, and David the shoulders of a Jonathan on which to stand, what does that say about our need of the same?

"When you meet a man or woman who puts Jesus Christ first, knit that one to your soul."[631]
Oswald Chambers

November 29

When God Seems Absent

"He stayed where he was for the next two days and made no move to go to them" (John 11:6 TLB).

In Jesus' physical absence from Bethany (when Lazarus was sick), He was yet there orchestrating all that happened for His greater glory and Mary and Martha's best good. The unseen hand of Christ starts to work at the first cry of desperation, only later to be evidenced visibly. In the silences of Christ there are unknown divine intentions and designs at play (as was the case then). See John 11:1–6.

G. Campbell Morgan said, "The people of God in the day of affliction are not abandoned by God. He is nigh when He seems absent. He is watching when He seems blind. He is active when He seems idle."[632] Our Christian forefathers spoke of "spiritual desertion"—the sense of divine abandonment. But despite what their emotions testified; the promises of God affirm that shall never be the case for the child of God.

The prophet makes clear that God exults over us in joy, even when He is "quiet in His love" (Zephaniah 3:17 AMP). Saith Randy Alcorn, "Many of us have walked the Emmaus Road. Overwhelmed by sorrow, plagued by questions, we wonder where God is. When all along He walks beside us."[633]

To quote Winslow: "God's silence to you in this overwhelming calamity, in this crushing affliction, in this overshadowing cloud, in this bitter trial, is the silence of infinite and unchangeable love. Wait and He

November

will speak anon, and sweet, assuring, and soothing will be the words that shall break that silence, the stillness of which has filled your mind with forebodings so painful and with an awe so profound—'It is I; do not be afraid!' Your bounding heart shall respond, 'It is the voice of my Beloved!'"[634]

"God sometimes brings us to the place where he brought Job to show us not only is God necessary, but God is enough."[635]
Adrian Rogers

November 30

What Is Seen Is Not Enough

"While we look not at the things which are seen, but at the things which are not seen: for the things which are seen are temporal; but the things which are not seen are eternal" (2 Corinthians 4:18).

Things that are seen are transitory and void of power to satisfy the deepest longing of the soul. Just ask Solomon. Having garnered mass possessions, fortune, fame, knowledge, and having engaged in every desired wanton pleasure "under the sun," he said, "So life came to mean nothing to me, because everything in it had brought me nothing but trouble. It had all been useless; I had been chasing the wind" (Ecclesiastes 2:17 GNT). It is the regrettable testimony of many, like Solomon, that their ladder in the quest for meaning and happiness leaned against the wrong wall.

The invisible in man, the soul, cannot be satisfied with the visible (temporal) of earth, only with the invisible (eternal) spiritual work of God. "There is a hole in my heart that cannot be filled with the things that I do. There is a hole in my heart that can only be filled with YOU." The emptiness of the heart is incessant despite exhaustive and costly efforts to fill it. No matter what one does, he cries, "I need more." Christ alone fills and satisfies the famished soul.

The psalmist says, "For he satisfies the longing soul, and the hungry soul he fills with good things" (Psalm 107:9 ESV). Christ says to the longing soul that which He declared to the woman at Jacob's Well: "Whosoever drinketh of this water shall thirst again: But whosoever drinketh of the water that I shall give him shall never thirst; but the water that I shall give him shall be in him a well of water springing up into everlasting life" (John 4:13–14).

"Christ liveth in me. And how great the difference...instead of bondage, liberty; instead of failure, quiet victories within; instead of fear and weakness, a restful sense of sufficiency in Another."
Hudson Taylor

December 1

When the Brook Dries Up (Part One)

"And it came to pass after a while, that the brook dried up, because there had been no rain in the land" (1 Kings 17:7).

Elijah witnessed the gradual drying of the stream into a narrow thread until it gradually disappeared. Maclaren says, "God makes us sometimes wait on beside a diminishing rivulet, and keeps us ignorant of the next step, till it is dry. Patience is an element in strength." Elijah refuses to bulge from the brook until he hears from God. Once the word is received, he proceeds immediately to the new post. A dried-up brook suggests one of several things.

The work is disapproved. Theological compromise and unscriptural principles of governance cause the brook to dry up (Jeremiah 3:3). God cannot bless and prosper that which goes against His Word.

The work is diminished. Brooks dry up because their season is ended. History attests to ministries that flourished greatly in one era only to languish in the next. Churches that prospered yesterday are floundering today in part because of diminished potential (no fault of their own), eroding pertinence (the community in which it's located has changed its ethnic, racial, or socioeconomic makeup, but the church hasn't), and, obviously, the decline of people. Their season of strong growth has ended. Now they are in the season of marked maintenance.

The work is deficient. Brooks dry up when the worker is slothful and lazy in duty and spiritual discipline. Such a worker is depicted in Proverbs 24:30–31. "The owner of this miserable garden was a sluggard. He would not work. So, the deterioration went on unchecked, until what was once a beautiful, productive, cleanly kept garden became a place of the rankest weeds."[636]

Disloyalty to God by failure to do that which was entrusted to us because of laziness and apathy will be met with the gravest of consequences.

"Dried-up brooks in no way cancel out God's providential plan. Often, they cause it to emerge."[637]

Chuck Swindoll

December 2

When the Brook Dries Up (Part Two)

"And it came to pass after a while, that the brook dried up, because there had been no rain in the land" (1 Kings 17:7).

The work is dead. "Ephraim is joined to idols: let him alone." God has written over numerous brooks, *Ichabod*, "the glory [of the Lord] is departed" (1 Samuel 4:21) in the pronouncement of their permanent dearth and emptiness of His manifold blessings. Various brooks (churches) have a name that they are alive but are dead (Revelation 3:1).

To witness a brook that once was streaming with torrents of living water (fruitful and flourishing) only to see it dried up is heartwrenching. When God shuts down the "water source" to a brook, no substitute, regardless of giftedness or power, can sustain it. Nothing can make alive that which God pronounces as dead, save He.

The work is disabled. Persecution, confinement (prison, hospital, home), withdrawal from the mission field, retirement, and grave illness often force a stream to go dry.

The work is done. Meyer says, "There comes a command clear and unmistakable. We must leave some beloved Cherith and go to some unwelcome Zarephath."[638] Dried up brooks may mean that the work assigned is finished and a new brook (ministry, work) is being readied. A worker can stubbornly stay when God says depart but will forfeit the power of God and lose out on the miracles in store for him at Zarephath. Had Elijah stayed at the brook Cherith, he would have missed the miracles at Zarephath. The worker that submissively goes to Zarephath "at the word of the Lord" in time will testify it was best for him to let God have His way.

"Our supreme thought should be: "Am I where God wants me to be?"[639]
F. B. Meyer

December 3

Minimalization of the Word

"And thou shalt set them in two rows, six on a row, upon the pure table before the LORD" (Leviticus 24:6).

The priests ate only bread while in the Tabernacle. Twelve loaves of bread stacked side by side on the Table of Showbread satisfied their hunger. They added nothing to it. No spices, no catsup or pickles. They were content with the Bread. The bread stacked 6 by 6 symbolizes the Bible, its 66 books, the manna, the Bread of God.

Like the priests, are you hungry for the Bread and it alone? Too many crave the "extras" and too little "Bread." They want music on the Bread, entertainment mingled with the Bread, certain emotional feelings to accompany the Bread, or the Bread to be merely an addition to the extras. The Bread, they say, is not sufficient alone.

What an insult to and contempt for the Word of God. The soul satisfied with the Bread, without the extras, is the mature soul. Note, extras, the right kind, are beneficial, provided they don't compete with or overshadow the Bread. Guard against feasting on the extras while allowing the soul to famish for deprivation of the Bread.

Peter exhorts, "As newborn babes, desire the sincere milk of the word, that ye may grow thereby" (1 Peter 2:2). "Strong desires and affections to the word of God," asserts Matthew Henry, "are a sure evidence of a person's being born again. If they be such desires as the babe has for the milk, they prove that the person is new born. They are the lowest evidence, but yet they are certain."[640]

"By catering our worship to the worshippers and not to the Object of our worship, I fear we have created human-centered churches."[641]
Francis Chan

December 4

Success in the Lord's Work (Part One)

"I am doing a great work, so that I cannot come down: why should the work cease, whilst I leave it, and come down to you?" (Nehemiah 6:3).

Nehemiah refused to come down, back down or get down. And in 52 days he got that which was down languishing back up flourishing (Nehemiah 6:15). Ten factors emerge that enabled Nehemiah's success. Adaptation of them by the pastor and Christian worker will prove equally successful in their work.

1. The work was not chosen by Nehemiah but divinely assigned by God (Nehemiah 2:12). Spurgeon says, "If you are not certain that the work you are about was given to you of God...you have no business to enter upon the work at all, for your whole strength will lie in a full conviction that your Master has sent you."[642]

2. The work was undertaken with the right attitude (Nehemiah 6:3). To every effort of the enemy to deter Nehemiah from the work he said, "I'm doing a great work."

3. The work was counted a priority (Nehemiah 6:3–4). A key principle to him in the work was never leave the building for the battling.[643]

4. The work was undertaken with a sense of urgency (Nehemiah 6:3). The clock is ticking on the time available to accomplish the task assigned. We tend to forget that. Nehemiah didn't.

5. The work was undergirded with prayer (Nehemiah 6:9). The work was bathed in prayer from its start (Nehemiah 1:4) to completion (Nehemiah 6:14–15). Redpath states, "In Christian work organizing and agonizing should go together."[644]

"Let those that are tempted to idle merry meetings by their vain companions thus answer the temptation, 'We have work to do, and must not neglect it.'"[645]

Matthew Henry

December 5

Success in the Lord's Work (Part Two)

"I am doing a great work, so that I cannot come down: why should the work cease, whilst I leave it, and come down to you?" (Nehemiah 6:3).

6. The work was graphed by a vision of what needed to be done and how (Nehemiah 2:13–15). The servant of God, in surveying the rubbish and broken-down walls of the church, is to be inflamed with a vision for undertaking its restoration.

7. The work was sustained through perseverance (Nehemiah 6:3). Nehemiah and the people endured the slander (Nehemiah 6:6–7), ridicule (Nehemiah 4:3), and physical assault (Nehemiah 4:7–8) through God's

enabling strength (Nehemiah 6:9). "Men in high place are little to be envied. They are often exposed to special dangers, both in principle and person."[646]

8. The work was shouldered by most of the people (Nehemiah 2:18). Nehemiah didn't believe in a one-man ministry. Success in the minister's work in part hinges on the participation and co-operation of church members. Spurgeon said, "Union is strength."[647]

9. The work was preserved through Nehemiah's discernment (Nehemiah 6:12). Nehemiah discerned Shemaiah's plot. The minister must "test the spirits" to see if they be of God to safeguard reputation, the work, and ministry.

10. The work was orchestrated and "wrought" by God from start to finish (Nehemiah 6:16). Nehemiah didn't have a *How to Build a Wall* handbook. But he did have God's divine authorization, supervision, and empowerment for the work. Redpath states, "Nehemiah triumphed because he was doing a work which God initiated; and because God initiated it, God Himself empowered it. It never would have succeeded had God not begun it."[648]

"Hard work will do almost everything; but in God's service it must not only be hard work, but hot work. The heart must be on fire."
C. H. Spurgeon

December 6

Ministry in Confinement

"The things which happened unto me [chains, imprisonment] have fallen out rather unto the furtherance of the gospel" (Philippians 1:12).

Paul used his confinement for great gain. Instead of wallowing in self-pity, envy, complaint, and frustration, he resolved to use it wisely and beneficially for the Gospel. He said, "[This imprisonment that was meant to stop me] has actually served to advance [the spread of] the good news [regarding salvation]" (Philippians 1:12 AMP). That is, the chains that brought constraints, loss, and pain gave Paul advantages, profit, and cheer. He enumerates the gain in Philippians 1:13–14.

1. Paul's chains brought notoriety to the cause of Christ in Rome.

2. Paul's personal guards (Praetorian guards) to whom he was chained were impacted with the Gospel in three ways. They often heard him speak the Gospel not only to them personally, but to visitors, and thereby they were changed or converted. Chained to Paul twenty-four/seven, they viewed his life up-close (character, disposition, attitude and actions) and discerned that the only crime he was guilty of was "allegiance" to Jesus Christ.

Note, how we respond to being confined to a sickbed, hospital ward, or jail cell bears a loud witness to the world positively or negatively for the Gospel.

3. Christians outside the prison were emboldened to testify for Christ by Paul's fearlessness and steadfastness to the Gospel. Join Paul in using suffering, confinement and pain for great gain.

"Trouble rightly borne honors God."[649]
George W. Truett

December 7

A Wandering Bird

"As a bird that wandereth from her nest [place of safety], so is a man that wandereth from his place" (Proverbs 27:8).

A bird (believer) that wanders from its nest is exposed to danger and hardship. Incalculable are the losses incurred in carelessly wandering away from Christ.

To wander away from Christ is to forsake *the safest refuge.*

To wander away from Christ is to forsake *the supremest friend.*

To wander away from Christ is to forsake *the surest hope.*

To wander away from Christ is to forsake *the strongest love.*

To wander away from Christ is to forsake *the soundest message* (the Word of God).

Stay put ("abide in me") in the nest of spiritual fellowship with the Lord, steadfastness to His Word, and His assigned post of duty. To borrow Paul's words, "Except these [you] abide in the ship, ye cannot be saved" (Acts 27:31).

December

"Are you not like a bird that has wandered from her nest? Believe me, there is no solid joy, no seraphic rapture, no hallowed peace this side of Heaven, except by living close under the shadow of the cross and nestling in the wounds of Jesus. Oh! That we should be so foolish! The bird doth not forget her nest, but we do forget our Lord."[650]

C. H. Spurgeon

December 8

The Church's Role Toward the Pastor (Part One)

"Be shepherds of the church of God, which he bought with his own blood" (Acts 20:28 NIV).

What ought the church to do in behalf of the pastor?

Accept him. Embrace him with his particular giftedness for the task. Don't play the compare game. The pastor must wear his own armor, not that of King Saul (former pastor or TV preacher). Expect him above all to possess giftedness in preaching the Word soundly and simply, manage his household biblically, and walk in obedience and holiness before the Lord. You don't have the right to expect him to bear angel wings and not have feet of clay. Set realistic and biblical expectations for him.

Pray for him. Paul requested prayer of the Ephesus church (Ephesians 6:19). Nothing is more important than to stand in the gap for the pastor in prayer. Spurgeon speaks for the minister when he says, "No man can do me a truer kindness in this world than to pray for me."[651] Pray daily and specifically for him. Pray as he prepares and delivers sermons, as he leads the church, as he resolves conflict and trouble, for his divine protection, for heavenly power in ministry, for traveling safety, for personal integrity, for his family, for his success as your pastor.

A young preacher had just settled into a new pastorate when some members shared their concerns to him over his weakness in preaching and potential failure as their pastor. But they said to him, "A little group of us have agreed to meet every Sunday morning to pray for you." That small group eventually became 1,000. The pastor's name was J. Wilbur Chapman (a renowned pastor/evangelist of the late 19th century).

Prayer fits the man of God for success and equips, enables and empowers him for the task.

Protect him.

1. Protect his person. Every minister has a huge "bull's eye target" on his back placed there by the Devil. Man and demons will ceaselessly seek to destroy the man and his ministry. Manifest the attitude, "To get to him, the enemy has to come through me."

2. Protect his priorities. Don't overload him with stuff that will jeopardize the time necessary for sermon preparation and prayer—like expecting him to attend every committee meeting and church function, and to show up at every Sunday school class outing.

"The first and principal duty of a pastor is to feed the flock by diligent preaching of the word."
                                        John Owen

December 9

The Church's Role Toward the Pastor (Part Two)

"Be shepherds of the church of God, which he bought with his own blood" (Acts 20:28 NIV).

Provide for him. The pastor has a right to an honorable remuneration (Luke 10:7). D. A. Carson says, "The church does not pay its ministers; rather it provides them with resources so that they are able to serve freely."[652] Instead of asking the new pastor, "What can you do for me?" ask often, "Pastor, what can I do for you?" Occasionally grease his palm with a twenty-dollar bill or a gift card to assist him.

Partner with him.

1. In vision. As he maps out the path for church progress, say to him as the people did to Nehemiah, "Let us rise up and build" (Nehemiah 2:18), not like the nobles that refused to co-operate in the work Nehemiah planned (Nehemiah 3:5).

2. In service. Do for him things you can do and are qualified to do, freeing his hands and time to do other things.

3. In biblical study and sermon preparation. Help build his library with books that will be profitable to his sermon study and spiritual growth. Provision of theological books and commentaries will enable him to be a better pastor, theologian, servant, and counselor.

4. In prayer (the greatest of works).

Praise him. Show gratitude for and to him through cards, letters, Christmas bonuses, etc. Share a heart-felt thank you for a sermon preached, a service rendered, a prayer uttered, a kindness manifested that was beyond the expected, and a visit made. Compliment the hard work in sermon preparation. Express appreciation for that which is learned under his ministry. Pass on second-hand compliments that others share with you about him.

Billy Graham recommended a minister to a church to be their pastor. In the letter he stated, "He will make you a great pastor." The committee wrote back with the reply, "Respectfully, we are not looking for a great pastor, but a pastor we can make great." In doing those things mentioned, you will make the new pastor a "great pastor."

"One crushing stroke has sometimes laid the minister very low."
C. H. Spurgeon

December 10

Benefits of Affliction

"It is good for me that I have been afflicted" (Psalm 119:71).

In whatever form affliction or trial comes it is intended to work for the believer's good.

It restrains evil appetites. Piper said, "Affliction mortifies deceitful and distracting fleshly desires, and so brings us into a more spiritual frame. Suffering has a great sin-killing effect."[653]

It refines the dim gold. Affliction is a crucible that purges the saint of impurities (Job 23:10).

It illuminates the mind. Spurgeon states, "Trial is our school where God teaches us on the blackboard. This schoolhouse has no windows to let in the cheerful light. It is very dark, and so we cannot look out and get distracted by external objects; but God's grace shines like a candle within, and by that light we see what else we had never seen."[654]

It awakens from spiritual dormancy. Affliction (at times) is God's grappling hook, fabricated in love, to recover the straying wanderer from grave danger in the "far country" (Luke 15:13).

It compels the search of Scripture. Invaluable biblical truth from the Master is taught or clarified while in the midst of a storm.

It enhances growth. Adrian Rogers testified, "I have grown the most in my own life in times of deepest despair....God stretched my life. And I'm here to tell you that I'm a better person because of it."[655]

It enhances the preciousness of Christ. Apart from affliction, Jesus is seen as the fairest of ten thousand to our soul, but in the furnace, He is felt to be more precious, valued, and prized.

It humbles the proud. Affliction brings arrogance to its knee.

It witnesses. History attests to the many who were brought to faith through observing a suffering saint.

It increases the longing for Heaven. Amidst suffering and pain, the present world loses its appeal and Heaven becomes a greater yearning. The prospect of a land free from pain and sorrow fires up the soul to want to go there (Revelation 21:4).

"The furnace of affliction is a good place for you, Christian; it benefits you; it helps you become more like Christ, and it is fitting you for Heaven."[656]
C. H. Spurgeon

December 11

When Things Don't Make Sense (Part One)

"O the depth of the riches both of the wisdom and knowledge of God! How unsearchable [undiscoverable] are His judgments, and His ways past finding out [untraceable]" (Romans 11:33).

Swindoll says, "God's heavenly plan doesn't always make earthly sense."[657] The godliest of saints have episodes in life when that which happens doesn't make sense. It didn't make sense to Mary and Martha why Jesus delayed His coming to heal their brother Lazarus. It didn't make sense to Job why he experienced such devastating loss and physical suffering. It didn't make sense to Abraham why God told him to slay his son Isaac. It didn't make sense to Sara how she would have a child at the age of ninety.

What do we do when God doesn't make sense? The concise answer is that we hold our ground in trusting to His unfailing compassionate love and caring protection, saying, "Though He slay me, yet will I trust in Him" (Job 13:15). We walk by faith, not by sight; trust, not understanding.

December

Spurgeon strikingly says, "It is a poor faith which can trust God only when friends are true, the body full of health, and the business profitable; but that is true faith which holds by the Lord's faithfulness when friends are gone, when the body is sick, when spirits are depressed and the light of our Father's countenance is hidden. A faith which can say in the direst trouble, 'Though he slay me, yet will I trust in him,' is Heaven-born faith."[658]

We go on believing and trusting in His mighty hand of deliverance, as we did in the past, for He alone is able to bring us through the most turbulent of storms.

"If God did not cause this, who did? Could God have prohibited it? Obviously, He could have; obviously He did not. So, God did not cause it, but God allowed it. Why did God allow it if He could have stopped it? Evidently, in His wisdom, He had some reason to allow it."[659]
Adrian Rogers

December 12

When Things Don't Make Sense (Part Two)

"O the depth of the riches both of the wisdom and knowledge of God! How unsearchable [undiscoverable] are His judgments, and His ways past finding out [untraceable]" (Romans 11:33).

What do we do when things don't make sense? We stop trying to figure God and His ways out and simply trust Him with the unknown. Francis Chan said, "It's not about figuring out all of the mysteries of God, but embracing Him and cherishing Him—even when He doesn't make perfect sense to us."[660] When God doesn't make sense, we grip tightly His never faltering Word and cling to His unfailing promises. We trust in the fact that He does not make mistakes and that there are no surprises to Him. Our heart clings to Romans 8:28 like a grappling hook. We remember that Paul said a day will come when the hazy and blurred events of life will become unclouded and clear. We give no place to the Devil to work doubt and fear in our mind (Ephesians 4:27). We acknowledge that He owes us no explanation or blueprint for what is transpiring, nor is either necessary.

What do we do when God doesn't make sense? When we can't trace His hand, we trust His heart. We acknowledge that God is in absolute control (Sovereign) of all that happens (permits or orders), though it may be incomprehensible, and promises somehow to bring good out of it (Romans 8:28). Saith Criswell, "Mystery may engulf us, enemies may assail us, friends may desert us, Satan may buffet us, sorrows may overwhelm us, poverty may threaten us, sickness may weaken us, despair may overtake us, dark clouds may swallow us up, but Paul says that all things—those things and a thousand other unnamable things—they all work together for good to them that love God."[661]

"Suffering is actually at the heart of the Chrstian story."
Timothy Keller

December 13

Haughtiness in the Pulpit
"An high look, and a proud heart,...is sin" (Proverbs 21:4).

Spiritual arrogance and egotism are repulsive and sickening to behold and turn both believers and sinners "off." "There is usually a motive behind the habit of self-praise; it carries with it a desire for exciting the admiration of others; it aims at reaping a harvest of laudation."[662] Arrogant pride among ministers (pastors, musicians, singers, evangelists) is escalating. *Showmanship* on stage is staggering and hindering the cause of Christ. Worship can easily descend into the parading of the flesh, mere entertainment, if the heart is not humble before the Lord.

With regard to a preacher's pride and arrogance, Spurgeon said, "Oh, dear, dear, the lofty ministerial airs that one has seen assumed by men who ought to have been meek and lowly! What a grand set of men some of the preachers of the past age thought themselves to be! The grand divines never shook hands with anybody except, indeed, with the deacons and a little knot of evidently superior persons. Now, all that kind of *stuck-uppishness* is altogether wrong."[663]

Too many young ministers perfume the air with the nauseating smell of being too good to associate or fellowship with someone they count below their status. "Self-praise silences the lips of admiration from others. The truly humble man will not crave such admiration."[664]

December

"None are more unjust in their judgments of others than those who have a high opinion of themselves."
C. H. Spurgeon

December 14

Divine Protection

"He keeps his eye upon you as you come and go and always guards you" (Psalm 121:8 TLB).

A traveler crossed what he thought was a safe bridge during a terrific storm at night. The bridge keeper in seeing him said, "In the name of God, where did you come from?"

The traveler replied, "I crossed the bridge." The man lodged with the bridge keeper for the night. The next morning, he took him back to the bridge which he had crossed. All the planks of the bridge had been torn away by the storm, and nothing remained except several beams stretching from one side to the other of the chasm. Somehow the traveler walked in the center of one of those beams the distance of a hundred feet, below which was a rushing swollen river. The man in seeing how near he came to death, fainted.

All of God's children can look back and see that grace time and again has carried them safely across unknown dilapidated "bridges" on a single beam, sparing them from grievous hurt and harm.

"The good man, during his journey through life, shall be under God's protection at all seasons as Israel in the wilderness was defended from the burning heat of the sun by the moist and refreshing shadow of the cloud and secured against the inclement influences of the nocturnal heavens by the kindly warmth and splendor diffused from the pillar of fire."[665]
George Horne

December 15

Psalm 23 (Part One)

"The LORD is my shepherd" (Psalm 23:1).

The Good Shepherd justifies the sheep (v. 1a). Spurgeon says, "No man has a right to consider himself the Lord's sheep unless his nature has been renewed, for the scriptural description of unconverted men does not picture them as sheep, but as wolves or goats."[666]

The Good Shepherd supplies the sheep (v. 1b–2). Sheep, though animals that flock together, receive individualized care from the Shepherd. He makes sure no sheep in the fold lacks any needful thing ("shall not want"). Abundant food in green pastures, refreshing water in quiet streams and brooks, and proper shelter to rest are always provided. The Good Shepherd, through the Holy Scripture, provides His sheep spiritual nourishment, renewal, rest, and direction.

The Good Shepherd quiets the sheep (v. 2). "He maketh me to lie down." Green pastures and still waters are pictures of tranquility and peace. The Lord's sheep often have to be compelled to lie down lest they fall down. We must "come apart" so that we don't "fall apart."

The Good Shepherd revives the sheep (v. 3). "He restoreth my soul." He grants the sheep reinvigoration spiritually and mentally. Alexander says, "To restore the soul here is to vivify or quicken the exhausted spirit."[667]

The Good Shepherd guides the sheep (v. 3). He leads the sheep in the right paths, the way of uprightness in heart and faithfulness in duty. He orchestrates the entirety of their life to their delight and His glory.

Matthew Henry says, "In these paths we cannot walk unless God, both lead us into them and lead us in them."[668] "Yea though I walk in the valley of the shadow of death."

"Observe," Spurgeon asserts, "that it is not walking *in* the valley, but *through* the valley. We go through the dark tunnel of death and emerge into the light of immortality. We do not die; we do but sleep to wake in glory. Death is not the house but the porch, not the goal but the passage to it."[669]

"This Psalm breathes throughout a spirit of the calmest and most assured trust in God; it speaks of a peace so deep, serenity so profound, that even the thought of the shadow of death cannot trouble it."
                                J. J. Perowne

December 16

Psalm 23 (Part Two)

"The LORD is my shepherd" (Psalm 23:1).

The Good Shepherd chides the sheep (v. 2a). Sheep, by nature prone to wander, stray from the sheepfold, and once lost are incapable of finding their way back. It's the shepherd's task to search for and restore them to the sheepfold. Likewise, when a sheep of the flock of the Lord strays into the "far country," He diligently pursues it until it is found. Upon finding it, He rebukes, corrects and restores it—graciously and mercifully forgives sin when confessed and restores the confessor.

The Good Shepherd abides with the sheep (v. 4b). Parker says, "My hand is locked in Thine; my life is drawn from Thine; my future is involved in Thine; God and the saint are one."[670] W. S. Plumer says, "The safety of God's people in this life does not consist in exemption from troubles and perils, but in the care and protection of Him who hides them in His pavilion and in His tabernacle and sets them upon a rock."[671]

The Good Shepherd satisfies the sheep (v. 6). The sheep of the Good Shepherd testify of the bountiful goodness throughout life received from His hand. Barnes observes, "The language is the utterance of a heart overflowing with joy and gratitude in the recollection of the past, and full of glad anticipation (as derived from the experience of the past) in regard to the future."[672]

"I will dwell in the house of the LORD forever." At the last Christ's sheep will be satisfied with their new home prepared in Heaven by the Lord. Maclaren wrote, "God will bring those whom He has fed and guided in journeying and conflict to an unchanging mansion in a home beyond the stars."[673] This He promised (John 14:1–3).

"Depth and strength underlie the simplicity of this psalm. Its peace is not escape; its contentment is not complacency. There is readiness to face deep darkness and imminent attack, and the climax reveals a love which homes towards no material goal but to the Lord Himself."[674]
Derek Kidner

December 17

Meet Me at the Fountain

"I go to prepare a place for you" (John 14:2).

Heaven.

It is a physical place (John 14:2). It is a place where streets are paved with pure gold, walls are framed with jasper, foundations are made with twelve precious stones, and gates are constructed of pearl.

It is a promised place (John 14:3). Paul affirms the truth, "In hope of eternal life, which God, that cannot lie, promised before the world began" (Titus 1:2).

It is a perfect place (Revelation 22:3–5). It is free from the curse of sin and the railing and ravaging of Satan and his cohorts.

It is a pleasurable place (Revelation 5:9). Courson observes, "When Jesus says, 'I go to prepare a place for you,' He is not speaking generically, but specifically. Jesus is preparing a place for you specifically. Think through this. What do you enjoy? What has God built into your being? Whatever it is, know this. Jesus is preparing a place for you to fulfill the elements He's woven into the fabric of your personality uniquely and specifically."[675]

It is a permanent place (2 Corinthians 5:8). Paul states, "Then we which are alive and remain shall be caught up together with them in the clouds, to meet the Lord in the air: and so shall we *ever* be with the Lord" (1 Thessalonians 4:17). With all that is known to man about Heaven, there is so much that is unknown that only adds to its grandeur.

At the industrial exposition in Chicago many years ago was a fountain which served as a meeting place for friends. One would say to a friend, "Will you meet me at the fountain?"

The reply was, "All right; I will meet you at the fountain."

P. P. Bliss wrote a gospel song based on the fountain, elevating the thought from the physical (exposition grounds) to the spiritual (Heaven). "Will you meet me at the fountain when I reach the glory-land? When you meet me at the fountain, shall I clasp your friendly hand? Other friends will give you welcome; other loving voices, cheer. There'll be music at the fountain—will you, will you meet me there?"

Will you?

December

"Our imaginations simply cannot comprehend the grandeur of this wonderful home, a place of everlasting joy, contentment, and peace."[676]
Billy Graham

December 18

The Devil's Big Lie

"There is forgiveness with thee" (Psalm 130:4).

The Devil entices man to sin and then, in its aftermath, tells him it is greater than may be forgiven by God. But that's a big lie. The psalmist refutes him, saying plenteous mercy and forgiveness is available at the throne of God.

Its surety. The Bible says, "There is forgiveness." The verb *is* in the verse is not in the original Hebrew. Therefore, without harm, the text might be translated, "There was forgiveness. There is forgiveness. There will be forgiveness as long as life remains." But it's just fine the way the verse now stands, "There is forgiveness with thee." These words are the uniform language of all the Scripture.

Its source. "There is forgiveness *with thee.*" Some translate it to read, "There is propitiation with thee." Jesus made appeasement with God for man's sin in His death at Calvary. God's wrath was poured out upon Him for sin, that man might not have to pay its penalty of eternal separation from God.

Its scope. The forgiveness of God has broad boundaries and covers every transgression. "There is forgiveness." No restriction is placed upon the sin that may be cleansed away. Why? The psalmist says, "And with him is plenteous redemption" (Psalm 130:7b). Is there hope for forgiveness for the drunkard? the adulterer? the backslider? the murderer? Indeed. The psalmist says because of the love of God and the plenitude of forgiveness, there is hope for every sinner (Psalm 130:7a). "The power of pardon is permanently resident with God; He has forgiveness ready to His hand at this instant."[677] And that's the Good News of the Gospel.

"It's Satan's delight to tell me that once he's got me, he will keep me. But at that moment I can go back to God. And I know that if I confess my sins, God is faithful and just to forgive me."
Alan Redpath

December 19

Real Rest for the Soul

"Come [keep coming] to Me, all of you who work and have heavy loads [weary, troubled, burdened]. I will give you rest" (Matthew 11:28 NLV).

Robertson says, "Let us keep on coming to" our high priest, this sympathizing and great high priest. Instead of deserting him, let us make daily use of him."[678] You can never come too often, request too much, or stay too long at the throne of grace. The storehouse of grace is limitless and inexhaustible.

Brooks wrote, "'Come,' saith Christ—that is, believe in Me, and 'I will give you rest'; I will give you peace with God and peace with conscience. I will turn your storm into an everlasting calm; I will give you such rest that the world can neither give to you nor take from you."[679]

A monument in Newport Church (Isle of Wight) erected by Queen Victoria portrays the manner in which Princess Elizabeth met with death. The Princess from her youth had been imprisoned, separated from family and friends until she died. Upon her death she was found with her head reclining on a Bible opened to the Scripture that read, "Come unto Me, all ye that labor and are heavy laden, and I will give you rest."

What a sermon in stone that monument preaches, reminding all that ultimate rest is found not in status or possession, but in the grace of the Lord Jesus Christ.[680]

"In place of our exhaustion and spiritual fatigue, God will give us rest. All He asks is that we come to Him...that we spend a while thinking about Him, meditating on Him, talking to Him, listening in silence, occupying ourselves with Him—totally and thoroughly lost in the hiding place of His presence."
Chuck Swindoll

December 20

Christian Hope

"May overflow with hope by the power of the Holy Spirit" (Romans 15:13 NIV).

December

"Optimism hopes for the best," states J. I. Packer, "without any guarantee of its arriving and is often no more than whistling in the dark. Christian hope, by contrast, is faith looking ahead to the fulfillment of the promises of God, as when the Anglican burial service inters the corpse 'in sure and certain hope of the Resurrection to eternal life, through our Lord Jesus Christ.' Optimism is a wish without warrant; Christian hope is a certainty, guaranteed by God himself. Optimism reflects ignorance as to whether good things will ever actually come. Christian hope expresses knowledge that every day of his life, and every moment beyond it, the believer can say with truth, on the basis of God's own commitment, that the best is yet to come."[681]

Most certainly the person who knows Jesus Christ personally as Lord and Savior and embraces the Christian hope He espoused will age biblically and joyfully without fear of becoming a grouchy old man or woman. Why? Billy Graham said, "Only the forward-looking Christian remains sincerely optimistic and joyful, knowing that Christ will win in the end."[682]

"Hope is not simply a 'wish' (I wish that such-and-such would take place); rather, it is that which latches on to the certainty of the promises of the future that God has made."
R. C. Sproul

December 21

Shining Saints

"Let your light so shine before men, that they may see your good works, and glorify your Father which is in Heaven" (Matthew 5:16).

Why shine. Shine to magnify Christ. The candle is to display Christ, not the Christian; the work and wonders, not the worker and wrappings. The light that calls attention to itself is haughty and vain, depriving God of the glory due His name. Shine to be winsome. Beecher said, "The success of the Gospel was made to depend not on preaching, but upon living men."[683] Shining saints reveal Christ to the people in darkness, making known the need of salvation and the way to it.

How shine. Shine through a life of "good works" and good example. "Whoever is a believer in Christ is a new creation. The old way of living has disappeared. A new way of living has come into existence" (2

Corinthians 5:17 GW). God is glorified most when others witness His work of grace manifest in our lives.

Where shine. We do not shine shut up in a monastery or church building, but in the world, "before men." To be lights to the world we must mingle with the world. It's impossible to impact the world for Christ in a telephone booth of solitariness. Saints are to let their light shine at home before spouse and children, in the workplace and at the water fountain, at the school house and playground, at the restaurant and social activity.

When shine. We are to shine all the time. "Let it shine till Jesus comes; I'm gonna let it shine."

Hidden shine. A bushel basket, to the degree it envelopes a light, causes the light's beam to wane and flicker, its luster and radiance to dampen, and its purpose to be impeded. For example, the bushel basket of cowardly silence and/or the least transgression negates or suffocates the entire profession. "While passing through this world of sin, and others your life shall view, be clean and pure without, within; let others see Jesus in you."

Note, there are times when secrecy in doing good works is profitable in order not "to be seen of [men]" (Matthew 6:1). The motivation for the good deed or work (exalt God or extol self) is the determining factor.

"Do not be as a dark lantern, burning with the shades down and illuminating nothing and nobody."[684]
Alexander Maclaren

December 22

Saltshakers
"Ye are the salt of the earth" (Matthew 5:13).

The metaphor of salt from the lips of Christ to the saints depicts their indispensable and pivotal role in the world. Christians as salt are to be the antidote to the corruption and decay of the world. This they are by the bold and brazen profession and declaration of the faith, protest of the deeds of darkness, and life of godliness they exhibit. Salt cleanses society of the causes of its stinking decay—sin and evil. It diminishes their presence and power.

During the COVID-19 pandemic, disinfectants were used heavily and broadly to destroy the spread of the virus. Saints are Heaven's disinfectant (salt) to prevent the spread of the deadly virus of sin.

The Christian as salt is to be the antidote to the tastelessness of life in the world. Saints are to permeate the world with sweetness, joy, peace, hope, love, and cheer, making it more palatable (enriching, enjoyable), especially to the disappointed, disparaged, and disheartened. Note, salt improves that upon which it is sprinkled.

Efficacious salt.

1. To be effective salt to the world the Christian must maintain saltiness, which is gained from abiding in Christ, spending time in His Word, and leading a holy life. Without this saltiness, the Christian is good for nothing. He has no power to remedy the world's sickness.

2. To be effective salt to the world the salt must be dispensed to the world, not stored up in a salt cellar (church). It must be shaken out of the saltshaker onto the world. Havner says, "Salt must be brought into close contact with whatever it is meant to affect if it is to do any good. Christians are the salt of the earth. We must be willing to be rubbed into the decaying carcass of an unregenerate society. Most of us are content to sit in our little saltshakers, far removed from a needy and lost humanity."[685]

"People don't enjoy salt. They enjoy what is salted. We are the salt of the earth. We do not exist for ourselves."
John Piper

December 23

What It Means to Follow Christ

"If any man will come after me, let him deny himself, and take up his cross, and follow me" (Matthew 16:24).

Following Christ means no rival to His worship. The believer's first and utmost love and loyalty belong to Christ. He is to be preeminent in our life, above spouse, child, and friend. Jesus said, "Anyone who wants to be my follower must love me far more than he does his own father, mother, wife, children, brothers, or sisters—yes, more than his own life—otherwise he cannot be my disciple" (Luke 14:26 TLB).

Following Christ means no refusal to His word. Christ frankly said, "If ye love me, keep my commandments" (John 14:15). The servant obeys the instruction of the master regardless of cost or consequence. That which Mary said to the attendants at the wedding feast at Cana is applicable to all: "Do whatever He tells you" (John 2:5 NIV). The servant has no discretionary power as to what part of the word of the Master is obeyed. It is all to be heeded. Adrian Rogers states, "Discipline says, 'I need to.' Duty says, 'I ought to.' Devotion says, 'I want to.'"

Following Christ means no retreat from His work. "Whosoever he be of you that forsaketh not all that he hath, he cannot be my disciple" (Luke 14:33). Stephen Olford said, "Forsaking all is following the Lord Jesus Christ without retreat."[686] The servant of the Lord burns his bridges behind him. "I have decided to follow Jesus, no turning back."

Following Christ means no regret about the walk. He that travels the journey of life with Christ testifies that it grows sweeter every step of the way. In my nearly sixty years of ministry, I never once met a Christian that told me he regretted his decision to follow Christ.

"God, send me anywhere, only go with me. Lay any burden on me, only sustain me. And sever any tie in my heart except the tie that binds my heart to Yours."
David Livingstone

December 24

No Room for You

"There was no room for them in the inn" (Luke 2:7).

The denial of love and acceptance in our lives by people who matter to us wounds, crushes the spirit. Their rejection infuses feelings of unworthiness, hopelessness, shame, and despair. Nothing, not even the grief of death, compares to the anguish and pain in hearing the horrendous message repeatedly, "You don't measure up to our standards. You are unwanted and unwelcome."

Joseph and Mary tried to find a room in Bethlehem's inn, but the innkeeper said he had no room for them (Luke 2:7). Have you ever been

December

told, "I don't have room for you?" If so, you know how badly hearing those words hurt.

Jesus knows how deeply these few words hurt, for He heard them time and again throughout His life. While He was in the womb of Mary, He heard them from the innkeeper. When He was nailed to the cross, Jesus heard the world saying, "We don't have room for you." Scripture tells us, "He [Jesus] came unto his own, and his own received him not" (John 1:11).

Jesus still hears the same words as He seeks entrance into men's hearts. "We don't have room for you." Jesus sympathizes with everyone who hears these words and gives assurance that no one will ever hear these painful words of rejection from Him. With open arms, Jesus says to you, "I have room for you and always will, no matter what happens."[687] That's the overwhelming message of the cradle that extended throughout Jesus' life to the Cross.

His invitation of old rings as true as ever when He says, "Him that cometh to me I will in no wise [under no circumstance] cast out [turn away, ignore, or refuse]" (John 6: 37). May I say to YOU, there is room for you at the table with Jesus. "There is room at the Cross for you."

"Come, and He will give you rest. Trust Him, for His word is plain. He will take the sinfulest; Christ receiveth sinful men."
Erdmann Neumeister

December 25

Why Christ Came

"And we have seen and testify that the Father has sent his Son to be the Savior of the world" (1 John 4:14 ESV).

What was the purpose for the divine incarnation 2,000 years ago in Bethlehem's manger? John cites three primary reasons for Christ's coming.

1. He "appeared in order to take away our sins" (1 John 3:5 GW); that is, to forgive them that we might be reconciled to God and given power to abstain from them. The person that continues to sin disregards the purpose of the incarnation.

2. It was to display God's love for man and grant to the lost eternal life (1 John 4:9; John 3:16).

3. It was to destroy the works of the Devil (1 John 3:8) the root of which is sin and the fruit of which is detestable and abominable acts, aspirations, and attitudes. Satan's work began in his rebellious revolt in Heaven and was initiated on earth in the garden when he seduced Adam and Eve to sin.

God and man walked in harmony until Satan severed this fellowship (Isaiah 59:2). Satan's deception of them about right and wrong (he is the world's biggest liar, the "Father of lies") and discreditation of the authority of God to control man spread from Adam and Eve into all the world (false religions, heretical preachers, unbiblical ideologies, etc.).

Matthew Henry asserts, "The Devil has designed and endeavored to ruin the work of God in this world. The Son of God has undertaken the holy war against him. He came into our world and was manifested in our flesh that He might conquer him and dissolve his works. Sin will He loosen and dissolve more and more, till He has quite destroyed it. Let not us serve or indulge what the Son of God came to destroy."[688]

Note, the word "destroy" means "to render inoperative, to rob of power," not annihilate.[689] Wiersbe states, "Satan has not been annihilated, but his power has been reduced and his weapons have been impaired. He is still a mighty foe, but he is no match for the power of God."[690]

How did Jesus demolish the works of the devil? The author of Hebrews says, "Forasmuch then as the children are partakers of flesh and blood, He also Himself likewise took part of the same; *that through death He might destroy him that had the power of death,* that is, the devil" (Hebrews 2:14).

Christ fulfilled the divine purposes for the incarnation through His suffering, shed blood, death at Calvary, and subsequent resurrection. Hallelujah!

Spurgeon advises, "If we want to destroy the works of the Devil, our best method is to manifest more and more the Son of God."[691]

"Satan is a decided fact and a destructive force, but he is also defeated foe."
Adrian Rogers

December 26

Assurance of Salvation

"Examine yourselves to see if your faith is genuine" (2 Corinthians 13:5 NLT).

The assurance of salvation must be based firmly upon God's Word to me, God's Work for me, and God's Witness in me.

God's Word to Me. "These things have I written unto you that believe on the name of the Son of God; that ye may know that ye have eternal life" (1 John 5:13). The bottom line about salvation is what God states in Scripture. Man accepts the witness of pharmacists about prescription medication, and the U.S. Treasury regarding the value of a dollar (a dollar is worth a dollar). John emphatically declares that "the witness [word] of God is greater [more sure, certain, reliable]" than that of man (1 John 5:9).

God's Work for Me. Jesus' atoning death at Calvary and His subsequent resurrection makes salvation possible. Man's work and morality don't come into play at all (Ephesians 2:8–9). Salvation is of Him, by Him, through Him, and in Him alone. It happens instantaneously the moment a sinner comes to Christ in faith and godly sorrow (repentance).

God's Witness in Me. The witness is two-fold.

1. The witness of the Holy Spirit. At conversion, the Holy Spirit takes up residence in the heart and bears witness to the transformation by grace (Romans 8:16).

2. The witness of a changed life. Conversion leads to a change in life (2 Corinthians 5:17). An old African-American saying undergirds this truth: "The day I got saved, my feet got a brand-new walk, and my speech got a brand-new talk." A difference occurs at salvation that continues to progress throughout the Christian's life.

To summarize: God's Word makes the believer *sure,* God's Work makes the believer *safe,* and God's Witness makes the believer *secure.*

"Our salvation is fastened with God's own hand, and with Christ's own strength, to the strong stake of God's unchangeable nature."
Samuel Rutherford

December 27

The Goal-Line Stand

"But put ye on the Lord Jesus Christ, and make not provision for the flesh, to fulfil the lusts thereof" (Romans 13:14).

Don't give Satan another inch of ground. Draw a line in the sand and say, "Enough is enough." Then take back all Satan took, in the authority of Jesus' name.

During football season, when the opposing team is on the one-yard line seeking to score, the great cry from fans that reverberates throughout the stadium is: "Hold that line!" You may have let them drive the ball 90 yards, played sluggishly, missed key tackles, and made senseless mistakes resulting in penalties; but, at the one-yard line, you set your cleats firmly in the sod and determine enough is enough.

Life is like football in this regard. You get pushed back, knocked down, and run over by sins and mistakes you make; and just as the enemy is about to deliver the final blow, you set your cleats in the sod at the goal line and say, "No further!" You have been beaten down but not defeated. There are not enough demons in Hell to drag you over the one-yard line into eternal bleakness, hopelessness, and Hell, if you cling to Jesus Christ.

Peter gave up much ground to the enemy by denying the Lord three times, but at the one-yard line, strength from the Lord was tapped to "hold that line" and not let Satan score a sweeping victory. David fumbled the ball big time with Bathsheba and let Satan beat him to a pulp, but he triumphed in the Lord in a goal-line stand (Psalm 51:1–17). Joseph's one-yard-line stand is one of the greatest in the Bible. Mrs. Potiphar made daily seductive advances toward him (Genesis 39:7, 10). Finally, the moment came when he was at the one-yard line. His purity and walk with God were on the line. He made an unforgettable goal-line stand, refusing to let her make any further advancement, and won the day (Genesis 39:11–13). The knockout punch came when Joseph told her, "How then can I do this great wickedness, and sin against God?" (Genesis 39:9).

You have a one-yard-line stand to make against a sinful indulgence. You have been pushed back, overrun, outplayed, and fooled by the play calls of Satan. He has beaten you hand over fist to this moment. Now your back is to the wall, and you must make the goal-line stand or else suffer utter defeat. Don't quit. Don't despair. Don't allow what you have

December

done, the defeats you have suffered, to break your spirit, resulting in an attitude of hopelessness. You can win. Like others, you can make an unforgettable goal-line stand that will change everything.

"Soon the battle will be over. It will not be long now before the day will come when Satan will no longer trouble us. There will be no more domination, temptation, accusation, or confrontation."
Thomas Watson

December 28

Not Far Away, but Still Lost
"Thou art not far from the Kingdom of God" (Mark 12:34).

What a tragedy, to be almost saved, but eternally lost!

Marks of those who are "not far away."

1. They are Teachable. They are openminded to the truth of the Gospel.
2. They are Knowledgeable. They know the why and way of it.
3. They are Desirous. They are interested in it.
4. They are Perceptive. They discern the truth and need of it.
5. They are Compatible. Their beliefs align with it.

Dangers for those who are "not far away."

1. They become complacent about it.
2. They become satisfied without it.
3. They become indifferent toward it.
4. They become resistant and die in their damnable condition.

Decision for those who are "not far away."

While the heart is warm and receptive to the Gospel, respond to its invitation. Delay today may mean Hell tomorrow. Procrastination is not only the thief of time, but of salvation. The road to Hell is paved with good intentions, as it is with sin. The Bible says, "now is the accepted time; behold, now is the day of salvation" (2 Corinthians 6:2).

"Tremble lest the decisive step be never taken. Decide at once."
C. H. Spurgeon

December 29

Immoveable Saints
"Be not moved away from the hope of the gospel" (Colossians 1:23).

Spurgeon states, "If Satan spends great power in keeping us from the hope, he uses equal force in endeavoring to drag us away from it, and equal cunning in endeavoring to allure us from it. Hence the apostle tells us not to be moved away from the hope of the Gospel. The exhortation is needful in presence of an imminent danger."[692]

What things might Satan use to move us away from hope and faith in Christ Jesus? Included are liberal and false religious teachers (Psalm 1:1), improper associations (2 Corinthians 6:14; 1 Kings 11:1–4), opposition and persecution for living the Christian life (John 16:33; 2 Timothy 3:12), disappointment in a Christian we admired (2 Peter 2:21; Hebrews 2:1–2), severe hardship and sorrow that devastates us (Deuteronomy 1:27–36; Luke 7:23), neglect of abiding fellowship with Christ and the church (Hebrews 10:25; John 15:4), and inexplicable sickness and suffering (Job 13:15).

To be forewarned is to be forearmed (1 Peter 5:8). An experienced old seaman told Richard Fuller, "In fierce storms, we must put the ship in a certain position and keep her there."

Said Fuller, "This, Christian, is what you must do....You must put your soul in one position and keep it there. You must stay upon the Lord, and, come what may—winds, waves, cross seas, thunder, lightning, frowning rocks, roaring breakers—no matter what, you must hold fast your confidence in God's faithfulness and His everlasting love in Christ Jesus."

"Who stands firm? Only the one for whom the final standard is not his reason, his principles, his conscience, his freedom, his virtue, but who is ready to sacrifice all these, when in faith and sole allegiance to God he is called to obedient and responsible action: the responsible person, whose life will be nothing but an answer to God's question and call."
                    Dietrich Bonhoeffer

December 30

Broken Vows

"When thou vowest a vow unto God, defer not to pay it" (Ecclesiastes 5:4).

The vow is a voluntary promise to abstain from something or to do something on the condition that God does something in return (delivers from death, heals an illness, opens a shut door, grants success in an undertaking). Unlike a resolution, it is binding to and punitive by God.

Vows must be legitimate in principle. Some vows ought not to be made, especially those that violate the Scripture and moral law. For example, to vow to commit a sinful or wrong act or to get even with someone that offended you is insensible, foolish and unacceptable.

Vows must be doable in practice. Don't make a vow until you are confident that which you committed to can be done. It is ludicrous to rashly vow to do a task beyond your ability, time, location or health.

Vows must be thoughtful in pledge. Devout deliberation is crucial regarding the cost of keeping a vow and the consequence of not keepint it. It's a serious blunder to fail to do what you have vowed for three reasons: it offends God, it injures the soul, and it brings judgment. Once a vow is made, it's irretrievable. It must not be evaded, denounced or excused.

Vows must be timely in performance. "Defer not to pay it; for God hath no pleasure in fools." The longer the obligation is postponed, the less likely is its fulfillment. Thomas Fuller said, "Vows made in storms are forgotten in calm."

Delay breeds forgetfulness of that which was promised, as seen in the case of the chief butler's vow to Joseph in Potiphar's jail. "If it be in the power of thy hands to pay it today," saith Matthew Henry, "leave it not till tomorrow; do not beg a day nor put it off to a more convenient season. By delay the sense of the obligation slackens and cools and is in danger of wearing off."[693]

Wonder of wonders are the many unkept vows man has made to God or to another due to mere forgetfulness. Norman Vincent Peale said, "Promises are like crying babies in a theater; they should be carried out at once."[694] Recall them and keep them. "Now I come to your Temple with burnt offerings to fulfill the vows I made to you—yes, the sacred vows that I made when I was in deep trouble" (Psalm 66:13–14 NLT).

"Hasty resolutions are of the nature of vows, and to be equally avoided."
William Penn

December 31

An End Is Come

"An end is come, the end is come: it watcheth for thee; behold, it is come" (Ezekiel 7:6).

An end will come to the opportunities of life. Opportunity is a divinely orchestrated conjuncture of happenings to facilitate and effectuate the plan of God. An ancient Greek sculptor entitled a piece of his work *Opportunity*. A visitor viewing the sculpture inquired, "Why is its face veiled?"

"Because men seldom know her when she comes to them," was the reply.

"And why does she stand upon her toes, and why the wings?"

"Because," said the sculptor, "when once she is gone, she can never be overtaken."[695]

An end will come to the offer of salvation. Salvation's invitation to a person ends at the moment of death, to all the world at the end of the age of grace (when Christ returns). See Hebrews 3:7.

An end will come to life's work. "Night is coming when no one can work" (John 9:4 CSB). That which God assigned must be done, lest at the judgment we be "weighed and found wanting." Good intentions don't count; the deed and duty must be engaged in. Delay must be thwarted. The sand in the hourglass is quickly dissipating.

An end will come to life. "It is appointed unto men once to die" (Hebrews 9:27). Life is like a mere vapor that appears momentarily before it vanishes (James 4:14). William Tiptaft says, "Fit or not fit, we must all die, and we know not how soon. As death leaves us, the judgment must find us." Prepare for it.

"Time is broken into periods; and every period, long or short, has its certain end."[696]

W. F. Adeney

Endnotes

[1] Truett, George W. *A Quest for Souls*. (New York and London: Harper & Brothers, Publishers, 1917), 50.
[2] Spurgeon, C. H. *Morning and Evening*. (London: Passmore & Alabaster), September 11 (Morning).
[3] Ellicott's Commentary for English Readers, I Corinthians 9:27.
[4] MacArthur, J., Jr. (Ed.). *The MacArthur Study Bible* (electronic ed.). (Nashville, TN: Word Pub., 1997), 1805.
[5] "Archaeology and the Bible." Christiananswers.net/archaeology, accessed December 27, 2010.
[6] Ibid.
[7] Ibid.
[8] Ibid.
[9] "Facing the Challenge." www.facingthechallenge.org, accessed December 22, 2010.
[10] McFarland, Alex. *10 Answers for Skeptics*, 49.
[11] MacArthur, John. "What Jesus' Death Meant to Him" (August 1, 1971). Gty.org, accessed June 14, 2011.
[12] Wilson, Larry. *Daily Devotional*. January 23, 2011. www.opc.org/devotional.html?devotion, accessed June 17, 2011.
[13] Knight, G. W. *The Pastoral Epistles: A Commentary on the Greek Text*. (Grand Rapids, MI; Carlisle, England: W. B. Eerdmans; Paternoster Press, 1992), 459.
[14] Barclay, W. (Ed.). *The Letters to Timothy, Titus, and Philemon*. (Philadelphia: Westminster John Knox Press, 1975), 210.
[15] Ibid.
[16] Zodhiates, S. *The Complete Word Study Dictionary: New Testament* (electronic ed.). (Chattanooga, TN: AMG Publishers, 2000).
[17] Wuest, K. S. *Wuest's Word Studies from the Greek New Testament: For the English Reader* (Vol. 12). (Grand Rapids: Eerdmans, 1997), 24.
[18] Simeon, C. *Horae Homileticae: 2 Timothy to Hebrews* (Vol. 19). (London: Holdsworth and Ball, 1833), 80.
[19] Spurgeon, C. H. *An All-Round Ministry*, 33.
[20] Arterburn, Stephen. *Walking Into Walls*. (Brentwood, TN: Worthy Publishing, 2011).
[21] MacArthur, J. F. *The Freedom and Power of Forgiveness* (electronic ed.). (Wheaton, IL: Crossway Books, 1998), 97.
[22] Adams, Jay. *From Forgiven to Forgiving*. (Amityville, NY: Calvary, 1994), 25.
[23] Spurgeon, C. H. "Healing for the Wounded." A sermon delivered November 11, 1865, New Park Street Chapel.

[24] Exell, J. S. *The Biblical Illustrator: The Psalms* (Vol. 5). (New York; Chicago; Toronto; London; Edinburgh: Fleming H. Revell Company; Francis Griffiths, 1909), 347.
[25] Spurgeon, C. H. "Concern for Other Men's Souls." Sermon delivered 1878, Metropolitan Tabernacle.
[26] Ibid.
[27] "10 Quotes from Billy Graham on Easter," April 11, 2017.
[28] The Hand of the Lord | Precept Austin. https://www.preceptaustin.org/the_hand_of_the_lord, accessed January 17, 2021.
[29] Ibid.
[30] Ibid.
[31] Exell, J. S. *The Biblical Illustrator: Exodus.* (New York: Anson D. F. Randolph & Company, n.d.), 545.
[32] Spurgeon, C. H. "The Wailing of Risca." Sermon delivered on Sunday morning, December 9, 1860, at Exeter Hall, Strand.
[33] VanGemeren, *The Expositor's Bible Commentary,* cited in J. E. Smith. *The Wisdom Literature and Psalms* (Ps 11:3). (Joplin, MO: College Press Pub. Co., 1996), 132.
[34] Spurgeon, C. H. *Psalms.* (Wheaton, IL: Crossway Books, 1993), 32.
[35] Henry, M. *Matthew Henry's Commentary on the Whole Bible: Complete and Unabridged in One Volume.* (Peabody: Hendrickson, 1994), 758.
[36] Boice, J. M. *Psalms 1–41: An Expositional Commentary.* (Grand Rapids, MI: Baker Books, 2005), 93.
[37] Spence-Jones, H. D. M. (Ed.). *Psalms* (Vol. 1). (London; New York: Funk & Wagnalls Company, 1909), 79.
[38] Simeon, C. *Horae Homileticae: Psalms, I–LXXII* (Vol. 5). (London: Samuel Holdsworth, 1836), 47.
[39] Exell, J. S. *The Biblical Illustrator: Exodus.* (New York: Anson D. F. Randolph & Company, n.d.), 307.
[40] Spurgeon, C. H. "The Certainty and Freeness of Divine Grace." Sermon delivered November 13, 1864, Metropolitan Tabernacle.
[41] Criswell, W. A., P. Patterson, E. R. Clendenen, D. L. Akin, M. Chamberlin, D. K. Patterson, and J. Pogue (Eds.). *Believer's Study Bible* (electronic ed.). (Nashville: Thomas Nelson, 1991), Ps 127:3.
[42] Plumer, W. S. *Studies in the Book of Psalms: Being a Critical and Expository Commentary, with Doctrinal and Practical Remarks on the Entire Psalter.* (Philadelphia; Edinburgh: J. B. Lippincott Company; A & C Black, 1872), 1115.
[43] Henry, Matthew. *Matthew Henry's Concise Bible Commentary,* Psalm 77:11.
[44] Plumer, W. S. *Studies in the Book of Psalms: Being a Critical and Expository Commentary, with Doctrinal and Practical Remarks on the Entire Psalter.* (Philadelphia; Edinburgh: J. B. Lippincott Company; A & C Black, 1872), 729.

Endnotes

[45] Spurgeon, C. H. "The Peace of God." (Sermon Delivered January 6, 1878). https://www.spurgeon.org/resource-library/sermons/the-peace-of-god/#flipbook/, accessed September 21, 2021.

[46] O'Brien, P. T. *The Epistle to the Philippians: A Commentary on the Greek Text.* (Grand Rapids, MI: Eerdmans, 1991), 495–496.

[47] MacArthur, J., Jr. (Ed.). The MacArthur Study Bible (electronic ed.). (Nashville, TN: Word Pub., 1997), 1828.

[48] Chambers, Oswald. *My Utmost for His Highest,* November 24.

[49] Henry, M. *Matthew Henry's Commentary on the Whole Bible: Complete and Unabridged in One Volume*. (Peabody: Hendrickson, 1994), 931.

[50] Manton, Thomas. *One Hundred and Ninety Sermons on the Hundred and Nineteenth Psalm,* Vol. 2. (London: William Brown, 1845), 585–586.

[51] Exell, J. S. *The Biblical Illustrator: Joshua, Judges, and Ruth* (Vol. 1). (New York; Chicago; Toronto: Fleming H. Revell Company, n.d.), 2.

[52] Criswell, W. A. "Grief at the Death of Family/Friends" (sermon), First Baptist Church, Dallas, Texas, January 12, 1958 a.m.

[53] Hallesby, Ole. *Prayer.* (London: Hodder & Stoughton, 1936).

[54] Spurgeon, C. H. *An All-Around Ministry,* Chapter One.

[55] https://www.inspiringquotes.us/author/8177-f-b-meyer/about-prayer, accessed June 22, 2022.

[56] https://wmpl.org/quote/, accessed May 26, 2018.

[57] Thomas, W. H. G. *Life Abiding and Abounding: Bible Studies in Prayer and Meditation.* (Chicago: The Bible Institute Colportage Association, n.d.), 12.

[58] Redpath, Alan. *Victorious Christian Service.* (Old Tappan, NJ: Fleming H. Revell Company, 1958), 24.

[59] Spurgeon, C. H. "Behold, He Prayeth." Sermon Delivered September 20, 1885.

[60] Spurgeon, C. H. *Exploring the Mind and Heart of the Prince of Preachers* (Kerry James Allen, Ed.). (Oswego, Ill: Fox River Press, 2005), 30.

[61] Lutzer, Erwin and David Jeremiah. *We Will Not Be Silenced.* (Eugene, Oregon: Harvest House Publishers, 2020), 247.

[62] *I Have Walked Alone with Jesus: Day by Day Meditations of Oswald J. Smith*

[63] Nee, Watchman. *The Spiritual Man.* (Christian Fellowship Publishers, 2009), 343.

[64] O'Brien, P. T. *The Letter to the Ephesians.* (Grand Rapids, MI: W.B. Eerdmans Publishing Co., 1999), 462.

[65] Roberts, John Owen. "How to Hold a Solemn Assembly." *The Solemn Assembly,* 1989.

[66] Taylor, Jack R. *Victory over the Devil.* (Nashville: Broadman Press, 1973), 9.

[67] Henry, M. *Matthew Henry's Commentary on the Whole Bible: Complete and Unabridged in One Volume.* (Peabody: Hendrickson, 1994), 2433.

68 Rogers, Adrian. "How to Handle Temptation." *Preaching and Teaching Resources*.
69 Criswell, W. A. "The Attack of Satan." *Daily Word,* October 28.
70 Spurgeon, C. H. "Runaway Jonah and the Convenient Ship." Sermon delivered August 10, 1890, Metropolitan Tabernacle.
71 Mother Teresa. https://www.christianquotes.info/top-quotes/17-amazing-quotes-power-words/, assessed January 31, 2021.
72 Exell, J. S. *Proverbs*. (New York; Chicago; Toronto: Fleming H. Revell Company, n.d.), 405.
73 Ironside, H. A. *Notes on the Book of Proverbs*. (Neptune, NJ: Loizeaux Bros., 1908), 186.
74 Fitzgerald, F. Scott. https://www.goodreads.com/quotes/212686-it-was-only-a-sunny-smile-and-little-it-cost, accessed January 31, 2021.
75 Henry, M. *Matthew Henry's Commentary on the Whole Bible: Complete and Unabridged in One Volume*. (Peabody: Hendrickson, 1994), 988.
76 https://www.christianquotes.info/top-quotes/17-amazing-quotes-power-words/, assessed January 31, 2021.
77 Spurgeon, C. H. "The Second Time." Sermon delivered May 24, 1874, Metropolitan Tabernacle.
78 Exell, J. S. *The Biblical Illustrator: Isaiah* (Vol. 3). (New York; Chicago; Toronto; London; Edinburgh: Fleming H. Revell Company, 1905), 259.
79 Ibid., Jeremiah (Vol. 1), 54.
80 http://www.whatchristianswanttoknow.com/20-amazing-quotes-about-serving, accessed November 18, 2013.
81 Ortberg, John. *The Life You've Always Wanted: Spiritual Disciplines for Ordinary People*. (Grand Rapids: Zondervan; Revised edition, September 17, 2002), 250.
82 Stanley, Charles. "Warning Against Spiritual Drifting" (In Touch Daily Devotional, April 14, 2008).
83 Packer, J. I. *The J. I. Packer Classic Collection*. (Colorado Springs: NavPress, 2010), 251.
84 Bruce, F. F. *The Epistle to the Hebrews* (Rev. ed.). (Grand Rapids, MI: Wm. B. Eerdmans Publishing Co., 1990), 66.
85 Orton, J., cited in J. S. Exell, *Proverbs*. (New York; Chicago; Toronto: Fleming H. Revell Company, n.d.), 632.
86 Piper, John. "The Danger of Drifting from the Word," April 28, 1996.
87 Spurgeon, C. H. "Samuel: An Example of Intercession." Sermon delivered May 9, 1880, Metropolitan Tabernacle.
88 Spurgeon, C. H. "Samuel: An Example of Intercession." Sermon delivered May 9, 1880, Metropolitan Tabernacle.
89 Hallesby, Ole. *Prayer*. (London: Hodder & Stoughton, 1936).
90 https://biblereasons.com/prayer-quotes/, accessed May 20, 2022.

Endnotes

[91] Spurgeon, C. H. "Samuel: An Example of Intercession." Sermon delivered May 9, 1880, Metropolitan Tabernacle.
[92] https://www.azquotes.com/quotes/topics/intercessory-prayer.html, accessed May 24, 2022.
[93] https://djameskennedy.org/devotional-detail/20150225-a-checklist-for-your-prayer-life, accessed May 9, 2017.
[94] Blackaby, Henry. *Experiencing God,* 194.
[95] Ibid.
[96] Henry, M. *Matthew Henry's Commentary on the Whole Bible: Complete and Unabridged in One Volume.* (Peabody: Hendrickson, 1994), 2324.
[97] Cited in Holiness, J.C. Ryle, Moody Publishers, 2010, p. 106.
[98] Sanders, Oswald J. *The Revival We Need.* (New York: The Christian Alliance Publishing Company, 1925), Chapter 3.
[99] https://www.christianquotes.info/quotes-by-topic/quotes-about-death/, accessed June 23, 2020.
[100] Henry, M. *Matthew Henry's Commentary on the Whole Bible: Complete and Unabridged in One Volume.* (Peabody: Hendrickson, 1994), 1007.
[101] Ironside, H. A. *Notes on the Book of Proverbs.* (Neptune, NJ: Loizeaux Bros., 1908), 324.
[102] Lawson, G. *Exposition of the Book of Proverbs,* Vol. 1. (Edinburgh; Glasgow; London: David Brown; W. Oliphant; F. Pillans; M. Ogle; Ogle, Duncan, and Co.; J. Nisbet, 1821), 438.
[103] Spurgeon, C. H. "Our Stronghold." Sermon delivered October 26, 1862, Metropolitan Tabernacle.
[104] Lawson, G. *Exposition of the Book of Proverbs,* Vol. 1. (Edinburgh; Glasgow; London: David Brown; W. Oliphant; F. Pillans; M. Ogle; Ogle, Duncan, and Co.; J. Nisbet, 1821), 438.
[105] MacArthur, J., Jr. (Ed.). The MacArthur Study Bible (electronic ed.). (Nashville, TN: Word Pub., 1997), 1829.
[106] Henry, M. *Matthew Henry's Commentary on the Whole Bible: Complete and Unabridged in One Volume.* (Peabody: Hendrickson, 1994), 2459.
[107] Exell, J. S. *The Biblical Illustrator: Hebrews* (Vol. 2). (New York; Chicago; Toronto: Fleming H. Revell Company, n.d.), 560.
[108] Exell, J. S. *The Biblical Illustrator: Hebrews* (Vol. 2). (London: James Nisbet & Co., n.d.), 564.
[109] Spurgeon, *Morning and Evening,* May 30 (Morning).
[110] Criswell, W. A., P. Patterson, E. R. Clendenen, D. L. Akin, M. Chamberlin, D. K. Patterson, and J. Pogue (Eds.). *Believer's Study Bible* (electronic ed.). (Nashville: Thomas Nelson, 1991), Mt. 13:3–9.
[111] O'Brien, P. T. *The Epistle to the Philippians: A Commentary on the Greek Text.* (Grand Rapids, MI: Eerdmans, 1991), 520.

[112] Exell, J. S. *The Biblical Illustrator: Philippians–Colossians, Vol. 1.* (New York; Chicago; Toronto; London; Edinburgh: Fleming H. Revell Company), 347.
[113] Cowman, L. B. *Streams in the Desert.* (Grand Rapids: Zondervan, 1997), January 5.
[114] Pink, A. W. *Comfort for Christians.* (Lafayette, IN: Sovereign Grace Publishers, 2007), 74.
[115] Exell, J. S. *The Biblical Illustrator:* Exell, J. S. *The Biblical Illustrator: Hebrews* (Vol. 2). (New York; Chicago; Toronto: Fleming H. Revell Company, n.d.), 186.
[116] Criswell, W. A. *What to Do Until Jesus Comes Back.* (Nashville: Broadman Press, 1975), 20.
[117] Ibid., 44.
[118] The Return of the Lord. http://preceptaustin.org/second_coming_of_christ.htm, accessed March 29, 2014.
[119] Friberg, T., B. Friberg, and N. F. Miller. *Analytical Lexicon of the Greek New Testament* (Vol. 4). (Grand Rapids, MI: Baker Books, 2000), 325.
[120] Henry, M. *Matthew Henry's Commentary on the Whole Bible: Complete and Unabridged in One Volume.* (Peabody: Hendrickson, 1994), 1901.
[121] Havner, Vance. "By Him All Things Consist," a sermon. http://www.sermonindex.net, accessed December 20, 2013.
[122] Criswell, W. A. *What to Do Until Jesus Comes Back.* (Nashville: Broadman Press, 1975), 94.
[123] https://journeyonline.org/never-doubt-in-the-dark-what-god-told-you-in-the-light/, accessed October 1, 2021.
[124] Wilkinson, Bruce H. "The Prayer of Jabez: Breaking Through to the Blessed Life."
[125] Spurgeon, C. H. "A Lesson and a Fortune for Christian Men of Business." Exell, J. S. *The Biblical Illustrator: Hebrews* (Vol. 2). (New York; Chicago; Toronto: Fleming H. Revell Company, n.d.), 612.
[126] https://www.brainyquote.com/quotes/thomas_aquinas_163328, accessed November 7, 2021.
[127] Lawson, G. *Exposition of the Book of Proverbs* (Vol. 1). (Edinburgh; Glasgow; London: David Brown; W. Oliphant; F. Pillans; M. Ogle; Ogle, Duncan, and Co.; J. Nisbet, 1821), 220.
[128] Henry, M. *Matthew Henry's Commentary on the Whole Bible: Complete and Unabridged in One Volume.* (Peabody: Hendrickson, 1994), 647.
[129] Ibid.
[130] Criswell, Criswell's Guidebook For Pastors, 232.
[131] Jowett, J. Henry. *The Secrets of Effective Preaching: Sin & Sympathy.* (London: Hodder & Stoughton, 1901), Chapter 20.
[132] https://www.pinterest.com/oxkr/adrian-rogers/, accessed January 7, 2017.

Endnotes

[133] http://www.goodreads.com/quotes/tag/apology, accessed January 7, 2017.
[134] http://www.goodreads.com/quotes/tag/ingratitude, accessed January 7, 2017.
[135] https://www.brainyquote.com/quotes/authors/m/max_lucado.html, accessed January 9, 2017.
[136] Lucado, Max. *Every Day Deserves a Chance: Wake Up to the Gift of 24 Hours.* (Nashville: Thomas Nelson, 2007).
[137] Spurgeon, C. H. "Jehovah-Shammah: A Glorious Name for the New Year." Sermon delivered January 4, 1891, Metropolitan Tabernacle.
[138] Ibid.
[139] Spurgeon, C. H., Morning and Evening, February 17.
[140] Spurgeon, C. H. "Harvest Men Wanted." Sermon was delivered August 17, 1873. Metropolitan Tabernacle.
[141] Murray, Andrew. *With Christ in the School of Prayer.* (Peabody, Massachusetts: Hendrickson Publishers, 2007), 55.
[142] Ibid.
[143] http://davidwilkersontoday.blogspot.com/2008/08/pray-lord-of-harvest.html, accessed June 20, 2017.
[144] Exell, J. S. *The Biblical Illustrator: I Corinthians* (Vol. 2). (New York; Chicago; Toronto: Fleming H. Revell Company, n.d.), 47.
[145] Henry, M. and T. Scott. *Matthew Henry's Concise Commentary.* (Oak Harbor, WA: Logos Research Systems, 1997), Acts 16:25.
[146] McGee, J. V. *Thru the Bible Commentary* (electronic ed., Vol. 4). (Nashville: Thomas Nelson, 1997), 585.
[147] Spurgeon, C. H. "Household Salvation." Sermon delivered November 5, 1871, Metropolitan Tabernacle.
[148] Simeon, C. *Horae Homileticae: John XIII to Acts* (Vol. 14). (London: Holdsworth and Ball, 1833), 457.
[149] Hendricks, Howard G. and William D. Hendricks. *Living by the Book/Living by the Book Workbook Set.* (Moody Publishers, 2007), 13.
[150] MacArthur, J. *In the Footsteps of Faith : Lessons from the Lives of Great Men* (electronic ed.). (Wheaton, IL: Crossway Books, 1998), 7.
[151] https://www.christianquotes.info/quotes-by-topic/quotes-about-examples/, accessed May 11, 2022.
[152] Spence-Jones, H. D. M. (Ed.). *Proverbs.* (London; New York: Funk & Wagnalls Company, 1909), 527.
[153] Henry, M. *Matthew Henry's Commentary on the Whole Bible: Complete and Unabridged in One Volume.* (Peabody: Hendrickson, 1994), 1016.
[154] Walvoord, J. F., and R. B. Zuck. *The Bible Knowledge Commentary: An Exposition of the Scriptures* (Vol. 1.). (Wheaton, IL: Victor Books, 1985), 964.
[155] Torrance, *The Christian Doctrine of God.* (Edinburgh: T&T Clark, 1996), 51.
[156] Sproul, R. C., John Gerstner, and Arthur Lindsley. *Classical Apologetics,* 161.

[157] Criswell, W. A. *Criswell Study Bible,* 1 John 2: 2.
[158] Spurgeon, C. H. "Samson Conquered." Sermon delivered November 21, 1858, New Park Street Chapel.
[159] Rice, John R. *Soul Winner's Fire,* 41.
[160] Barber, Fred. "Travail for Souls." (Murfreesboro, TN: *The Sword of the Lord,* 8 Oct. 2004), 201.
[161] Hutson, Curtis. *Great Preaching on Soulwinning,* 61.
[162] Henry, M. *Matthew Henry's Commentary on the Whole Bible: Complete and Unabridged in One Volume.* (Peabody: Hendrickson, 1994), 2433.
[163] MacArthur, J., Jr. (Ed.). The MacArthur Study Bible (electronic ed.). (Nashville, TN: Word Pub., 1997), 1949.
[164] Spurgeon, Charles. *The Soul Winner.* (Wm. B. Eerdmans Publishing, 1989), 15.
[165] Spurgeon, C. H. "Songs in the Night." Sermon published February 28, 1898, delivered at Metropolitan Tabernacle.
[166] Piper, John. "Singing, Suffering, and Scripture: How God Keeps Us Through Song" (Sermon), November 8, 2020.
[167] Henry, M. *Matthew Henry's Commentary on the Whole Bible: Complete and Unabridged in One Volume.* (Peabody: Hendrickson, 1994), 2048.
[168] Ironside, H. A. *Notes on the Book of Proverbs.* (Neptune, NJ: Loizeaux Bros., 1908), 315.
[169] *Lives of the Artists: Michelangelo.* (Milwaukee, Wisconsin: Garth Stevens Publishing, 2004). 41–42.
[170] Henry, M. *Matthew Henry's Commentary on the Whole Bible: Complete and Unabridged in One Volume.* (Peabody: Hendrickson, 1994), 315.
[171] Exell, J. S. *The Biblical Illustrator: II Kings.* (New York; Chicago; Toronto: Fleming H. Revell Company, n.d.), 68.
[172] *Experiencing God.*
[173] Duwel, Wesley. *Touch the World through Prayer.* (Grand Rapids: Zondervan Publishing Company, 1986), 60.
[174] Bounds. *Purpose in Prayer.* (Revell, 1920).
[175] Wiersbe, Warren W. and David W. Wiersbe. *10 Power Principles for Christian Service.* (Grand Rapids: Baker Books, 2010), 86.
[176] https://www.azquotes.com/author/22604-Woodrow_M_Kroll, accessed June 25, 2022.
[177] Spurgeon, C. H. *The Treasury of David: Psalms 27–57* (Vol. 2). (London; Edinburgh; New York: Marshall Brothers, n.d.), 214.
[178] Henry, M. *Matthew Henry's Commentary on the Whole Bible: Complete and Unabridged in One Volume.* (Peabody: Hendrickson, 1994), 798.
[179] MacArthur, John. *The MacArthur New Testament Commentary: Romans, Vol. 1.* (Chicago: Moody Press, 1991), 473.
[180] Spurgeon. *Morning and Evening,* February 23 (Morning).

Endnotes

[181] Ibid.
[182] Spurgeon. *Faith's Checkbook,* January 3.
[183] Ibid.
[184] Burroughs, Dillon. *Hunger No More: A 1-Year Devotional Journey Through the Psalms.*
[185] Spurgeon, Charles Haddon. *Spurgeon at His Best: Over 2200 Striking Quotations from the World's Most Exhaustive and Widely Read Sermon Series.* (Baker Publishing Group, 1988).
[186] Kidner, Derek. *The Proverbs: An Introduction and Commentary. Tyndale Old Testament Commentary.* (Downers Grove: InterVarsity, 1964), 129.
[187] https://www.deseretnews.com/top/2752/0/40-inspiring-quotes-about-education-in-the-classroom-education-in-life.html, accessed October 11, 2017.
[188] https://www.deseretnews.com/top/2752/0/40-inspiring-quotes-about-education-in-the-classroom-education-in-life.html, accessed October 11, 2017.
[189] https://quotefancy.com/quote/1588044/Woodrow-M-Kroll-Treat-the-elderly-as-a-nonrenewable-resource-they-care.
[190] Plumer, W. S. *Studies in the Book of Psalms: Being a Critical and Expository Commentary, with Doctrinal and Practical Remarks on the Entire Psalter.* (Philadelphia; Edinburgh: J. B. Lippincott Company; A & C Black, 1872), 419.
[191] Gill, John. *Gill's Exposition of the Entire Bible,* Psalm 34:8.
[192] https://www.goodreads.com/quotes/232403-friendship-is-one-of-the-sweetest-joys-of-life-many, accessed October 19, 2017.
[193] Spurgeon, C. H. "Paul—His Cloak and His Books." Sermon delivered November 29, 1863, Metropolitan Tabernacle.
[194] Exell, J. S. *The Biblical Illustrator: St. John* (Vol. 1). (New York; Chicago; Toronto: Fleming H. Revell Company, n.d.), 250.
[195] Henry, M. *Matthew Henry's Commentary on the Whole Bible: Complete and Unabridged in One Volume.* (Peabody: Hendrickson, 1994), 1930.
[196] Exell, J. S. *The Biblical Illustrator: Second Corinthians.* (New York; Chicago; Toronto: Fleming H. Revell Company, n.d.), 293.
[197] MacArthur, J., Jr. (Ed.). The MacArthur Study Bible (electronic ed.). (Nashville, TN: Word Pub., 1997), 1771.
[198] Spurgeon, C. H. "The Cry of the Heathen." Sermon delivered April 25, 1858, at the New Park Street Chapel.
[199] Henry, M. *Matthew Henry's Commentary on the Whole Bible: Complete and Unabridged in One Volume.* (Peabody: Hendrickson, 1994), 2135.
[200] Ibid., 2181.
[201] Spurgeon, C. H. "Before Sermon, at Sermon, and After Sermon." Sermon delivered June 28, 1885, Metropolitan Tabernacle.
[202] Beasley-Murray, G. R. *John* (Vol. 36). (Dallas: Word, Incorporated, 1999), 272.

[203] Hindson, E. E. and W. M. Kroll (Eds.). *KJV Bible Commentary.* (Nashville: Thomas Nelson, 1994), 2112.
[204] Spurgeon, C. H. "Peter After His Restoration." Sermon delivered July 26, 1888, Metropolitan Tabernacle.
[205] McKane, William. *Proverbs, Old Testament Library.* Cited in NET Bible First Edition Notes. (Biblical Studies Press, 2006), Prov. 16:18.
[206] http://izquotes.com/quote/319561, accessed October 25, 2017.
[207] *The Biblical Illustrator,* Vol. 7, Proverbs 16:18
[208] Anders, Max. *Defending Your Faith,* 47.
[209] Criswell, W. A. *Why I Preach the Bible Is Literally True,* 19–20.
[210] MacArthur, J., Jr. (Ed.). The MacArthur Study Bible (electronic ed.). (Nashville, TN: Word Pub., 1997), 1625.
[211] Schep, J. A. *Resurrection of Jesus Christ, Zondervan Pictorial Bible Encyclopedia,* vol. 5. (www.zondervan.com, 1975), 83.
[212] Simeon, C. *Horae Homileticae: Jeremiah to Daniel,* Vol. 9. (London: Samuel Holdsworth, 1836), 86–87.
[213] https://www.azquotes.com/quote/703860, accessed July 14, 2020.
[214] Spurgeon, C. H. *Morning and Evening.* (London: Passmore & Alabaster), May 31 (Evening).
[215] McConkey, James. *The Three-fold Secret of the Holy Spirit.* (Pittsburgh: Silver Publishing Society, 1922), 106.
[216] Henry, M. *Matthew Henry's Commentary on the Whole Bible: Complete and Unabridged in One Volume.* (Peabody: Hendrickson, 1994), 2018.
[217] 43 Great Quotes on the Power and Importance of Reading, September 13, 2013. https://bilingualmonkeys.com/43-great-quotes-on-the-power-and-importance-of-reading/, accessed September 23, 2022.
[218] Criswell, W. A. "He Being Dead Yet Speaketh." Sermon delivered 2-14-60 (10:50 a.m.), First Baptist Church, Dallas, Texas.
[219] Spurgeon, C. H. "A Last Look-Out." Sermon delivered in 1871, Metropolitan Tabernacle.
[220] Lucado, Max. "The Gospel of Second Chances," Maxlucado.com, accessed July 19, 2021.
[221] Bunyan, John. *The Commemorative Edition of the Works of John Bunyan,* Volume 2. (London: The London Printing and Publishing Company, 1859), 1206.
[222] Henry, M. *Matthew Henry's Commentary on the Whole Bible: Complete and Unabridged in One Volume.* (Peabody: Hendrickson, 1994), 2484.
[223] Ibid., 2365.
[224] Ibid., 2382.
[225] Graham, Billy. "The Holy Spirit: Activating God's Power in Your Life."
[226] Spurgeon, C. H. "Thoughts on the Last Battle." (Sermon, May 13, 1855).

Endnotes

[227] Exell, J. S. *The Biblical Illustrator: 1 Samuel,* Vol. 2. (New York; Chicago; Toronto; London; Edinburgh: Fleming H. Revell Company), 523.

[228] Graham, Billy. *Peace with God.* (Waco, TX: Word, 1953), 83.

[229] MacDonald, W. *Believer's Bible Commentary: Old and New Testaments.* (A. Farstad, Ed.). (Nashville: Thomas Nelson, 1995), 1430.

[230] MacArthur, J., Jr. (Ed.). The MacArthur Study Bible (electronic ed.). (Nashville, TN: Word Pub., 1997), 1546.

[231] Yates, *Preaching from the Prophets,* 30.

[232] Henry, M. *Matthew Henry's Commentary on the Whole Bible: Complete and Unabridged in One Volume.* (Peabody: Hendrickson, 1994), 1839.

[233] McGee, J. V. *Thru the Bible Commentary: The Gospels (Luke),* (electronic ed., Vol. 37). (Nashville: Thomas Nelson, 1991), 76.

[234] Exell, J. S. *The Biblical Illustrator: St. Luke* (Vol. 1). (New York; Chicago; Toronto: Fleming H. Revell Company, n.d.), 468.

[235] Courson, J. *Jon Courson's Application Commentary.* (Nashville, TN: Thomas Nelson, 2003), 320.

[236] Henry, M. *Matthew Henry's Commentary on the Whole Bible: Complete and Unabridged in One Volume.* (Peabody: Hendrickson, 1994), 1800.

[237] Wiersbe, W. W. *Wiersbe's Expository Outlines on the New Testament.* (Wheaton, IL: Victor Books, 1992), 128.

[238] Morgan, G. Campbell. *The Acts of the Apostles,* 389–390.

[239] Fasol, et al., *Preaching Evangelistically,* 76.

[240] Wright, N. T. "Simply Good News: Why the Gospel Is News and What Makes It Good."

[241] Courson, J. *Jon Courson's Application Commentary.* (Nashville, TN: Thomas Nelson, 2003), 1158.

[242] MacArthur, J., Jr. (Ed.). The MacArthur Study Bible (electronic ed.). (Nashville, TN: Word Pub., 1997), 1823.

[243] Spurgeon, Morning and Evening, Oct. 20 (Morning).

[244] Exell, J. S. *The Biblical Illustrator: Matthew.* (New York; Chicago; Toronto: Fleming H. Revell Company, n.d.), 105.

[245] Ibid., Proverbs, 596.

[246] Ibid., The Psalms (Vol. 3), 314.

[247] Spurgeon, C. H. *Psalms.* (Wheaton, IL: Crossway Books, 1993), 149.

[248] Henry, M. *Matthew Henry's Commentary on the Whole Bible: Complete and Unabridged in One Volume.* (Peabody: Hendrickson, 1994), 795.

[249] Cowper. *Streams in the Desert,* August 16.

[250] Exell, J. S. *The Biblical Illustrator: First Chronicles, Second Chronicles, Ezra, Nehemiah, and Esther* (Vol. 2). (New York; Chicago; Toronto: Fleming H. Revell Company, n.d.), 107.

[251] Spurgeon, C. H. "Joash and His Friend Jehoiada."

[252] MacArthur, J., Jr. (Ed.). The MacArthur Study Bible (electronic ed.). (Nashville, TN: Word Pub., 1997), 743.

[253] Alexander, J. A. *The Psalms Translated and Explained.* (Edinburgh: Andrew Elliot; James Thin, 1864), 9.

[254] Exell, J. S. *The Biblical Illustrator: The Psalms* (Vol. 1). (New York; Chicago; Toronto: Fleming H. Revell Company, n.d.), 4.

[255] Henry, M. *Matthew Henry's Commentary on the Whole Bible: Complete and Unabridged in One Volume.* (Peabody: Hendrickson, 1994), 2284.

[256] *Barnes Notes on the Bible,* Psalms 66:16.

[257] Leavell, Roland Q. *Winning Others to Christ.* (Nashville, TN: The Sunday School Board of the Southern Baptist Convention, 1936), 39.

[258] Blackwood, Andrew. *Evangelical Sermons of our Day.* (New York, NY: Harper & Brothers, 1959), 272–278.

[259] Schaeffer, Francis. *Complete Works,* Volume 5, 252.

[260] MacArthur, John. "How to Treat False Teachers, Part 1." October 6, 1985. www.gty.org, accessed January 2, 2015.

[261] Swindoll, Charles R. *Conquering Through Conflict.* W Publishing Group.

[262] Plumer, W. S. *Studies in the Book of Psalms: Being a Critical and Expository Commentary, with Doctrinal and Practical Remarks on the Entire Psalter.* (Philadelphia; Edinburgh: J. B. Lippincott Company; A & C Black, 1872), 918.

[263] Spurgeon, C. H. "At Evening Time It Shall Be Light." October 25, 1857.

[264] http://www.bartleby.com/348/44.html, accessed February 12, 2017.

[265] http://www.thoughts-about-god.com/quotes/quotes-aging.html, accessed February 4, 2017.

[266] Spence-Jones, H. D. M. (Ed.). *Song of Solomon.* (London; New York: Funk & Wagnalls Company, 1909), 208.

[267] Spurgeon, C. H. "The Shulamite's Choice Prayer." Sermon delivered February 25, 1861, Metropolitan Tabernacle.

[268] Deere, J. S. *Song of Songs.* In J. F. Walvoord & R. B. Zuck (Eds.). *The Bible Knowledge Commentary: An Exposition of the Scriptures* (Vol. 1). (Wheaton, IL: Victor Books, 1985), 1024.

[269] Ibid.

[270] Criswell, *Study Bible,* 1459.

[271] Dixon, Francis. June 9, 1964.

[272] Moody, D. L. *Pleasures and Profit,* 32–33.

[273] Spurgeon, C. H. "The Best Christmas Fare." Sermon delivered December 25, 1881, Metropolitan Tabernacle.

[274] Plumer, W. S. *Studies in the Book of Psalms: Being a Critical and Expository Commentary, with Doctrinal and Practical Remarks on the Entire Psalter.* (Philadelphia; Edinburgh: J. B. Lippincott Company; A & C Black, 1872), 1066.

[275] Spurgeon, C. H. "The Heaven of Heaven." Sermon delivered August 9, 1868, Metropolitan Tabernacle.

Endnotes

[276] Rogers, Adrian. "A Place Called Heaven" (sermon).
[277] Exell, J. S. *Isaiah* (Vol. 3). (New York; Chicago; Toronto; London; Edinburgh: Fleming H. Revell Company, n.d.), 310.
[278] Spurgeon, C. H. *Morning and Evening,* December 27 (Evening).
[279] Henry, M. *Matthew Henry's Commentary on the Whole Bible: Complete and Unabridged in One Volume.* (Peabody: Hendrickson, 1994), 1197.
[280] https://quotestats.com/topic/quotes-about-gods-guidance/, accessed December 29, 2021.
[281] Exell, J. S. *The Biblical Illustrator: Hebrews* (Vol. 2). (New York; Chicago; Toronto: Fleming H. Revell Company, n.d.), 223.
[282] https://www.stresslesscountry.com/valentines-quotations/, accessed February 1, 2022.
[283] https://parade.com/1089418/kimberlyzapata/grief-quotes/, accessed March 9, 2022.
[284] Exell, J. S. *The Biblical Illustrator: Hebrews* (Vol. 2). (New York; Chicago; Toronto: Fleming H. Revell Company, n.d.), 230.
[285] Horne, G. *A Commentary on the Book of Psalms.* (New York: Robert Carter & Brothers, 1856), 118.
[286] "The Homilist," cited in *The Biblical Illustrator*, Psalm 26:8.
[287] Dixon, Francis. "Highlights in Hebrews," Study 10 (Series 60).
[288] Exell, J. S. *The Biblical Illustrator: Hebrews,* Vol. 1. (London: James Nisbet & Co.), 172.
[289] Ritzema, E. and E. Vince, (Eds.). *300 Quotations for Preachers from the Puritans.* (Bellingham, WA: Lexham Press, 2013).
[290] Talmage, T. De Witt. "The Ferry Boat of the Jordan" (sermon), http://biblehub.com/sermons/auth/talmage/the_ferry-boat_of_the_jordan.htm, accessed January 2, 2017.
[291] Malphurs, Aubrey and Keith Willhite. *A Contemporary Handbook for Weddings and Funerals and other Occasions.* (Grand Rapids, Michigan: Kregal Publications, 2006), 238. (adapted)
[292] Spurgeon, C. H. Sermon 3125. "Fear of Death," December 17, 1874.
[293] Spurgeon, C. H. *Psalms.* (Wheaton, IL: Crossway Books, 1993), 332.
[294] Henry, M. *Matthew Henry's Commentary on the Whole Bible: Complete and Unabridged in One Volume.* (Peabody: Hendrickson, 1994), 856.
[295] Frank Shivers, 2021
[296] Janzen, W. *Exodus.* (Waterloo, ON; Scottdale, PA: Herald Press, 2000), 261.
[297] Exell, J. S. *The Biblical Illustrator: Exodus.* (New York; Chicago; Toronto: Fleming H. Revell Company, n.d.), 371.
[298] Waltke, B. K. *The Book of Proverbs,* Chapters 1–15. (Grand Rapids, MI: Wm. B. Eerdmans Publishing Co., 2004), 606.

299 Buzzell, S. S. *Proverbs*. In J. F. Walvoord & R. B. Zuck (Eds.). *The Bible Knowledge Commentary: An Exposition of the Scriptures* (Vol. 1). (Wheaton, IL: Victor Books, 1985), 936.
300 https://gracequotes.org/author-quote/henry-ward-beecher/, accessed April 21, 2021.
301 Swindoll, Chuck. *Insight for Today: A Daily Devotional.* "Give God Your Worries," March 17, 2017.
302 https://www.godtube.com/news/top-27-christian-quotes-about-faith.html, accessed February 4, 2021.
303 www.brainyquote.com/quotes/keywords/anxiety.html, accessed September 4, 2017.
304 Rogers, Adrian. "God's Answer to Loneliness." http://www.oneplace.com/ministries/love-worth-finding/read/articles/gods-answer-to-loneliness-9028.html, accessed February 18, 2017.
305 Dobson, James C. "Life on the Edge: The Next Generation's Guide to a Meaningful Future." https://www.goodreads.com/quotes/7951819-29-most-loneliness-results-from-insulation-rather-than-isolation-in, accessed February 17, 2017.
306 https://www.brainyquote.com/quotes/quotes/l/lordbyron150314.html, accessed February 25, 2017.
307 Exell, J. S. *The Biblical Illustrator: I Corinthians* (Vol. 2). (New York; Chicago; Toronto: Fleming H. Revell Company, n.d.), 554.
308 Ibid., Isaiah (Vol. 3), 55.
309 Gill, John. *Exposition of the Entire Bible,* Isaiah 52:1.
310 https://www.barna.com/research/millions-of-unchurched-adults-are-christians-hurt-by-churches-but-can-be-healed-of-the-pain/?fbclid=IwAR3du2gIoPZvMKHkU96PmgZ9M2anNviKUV2pJ8jYZ1BZ-wphjfjINAPb2yo, accessed August 10, 2021.
311 Piper, John. "Did the Church Hurt You?" December 16, 2017. https://www.desiringgod.org/articles/did-the-church-hurt-you, accessed August 10, 2021.
312 This meditation is adapted from a personal letter from Dr. Jim Palmer, Miles Road Baptist Church, Summerville, SC. Undated (2021).
313 Spurgeon, C. H. *Morning and Evening,* January 2 (Morning).
314 Henry, M. *Matthew Henry's Commentary on the Whole Bible: Complete and Unabridged in One Volume.* (Peabody: Hendrickson, 1994), 2200.
315 Ferguson, Sinclair. *The Whole Christ: Legalism, Antinomianism, and Gospel Assurance—Why the Marrow Controversy Still Matters.* (Crossway, 2016), 110.
316 Spurgeon, C. H. "Household Salvation." Sermon delivered November 5, 1871, Metropolitan Tabernacle.
317 MacArthur, J., Jr. (Ed.). The MacArthur Study Bible (electronic ed.). (Nashville, TN: Word Pub., 1997), 1914.

Endnotes

[318] Spurgeon, C. H. "Faith's Ultimatum," (Sermon delivered July 18, 1875).
[319] https://www.christianquotes.info/top-quotes/19-amazing-quotes-about-living-by-faith/, accessed June 12, 2021.
[320] Morgan, R. J. *Nelson's Annual Preacher's Sourcebook,* 2002 Edition. (Nashville: Thomas Nelson Publishers, 2001), 397.
[321] https://www.christianquotes.info/top-quotes/19-amazing-quotes-about-living-by-faith/, accessed June 12, 2021.
[322] Jeremiah, David. *The Jeremiah Study Bible.*
[323] Packer, J. I. *Knowing God.* https://www.goodreads.com/work/quotes/276686-knowing-god?page=5, accessed May 15, 2021.
[324] MacArthur, John. *Hebrews,* 10:26–27.
[325] https://gracequotes.org/quote/remember-that-if-you-are-a-child-of-god-you-wil, accessed October 19, 2017.
[326] https://www.christianquotes.info/quotes-by-topic/quotes-about-forgiveness/, accessed May 13, 2021.
[327] *The NET Bible First Edition Notes.* (Biblical Studies Press, 2006), Pr 12:25.
[328] https://www.jonbeaty.com/21-of-the-most-inspirational-quotes-about-trusting-god/, accessed February 2, 2021.
[329] https://www.christianquotes.info/quotes-by-topic/quotes-about-anxiety/, accessed May 1, 2021.
[330] Barclay, W. (Ed.). *The letters to the Philippians, Colossians, and Thessalonians* (electronic ed.) (Philadelphia: The Westminster John Knox Press, 1975), 77.
[331] Henry, M. *Matthew Henry's Commentary on the Whole Bible: Complete and Unabridged in One Volume.* (Peabody: Hendrickson, 1994), 981.
[332] https://www.christianquotes.info/quotes-by-topic/quotes-about-anxiety/
[333] www.whatchristianswanttoknow.com/top-15-christian-quotes-about-overcoming-anxiety/#ixzz6tby7estG, accessed May 1, 2021.
[334] 40 Charles Spurgeon Quotes on Anxiety, Fear, and Worry. http://www.cross-points.org/charles-spurgeon-quotes-on-anxiety-fear-and-worry/, accessed November 1, 2017.
[335] https://www.christianquotes.info/quotes-by-topic/quotes-about-anxiety/, accessed May 1, 2021.
[336] Scarborough, L. R. "Lost!" (Sermon)
[337] Appelman, Hyman J. *The Savior's Invitation and Other Evangelistic Sermons.* (Grand Rapids, MI: Baker Book House, 1981), 35–42.
[338] Packer, J. I. *Evangelism & the Sovereignty of God.*
[339] Talmage, DeWitt. "The Ministry of Tears" (sermon). https://www.gracegems.org/SERMONS2/ministry_of_tears.htm, accessed March 18, 2023.
[340] Tozer, A. W. *I Talk Back to the Devil,* 12–13.

[341] Henry, M. *Matthew Henry's Commentary on the Whole Bible: Complete and Unabridged in One Volume.* (Peabody: Hendrickson, 1994), 990.
[342] Arndt, W., F. W. Danker, W. Bauer, & F. W. Gingrich. *A Greek-English Lexicon of the New Testament and Other Early Christian Literature,* (3rd ed.). (Chicago: University of Chicago Press, 2000), 1039.
[343] Ironside, H. A. *Lectures on the Book of Revelation.* (Neptune, N. J.: Loizeaux Brothers, 1920), 71.
[344] *Criswell Study Bible,* Jude 1:3.
[345] MacArthur, John. "How to Handle Persecution, Part 1." https://www.gty.org/library/study-guides/116/how-to-handle-persecution, accessed January 28, 2021.
[346] Spurgeon, C. H. "Refusing to be Comforted" (Sermon), March 18, 1883. Psalm 77:2
[347] https://quotefancy.com/quote/1604381/Alexander-Whyte-You-do-not-really-care-for-God-s-mercy-or-His-comfort-either-so-long-as, accessed March 7, 2021.
[348] Spurgeon, C. H. "Refusing to be Comforted" (Sermon), March 18, 1883. Psalm 77:2
[349] MacArthur, John. "The Gift of Peace." gty.org, accessed January 25, 2021.
[350] Wiersbe, W. W. *Wiersbe's Expository Outlines on the New Testament.* (Wheaton, IL: Victor Books, 1992), 251.
[351] https://viralbeliever.com/christian-quotes-about-peace/, accessed January 24, 2021.
[352] Exell, J. S. *The Biblical Illustrator:* St. John (Vol. 2). (New York; Chicago; Toronto: Fleming H. Revell Company, n.d.), 589.
[353] https://www.christianquotes.info/top-quotes/19-beautiful-quotes-about-gods-peace/, accessed January 24, 2021.
[354] Spurgeon, C. H. "Spiritual Peace" (Sermon), February 19, 1860.
[355] https://viralbeliever.com/christian-quotes-about-peace/, accessed January 24, 2021.
[356] MacArthur, John. "The Gift of Peace." gty.org, accessed January 25, 2021.
[357] Ibid.
[358] Courson, J. *Jon Courson's Application Commentary.* (Nashville, TN: Thomas Nelson, 2003), 557.
[359] Henry, M. *Matthew Henry's Commentary on the Whole Bible: Complete and Unabridged in One Volume.* (Peabody: Hendrickson, 1994), 686.
[360] https://www.goodreads.com/quotes/17247-i-am-not-what-i-ought-to-be-i-am, accessed June 2, 2021.
[361] Arndt, W., F. W. Danker, W. Bauer, & F. W. Gingrich. *A Greek-English Lexicon of the New Testament and Other Early Christian Literature* (3rd ed.). (Chicago: University of Chicago Press, 2000), 909.

[362] Exell, J. S. *The Biblical Illustrator: Hebrews* (Vol. 1). (New York; Chicago; Toronto: Fleming H. Revell Company, n.d.), 322.
[363] Henry, M. *Matthew Henry's Commentary on the Whole Bible: Complete and Unabridged in One Volume*. (Peabody: Hendrickson, 1994), 2386.
[364] Exell, J. S. *The Biblical Illustrator: Hebrews* (Vol. 1). (New York; Chicago; Toronto: Fleming H. Revell Company, n.d.), 322.
[365] Ibid.
[366] Spurgeon, C. H. *Morning and Evening*. January 18 (Morning).
[367] Hobbs, H. H. *My Favorite Illustrations*. (Nashville, TN: Broadman Press, 1990), 133.
[368] Cited in Warren Wiersbe. *With the Word*. (Nashville: Oliver Nelson Books, 1991), 176.
[369] Spurgeon, C. H. *The Soul Winner*. (Whitaker House, 1995), 282.
[370] Spurgeon, C. H. *The Soul Winner*. (Wm. B. Eerdmans Publishing, 1989), 238.
[371] Henry, M. *Matthew Henry's Commentary on the Whole Bible: Complete and Unabridged in One Volume*. (Peabody: Hendrickson, 1994), 1664.
[372] Barclay, W. (Ed.). *The Gospel of Matthew* (Vol. 1). (Philadelphia, PA: The Westminster John Knox Press.1976), 392.
[373] Barna.org., October 6, 2008.
[374] Access the 52 Sundays of Missionary moments at https://www.sbcv.org/52sundays/.
[375] Spurgeon, C. H. "The Lord is Risen Indeed." Sermon delivered April 12, 1873, Metropolitan Tabernacle.
[376] Spurgeon, C. H. *The Treasury of David,* Psalm 16:10.
[377] https://www.communicatejesus.com/40-quotes-life-changing-power-resurrection/ accessed October 25, 2020.
[378] Spurgeon, C. H. "Paul the Ready." Sermon Delivered May 22, 1890, Metropolitan Tabernacle.
[379] Raleigh, A. "Faithful unto Death." *The Biblical Illustrator,* Revelation 2:10.
[380] Spurgeon, C. H. "Paul the Ready." Sermon Delivered May 22, 1890, Metropolitan Tabernacle.
[381] Horne, G. *A Commentary on the Book of Psalms*. (New York: Robert Carter & Brothers, 1856), 521.
[382] Spence-Jones, H. D. M. (Ed.). *Psalms* (Vol. 3). (London; New York: Funk & Wagnalls Company, 1909), 371.
[383] Pope, W. B. *The Inward Witness,* 160.
[384] Spurgeon, C. H. *Psalms*. (Wheaton, IL: Crossway Books, 1993), 329.
[385] Henry, M. *Matthew Henry's Commentary on the Whole Bible: Complete and Unabridged in One Volume*. (Peabody: Hendrickson, 1994), 948.
[386] Spurgeon, C. H. "Flowers from a Puritan's Garden" (New York: Funk & Wagnalls, 1883). Taken from the Preface.

[387] Spurgeon, Charles. *The Complete Works of C. H. Spurgeon,* Volume 35: Sermons 2062–2120. (Delmarva Publications, Inc., 2015), 332.
[388] Spurgeon, C. H. *Morning and Evening,* February 20 (Morning).
[389] Spurgeon, C. H. *The Treasury of David: Psalms 1–26* (Vol. 1). (London; Edinburgh; New York: Marshall Brothers, n.d.), 269.
[390] Swindoll, Chuck. "Encouragement Takes the Sting Out of Life," April 17, 2014. https:// insight.org/resources/article-library/individual/encouragement-takes-the-sting-out-of-life, accessed September 19, 2020.
[391] Lawson, George. *A Practical Exposition of the Book of Proverbs,* 1821.
[392] Spurgeon, C. H. "Jude's Doxology." Sermon delivered November 7, 1875, Metropolitan Tabernacle.
[393] Spurgeon, C. H. "Noah's Flood." Sermon delivered March 5, 1868, at Metropolitan Tabernacle.
[394] Spurgeon, C. H. "The Cause and Cure of Weariness in Sabbath-School Teachers." Sermon delivered November 8, 1887, Metropolitan Tabernacle.
[395] Spurgeon, C. H. *The Treasury of David: Psalms 120–150* (Vol. 6). (London; Edinburgh; New York: Marshall Brothers, n.d.), 70–71.
[396] Spurgeon, C. H. "The Cause and Cure of Weariness in Sabbath-School Teachers." Sermon delivered November 8, 1887, Metropolitan Tabernacle.
[397] Exell, J. S. *Isaiah* (Vol. 3). (New York; Chicago; Toronto; London; Edinburgh: Fleming H. Revell Company, n.d.), 258.
[398] Ibid., 260.
[399] Exell, J. S. *Ecclesiastes & The Song of Solomon* (Vol. 1). (New York; Chicago; Toronto; London; Edinburgh: Fleming H. Revell Company, n.d.), 270.
[400] Spurgeon, C. H. "Christ's Loneliness and Ours." Sermon published August 8, 1907, Metropolitan Tabernacle.
[401] Melvill, Henry. *The Preacher in Print. The Golden Lectures,* (1855). (London: James Paul, 1, Chapter House Court, 1856), 345.
[402] Spurgeon, C. H. *Lectures to My Students: A Selection from Addresses Delivered to the Students of the Pastors' College, Metropolitan Tabernacle.* (Vol. 1). (London: Passmore and Alabaster, 1875), 189.
[403] Spurgeon, C. H. "The Cause and Cure of Weariness in Sabbath-School Teachers." Sermon delivered November 8, 1887, Metropolitan Tabernacle.
[404] Spurgeon, C. H. *The Treasury of David: Psalms 120–150* (Vol. 6). (London; Edinburgh; New York: Marshall Brothers, n.d.), 70.
[405] Exell, J. S. *The Biblical Illustrator:* Jeremiah (Vol. 1). (New York; Chicago; Toronto: Fleming H. Revell Company, n.d.), 425.
[406] Henry, M. *Matthew Henry's Commentary on the Whole Bible: Complete and Unabridged in One Volume.* (Peabody: Hendrickson, 1994), 1263.
[407] Simeon, C. *Horae Homileticae: Jeremiah to Daniel* (Vol. 9). (London: Holdsworth and Ball, 1832), 162.
[408] Ibid.

Endnotes

[409] "The Printed Page." *Sword of the Lord,* August 7, 2009.
[410] "Paul, I Found Christ Through Your Writings" (Murfreesboro, TN: Sword of the Lord, Aug 7, 2009), 18.
[411] Boswell, James. *The Life of Samuel Johnson,* (vol. 4), 29.
[412] Hammond, Peter. "You Are What You Read," 6/15/2021. ReformationSA.org., accessed December 27, 2022.
[413] Has God Called Me to Write? An interview with John Piper, June 9, 2015. https://www.desiringgod.org/interviews/has-god-called-me-to-write, accessed October 13, 2022.
[414] West, Mary Jessamyn. https://graciousquotes.com/journaling-quotes/, accessed September 29,2022.
[415] Spurgeon, C. H. *Flowers from a Puritan's Garden.* (New York: Funk & Wagnalls, 1883). Taken from the Preface.
[416] Wiersbe, Warren. *Best of Tozer.* (Grand Rapids, MI: Baker Book House, 1978), 151–152.
[417] Ibid.
[418] https://www.quotemaster.org/Hearing+God, accessed September 28, 2021.
[419] Spurgeon, C. H. "A Voice from Heaven." Sermon delivered APRIL 17, 1887, Metropolitan Tabernacle.
[420] Barclay, W. (Ed.). *The Letters to Timothy, Titus, and Philemon.* (Philadelphia: Westminster John Knox Press, 1975), 156.
[421] Spurgeon, C. H. "'The Day' and Its Disclosures." (Sermon delivered February 18, 1872). https://www.spurgeongems.org/sermon/chs3531.pdf, accessed November 13, 2021.
[422] Curtis Hutson, Ed. *Great Preaching on Thanksgiving.* (Murfreesboro, TN: Sword of the Lord Publishers, 1987), 11.
[423] https://www.inc.com/jeff-haden/40-inspiring-motivational-quotes-about-gratitude.html, accessed September 13, 2021.
[424] Spurgeon, C. H. *Psalms.* (Wheaton, IL: Crossway Books, 1993), 149.
[425] MacDonald, W. *Believer's Bible Commentary: Old and New Testaments,* (A. Farstad, Ed.). (Nashville: Thomas Nelson, 1995), 606.
[426] Graham, Billy. *Hope for the Troubled Heart.* (Dallas: Word, 1991), 96.
[427] Cowman, *Streams in the Desert,* January 3.
[428] Raleigh, Alexander. *From Dawn to the Perfect Day.* (Edinburgh: Adam & Charles Black, 1883), 225.
[429] McGee, J. V. *Thru the Bible Commentary* (electronic ed., Vol. 1). (Nashville: Thomas Nelson, 1997), 609.
[430] Spurgeon, C. H. *Lectures to My Students: Addresses Delivered to the Students of the Pastors' College, Metropolitan Tabernacle,* Second series, (Vol. 2). (New York: Robert Carter and Brothers, 1889), 20.
[431] Spurgeon, C. H. *An All-Round Ministry,* 236.
[432] *Ellicott's Commentary for English Readers,* 2 Corinthians 2:4.

[433] Ironside, H. A. *Notes on the Book of Proverbs.* (Neptune, NJ: Loizeaux Bros, 1908), 333.
[434] Waltke, B. K. *The Book of Proverbs,* Chapters 15–31. (Grand Rapids, MI: Wm. B. Eerdmans Publishing Co., 2005), 276.
[435] Jeremiah, David. "Christ's Message for the Seven Churches and Today." https://davidjeremiah.blog/christs-message-for-the-seven-churches-of-revelation-and-today/, accessed February 5, 2023.
[436] Ibid.
[437] Exell, J. S. *The Biblical Illustrator: Revelation.* (New York; Chicago; Toronto: Fleming H. Revell Company, n.d.), 96).
[438] Rogers, Adrian. *Unveiling the End Times in Our Time.* (Nashville: Broadman Press, 2004), 64–65.
[439] Rainer, Thom S. "I Am a Church Member: Discovering the Attitude that Makes the Difference."
[440] Spence-Jones, H. D. M. (Ed.). *Proverbs.* (London; New York: Funk & Wagnalls Company, 1909), 533.
[441] www.whatchristianswanttoknow.com/bible-verses-about-worry-20-comforting-scripture-quotes, accessed September 4, 2017.
[442] Exell, J. S. *The Biblical Illustrator: Revelation.* (New York; Chicago; Toronto: Fleming H. Revell Company, n.d.), 261.
[443] Ibid., 262.
[444] Gaebelein, F. E. (Ed.). *The Expositor's Bible Commentary: Matthew, Mark, Luke* (Vol. 8). (Grand Rapids, MI: Zondervan Publishing House, 1984), 76.
[445] Wiersbe, Warren W. *The Names of Jesus.*
[446] Names for Jesus according to Cruden's Concordance total 198. Sunday's count may have included additional titles for Jesus.
[447] Spurgeon, C. H. "Our Sympathizing High Priest." Sermon delivered October 31, 1886, Metropolitan Tabernacle.
[448] Twitter post from Dec 21, 2015.
[449] Spurgeon, C. H. "Our Sympathizing High Priest." Sermon delivered October 31, 1886, Metropolitan Tabernacle.
[450] Graves, Stephen; Thomas Addington; Sean Womack. *The Mentoring Blueprint.* (Nashville: Word Publishing, 2000), 2.
[451] Ibid., 32.
[452] Henry, M. *Matthew Henry's Commentary on the Whole Bible: Complete and Unabridged in One Volume.* (Peabody: Hendrickson, 1994), 1412.
[453] Maclaren, Alexander. *Expositions of Holy Scripture,* Ezekiel 37:1–14.
[454] Ibid., 1412.
[455] Yates, Kyle. *Preaching,* 184.
[456] Simeon, C. *Horae Homileticae: Mark–Luke* (Vol. 12). (London: Holdsworth and Ball, 1832), 548).

Endnotes

[457] Henry, M. *Matthew Henry's Commentary on the Whole Bible: Complete and Unabridged in One Volume.* (Peabody: Hendrickson, 1994), 975.
[458] Cited in Drummond, Lewis. *The Canvas Cathedral.* (Word Publishing, 2003), 428.
[459] Barnes, Albert. *Notes on the Bible.* (1834), Philippians 4:7.
[460] MacArthur, J., Jr. (Ed.). The MacArthur Study Bible (electronic ed.). (Nashville, TN: Word Pub., 1997), 1828.
[461] Courson, J. *Jon Courson's Application Commentary.* (Nashville, TN: Thomas Nelson, 2003), 557.
[462] Wuest, K. S. *Wuest's Word Studies from the Greek New Testament: for the English Reader* (Vol. 5). (Grand Rapids: Eerdmans, 1997), 110.
[463] Exell, J. S. *The Biblical Illustrator: Philippians–Colossians* (Vol. 1). (New York; Chicago; Toronto: Fleming H. Revell Company, n.d.), 330.
[464] http://izquotes.com/quote/319561, accessed October 25, 2017.
[465] Bonar, Horatius. *Looking to the Cross,* Preface, 1851.
[466] Ibid., 114.
[467] Spurgeon, C. H. "Preaching! Man's Privilege and God's Power!," Sermon Delivered November 25, 1860, New Park Street Pulpit.
[468] https://www.goodreads.com/quotes/tag/books?page=14, accessed September 26, 2022.
[469] Ibid.
[470] https://www.azquotes.com/author/8805-C_S_Lewis/tag/reading, accessed September 27, 2022.
[471] https://www.christianquotes.info/quotes-by-topic/quotes-about-books/, accessed September 27, 2022.
[472] Butler, Samuel. *The Notebooks of Samuel Butler.*
[473] Spurgeon, C. H. "Paul—His Cloak and His Books." Sermon Delivered November 29, 1863, Metropolitan Tabernacle.
[474] Baudelaire, Charles https://www.brainyquote.com, accessed September 28, 2022.
[475] 50 Most Convincing Quotes About the Importance of Books and Libraries. https://ebookfriendly.com/best-quotes-importance-books-libraries/, accessed September 23, 2022.
[476] https://www.azquotes.com/quote/349883, accessed September 29, 2022.
[477] https://www.goodreads.com/quotes/tag/books?page=9, accessed September 26, 2022.
[478] Goold, William H. (ed.). *The Church and the Bible, The Works of John Owen,* 16, "The True Nature of a Gospel Church and Its Government." (Edinburgh: Banner of Truth, 1991), 74.
[479] Ibid., "The Duty of a Pastor," 453.
[480] Henry, M. *Matthew Henry's Commentary on the Whole Bible: Complete and Unabridged in One Volume.* (Peabody: Hendrickson, 1994), 2407.

481 Spurgeon. *Lectures to My Students,* 314.
482 Ibid., 30.
483 Lutzer, Erwin. *Pastor to Pastor.* (Kregel, 1998), 11.
484 https://covenantlifetampa.org/2014/07/matthew-935-38-prayer-for-laborers-for-the-harvest/, accessed June 20, 2017.
485 Bunyan, John. *Israel's Hope Encouraged.* (Bellingham, WA: Logos Bible Software), 1:578.
486 Ibid.
487 Graham, Billy. "In His Own Words: The Hope of Heaven." March 21, 2017. https:// billygrahamlibrary.org/in-his-own-words-the-hope-of-heaven/, accessed October 20, 2020.
488 Criswell, W. A. & Paige Patterson. *Heaven.* (Wheaton, Ill: Tyndale House Publications, Inc., 1991), 162.
489 Packer, J. I. *The J. I. Packer Classic Collection.* (Colorado Springs: NavPress, 2010), 170.
490 Drummond, Lewis. *The Word of the Cross.* (Nashville: Broadman Press, 1992), 337.
491 Stewart, *Heralds of God,* 41.
492 MacArthur, *Rediscovering Expository Preaching,* 3.
493 Whitesell, *Basic New Testament Evangelism,* 106.
494 Spurgeon, C. H. "Good Earnests of Great Success." Sermon delivered January 12, 1868, Metropolitan Tabernacle.
495 Cowman, L. B. *Streams in the Desert, Updated Edition.* (Grand Rapids: Zondervan, 1977), 217.
496 Boice, J. M. *Psalms 42–106: An Expositional Commentary.* (Grand Rapids, MI: Baker Books, 2005), 370.
497 Ibid.
498 Maclaren, Alexander. *The Book of Psalms:* Book II, 48.
499 Exell, J. S. *The Biblical Illustrator:* The Psalms (Vol. 3). (New York; Chicago; Toronto: Fleming H. Revell Company, n.d.), 404.
500 Ibid.
501 Spurgeon, C. H. *Morning and Evening,* January 6 (Morning).
502 Adrian Rogers. "Do You Need Comforting?," September 30. https://www.christianity.com/devotionals/love-worth-finding-adrian-rogers/love-worth-finding-september-30-2019.html, accessed January 26, 2021.
503 https://www.azquotes.com/quote/573620?ref=power-of-god, accessed February 3, 2021.
504 https://faithunlocked.wordpress.com/2014/10/18/quotes-on-gods-promises/, accessed February 3, 2021.
505 Francis Chan, Crazy Love: Overwhelmed by a Relentless God.
506 https://faithunlocked.wordpress.com/2014/10/18/quotes-on-gods-promises/, accessed February 3, 2021.

Endnotes

507 https://www.azquotes.com/quote/573620?ref=power-of-god, accessed February 3, 2021.
508 https://www.azquotes.com/quotes/topics/power-of-god.html?p=2, accessed February 3, 2021.
509 Pink, A. W. *The Attributes of God.*
510 Ryle, J. C., on Zechariah's Song in Luke 1:67–80.
511 Spurgeon, C. H. "The Sound in the Mulberry Trees." Sermon delivered May 31, 1857, New Park Street Chapel.
512 Spurgeon. *Lectures to My Students,* 39.
513 Bridges, Charles. *Christian Ministry,* 1830.
514 Spurgeon, *Lectures to My Students,* 40.
515 Kulp, George. *The Making of a Preacher,* "The Preacher's Call," Chapter 1.
516 "Still Called to the Ministry," *Moody Monthly* 83, no. 7. (March 1983), 133.
517 Spurgeon, C. H. "Fear Not" (Sermon No. 156). Delivered on Sabbath Morning, October 4, 1857.
518 Henry, M. *Matthew Henry's Commentary on the Whole Bible: Complete and Unabridged in One Volume.* (Peabody: Hendrickson, 1994), 1154.
519 Watts, J. D. W. *Isaiah 34–66* (Vol. 25). (Dallas: Word, Incorporated, 1987), 106.
520 Spurgeon, C. H. *The Treasury of David: Psalms 120–150* (Vol. 6). (London; Edinburgh; New York: Marshall Brothers, n.d.), 336.
521 Simeon, C. *Horae Homileticae: Isaiah, XXVII–LXVI* (Vol. 8). (London: Holdsworth and Ball, 1832), 147.
522 Henry, M. *Matthew Henry's Commentary on the Whole Bible: Complete and Unabridged in One Volume.* (Peabody: Hendrickson, 1994), 921–922.
523 Morgan, R. J. *Nelson's Complete Book of Stories, Illustrations, and Quotes* (electronic ed.). (Nashville: Thomas Nelson Publishers, 2000), 645–646.
524 Spurgeon, C. H. *Morning and Evening.* (London: Passmore & Alabaster), February 21 (Morning).
525 Exell, J. S. *The Biblical Illustrator:* The Psalms (Vol. 5). (New York; Chicago; Toronto: Fleming H. Revell Company, n.d.), 86.
526 Barnes, Albert. *Barnes Notes on the Bible,* Psalm 119:11.
527 *Gill's Exposition of the Entire Bible,* Psalm 119:11.
528 Bridges, Charles. *Exposition of the Book of Proverbs,* 486.
529 Exell, J. S. *The Biblical Illustrator: Jeremiah* (Vol. 2). (New York; Chicago; Toronto: Fleming H. Revell Company, n.d.), 67.
530 Spurgeon, *Morning and Evening,* March 6 (Morning).
531 Hindson, E. E., & W. M. Kroll, (Eds.). *KJV Bible Commentary.* (Nashville: Thomas Nelson, 1994), 2082.
532 Meyer, F. B. "Secret of Guidance 9—THE FULLNESS OF THE SPIRIT," http://articles.ochristian.com/article11792.shtml. Accessed July 25, 2021.

⁵³³ Meyer, F. B. "Be Filled With the Holy Spirit." Decision Magazine, May 12, 2010. https://decisionmagazine.com/filled-with-holy-spirit/, accessed July 24, 2021.
⁵³⁴ Three of the contrasts adapted from F. B. Meyer, "The Infilling of the Holy Spirit." https://www.sermonindex.net/modules/articles/index.php?view=article&aid=18555, accessed July 25, 2021.
⁵³⁵ MacArthur, John. *The MacArthur New Testament Commentary, Ephesians*. (Moody Press), 256.
⁵³⁶ Exell, J. S. *The Biblical Illustrator: Matthew*. (New York; Chicago; Toronto: Fleming H. Revell Company, n.d.), 222.
⁵³⁷ Ibid., 224.
⁵³⁸ Spurgeon, C. H. "A Special Invitation." (Sermon)
⁵³⁹ Exell, J. S. *The Biblical Illustrator:* Matthew. (New York; Chicago; Toronto: Fleming H. Revell Company, n.d.), 224.
⁵⁴⁰ Ibid., 224.
⁵⁴¹ Simeon, C. *Horae Homileticae: Matthew* (Vol. 11). (London: Holdsworth and Ball, 1832–1863), 349.
⁵⁴² https://www.christianquotes.info/quotes-by-topic/quotes-about-church/#ixzz5ELCPHpC0, accessed May 2, 2018.
⁵⁴³ Exell, J. S. *The Biblical Illustrator: The Psalms* (Vol. 5). (New York; Chicago; Toronto: Fleming H. Revell Company, n.d.), 181.
⁵⁴⁴ Spurgeon, C. H. *The Treasury of David: Psalms 120–150* (Vol. 6). (London; Edinburgh; New York: Marshall Brothers, n.d.), 49.
⁵⁴⁵ https://www.goodreads.com/quotes/549103-only-one-life-twill-soon-be-past-only-what-s-done, accessed August 28, 2021.
⁵⁴⁶ Spence-Jones, H. D. M. (Ed.). *Psalms* (Vol. 3). (London; New York: Funk & Wagnalls Company, 1909), 210.
⁵⁴⁷ Horne, G. *A Commentary on the Book of Psalms*. (New York: Robert Carter & Brothers, 1856), 473.
⁵⁴⁸ *Matthew Henry's Commentary on the Bible,* Psalm 124:1.
⁵⁴⁹ Spurgeon. *The Treasury of David,* Psalm 124:1.
⁵⁵⁰ Longman III, T, & D. E. Garland (Eds.). *The Expositor's Bible Commentary: Psalms* (Revised Edition), (Vol. 5). (Grand Rapids, MI: Zondervan, 2008), 903.
⁵⁵¹ *The Criswell Study Bible,* Ephesians 5:18.
⁵⁵² https://www.christianquotes.info/top-quotes/22-motivating-quotes-about-prayer/, accessed September 4, 2021.
⁵⁵³ https://www.goodreads.com/quotes/322408-our-praying-needs-to-be-pressed-and-pursued-with-an, accessed September 5, 2021.
⁵⁵⁴ Spurgeon, *Morning and Evening,* September 26 (Evening).
⁵⁵⁵ *Promises and Prayers for a Christian Friend.* (Brentwood, TN: Freeman-Smith, 2012), 51.

Endnotes

[556] Swindoll, Chuck. *Abraham.* (Carol Stream, Illinois: Tyndale House Publishers, Inc., 2014), 8.

[557] Exell, J. S. *The Biblical Illustrator: The Psalms,* Vol. 2. (New York; Chicago; Toronto; London; Edinburgh: Fleming H. Revell Company), 46.

[558] Spurgeon, *Morning and Evening,* August 30 (Morning).

[559] https://www.christianquotes.info/quotes-by-topic/quotes-about-restoration/, accessed May 13, 2021.

[560] https://www.christianquotes.info/quotes-by-topic/quotes-about-forgiveness/, accessed May 13, 2021.

[561] https://www.christianquotes.info/quotes-by-topic/quotes-about-forgiveness/, accessed May 13, 2021.

[562] Henry, M. *Matthew Henry's Commentary on the Whole Bible: Complete and Unabridged in One Volume.* (Peabody: Hendrickson, 1994), 1018.

[563] https://www.treasurequotes.com/quotes/friendship-isnt-about-who-youve-known-the-lo, accessed November 7, 2021.

[564] https://thinkaboutsuchthings.com/christian-friendship-quotes/, accessed November 7, 2021.

[565] MacDonald, W. *Believer's Bible Commentary: Old and New Testaments* (A. Farstad, Ed.). (Nashville: Thomas Nelson, 1995), 835.

[566] Keller, Timothy. *God's Wisdom for Navigating Life.* (New York, New York: Viking, 2017), 167.

[567] Green, Michael. *Who Is This Jesus?* (Eastbourne, England: Kingsway Publications, 1992), 63.

[568] McConkey, James. *The Three-fold Secret of the Holy Spirit.* (Pittsburgh: Silver Publishing Society, 1922), 106.

[569] Exell, J. S. *The Biblical Illustrator: Genesis* (Vol. 1). (New York; Chicago; Toronto: Fleming H. Revell Company, n.d.), 39.

[570] Keil, C. F. & F. Delitzsch. *Commentary on the Old Testament* (Vol. 1). (Peabody, MA: Hendrickson, 1996), 30.

[571] Henry, M. *Matthew Henry's Commentary on the Whole Bible: Complete and Unabridged in One Volume.* (Peabody: Hendrickson, 1994), 4.

[572] Ibid., 2012.

[573] Spurgeon, C. H. *The Treasury of David: Psalms 88–110* (Vol. 4). (London; Edinburgh; New York: Marshall Brothers, n.d.), 65.

[574] Henry, M. *Matthew Henry's Commentary on the Whole Bible: Complete and Unabridged in One Volume.* (Peabody: Hendrickson, 1994), 876.

[575] Smith, Hannah Whitall. "The God of All Comfort." https://biblehub.com/library/smith/the_god_of_all_comfort/chapter_11_things_that_cannot.htm, accessed July 5, 2020.

[576] Seven of the eight headers come from the book *Why Do Christians Suffer* by Anthony Zeoli and cited by Billy Graham in the pamphlet "Why Christians Suffer," 1953.

[577] https://www.christianquotes.info/quotes-by-topic/quotes-about-patience/, assessed December 22, 2021.
[578] Bridges, Jerry. *The Practice of Godliness.* (NavPress, 1996), 175.
[579] Graham, Billy. "Why Christians Suffer" (pamphlet). (Billy Graham Evangelistic Association, 1953), 7.
[580] Pithy gems from Charles Spurgeon!, https://www.gracegems.org/30/short_pithy_gems_Spurgeon.htm, accessed January 23, 2022.
[581] Spurgeon, C. H. *Morning and Evening.* (London: Passmore & Alabaster), May 31 (Evening).
[582] Chadwick, Samuel. *Path to Prayer.* (1931), Chapter 11.
[583] Hutson, Curtis. (Ed.). *Great Preaching on Prayer.* (Murfreesboro, TN: Sword of the Lord Publishers, 1988), 235.
[584] Spurgeon, C. H. "Boldness at the Throne." Sermon delivered September 14, 1873, at the Metropolitan Tabernacle.
[585] Bounds, E. M. cited in *How to Live a Life of Prayer,* 112.
[586] Parsons, Charles R. "An Hour With George Müller, the Man of Faith to Whom God Gave Millions" (Interview with Müller at the close of his life).
[587] Spurgeon, C. H. "The Thorn in the Flesh." Sermon delivered December 8, 1872, Metropolitan Tabernacle.
[588] Hughes, Philip Edgcumbe. *Paul's Second Epistle to the Corinthians* (NICNT). (Grand Rapids: Eerdmans, 1962), ad loc.
[589] Spurgeon, C. H. "The Thorn in the Flesh." Sermon delivered December 8, 1872, Metropolitan Tabernacle.
[590] Barclay, W. (Ed.). *The Letters to the Philippians, Colossians, and Thessalonians* (electronic ed). (Philadelphia: The Westminster John Knox Press, 1975), 175.
[591] Laurie, Greg. Devotion: "For Righteousness' Sake," March 01, 2019. https://harvest.org/resources/devotion/for-righteousness-sake-2019/, accessed April 10, 2021.
[592] Dixon, A. C. *Through Night to Morning.* (Greenville, South Carolina: The Gospel Hour, Inc., no copyright date), Sermon #19: "Comfort for Shut-Ins".
[593] https://www.goodreads.com/quotes/tag/intercession?page=4, accessed March 3, 2022.
[594] Henry, M. *Matthew Henry's Commentary on the Whole Bible: Complete and Unabridged in One Volume.* (Peabody: Hendrickson, 1994), 2317.
[595] Spurgeon, C. H. *The Treasury of David: Psalms 56–87* (Vol. 3). (London; Edinburgh; New York: Marshall Brothers, n.d.), 434.
[596] Fitchett, W. H. *The Beliefs of Unbelief.* (New York: Jennings & Graham, 1907), 38.
[597] Chafer, Lewis Sperry. *Systematic Theology,* 8 vols. (Dallas: Dallas Seminary, 1947), 1:155, 157.

Endnotes

[598] Criswell, W. A. "The Reality of God" (sermon), April 16, 1973, First Baptist Church, Dallas, Tx.

[599] Elliot, Elizabeth. "Suffering Is Never for Nothing."

[600] https://www.crosswalk.com/faith/spiritual-life/inspiring-quotes/30-inspiring-christian-quotes.html, accessed May 17, 2022.

[601] Wiersbe, W. W. *Prayer: Basic Training.* (Wheaton, IL: Tyndale, 1988), 14.

[602] Spurgeon, C. H. *Metropolitan Tabernacle Pulpit Sermons* (Vol. 50), "David's First Victory." (London: Passmore & Alabaster, 1904), 596.

[603] Exell, J. S. *The Biblical Illustrator: I Samuel.* (New York; Chicago; Toronto: Fleming H. Revell Company, n.d.), 471.

[604] Ibid., *Exodus,* 94.

[605] Exell, J. S. *The Biblical Illustrator: Romans* (Vol. 2). (New York; Chicago; Toronto: Fleming H. Revell Company, n.d.), 17.

[606] Murray, Andrew. *The Secret of Believing Prayer,* Chapter 12.

[607] Spurgeon, C. H. "A Prayer for Revival," a sermon Delivered August 14, 1887.

[608] Ibid.

[609] Spence-Jones, H. D. M. (Ed.). *Proverbs.* (London; New York: Funk & Wagnalls Company, 1909), 270.

[610] Ibid.

[611] *Fraser's Magazine for Town and Country,* Volume 34. (London: printed by George Barclay, 1846), 131.

[612] Maclaren, Alexander. *The Psalms,* 408.

[613] Henry, M. *Matthew Henry's Commentary on the Whole Bible: Complete and Unabridged in One Volume.* (Peabody: Hendrickson, 1994), 985.

[614] Maclaren, Alexander. *The Psalms,* 408.

[615] Shakespeare, William. *King Lear,* (Act I, Scene IV), 13. nfs.sparknotes.com, accessed May 25, 2011.

[616] Henry, M. *Matthew Henry's Commentary on the Whole Bible: Complete and Unabridged in One Volume.* (Peabody: Hendrickson, 1994), 522.

[617] Simeon, C. *Horae Homileticae: Judges to 2 Kings* (Vol. 3). (London: Samuel Holdsworth, 1836), 458.

[618] Henry, M. *Matthew Henry's Commentary on the Whole Bible: Complete and Unabridged in One Volume.* (Peabody: Hendrickson, 1994), 1441.

[619] Ibid.

[620] MacDonald, W. *Believer's Bible Commentary: Old and New Testaments* (A. Farstad, Ed.). (Nashville: Thomas Nelson, 1995), 1216.

[621] Lloyd-Jones, Martyn. *Studies in the Sermon on the Mount,* (Vol. 1). (InterVarsity Press, 1977), 81.

[622] MacDonald, W. *Believer's Bible Commentary: Old and New Testaments* (A. Farstad, Ed.). (Nashville: Thomas Nelson, 1995), 1216.

[623] Lloyd-Jones, Martyn. *Studies in the Sermon on the Mount,* (Vol. 1). (InterVarsity Press, 1977).

[624] Bonar, Andrew A. *Christ and His Church in the Book of Psalms.* (1859).
[625] Spurgeon. *The Treasury of David,* Psalm 124:1.
[626] Spence-Jones, H. D. M. (Ed.). *Psalms* (Vol. 3). (London; New York: Funk & Wagnalls Company, 1909), 206.
[627] Walvoord, J. F. & R. B. Zuck (Eds.). *The Bible Knowledge Commentary: An Exposition of the Scriptures, Job* (Vol. 1). (Wheaton, IL: Victor Books, 1985), 775.
[628] Keller, Tim. *Walking with God through Pain and Suffering.* (New York: Riverhead Books, 2015), 58.
[629] Exell, J. S. *The Biblical Illustrator: Ephesians* (Vol. 2). (New York; Chicago; Toronto: Fleming H. Revell Company, n.d.), 371.
[630] MacArthur, John. *Ephesians.* (Moody, 1986), 137.
[631] Chambers, Oswald. "So Send I You / Workmen of God: Recognizing and Answering God's Call to Service." (Our Daily Bread Publishing, 2015).
[632] Morgan, G. Campbell. *The Westminster Pulpit* (Vol. 4). (Grand Rapids: Baker Book House, 2006), 194.
[633] Waiting When God Seems Silent, February 10, 2019. https://www.desiringgod.org/articles/waiting-when-god-seems-silent, accessed October 6, 2021.
[634] Winslow, Octavius. *The Sympathy of Christ,* Chapter 5: "The Silence of Christ."
[635] *Life Worth Finding Daily Devotional,* "Have You Found That God Is Enough?" November 24, 2019.
[636] Exell, J. S. *The Biblical Illustrator:* Proverbs. (New York; Chicago; Toronto: Fleming H. Revell Company, n.d.), 595.
[637] Swindoll, Charles R. *Great Days with the Great Lives.*
[638] Meyer, F. B. "Ordered to Zarephath" (sermon).
[639] Meyer, F. B. "Beyond the Drying Brook" (sermon).
[640] Henry, M. *Matthew Henry's Commentary on the Whole Bible: Complete and Unabridged in One Volume.* (Peabody: Hendrickson, 1994), 2425.
[641] Chan, Francis. *We Are Church.*
[642] Spurgeon, C. H. "Surveying the Field," (Sermon delivered March 7, 1867) at The Metropolitan Tabernacle, Newington.
[643] Redpath, Alan. *Victorious Christian Service.* (Old Tappan, New Jersey: Fleming H. Revell Company, MCMLVIII), 105.
[644] Ibid., 48.
[645] Henry, M. *Matthew Henry's Commentary on the Whole Bible: Complete and Unabridged in One Volume.* (Peabody: Hendrickson, 1994), 632.
[646] Exell, J. S. *The Biblical Illustrator: First Chronicles, Second Chronicles, Ezra, Nehemiah, and Esther* (Vol. 4). (New York; Chicago; Toronto: Fleming H. Revell Company, n.d.), 86.

Endnotes

[647] https://www.christianquotes.info/quotes-by-topic/quotes-about-unity/, accessed February 8, 2022.
[648] Redpath, Alan. *Victorious Christian Service*. (Old Tappan, New Jersey: Fleming H. Revell Company, MCMLVIII), 114.
[649] Truett, George W. *A Quest for Souls*. (New York and London: Harper & Brothers Publishers, 1917), 265, 267.
[650] Spurgeon, C. H. "The Wandering Bird" (Sermon #3453), Proverbs 27:8.
[651] https://www.christianquotes.info/quotes-by-topic/quotes-about-intercession/, accessed March 4, 2022.
[652] Carson, D. A. *When Jesus Confronts the World*. (Grand Rapids: Baker, 1987), 125.
[653] Piper, John. "Five Ways Affliction Helps," February 4 (Devotional). https://www.desiringgod.org/articles/five-ways-affliction-helps, accessed April 23, 2022.
[654] Exell, J. S. *The Biblical Illustrator: The Psalms* (Vol. 5). (New York; Chicago; Toronto: Fleming H. Revell Company, n.d.), 74–75.
[655] Rogers, Adrian. "Jesus—God's Answer to Man's Despair" (sermon). https://www.lightsource.com/ministry/love-worth-finding/articles/jesusgods-answer-to-mans-despair-16044.html, accessed April 29, 2022.
[656] Spurgeon, C. H. https://www.christianquotes.info/quotes-by-topic/quotes-about-affliction/, accessed July 7, 2020.
[657] https://quotestats.com/topic/when-god-doesnt-make-sense-quotes/, accessed September 16, 2021.
[658] Spurgeon, C. H. *Morning and Evening*. (London: Passmore & Alabaster), October 7.
[659] Rogers, Adrian. "A Time of Terror and a Word of Hope," Sermon, September 11, 2001. https://www.lifeway.com/en/articles/sermon-terror-hope-tragedy-september-11-adrian-rogers, accessed September 28, 2021.
[660] https://quotestats.com/topic/when-god-doesnt-make-sense-quotes/, accessed September 16, 2021.
[661] Criswell, W. A. "God's Providential Care" (Sermon). October 24, 1954. https://wacriswell.com/sermons/1954/god-s-providential-care/, accessed August 22, 2020.
[662] Spence-Jones, H. D. M. (Ed.). *Proverbs*. (London; New York: Funk & Wagnalls Company, 1909), 521.
[663] Spurgeon, C. H. "Approachableness of Jesus."
[664] Spence-Jones, H. D. M. (Ed.). *Proverbs*. (London; New York: Funk & Wagnalls Company, 1909), 522.
[665] Horne, G. *A Commentary on the Book of Psalms*. (New York: Robert Carter & Brothers, 1856), 467.
[666] Spurgeon. *The Treasury of David*, Psalm 23:1.

[667] Alexander, J. A. *The Psalms Translated and Explained.* (Edinburgh: Andrew Elliot; James Thin, 1864), 108.
[668] Henry, M. *Matthew Henry's Commentary on the Whole Bible: Complete and Unabridged in One Volume.* (Peabody: Hendrickson, 1994), 773.
[669] Spurgeon, C. H. *The Treasury of David: Psalms 1–26* (Vol. 1). (London; Edinburgh; New York: Marshall Brothers, n.d.), 355.
[670] Parker, Joseph. *The People's Bible,* Psalm 23:4.
[671] Plumer, W. S. *Studies in the Book of Psalms: Being a Critical and Expository Commentary, with Doctrinal and Practical Remarks on the Entire Psalter.* (Philadelphia; Edinburgh: J. B. Lippincott Company; A & C Black, 1872), 360.
[672] *Barnes Notes on the Bible,* Psalm 23:6.
[673] Maclaren, Alexander. *The Book of Psalms,* 232.
[674] Derek Kidner. Kidner Classic Commentaries – Psalms 1 – 72 (Downers Grove, Ill: InterVarsity Press, 2008), 127.
[675] Jon Courson. *Jon Courson's Application Commentary,* 556.
[676] Graham, Billy. *Where I Am: Heaven, Eternity, and Our Life Beyond.* (Nashville: Thomas Nelson, 2015).
[677] Spurgeon, C. H. *The Treasury of David: Psalms 120–150* (Vol. 6). (London; Edinburgh; New York: Marshall Brothers, n.d.), 119.
[678] Robertson, A. T. *Word Pictures in the New Testament.* (Nashville, TN: Broadman Press, 1933), Heb. 4:16.
[679] Exell, J. S. *The Biblical Illustrator: Matthew.* (New York; Chicago; Toronto: Fleming H. Revell Company, n.d.), 224.
[680] Ibid., 225.
[681] http://www.goodreads.com/quotes/275720-optimism-hopes-for-the-best-without-any-guarantee-of-its, accessed January 16, 2017.
[682] https://billygraham.org/story/9-ways-to-grow-in-your-faith/, accessed January 16, 2017.
[683] Exell, J. S. *The Biblical Illustrator: Matthew.* (New York; Chicago; Toronto: Fleming H. Revell Company, n.d.), 66.
[684] Ibid., 68.
[685] Havner, Vance. *Pepper 'N' Salt,* 18–19.
[686] Olford, Stephen. *Basics for Believers.* (Colorado Springs, Co: Victor, 2003), 253.
[687] Inspired, adapted, expanded from Max Lucado. Maxlucado.com/general/no-room/, accessed February 8, 2013.
[688] Henry, M. *Matthew Henry's Commentary on the Whole Bible: Complete and Unabridged in One Volume.* (Peabody: Hendrickson, 1994), 2448.
[689] Wiersbe, W. W. *The Bible Exposition Commentary* (Vol. 2). (Wheaton, IL: Victor Books, 1996), 506.
[690] Ibid.

Endnotes

[691] Spurgeon, C. H. "The Works of the Devil Destroyed." Sermon delivered July 1, 1883, Metropolitan Tabernacle.

[692] Spurgeon, C. H. "Stand Firm." Sermon Delivered August 27, 1882, Metropolitan Tabernacle.

[693] Henry, M. *Matthew Henry's Commentary on the Whole Bible: Complete and Unabridged in One Volume.* (Peabody: Hendrickson, 1994), 1039.

[694] http://www.wiseoldsayings.com/promises-quotes/, accessed December 8, 2017.

[695] Sanders, J. Oswald. *Divine Art of Soul Winning,* 68.

[696] Spence-Jones, H. D. M. (Ed.). *Ezekiel* (Vol. 1). (London; New York: Funk & Wagnalls Company, 1909), 121.

www.ingramcontent.com/pod-product-compliance
Lightning Source LLC
Chambersburg PA
CBHW030133170426
43199CB00008B/47